Patterns in Java™, Volume 1

Second Edition

Patterns in Java™, Volume 1

A Catalog of Reusable Design Patterns Illustrated with UML

Second Edition

MARK GRAND

Wiley Publishing, Inc.

Publisher: Robert Ipsen
Editor: Theresa Hudson
Developmental Editor: Kathryn Malin
Managing Editor: Angela Smith
New Media Editor: Brian Snapp
Text Design & Composition: North Market Street Graphics

This book is printed on acid-free paper. ☺

Published by Wiley Publishing, Inc., Indianapolis, Indiana

Published simultaneously in Canada.

Library of Congress Cataloging-in-Publication Data:
ISBN: 0-471-22729-3

Wiley also publishes its books in a variety of electronic formats. Some content that appears in print may not be available in electronic versions.
For more information about Wiley products, visit our web site at www.wiley.com.

10 9 8 7 6 5 4 3 2 1

C O N T E N T S

A C K N O W L E D G M E N T S

I would first like to acknowledge the patience of my wife, Nicole. Without her support, this second edition of *Patterns in Java, Volume 1* would not have been possible.

I would also like to acknowledge the feedback that I have received from many readers whose emails to me suggested improvements and corrections that have gone into this second edition. I would like to single out Ed Remmell, who organized a discussion group around my book and took the time to send me summaries of the discussions. Other readers who took the time and trouble to send me useful questions and comments are (in alphabetical order): Nader Afshar, Derrick Ampy, Barry W. Anderson, Paul E. Andrighetti, Kaushik Barot, Ted Beckett, Pablo Bellver, Davide De Benedictis, Dave Busse, Mike Carlin, Max Chandler, John Clarke, Charlie Crook, Christian Cryder, Carlos Devoto, Cyrus Doomasia, Rodrigo Figueiredo, Jeff French, Brent Fry, Srinivas Ganti, Daniel L. Gleneck, Satish Gupta, Barton W. Hammond, Shannon Harvey, Judy Housman, Hong Hsu, Rob Hulsebos, Gary Janes, Brian Krahmer, Erik Bak Kristensen, Robert Laganière, Laurene O. Laidlaw, Allen Lee, Roger Lee, Tim Lethbridge, Charles Magid, Kurt Matthys, Phil McGlauchlin, Barry

Middlebrook, Sadiq Mohammed, Thomas Moore, Raymond Naseef, Jaime Nino, Jeff Oakes, Sudesh Palekar, Greg Pearman, Jim Phipps, John Pinto, Jon Poploskie, Raj Prathinidhi, Andy Pryke, Tulsi Rai, Damith C. Rajapakse, Steven Ranieri, John Sargeant, Robert Allan Schwartz, Greg Scott, Joe Sharp, Mike Shivas, Eduardo Silva, Daniel Stainhauser, Steve Stephens, Christian Svenstrup, Oyvind Teig, Alan Thompson, Richard Tomlinson, Bruce Wallace, Dieter Wankmueller, Mark Waschkowski, Richard Williams, Joe Wissmann, Robert Wragg, Wayne Wylupski, and Hong Yan.

Acknowledgments from the First Edition

I want to thank Craig Larman, my most conscientious reviewer. He convinced me of the importance of patterns. Craig also provided me with much invaluable feedback on the use of UML and the presentation of patterns. His valuable suggestions greatly improved the way that I present the patterns in this book.

Jack Harich was another manuscript reviewer who made many useful suggestions about the organization of this book. He convinced me to expand my coverage of fundamental patterns. He also supplied the example that I use for the State pattern.

Brad Appleton provided me with the most voluminous and detailed comments.

The UIUC patterns group provided some insightful discussions for the patterns in this book. The participants in those discussions included Brian Foote, Ed Peters, Dragos Malonescu, Peter Hatch, Don Roberts, Joseph W. Yoder, Ralph Johnson, John Brant, James Overturf, Jean Pierre Briot, Eiji Nabika, Hiro Nakamura, and Ian Chai.

I also want to acknowledge some of my other reviewers, in particular Micheal Wheaton and Micheal Pair.

A B O U T   T H E   A U T H O R

Mark Grand is an Atlanta-based consultant with over 23 years of experience specializing in distributed systems, object-oriented design, and Java. He was the architect for the first commercial business-to-business (B2B) e-commerce product for the Internet. He is currently working on an open source framework for gluing components and programs into an application.

Mark Grand is most widely known for his best-selling *Patterns in Java* books. In addition to teaching Java for Sun and other training organizations, Mark has been involved in several large-scale commercial Java projects.

Prior to his involvement with Java, Mark spent over 11 years as a designer and implementer of fourth-generation languages (4GLs). His most recent role in that vein was as the architect and project manager for an electronic data interchange product. Mark has worked with a number of information technology (IT) organizations in capacities such as software architect, database architect, network designer and administrator, and Sun System administrator. He has been involved with object-oriented programming and design since 1982.

1

Introduction to
Software Patterns

Software patterns are reusable solutions to recurring problems that we encounter during software development. Because this book is all about software patterns, they are simply referred to as *patterns* throughout.

What makes a bright, experienced programmer much more productive than a bright, but inexperienced programmer? Experience. Experience gives programmers a wealth of wisdom. As programmers gain experience, they recognize the similarity of new problems to those they have solved in the past. With even more experience, they recognize that solutions to similar problems follow recurring patterns. With knowledge of these patterns, experienced programmers can recognize a problem to which specific patterns apply and immediately determine the solution without having to stop to analyze the problem first.

When a programmer discovers a pattern, it's just an insight. In most cases, to go from an unverbalized insight to a well-thought-out idea that the programmer can clearly articulate is surprisingly difficult. It's also an extremely valuable step. When we understand a pattern well enough to put it into words, we are able to intelligently combine it with other patterns. More important, once put into words, a pattern can be used in discussions among programmers who know the pattern. Such discussions allow programmers to more effectively collaborate and combine their wisdom. They can also help avoid the situation in which programmers argue over different solutions to a problem but find that they were actually thinking of the same solution, only expressing it in different ways.

Putting a pattern into words has an additional benefit for less experienced programmers who have not yet discovered the pattern. Once a pattern has been put into words, more experienced programmers can teach it to programmers who aren't familiar with the pattern.

The intended value of this book is that it provide experienced programmers with a common vocabulary to discuss patterns. It should also allow programmers who have not yet discovered a pattern to learn about the pattern.

Although this book includes a substantial breadth of patterns, you may discover additional patterns yourself. Some patterns that you discover may be highly specialized and of interest only to a small number of people. Other patterns may be of broad interest and worthy of inclusion in a future volume of this book. If you wish to communicate such a pattern to this book's author, you may send an email to mgrand@mindspring.com.

The patterns cataloged in this book convey constructive ways for organizing parts of the software development cycle. There are, however, nonconstructive patterns that can recur in programs. These are called *AntiPatterns* because they can cancel out the benefits of patterns. This book does not attempt to catalog AntiPatterns, for the subject is well covered in other books.

Patterns and AntiPatterns are similar but fundamentally different. The point of a pattern is to recognize when you have the opportunity to apply a good solution to a problem. The point of an AntiPattern is to recognize the nature of a bad situation and suggest solutions.

Patterns Description

Patterns are usually described using a format that includes the following information:

- A name that is commonly used for the pattern. Alternative names are given in cases where the pattern is known by more than one name.
- A description of the problem that includes a concrete example and a solution specific to the concrete problem.
- A summary of the considerations that lead to the formulation of a general solution or the avoidance of the solution.
- A general solution.

- The consequences—good and bad—of using the given solution to solve a problem.
- A list of related patterns.

Pattern books differ in how they present this information. The format used in this set of books varies with the phase of the software life cycle that the pattern addresses. The patterns in this volume are all related to the design phase. The descriptions of design-phase-related patterns in this volume are organized into sections with the following headings:

PATTERN NAME

The heading of this section consists of the name of the pattern. Most patterns don't have any additional text under this heading. For those that do, this section contains alternate names for the pattern or information about the derivation or general nature of the pattern.

SYNOPSIS

This section contains a brief description of the pattern. The synopsis conveys the essence of the solution provided by the pattern. The synopsis is primarily directed at experienced programmers who may recognize the pattern as one they already know but for which they may not have had a name.

Don't be discouraged if you don't recognize a pattern from its name and synopsis. Instead, carefully read through the rest of the pattern description to understand it.

CONTEXT

This section describes the problem that the pattern addresses. For most patterns, the problem is introduced in terms of a concrete example. After presenting the problem in the example, the Context section suggests a design solution to the problem.

FORCES

The Forces section summarizes the considerations that lead to the general solution presented in the Solution section. It may also present reasons to not use the solution. The reasons to use or not use the solution are presented as a bulleted list:

- ☺ Reasons to use the solution are bulleted with a happy face.
- ☹ Reasons to not use the solution are bulleted with a sad face.

SOLUTION

The Solution section is the core of the pattern. It describes a general-purpose solution to the problem that the pattern addresses.

IMPLEMENTATION

The Implementation section describes important considerations when using the solution. It may also describe some common variations or simplifications of the solution.

CONSEQUENCES

The Consequences section explains the implications—good and bad—of using the solution. Most consequences are organized into bullet points as follows:

- ☺ Good consequences are bulleted with a happy face.
- ● Neutral consequences are bulleted with a dot.
- ☹ Bad consequences are bulleted with a sad face.

JAVA API USAGE

When there is an appropriate example of the pattern in the core Java API, it's pointed out in this section. Those patterns that are not used in the core Java API do not have this section in their description.

CODE EXAMPLE

This section contains a code example that shows a sample implementation for a design that uses the pattern. In most cases, this design is described in the Context section.

RELATED PATTERNS

This section contains a list of patterns that are related to the pattern described.

A Brief History of Patterns

The idea of software patterns originally came from the field of architecture. Christopher Alexander, an architect, wrote two revolutionary books that describe patterns in building architecture and urban planning: *A*

Pattern Language: Towns, Buildings, Construction (Oxford University Press, 1977) and *The Timeless Way of Building* (Oxford University Press, 1979). The ideas presented in those books are applicable to a number of fields outside of architecture, including software development.

In 1987, Ward Cunningham and Kent Beck used some of Alexander's ideas to develop five patterns for user-interface design. They published a paper on the user-interface patterns at OOPSLA-87 entitled "Using Pattern Languages for Object-Oriented Programs."

In the early 1990s, Erich Gamma, Richard Helm, John Vlissides, and Ralph Johnson began work on one of the most influential computer books of the last decade: *Design Patterns*. Published in 1994 and often called the "Gang of Four," or GoF, book, it popularized the idea of patterns and was the greatest single influence on this book.

This book is a second edition. Additional patterns have been added that were not in the first edition. Many improvements suggested by readers of the first edition have been incorporated into the patterns. Examples have been changed to reflect more recent versions of Java.

Both editions of this book represent an evolution of patterns and objects since the GoF book was published. The GoF book used C++ and Smalltalk for its examples. This book uses Java and takes a rather Java-centric view of most things. When the GoF book was written, the Unified Modeling Language (UML) did not exist; now, it is widely accepted as the preferred notation for object-oriented analysis and design, and it is the notation used in this book.

Organization of This Book

This book is the first volume of a three-volume set that covers a wider range of patterns than previously published works.

This first volume focuses exclusively on design patterns that are used at the micro-architectural level. The second volume includes patterns used during user interface design, coding and testing. The third volume focuses on architectural and design patterns useful for enterprise and distributed applications.

All three volumes begin with a description of the subset of UML used in that volume. The following chapter contains an overview of the software life cycle, to provide the context in which the patterns are used. This chapter goes on to provide a case study that includes examples of using patterns in that volume. The remaining chapters describe different sorts of patterns.

There will be a Web site related to this book at http://mgrand.home .mindspring.com. The Web site will contain synopsis of the patterns that appear in this book. The Web site will also contain the code examples in this volume.

The Java examples that appear in this book are based on Java version 1.4.

2

Overview of UML

The *Unified Modeling Language* (UML) is a notation that you can use for object-oriented analysis and design. This chapter contains a brief overview of UML that introduces you to the subset of UML and the extensions to UML used in this book. For a complete description of UML, see www.omg.org/technology/documents/formal/uml.htm.

Books that are specifically about UML call the pieces of information stored in instances of a class *attributes*; they call a class's encapsulations of behavior *operations*. Those terms, as with UML, are not specific to any implementation language. This book is not language neutral; it assumes that you use Java as your implementation language. It also uses Java-specific terms in most places rather than terms that are language neutral but less familiar to Java programmers. For example, it uses the words *attribute* and *variable* interchangeably, with preference for the Java-specific term *variable*. This book also uses the words *operation* and *method* interchangeably, with preference for the Java-specific term *method*.

UML defines a number of different kinds of diagrams. The rest of this chapter is organized into sections that describe different kinds of UML diagrams and the elements that appear in them.

If you are experienced with object-oriented design, you will find most of the concepts underlying the UML notation to be familiar. If you find many concepts unfamiliar, read only as much of this chapter as you feel comfortable with. When you see a UML diagram in later chapters that contains something that you want explained, come back to this chapter and find a diagram that contains the UML element that you want explained.

Class Diagram

A *class diagram* is a diagram that shows classes, interfaces, and their relationships. The most basic element of a class diagram is a *class*. Figure 2.1 provides an example of a class, showing many of the features that a class can have within a class diagram.

Classes are drawn as rectangles. The rectangles can be divided into two or three compartments. The class rectangle shown in Figure 2.1 has three compartments: the top compartment contains the name of the class; the middle compartment lists the class's variables; and the bottom compartment lists the class's methods.

The symbols that precede each variable and method are called *visibility indicators*. The possible visibility indicators and their meanings are shown in Table 2.1

The variables in the middle compartment are shown as

```
visibilityIndicator name : type
```

Therefore, the two variables shown in the class are private variables. The name of the first variable is `instance` and its type is `AudioClipManager`. The name of the second variable is `prevClip` and its type is `AudioClip`.

Though not shown in Figure 2.1, an initial value can be indicated for a variable by following the variable's type with an equal (=) sign and the value like this:

```
shutDown:boolean = false
```

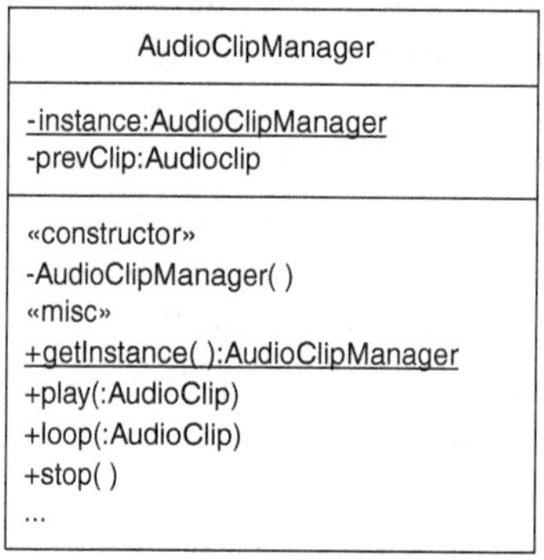

FIGURE 2.1 Basic class diagram.

TABLE 2.1 Visibility Indicators

Visibility Indicators	*Meaning*
+	Public
#	Protected
–	Private

Notice that the first variable shown in the class is underlined. An underlined variable denotes a static variable. The same applies to methods, too; underlined methods denote static methods.

The methods in the bottom compartment are shown as

```
visibilityIndicator name ( formalParameters ) : returnType
```

The `getInstance` method shown in the class above returns an `AudioClipManager` object.

UML indicates a void method by leaving out the ": returnType" from a method to indicate that it does not return anything. Therefore, the `stop` method shown in the class in Figure 2.1 does not return any result.

A method's formal parameters consist of a name and a type like this:

```
setLength(length:int)
```

If a method has multiple parameters, commas separate them like this:

```
setPosition(x:int, y:int)
```

Two of the methods in the class in Figure 2.1 are preceded by a word in guillemets, like this:

```
«constructor»
```

In a UML drawing, a word in guillemets is called a *stereotype*. A stereotype is used like an adjective to modify what comes after it. The constructor stereotype indicates that the methods following it are constructors. The `misc` stereotype indicates that the methods following it are regular methods. Additional uses for stereotypes are described later in this chapter.

One last element that appears in the class in Figure 2.1 is an ellipsis (. . .). If an ellipsis appears in the bottom compartment of a class, it means that the class has additional methods that the diagram does not show. If an ellipsis appears in the middle compartment of a class, it means that the class has additional variables that the diagram does not show.

Often, it is neither necessary nor helpful to show as many details of a class as were shown in the class in Figure 2.1. As shown in Figure 2.2, a class may be drawn with only two compartments: a top compartment,

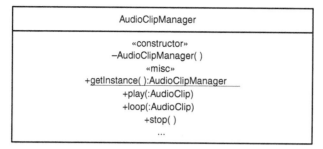

FIGURE 2.2 Two-compartment class.

which contains the class's name, and a bottom compartment, which shows the class's methods. A two-compartment class means only that its variables are not shown; it does not mean that the class lacks variables.

The visibility indicators may be omitted from methods and variables. A method or variable shown without a visibility indicator means that there is no indication of the method's or variable's visibility. It does not imply that the method or variable is public, protected, or private.

A method's parameters may be omitted if their return values are also omitted. For example, the visibility indicators and method parameters are omitted from the class shown in Figure 2.3.

The simplest form of a class has just one compartment that contains the class name, as shown in Figure 2.4. A one-compartment representation of a class merely identifies the class; it provides no indication about what variables or methods the class has.

Interfaces are drawn in a manner similar to classes. The difference is that the name in the top compartment is preceded by an `interface` stereotype. Figure 2.5 is an example of an interface.

Classes and interfaces are important elements of class diagrams. Other elements of a class diagram show relationships between classes and interfaces. Figure 2.6 is a typical class diagram.

```
AudioClipManager
─────────────────────────
instance:AudioClipManager
prevClip:Audioclip
─────────────────────────
‹‹constructor››
AudioClipManager
‹‹misc››
getInstance
play
loop
stop
...
```

FIGURE 2.3 Simplified class diagram.

```
┌─────────────────────────┐
│ AudioClipManager        │
└─────────────────────────┘
```

FIGURE 2.4 One-compartment class.

```
┌─────────────────────────┐
│     ‹‹interface››        │
│       AddressIF          │
├─────────────────────────┤
│ getAddress1             │
│ setAddress1             │
│ getAddress2             │
│ setAddress2             │
│ getCity                 │
│ setCity                 │
│ getState                │
│ setState                │
│ getPostalCode           │
│ setPostalCode           │
└─────────────────────────┘
```

FIGURE 2.5 Interface.

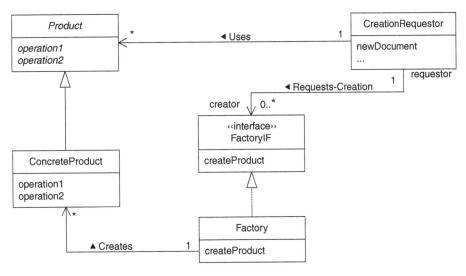

FIGURE 2.6 Class diagram.

The lines in Figure 2.6 indicate the relationships between the classes and an interface. A solid line with a closed hollow head, such as the one in Figure 2.7, indicates the relationship of a subclass that inherits from a superclass.

The class diagram in Figure 2.6 shows the abstract class Product as the superclass of the ConcreteProduct class. You can tell that it is abstract because its name is italicized. You can tell that its methods are abstract because they, too, are italicized.

A similar sort of line is used to indicate that a class implements an interface. It is a dotted or dashed line with a closed head like the one in Figure 2.8.

The class diagram in Figure 2.6 shows that the Factory class implements the FactoryIF interface.

The other lines show other types of relationships between the classes and interface. UML calls these other types of relationships *associations*. With associations can appear a number of things that provide information about the nature of an association. Although the following items are optional, this book consistently uses them wherever it makes sense to do so.

Association Name. Somewhere around the middle of an association there may be an association name. The name of an association is always capitalized. At one end of the association name there may be a triangle to indicate the direction in which you should read the association.

Looking at Figure 2.6, you will see that the association between the Factory and ConcreteProduct classes has the name Creates.

Navigation Arrows. Arrowheads that may appear at the ends of an association are called *navigation arrows*. Navigation arrows indicate the direction in which you may navigate an association.

Looking at the association named Creates in Figure 2.6, you will see a navigation arrow pointing from the Factory class to the ConcreteProduct class. Because of the nature of creation, it seems clear that it means the Factory class is responsible for creating instances of the ConcreteProduct class.

FIGURE 2.7 Subclass inherits from superclass.

FIGURE 2.8 Class implements an Interface.

The nature of some associations is less obvious. To make the nature of such associations clear, it may be necessary to supply additional information about the association. One common way to clarify the nature of an association is to name the role that each class plays in the association.

Role Name. To clarify the nature of an association, the name of the role each class plays in the association can appear at each end of an association, next to the corresponding class. Role names are always lowercase. That makes them easier to distinguish from association names, which are always capitalized.

In Figure 2.6, the `CreationRequester` class and the `FactoryIF` interface participate in an association named `Requests-Creation`. The `CreationRequester` class participates in that association in a role called `requester`. The `FactoryIF` interface participates in that association in a role called `creator`.

Multiplicity Indicator. Another helpful detail of an association is how many instances of each class participate in an occurrence of the association. A multiplicity indicator may appear at each end of an association to provide that information. A multiplicity indicator can be a simple number, like 0 or 1, or a range of numbers indicated like this:

    0..2

An asterisk as the high value of a range means an unlimited number of occurrences. The multiplicity indicator 1..* means at least one instance; 0..* means any number of instances. A simple * is equivalent to 0..*. Looking at the multiplicity indicators in Figure 2.6, you see that each one of the associations in the drawing is a one-to-many relationship.

Figure 2.9 is a class diagram that shows a class with multiple subclasses. Though the drawing in Figure 2.9 is perfectly valid, UML allows a more aesthetically pleasing way to draw a class with multiple subclasses. You can combine the arrowheads as is shown in Figure 2.10. The diagram in Figure 2.10 is identical in meaning to the diagram in Figure 2.9.

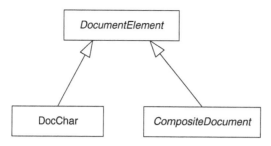

FIGURE 2.9 Multiple inheritance arrows.

Sometimes there is a need to convey more structure than is implied by a simple one-to-many relationship. The type of one-to-many relationship where one object contains a collection of other objects is called an *aggregation*. A hollow diamond at the end of the association indicates aggregation. The hollow diamond appears at the end of the association attached to the class that contains instances of the other class. The class diagram in Figure 2.11 shows an aggregation.

The class diagram in Figure 2.11 shows a class named Message-Manager. Each of its instances contains zero or more instances of a class named MIMEMsg.

UML has another notation to indicate a stronger relationship than aggregation. That relationship is called *composite aggregation*. For an aggregation to be composite, two conditions must be satisfied:

- Aggregated instances must belong to only one composite at a time.
- Some operations must propagate from the composite to its aggregated instances. For example, when a composite object is cloned, its clone method will typically clone the aggregated instances so that the cloned composite will own clones of the original aggregated instances.

Figure 2.12 is a class diagram that contains a composite aggregation.

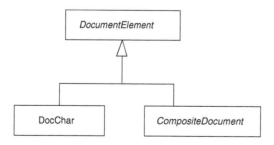

FIGURE 2.10 Single inheritance arrow.

FIGURE 2.11 Aggregation.

The class diagram in Figure 2.12 shows a Document class. Document objects can contain Paragraph objects; Paragraph objects can contain DocChar objects. Because of the composite aggregation, you know that Paragraph objects do not share DocChar objects and Document objects do not share Paragraph objects.

Some associations are indirect. Instead of classes being directly associated with each other, they are associated indirectly through a third class. Consider the class diagram in Figure 2.13.

The association in Figure 2.13 shows that instances of the Cache class refer to instances of the Object class through an instance of the ObjectID class.

There is another use for ellipsis in a class diagram. Some class diagrams need to show that a class has a large or open-ended set of subclasses, while only showing a few subclasses as examples of the sort of subclasses that the class has. The class diagram in Figure 2.14 shows how ellipsis can be used to show just that.

The class diagram in Figure 2.14 shows a class named DataQuery. The DataQuery class has subclasses named JDBCQuery, OracleQuery, Sybase-Query, and an indefinite number of other classes that are indicated by the ellipsis.

An association between classes or interfaces implies a dependency that involves an object reference connecting two objects. Other types of

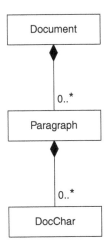

FIGURE 2.12 Composite aggregation.

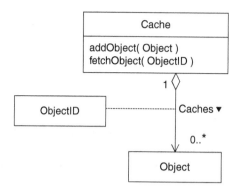

FIGURE 2.13 Association class.

dependencies are possible. A dashed line is used to indicate a dependency in the more general sense. Figure 2.15 shows an example of such a dependency.

The classes in a class diagram can be organized into packages. A package is drawn as a large rectangle above which lies a small rectangle containing the package name. The small and large rectangles are arranged to have an overall shape similar to that of a manila folder. The class diagram in Figure 2.16 contains a package.

Figure 2.16 shows a package named ServicePackage. A visibility indicator can precede the name of classes and interfaces that appear within a package. Public classes are accessible to classes outside of the package; private classes are not.

Sometimes there are aspects of a design that you cannot make sufficiently clear without a comment in a diagram. Comments in UML are drawn as a rectangle with its upper right corner turned down. Comments are attached to the diagram element to which they relate via a dashed line. The class diagram in Figure 2.17 contains a comment.

Figure 2.17 shows the static class MilestoneMemento, which is a private member of the GameModel class. There is no standard way in UML to

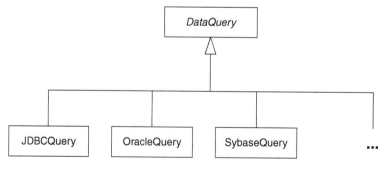

FIGURE 2.14 Open-ended subclasses.

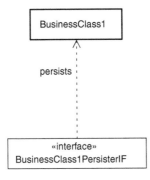

FIGURE 2.15 Dependency.

represent a static private member class. The diagram uses a stereotype as an extension to UML to indicate that the `MilestoneMemento` class is static. It uses an association to indicate that the `MilestoneMemento` is a private member of the `GameModel` class. To make the relationship even more clear, Figure 2.17 contains a comment about it.Class diagrams can include objects. Most of the objects in the class diagrams in this book are drawn as shown in Figure 2.18.

The object shown in Figure 2.18 is an instance of a class named `Area`. The underline tells you that it is an object. A name may appear to the left of the colon (:). The only significance of the name is that you can use it to identify the individual object.

Some diagrams indicate an object as just an empty rectangle. Obviously, blank objects cannot be used to identify any particular kind of object. However, they can be used in a diagram that shows a structure in which objects of unspecified types are connected. The class diagram in Figure 2.19 shows such a structure.

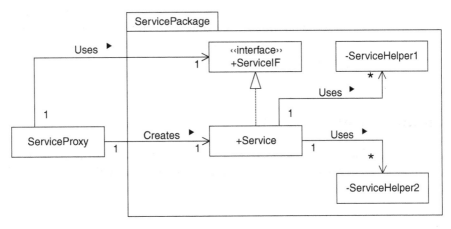

FIGURE 2.16 Package.

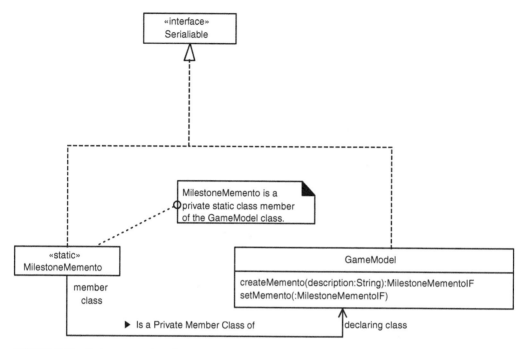

FIGURE 2.17 Private static classes.

The lines that connect two objects are not associations but links. Whereas links are connections between objects, associations are relationships between classes. A link is an occurrence of an association, just as an object is an instance of a class. Links can have association names, navigation arrows, and most of the other embellishments that associations can have. Because a link is a connection between two objects, it may not have multiplicity indicators or aggregation diamonds.

Some diagrams consist of just objects and links. Such diagrams are considered a kind of class diagram. However, there is a special name for this kind of diagram: *object diagram*. Figure 2.20 is an example of an object diagram.

Collaboration Diagram

Class and object diagrams show relationships between classes and objects. They also provide information about interactions between classes. They do

:Area

FIGURE 2.18 Object.

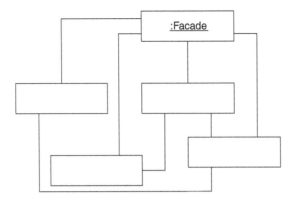

FIGURE 2.19 Blank objects.

not show the sequence in which the interactions occur or any concurrency that they may have.

Collaboration diagrams show objects, the links that connect them, and the interactions that occur over each link. They also show the sequence and concurrency requirements of each interaction. Figure 2.21 is a simple example of a collaboration diagram.

Any number of interactions can be associated with a link. Each interaction involves a method call. Next to each interaction or group of interactions is an arrow that points to the object whose method is called by the interaction. Collectively, the entire set of objects and interactions shown in a collaboration diagram is called a *collaboration*.

Each interaction shown in Figure 2.21 begins with a sequence number and a colon. Sequence numbers indicate the order in which method calls occur. An interaction with the number 1 must come before an interaction with the number 2, and so on.

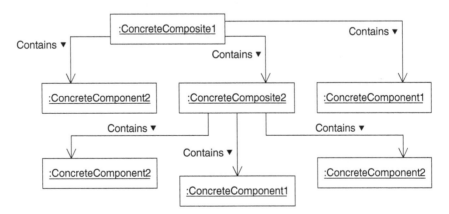

FIGURE 2.20 Object diagram.

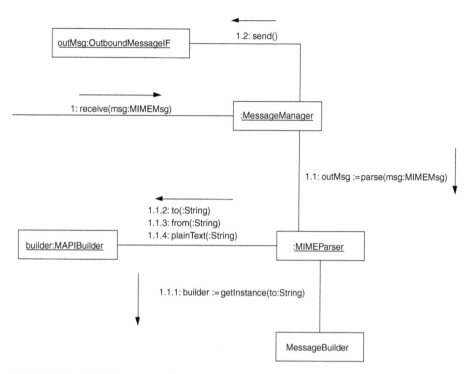

FIGURE 2.21 Collaboration diagram.

Multilevel sequence numbers consist of two or more numbers separated by a period. Notice that most of the sequence numbers in the diagram in Figure 2.21 are multilevel sequence numbers. Multilevel sequence numbers correspond to multiple levels of method calls. The portion of a multilevel sequence number to the left of its rightmost period is called its *prefix*. For example, the prefix of 1.3.4 is 1.3.

Interactions numbered with a multilevel sequence number occur during another interaction's method call. The other method call is determined by the interaction's prefix. The method calls of the interactions numbered 1.1 and 1.2 are made during the method call of interaction 1. Similarly, interactions numbered 1.1.1, 1.1.2, 1.1.3, and so forth, occur during the method call of interaction 1.1.

Among interactions numbered with the same prefix, their methods are called in the order determined by the last number in their sequence numbers. Therefore, the methods of interactions numbered 1.1.1, 1.1.2, 1.1.3, and so forth, are called in that order.

As mentioned earlier, links represent a connection between two objects. For this reason, links may not have any multiplicity indicators. That works well for links that represent an occurrence of an association

FIGURE 2.22 Multiobject.

between a definite number of objects. Associations that have a star multi-plicity indicator on either end involve an indefinite number of objects. There is no way to draw an indefinite number of links to an indefinite number of objects. UML provides a symbol, called a *multiobject,* that allows us to draw links for connecting an indefinite number of objects. A multiobject represents an indefinite number of objects. A multiobject looks like a rectangle behind a rectangle. The collaboration diagram in Figure 2.22 contains a multiobject.

The collaboration diagram in Figure 2.22 shows an ObservableIF object calling a Multicaster object's notify method. The Multicaster object's implementation of the notify method calls the notify method of an indefinite number of ObserverIF objects linked to the Multicaster object.

Objects created as a result of a collaboration may be marked with the property {new}. Temporary objects that exist only during a collaboration may be marked with the property {transient}.[1] The collaboration diagram in Figure 2.23 shows a collaboration that creates an object.

Some interactions happen concurrently rather than sequentially. A letter at the end of a sequence number indicates concurrent interactions.

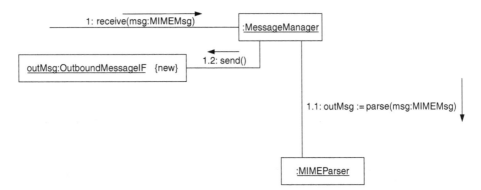

FIGURE 2.23 New object.

---

[1] UML's use of the word *transient* is very different from Java's use of the word. In UML, the word means that an object has a bounded lifetime; in Java, it means that a variable is not part of an object's persistent state.

For example, the methods of interactions numbered 2.2a and 2.2b would be called concurrently and each call would run in a separate thread. Consider the collaboration diagram in Figure 2.24.

In Figure 2.24, the top-level interaction is the one numbered 1. During that interaction, interaction 1.1 is invoked first; interactions 1.2a and 1.2b are then invoked at the same time. After that, interactions 1.3 and 1.4 are invoked, in that order.

An asterisk after a sequence number indicates a repeated interaction. Consider the collaboration diagram in Figure 2.25.

The collaboration in Figure 2.25 begins by calling the `TollBooth` object's `start` method. That method repeatedly calls the object's `collectNextToll` method. The `collectNextToll` method calls the `TollBasket` object's `collectToll` method and the `TollGate` object's `raiseGate` method.

One other thing to notice about the collaboration diagram in Figure 2.25 is the «self» stereotype that appears next to the link for interaction 1.1. It serves to clarify the fact that the link is a self-reference.

Unlike the example in Figure 2.25, most repetitive interactions occur conditionally. UML allows a condition to be associated with an interaction by putting it inside of square brackets before the colon. The collaboration diagram in Figure 2.26 shows an example of a conditional repetitive interaction.

Figure 2.26 shows an `Iterator` object being passed to a `DialogMediator` object's `refresh` method. Its `refresh` method, in turn, calls a `Widget` object's `reset` method and then repeatedly calls its `addData` method while the `Iterator` object's `hasNext` method returns true.

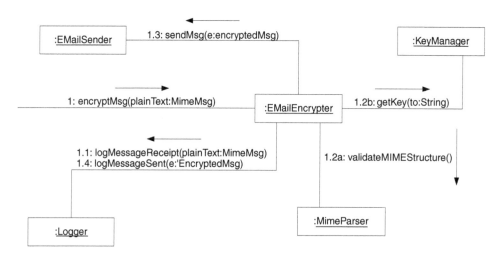

FIGURE 2.24 Email encrypter.

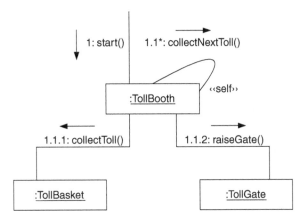

FIGURE 2.25 Toll booth.

It is important to note that the definition of UML does not define the meaning of conditions associated with repetitive interactions very precisely. In particular, the definition of UML says that what appears between the square brackets can be "expressed in pseudocode or an actual programming language." This book consistently uses Java for that purpose.

When dealing with multiple threads, something that often needs to be specified about methods is what happens when two threads try to call the same method at the same time. UML allows that to be specified by placing one of the following constructs after a method:

> {concurrency = sequential} This means that only one thread at a time should call a method. No guarantee is made about the correctness of the method's behavior if the method is called by multiple threads at a time.

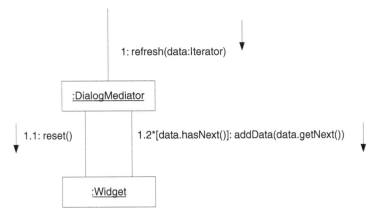

FIGURE 2.26 Refresh.

{concurrency = concurrent}   This means that if multiple threads call a method at the same time they will all execute it concurrently and correctly.

{concurrency = guarded}   This means that if multiple threads call a method at the same time, only one thread at a time will be allowed to execute the method. While one thread is executing the method, other threads will be forced to wait until it is their turn. This behavior is similar to that of synchronized Java methods.

The collaboration diagram in Figure 2.27 shows an example of a synchronized method.

There are refinements to thread synchronization used in this book for which there is no standard representation in UML. This book uses some extensions to the {concurrency = guarded} construct to represent those refinements.

Sometimes the object on which threads must synchronize is not the same object whose method is called by an interaction. Consider the collaboration diagram in Figure 2.28.

In Figure 2.28, {concurrency = guarded:lockObject} refers to the object labeled lockObject. Before the method call can actually take place, the thread that controls the call must own the lock associated with the out object. This is identical to Java's semantics for a synchronized statement.

Sometimes there are preconditions beyond acquiring ownership of a lock that must be met before a thread may proceed with a method call. Such preconditions are indicated by a vertical bar followed by the precondition. The collaboration diagram in Figure 2.29 shows such preconditions following guarded and a vertical bar.

The collaboration diagram in Figure 2.29 shows two asynchronous interactions. One interaction calls a PrintQueue object's addPrintJob method to add a print job to the PrintQueue object. In the other interaction, a PrintDriver object calls the PrintQueue object's getPrintJob

FIGURE 2.27 Synchronized method call.

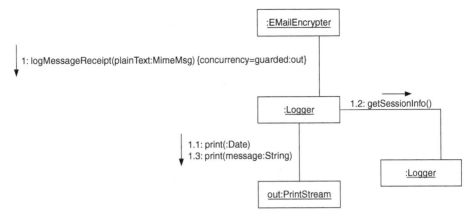

FIGURE 2.28 Synchronization using a third object.

method to get a print job from the PrintQueue object. Both interactions have synchronization preconditions. If the print queue is full, the interaction that calls the addPrintJob method will wait until the print queue is not full before proceeding to make the call to the addPrintJob method. If the print queue is empty, the interaction that calls the getPrintJob method will wait until the print queue is not empty before proceeding to make the call to the getPrintJob method.

A type of precondition not usually indicated with an expression is the requirement that an interaction not start until two or more other interactions finish. An implicit precondition in all interactions is that they not start before the directly preceding interaction finishes; for example, an interaction numbered 1.2.4 cannot start until the interaction numbered 1.2.3 completes.

Before they can start, some interactions are required to wait for additional, or *predecessor*, interactions to complete. Such additional predeces-

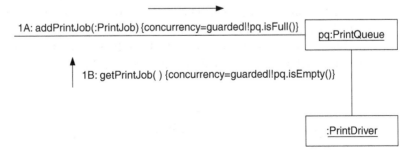

FIGURE 2.29 Print queue.

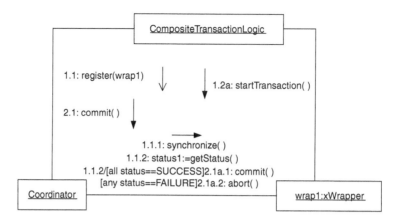

FIGURE 2.30 Additional predecessor interactions.

sor interactions are indicated by listing them at the left side of the interaction followed by a slash (/) and the rest of the interaction. The collaboration diagram in Figure 2.30 contains an example.

In Figure 2.30, the interaction labeled 2.1a.1 cannot start until interaction 1.1.2 finishes. If an interaction must wait for more than one additional predecessor interactions to finish before it starts, they appear before the slash and are separated from other such interactions by commas.

The mechanisms discussed so far determine when the methods of a collaboration are called. They do not, however, say anything about when method calls return. The arrows that point at the objects whose methods are called provide information about when the methods may return.

Most of the arrows in Figure 2.30 have a closed head, which indicates that the calls are synchronous. The method calls do not return until the method has completed doing whatever it does.

An open arrowhead indicates an asynchronous method call. An asynchronous method call returns to its caller immediately, while the method does its work asynchronously in a separate thread. The collaboration diagram in Figure 2.31 shows an asynchronous method call.

UML only defines arrowheads for synchronous and asynchronous calls. UML allows other types of arrows to indicate different types of method calls as extensions to UML. To indicate a balking call, this book uses a bent-back arrow, as shown in Figure 2.32.

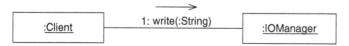

FIGURE 2.31 Asynchronous method call.

FIGURE 2.32 Balking call.

When a balking call is made to an object's method and there is no other thread executing that object's method, it will return when the method is finished doing what it does. However, when a balking call is made and another thread is currently executing that object's method, the method returns immediately without doing anything.

You may have noticed that the object that makes the top-level call that initiates a collaboration is not shown in all of the collaboration diagrams. If the object that initiates the collaboration is not part of a collaboration diagram, then it is not considered to be a part of the collaboration.

Up to this point, the objects discussed for modeling in UML have been passive in nature—that is, they do nothing until one of their methods is called.

Some objects are active. They have a thread associated with them that allows them to initiate operations asynchronously and independently of whatever else is happening in a program. An active object is indicated with a thick border. Figure 2.33 contains an example of an active object.

Figure 2.33 shows an active `Sensor` object that calls a `SensorObserver` object's method without another object first calling one of its methods.

Statechart Diagram

Statechart diagrams are used to model a class's behavior as a state machine. Figure 2.34 is an example of a simple state diagram.

A statechart diagram shows each state as a rounded rectangle. The states in Figure 2.34 are all divided into two compartments: The upper compartment contains the name of the state. The lower compartment contains a list of events to which the object responds while in that state but

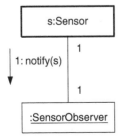

FIGURE 2.33 Active sensor.

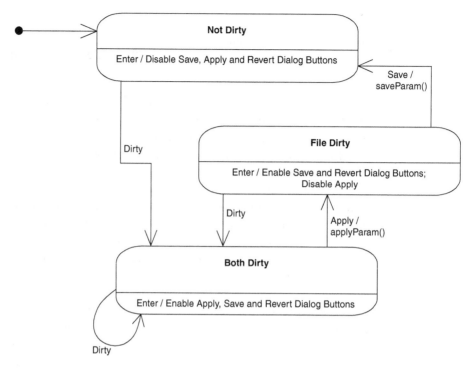

FIGURE 2.34 Statechart diagram.

without changing state. Each event in the list is followed by a slash and the action that it performs in response to the event. UML predefines two such events:

- The enter event, which occurs when an object enters a state
- The exit event, which occurs when an object leaves a state

If all events cause an object in a state to change to a different state, the state's rectangle is not divided into two compartments. Such a state is drawn as a simple rounded rectangle that contains only the state's name.

Every state machine has an initial state that an object is in before the first transition occurs. The initial state is drawn as a small, solid circle.

Transitions between states are shown in statechart diagrams as lines between states. Normally, transition lines are required to have a label that indicates the event that triggers the transition. The event may be followed by a slash and the action that occurs when the transition takes place.

If a statechart includes a final state, the final state is drawn as a small, solid circle inside of a larger circle.

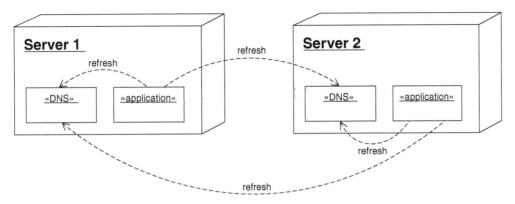

FIGURE 2.35 Deployment diagram.

Deployment Diagram

Deployment diagrams show how software is deployed onto computing elements. Figure 2.35 is an example of a deployment diagram.

Figure 2.35 shows two computing elements labeled Server1 and Server2. The UML terminology for computing element is *node*. However, because this book uses this word to mean other things, the term *computing element* is used instead.

The smaller boxes inside the computing elements are software components. A component is a collection of objects that are deployed together. Each computing element in the diagram contains two components: a DNS component and an application component.

Communications between components are indicated by dashed lines. In Figure 2.35, the dashed lines, labeled refresh, indicate that the application components send messages to the DNS components.

The Software Life Cycle

This volume is devoted to patterns used during the object-oriented design phase of the software life cycle. This chapter first describes the software life cycle; then it presents the object-oriented design portion of a case study.

There are a variety of activities that take place during the lifetime of a piece of software. Figure 3.1 shows some of the activities that lead to the deployment of a piece of business software.

Figure 3.1 is not intended to show all the activities that occur during a software project. It merely shows some common activities for the purpose of understanding the context for the patterns discussed in this book. The volumes of this work describe recurring patterns that occur during the portion of the software life cycle labeled in Figure 3.1 as "Build".

Figure 3.1 shows very clear boundaries between each activity. In practice, the boundaries are not always so clear. Sometimes it is difficult to say whether a particular activity belongs in one box or another. The precise boundaries are not important. What is important is to understand the relationships between these activities.

Earlier activities, such as defining requirements and object-oriented analysis, determine the course of activities that follow them, such as defining essential use cases or object-oriented design. In the course of those later activities, however, deficiencies emerge in the products of earlier activities.

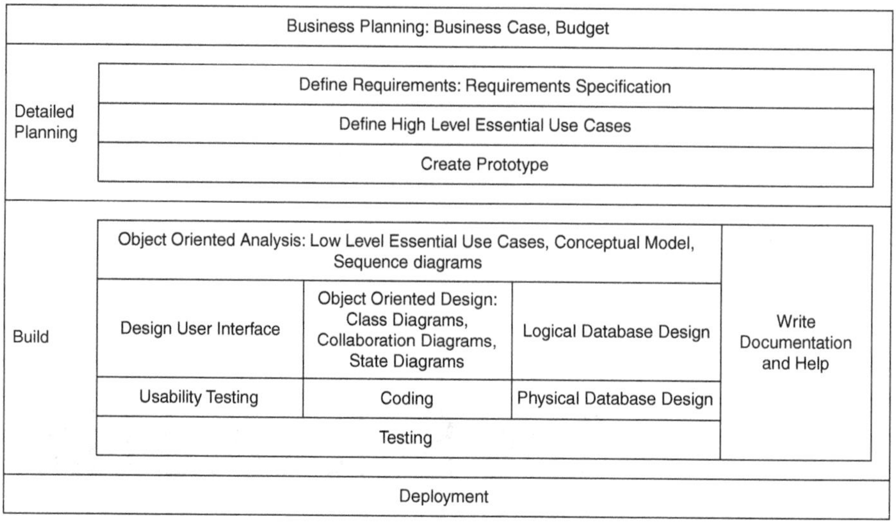

Business Planning: Business Case, Budget				

Detailed Planning	Define Requirements: Requirements Specification			
	Define High Level Essential Use Cases			
	Create Prototype			

Build	Object Oriented Analysis: Low Level Essential Use Cases, Conceptual Model, Sequence diagrams			Write Documentation and Help
	Design User Interface	Object Oriented Design: Class Diagrams, Collaboration Diagrams, State Diagrams	Logical Database Design	
	Usability Testing	Coding	Physical Database Design	
	Testing			

Deployment				

FIGURE 3.1 Activities leading to software deployment.

For example, in the course of defining a use case, it may become apparent that there is an ambiguous or conflicting requirement. Making the necessary changes to the requirements will generally result in the need to modify existing use cases or write new ones. You should expect such iterations. So long as the trend is for later iterations to produce fewer changes than earlier iterations, consider the iterations to be part of the normal development process.

What follows are brief descriptions of some of the activities shown in Figure 3.1. These descriptions provide only enough information about these activities to understand how the patterns discussed in this work apply to a relevant activity. The case study that follows the descriptions provides deeper insights into these activities.

> **Business Planning.**   This typically starts with a proposal to build or modify a piece of software. The proposal evolves into a *business case*. A business case is a document that describes the pros and cons of the software project and also includes estimates of the resources that will be required to complete the project. If a decision is made to proceed with the project, then a preliminary schedule and budget are prepared.
>
> **Define Requirements.**   The purpose of this activity is to produce a *requirements specification* that says what the software produced by the project will and will not do. This typically begins with goals and high-level requirements from the business case. Additional requirements are obtained from appropriate sources to produce an initial requirements specification.

As the requirements specification is used in subsequent activities, necessary refinements to the requirements are discovered. The refinements are incorporated into the requirements specification. The products of subsequent activities are then modified to reflect the changes to the requirements specification.

Define Essential Use Cases.   A use case describes the sequence of events that occurs in a specific circumstance between a system and other entities called *actors*. Developing use cases improves our understanding of the requirements, analysis, or design that the use case is based on. As we develop a better understanding of requirements, analysis, and design, we are able to refine them.

Essential use cases describe events in terms of the problem domain. Use cases that describe events in terms of the internal organization of software are called *real use cases*.

The type of use case most appropriate for refining requirements are high-level essential use cases. Such use cases are high-level in the sense that they explore the implications of what they are based on but do not try to add additional details.

Create Prototype.   Create a prototype of the proposed software. A prototype can be used to get reactions to a proposed project. Reactions to a prototype can be used to refine requirements and essential use cases.

Define High-Level System Architecture.   Determine the major components of the system that are obvious from the original proposal. Also determine their relationships.

Object-Oriented Analysis.   The purpose of this activity is to understand what the software produced by the project will do and how it will interact with other entities in its environment. The goal of analysis is to create a model of what the software is going to do but not how to do it. The products of object-oriented analysis model the situation in which the software will operate, from the perspective of an outside observer. The analysis does not concern itself with what goes on inside the software.

Object-Oriented Design.   The purpose of this activity is to determine the internal organization of software. The products of the design effort identify the classes that will comprise the internal logic of the software. They also determine the internal structure of the classes and their interrelationships.

More decisions are made during object-oriented design than during any other activity. For that reason, this work includes more patterns that apply to object-oriented design than any other activity.

Coding.   The purpose of this activity is to write the code that will make the software work.

Testing.   The purpose of this phase is to ensure that the software works as expected.

Case Study

What follows is a case study that involves the design and development of an employee timekeeping system for a fictitious business called Henry's Food Market. To keep the size of this case study reasonable, the artifacts of the development process are simplified and abbreviated. Details of deriving those artifacts are also abbreviated. The point of this case study is to set the stage for a situation where applications of design patterns can be demonstrated.

Business Case

Here is an abbreviated business case that lays out the motivation and schedule for building an employee timekeeping system.

Henry's Food Market operates five retail stores. To support those stores, it operates a warehouse, as well as a commercial bakery that produces the baked goods that the stores sell. Most of the company's employees are paid by the hour. The hours of employees are tracked by a time-clock system. When beginning work, going on break, returning from break, and ending work, all employees are supposed to slide their employee badges through a timekeeping clock that records their hours.

Henry's Food Market wants to expand, increasing the number of its stores from 5 to 21 over the next two years at a rate of two stores every three months. One challenge facing the company is that should it continue to use its existing timekeeping system, it will have to hire more employees to handle the system's administrative side. Currently, each location requires a person working half-time as a timekeeper to administer its timekeeping system. The timekeeper is required to perform the following activities:

- The timekeeper prints reports showing the number of hours that each employee worked the previous day, so supervisors can verify that their subordinates worked their stated number of hours. Some common errors that supervisors uncover while reviewing these reports include the following:
  - Employees not clocking out when going on break or leaving work
  - Employees clocking in employees who report late to work

- Employees clocking in before the beginning of their shift, hoping to be paid for the extra time
- The timekeeper enters corrections into the timekeeping system.
- The timekeeper prepares weekly reports showing the number of hours each employee works in a given location, and sends those reports to the payroll department.

Because the timekeeping system provides employee hours in the form of a printed report only, there is currently one person who works full-time to enter employee hours into the payroll system and review the entered hours. That person costs the company $24,000 per year. If the company continues to use the same system, it will have to hire another person, at an additional cost of $24,000 per year, to enter employee hours.

The cost of having a person working half-time as a timekeeper in each location is $9,000 per person per year. The current cost of paying people to be timekeepers is $63,000 per year.

The total current cost of labor for timekeeping is $87,000 per year. In two years, when the company's expansion is complete, that labor cost for timekeeping will have increased to $237,000.

The proposed project is to build a replacement timekeeping system that will keep the labor cost of timekeeping at current or lower levels after the expansion. The timekeeping system is expected to pay for itself in 18 months. It is expected to be deployed within 6 months of the beginning of the project.

Define Requirements Specification

Minimally, a requirements specification should specify the required functions and attributes of what a project produces. Required functions are things that the system must do, such as recording the time when an employee begins work. Required attributes are characteristics of the system that are not functions, such as requiring that users with just an eighth grade education are able to use the timekeeping terminals. There are some other things that are normally found in a requirements document that are not in the following example:

Assumptions. This is a list of things that are assumed to be true, such as the minimum educational level of employees or that the company will not become unionized.

Risks. This is a list of things that may go wrong, leading to delay or failure of the project. This list may include technical uncertainties, such as the availability of devices that are suitable for use as timekeeping terminals. It may also include nontechnical concerns, such as anticipated changes to labor laws.

Dependencies. This is a list of resources the project may depend on, such as the existence of a wide-area network.

It is helpful to number the requirements in a requirements specification. Doing so allows decisions based on a requirement to be easily noted in use cases, design documents, and even code. If inconsistencies are found later, it will be easy to trace them back to the relevant requirements. It is common to number requirements hierarchically by functions. The following are some required functions of the timekeeping system:

R1 The system must collect the times that employees start work, go on break, return from break, and leave work.

> **R1.1** In order to work with the timekeeping terminal, employees are required to identify themselves by sliding their employee badge through a badge reader on the timekeeping terminal.
>
> **R1.2** After an employee is identified to a timekeeping terminal, that employee will be able to press a button to indicate whether he or she is starting a work shift, going on break, returning from break, or ending a work shift. The timekeeping system will keep a permanent record of each such event in a form that it can later incorporate into a report of the employee's hours.

R2 Supervisors must be able to review the hours of subordinates at a timekeeping terminal without any need to get hard copy.

> **R2.1** Timekeeping terminals present options to supervisors that allow them to review and modify an employee's recorded hours.
>
> > **R2.1.1** All revisions made to an employee's timekeeping record leave an audit trail that retains the original records and identifies the person who made each revision.
>
> **R2.2** To ensure the simplest possible user interface for nonsupervisors, nonsupervisors will not see any options related to supervisory functions when they use a timekeeping terminal.
>
> **R2.3** Supervisors are able to modify the timekeeping records of only their own subordinates.

R3 At the end of each pay period, the timekeeping system must automatically transmit employee hours to the payroll system.

As we develop some use cases, you can expect to discover additional required functions.

Develop High-Level Essential Use Cases

When developing use cases, it is usually best to first focus on the most common cases and then develop use cases for less common cases. Use cases for common situations are called *primary use cases;* use cases for less common situations, *secondary use cases.* Here is a use case for the most common use of the timekeeping system:

Use case:	Employee Uses Timekeeping Terminal, version 1.
Actor:	Employee.
Purpose:	Inform timekeeping system of an employee's comings and goings.
Synopsis:	An employee is about to begin a work shift, go on break, return from break, or end a work shift. The employee identifies him- or herself to the timekeeping system and lets it know which of those four things he or she is about to do.
Type:	Primary and essential.
Cross-References:	Requirements R1, R1.1, R1.2, R1.3, and R2.2.

Course of Events

Employee	System
1. Employee slides his or her badge through a timekeeping terminal's badge reader.	2. The timekeeping terminal reads the employee ID from the badge and verifies that it is a legitimate employee ID. The timekeeping terminal then prompts the employee to tell it whether he or she is starting a work shift, going on break, returning from break, or ending a work shift.
3. The employee indicates to the timekeeping terminal whether he or she is starting a work shift, going on break, returning from break, or ending a work shift.	4. The timekeeping terminal makes a permanent record of the employee's indication. It then acknowledges the employee by displaying the current time, indicating that it is ready for use by the next employee.

Now we consider a larger use case that is less detailed:

Use case:	Employee Uses Multiple Timekeeping Terminals to Track Hours, version 1.
Actors:	Employee.

Purpose:	Inform timekeeping system of an employee's comings and goings during an entire shift.
Synopsis:	An employee who is not restricted to the use of a single timekeeping terminal notifies the time-keeping system when he or she starts a shift, goes on break, returns from break, and ends a shift.
Type:	Primary and essential.
Cross-references:	Requirements R1 and R1.2.

Course of Events

Employee	System
1. An employee uses a timekeeping terminal to notify the timekeeping system that he or she is beginning a shift.	2. The system makes a record of the time that the employee began the shift.
3. An employee uses a timekeeping terminal to notify the timekeeping system that he or she is going on break.	4. The system makes a record of the time that the employee went on break.
5. An employee uses a timekeeping terminal to notify the timekeeping system that he or she has returned from break.	6. The system makes a record of the time that the employee returned from break.
7. An employee uses a timekeeping terminal to notify the timekeeping system that he or she is ending a shift.	8. The system makes a record of the time that the employee ended the shift.

Analyzing the less detailed use case, we find a potential problem: The absence of a requirement that the timekeeping terminals all maintain the correct time. Employees are likely to notice if the time on different time-keeping terminals is not the same. They would want to start their shift on the terminal that shows the later time and end their shift on the terminal that shows the earlier time. To prevent employees from cheating the company in this way, we add another requirement:

R1.3 The times displayed and recorded by different timekeeping ter-minals must be within 5 seconds of each other.

As we develop additional essential use cases, additional refinements to the requirements will be found. However, this is all that we present in this case study.

Object-Oriented Analysis

Object-oriented analysis is concerned with building a model of the problem to be solved. It answers the question of what the software will do without being concerned with how it will do it.

The primary product of object-oriented analysis is a conceptual model of the problem that shows the proposed system and the real-world entities with which the system will interact. The conceptual model also includes the relationships and interactions between the entities and between the entities and the system.

Conceptual models are usually constructed in two phases:

1. Identify the entities that are involved in the problem. It is very important to identify all the entities involved. When in doubt, it is best to include an entity in the model. As the design develops, it will become apparent whether the entity is necessary for subsequent design activities. However, an entity missing from the analysis might not be detected later.
2. Build a conceptual model to identify relationships between the entities.

UML uses the same symbols to represent the entities and relationships of a conceptual model as it uses to represent classes and associations in a class model. Figure 3.2 is a diagram that shows just the entities that are apparent from the requirements and the use cases.

The entities in Figure 3.2 are in no particular order. The diagram in Figure 3.3 adds some of the more obvious relationships.

As you look at the diagram in Figure 3.3, you will notice two entities that are not involved in any of the indicated relationships: `TimekeepingSystem` and `EmployeeID`.

The diagram in Figure 3.3 is supposed to be a conceptual model of the problem to be solved. Because the `TimekeepingSystem` entity does not seem to have a relationship to anything else in the problem, we conclude that it is really part of the solution rather than the problem. For that reason, we will drop it from the model.

The `EmployeeID` entity is very closely related to the `Employee` entity. It is so closely related, in fact, to the `Employee` entity that it seems more appropriate to represent it as an attribute. The diagram in Figure 3.4 shows the conceptual model with attributes added.

The diagram in Figure 3.4 is as far as we will take the analysis of this problem.

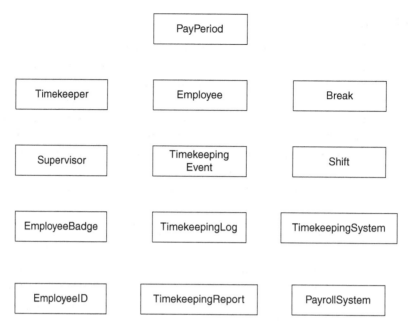

FIGURE 3.2 Conceptual model (entities only).

Object-Oriented Design

Object-oriented design is concerned with designing the internal logic of a program. In this case, we are concerned with the internal logic of the time-keeping system. Object-oriented design is concerned neither with how the user interface presents that logic nor with how data is stored in a database. Its ultimate goal is to provide a detailed design of the classes that will provide that internal logic.

There are various strategies for using the results of analysis to produce a design. The strategy we use here is to create a class diagram that models the structural relationships in the conceptual model. We then develop collaboration diagrams to model the behavioral relationships in the conceptual model, after which we refine the class diagrams with what we learned from the collaboration diagrams, then refine the collaboration and class diagrams with requirements not covered by the conceptual model. Throughout this process, we use design patterns to guide us.

We construct our first class diagram by assuming that there is a class to represent each entity in the conceptual model, as shown in Figure 3.5. Rather than assume the representation of the entity attributes in the conceptual model, the class diagram in Figure 3.5 indicates *accessor methods* for the attributes.

Next we consider the "Is-a" relationships in the conceptual model. Though an obvious way to represent "Is-a" relationship in a class diagram

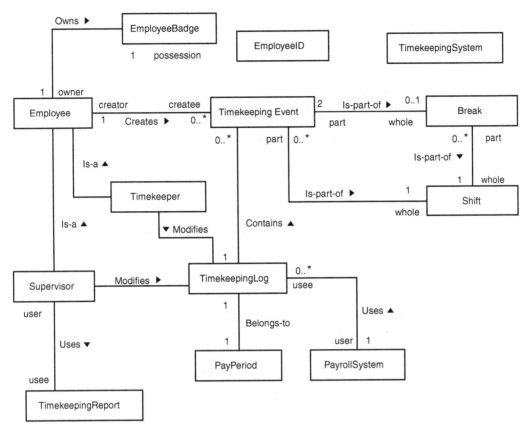

FIGURE 3.3 Conceptual model (with associations).

is through inheritance, the Delegation pattern tells us that it is not always the best way to represent "Is-a" relationships. In particular, it tells us to use delegation instead of inheritance to represent "Is-a" relationships to represent roles that instances of a class may play—if instances of the class play different roles at different times. Since a nonsupervisory employee may be promoted to supervisor, transferred from another job to the timekeeper job, or become a timekeeping supervisor, we use delegation to represent those roles. Figure 3.6 is a version of the class diagram that adds the role relationships.

The "Is-part-of" relationships in the conceptual diagram are another structural relationship that at this point we might consider designing into the class diagram. We notice that there is some redundancy between two sets of "Is-part-of" relationships: The "Is-part-of" relationship between Shift and TimekeepingEvent appears to have some redundancy with the set of "Is-part-of" relationships between Shift and Break and between Break and TimekeepingEvent. For that reason, we postpone including those rela-

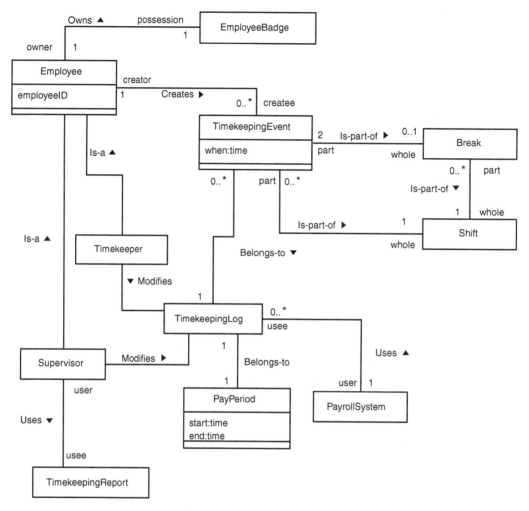

FIGURE 3.4 Conceptual model (with attributes).

tionships in the design until we clarify the relationships through the construction of collaboration diagrams.

Because we guide the construction of collaboration diagrams with use cases, we construct the following real use case to describe a day's use of the timekeeping system for a typical employee.

Use case:	Employee Uses Timekeeping Terminal to Track Hours, version 1.
Actors:	Employee.
Purpose:	Inform timekeeping system of an employee's comings and goings.
Synopsis:	An employee is about to begin a work shift, go

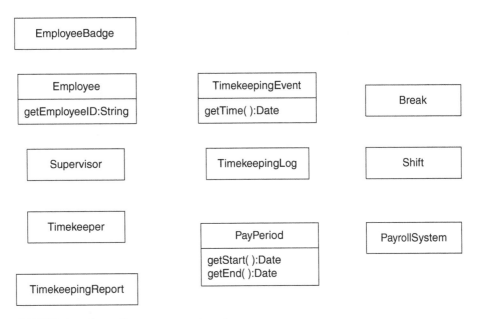

FIGURE 3.5 Class diagram, version 1.

on break, return from break, or end a work shift. He or she identifies him- or herself to the timekeeping system and lets it know which of those four things he or she is about to do.

Type:	Primary and real.
Cross-References:	Requirements R1, R1.1, R1.2, R1.3, and R2.2; essential use case "Employee Uses Timekeeping Terminal."

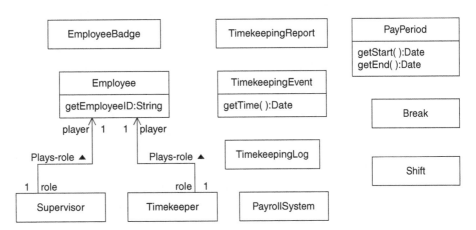

FIGURE 3.6 Class diagram, version 2.

Course of Events

Employee	*System*
1. Employee slides his or her badge through a timekeeping terminal's badge reader.	2. The timekeeping terminal replaces its display of the current time, indicating that it is looking up the employee ID detected by the badge reader. After the timekeeping terminal has looked up the employee's information, it first checks whether the employee is allowed to use this particular time-keeping terminal. It then prompts the employee to tell it whether he or she is starting a work shift, going on break, returning from break, or ending a work shift.
3. The employee indicates to the time-keeping terminal whether he or she is starting a work shift, going on break, returning from break, or ending a work shift.	4. The timekeeping terminal makes a permanent record of the employee's indication. It acknowledges the completion of the timekeeping transaction by displaying the current time, indicating that it is ready for use by the next employee.

We can see that the preceding use case involves classes that are not in Figure 3.6. This use case talks about a timekeeping terminal interacting with a user, so we include a user interface class in our design. We may later refine that into additional classes if it seems necessary.

The use case also mentions creating a permanent record of timekeeping events. To manage that and the employee information that the timekeeping terminal looks up, we infer the existence of a database object. Again, we leave open the possibility of later additional refinement.

We want to minimize the number of dependencies between the user interface and the classes that implement the timekeeping terminal's internal logic. Maintaining loose coupling between the user interface and the internal logic makes the software more maintainable. To achieve this, we use the Façade pattern. The Façade pattern tells us that we can maintain low coupling between a functionally related set of classes and their client classes by interposing an additional façade class between the set of classes and their clients. Most or all of the client's access to the set of classes is through the façade class. The façade class also encapsulates the common logic that is needed to use the set of classes.

The façade class that we add to the design is called `TimekeepingController`. It is responsible for controlling the sequence of events that occurs when a timekeeping terminal interacts with a user.

Based on the preceding use case, we construct the collaboration diagram shown in Figure 3.7.

Here is a description of the interactions shown in the collaboration diagram in Figure 3.7:

1. The `UserInterface` object begins the collaboration by passing an employee ID to the `TimekeepingController` object's `doTransaction` method.

> **1.1** The `TimekeepingController` object gets information about the employee associated with the employee ID by passing the employee ID to the `Database` object's `LookupEmployee` method. The `LookupEmployee` method returns an `Employee` object that encapsulates information about the employee.
>
> **1.2** The `TimekeepingController` object calls the `UserInterface` object's `getEventType` method, which causes the user interface to prompt the employee for the type of event that should be recorded. The method returns a value that indicates the type of event to record.
>
> **1.3** The `TimekeepingController` object passes the event type that it got from the user interface to the `TimekeepingEvent` class's `createEvent` method. The `createEvent` method returns an object that encapsulates the event.
>
> **1.4** The `TimekeepingController` object passes the event object to the Database object's `storeEvent` method so that it can be stored in the database.

What follows is some of the rationale behind the construction of the start-shift collaboration diagram in Figure 3.7.

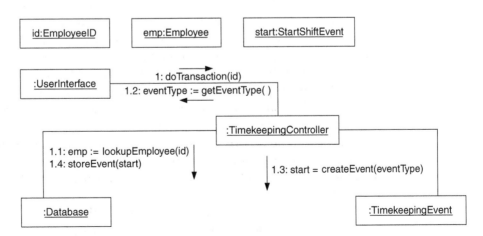

FIGURE 3.7 Start-shift collaboration.

- The `Database` class's `lookupEmployee` operation creates an object to encapsulate the employee information that it finds. The Creator pattern, described in *Patterns in Java, Volume 2,* says that if an object contains, aggregates, records instances of, or provides initializing data for instances of a class, then that object is a good choice of creator for instances of that class. Therefore, the objects that the `Database` class's `lookupEmployee` operation creates will be instances of the `Employee` class.

- Because a start-of-shift event is a kind of timekeeping event, objects that represent this event are an instance of a subclass of the `TimekeepingEvent` class. There are other subclasses of the `TimekeepingEvent` class to represent other kinds of timekeeping events. We don't want the user interface to know about the subclasses of the `TimekeepingEvent` class, because we want to minimize the dependencies between the user interface and the internal logic. To achieve this, we use the Factory Method pattern.

The Factory Method pattern puts one class in charge of creating instances of other classes that have a common superclass or implement a common interface. Following that pattern, we put the `TimekeepingEvent` class in charge of creating instances of its subclasses.

Figure 3.8 is another version of the class diagram that we have been working on. It includes refinements from what we have learned from the collaboration diagram in Figure 3.6.

The `EmployeeBadge` class has been removed from the design, because the mechanism for capturing an employee ID is part of the user interface, not part of the internal logic.

For the next refinement to the design, we will take a closer look at the `Database` class. The intent of the `TimekeepingLog` entity in the conceptual model was to maintain a log of all timekeeping events. We created a class that corresponds to it in our initial design. Now, we notice that the `Database` class has been given that responsibility. That means that we don't need the `TimekeepingLog` class in the design, so we will remove it.

An area of the design that we have not yet addressed is the generation of timekeeping reports. Supervisors use timekeeping reports to review the hours that their subordinates have worked. Specially formatted timekeeping reports are fed to the payroll system.

Timekeeping reports organize timekeeping events into shifts. A shift is a range of time during which an employee is at work. During a shift, an employee is supposed to be working, except for periods within a shift called *breaks*. Breaks are periods when an employee stops working for such reasons as eating lunch or going to the bathroom.

For the purpose of computing an employee's pay, the time during a shift is broken down into three categories.

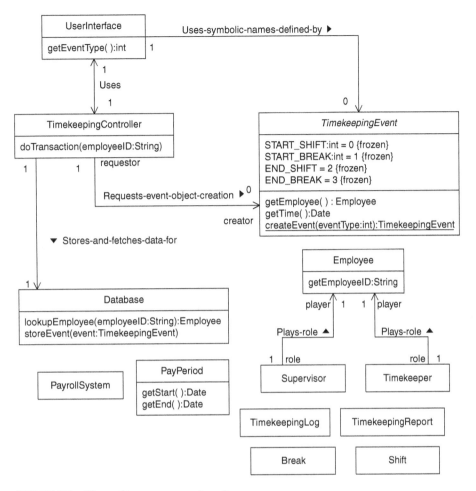

FIGURE 3.8 Class diagram, version 3.

- *Regular time* is time that an employee is paid at his or her usual hourly rate.
- *Overtime* is time beyond the time that an employee is normally expected to work. An employee is paid for overtime at a multiple of his or her regular-time rate.
- *Unpaid time* is time that an employee is not paid for. Some or all of an employee's break time may be unpaid time.

Timekeeping reports must break down the time that an employee has worked into these three categories and indicate the amount of money an employee has earned before taxes and other deductions.

The rules for classifying time as regular time, overtime, and unpaid time vary from state to state. The rules for computing the multiple of the regular rate that is paid for overtime also vary from state to state. Henry's

Food Market currently operates in only one state. However, there are plans to expand into other states. Therefore, the design must account for different rules used to classify an employee's hours and compute the employee's pay.

To allow different sets of rules to be selected for timekeeping computations, we need to devise a way to organize a set of rules as a set of objects. We can represent a set of rules as finite state machines that take timekeeping events as input and respond to the input by performing timekeeping computations. The statechart diagram in Figure 3.9 shows a sample state machine that, omitting states and transitions for error handling, models timekeeping rules for the state of Georgia.

To implement the state machine shown in Figure 3.9, we can use the State pattern. The State pattern tells us to implement the states of a state class as classes that implement a common interface. The class diagram in Figure 3.10 shows how the State pattern can be used to implement the state machine in Figure 3.9.

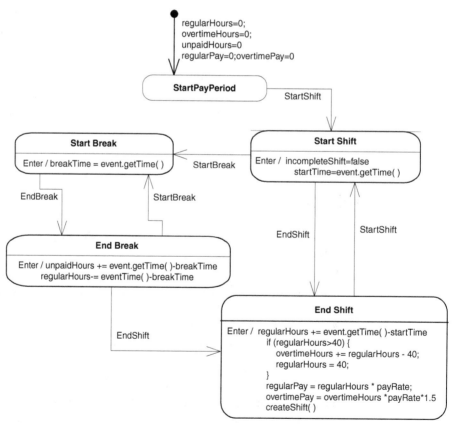

FIGURE 3.9 Sample state-based timekeeping computation.

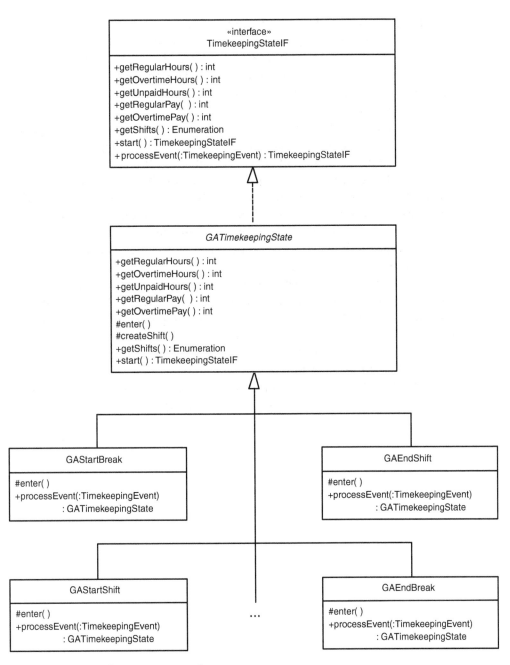

FIGURE 3.10 Timekeeping state classes.

Here is how the classes in Figure 3.10 are used. A program that gets an employee's timekeeping events from the database creates a GATimekeepingState object. It uses an instance of each of its subclasses to represent each of the state machine's states. The GATimekeepingState object's start method returns the state machine's initial state and makes that state the current state.

After a program creates an instance of GATimekeepingState, it calls its start method to get the initial state. Then the program begins fetching an employee's timekeeping events from the database. It passes each timekeeping event object it fetches to the processEvent method of the current state object. The processEvent method causes the state machine to transition to another state based on the type of timekeeping event that is passed to it. The processEvent method returns the new current state. When the processEvent method causes the state machine to enter a state, it calls that state object's enter method.

As the state machine shifts from state to state, it computes the employee's hours and gross pay. It also organizes the timekeeping events into shifts. When the program is finished passing an employee's timekeeping events to the state machine, it can call appropriate methods of the GATimekeepingState object to get the employee's hours, gross pay, or an Enumeration of the shifts that the employee worked.

This is as far as we take this case study. It is hoped that the case study has provided you with some insight about how to use design patterns.

4

Fundamental Design Patterns

The patterns in this chapter are the most fundamental and important design patterns to know. You will find these patterns used extensively in other design patterns.

The Delegation; Interface; Abstract Superclass; and Interface and Abstract Class patterns demonstrate how to organize relationships between classes. Most patterns use at least one of these patterns. They are so ubiquitous that they are often not mentioned in the Related Patterns sections for most patterns.

The Immutable pattern describes a way to avoid bugs and delays when multiple objects access the same object. Although the Immutable pattern is not explicitly part of the majority of other patterns, it can be used advantageously with most patterns.

The Marker Interface pattern describes a way to simplify the design of classes that have a constant boolean attribute.

The Proxy pattern is the basis for a number of patterns that share the common concept in which an object manages access to another object in a relatively transparent way.

Delegation (When Not to Use Inheritance)

SYNOPSIS

In some situations, using inheritance to extend a class leads to a bad design. Though less convenient, delegation is a more general-purpose way of extending classes. Delegation succeeds in many situations where inheritance does not work well.

CONTEXT

Inheritance is a common way to extend and reuse the functionality of a class. Delegation is a more general way for extending a class's behavior that involves a class calling another class's methods rather than inheriting them. Inheritance is inappropriate for many situations in which delegation is appropriate.

For example, inheritance is useful for capturing "is-a-kind-of" relationships because of their static nature. However, "is-a-role-played-by" relationships are awkward to model by inheritance. Instances of a class can play multiple roles. Consider the example of an airline reservation system that includes such roles as passenger, ticket-selling agent, and flight crew. It's possible to represent these role relationships as a class called `Person` that has subclasses corresponding to these roles, as shown in Figure 4.1.

The problem with the model in Figure 4.1 is that the same person can fill more than one of these roles. A person who is normally part of a flight crew can also be a passenger. Some airlines occasionally float flight crew members to the ticket counter, which means that the same person can fill

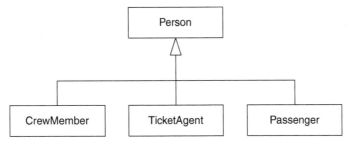

FIGURE 4.1 Modeling roles with inheritance.

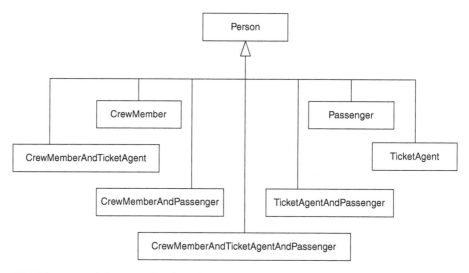

FIGURE 4.2 Modeling multiple roles with Inheritance.

any combination of these roles. To model this situation, you would need seven subclasses for Person, as shown in Figure 4.2. The number of subclasses needed increases exponentially with the number of roles. To model all the combinations of six roles would require 63 subclasses.

A more serious problem is that the same person may play different combinations of roles at different times. Inheritance relationships are static and do not change over time. To model different combinations of roles over time using inheritance relationships, it is necessary to use different objects at different times to represent the same person in order to capture changes in role. Modeling dynamically changing roles with inheritance gets complicated.

On the other hand, it is possible to represent persons in different roles using delegation without having any of these problems. Figure 4.3 shows how the model could be reorganized using delegation.

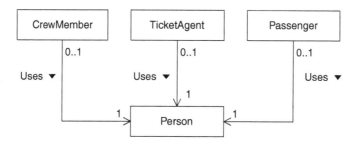

FIGURE 4.3 Modeling roles with delegation.

Using the organization shown in Figure 4.3, a `Person` object delegates the responsibility of filling a particular role to an object that is specific to that role. You need only as many objects as there are roles to fill. Different combinations do not require additional objects. Because delegation objects can be dynamic, role objects can be added or removed as a person fills different roles.

In the case of the airline reservation software, a predetermined set of role objects may become associated with different `Person` objects over time. For example, when a flight is scheduled, it will be determined that a certain number of flight crewmembers must be on board. When a flight is staffed, specific persons will be associated with crewmember roles. As schedules change, a person may be shifted from one crewmember role to another.

FORCES

☺ Inheritance is a static relationship; it does not change over time. If it is found that an object needs to be a different subclass of a class at different times, it should not have been made a subclass of that class in the first place. If an object is created as an instance of a class, it will always be an instance of that class. However, an object can delegate behavior to different objects at different times.

☺ If it is found that a class attempts to hide a method or variable inherited from a superclass from other classes, that class should not inherit from the superclass. There is no effective way to hide methods or variables inherited from a superclass. However, it is possible for an object to use another object's methods and variables while ensuring that it is the only object with access to the other object. This accomplishes the same thing as inheritance but uses dynamic relationships that can change over time.

☺ A class related to a program's problem domain should not be a subclass of a utility class. There are two reasons for this:

● If a class is declared a subclass of a class such as `ArrayList` or `HashMap`, there is risk that these classes not under your control will change in an incompatible way. Though the risk is low, usually there is no corresponding benefit to offset it.

● When a problem-domain-specific class as a subclass of a utility class is written, usually the intention is to use the functionality of the utility class for implementing problem-domain-specific functionality. The problem with using inheritance this way is that it weakens the encapsulation of the problem domain class's implementation.

Client classes that use the problem-domain-specific class may be written in a way that assumes the problem-domain-specific class to be a subclass of the utility class. If a change to the implementation of the problem domain class gives it a different superclass, client classes that rely on the problem-domain class having its original superclass will break.

An even more serious problem is that client classes can call the public methods of the utility superclass, thereby defeating its encapsulation.

☹ Delegation can be less convenient than inheritance, because it requires more code to implement.

☹ Delegation imposes less structure on classes than inheritance. In designs in which constraining the structure of classes is important, the structure and inflexibility of inheritance may be a virtue. This is often true in frameworks. See the discussion of the Template Method pattern for more details of this issue.

Some inappropriate uses of inheritance are sufficiently common to be classified as AntiPatterns. In particular, subclassing utility classes and using inheritance to model roles are common design flaws.

☺ Most reuse and extension of a class is not appropriately done through inheritance.

☺ The behavior that a class inherits from its superclass cannot be easily changed over time. Inheritance is not useful when the behavior on which a class should build is not determined until runtime.

SOLUTION

Use delegation to reuse and extend the behavior of a class. You do this by writing a new class (the *delegator*) that incorporates the functionality of the original class by using an instance of the original class (the *delegatee*) and calling its methods.

Figure 4.4 shows that a class in a `Delegator` role uses a class in the `Delegatee` role.

Delegation is more general purpose than inheritance. Any extension to a class that can be accomplished by inheritance can also be accomplished by delegation.

FIGURE 4.4 Delegation.

IMPLEMENTATION

The implementation of delegation is very straightforward, for it simply involves the acquisition of a reference to an instance of the class to which you want to delegate and call its methods.

The best way to ensure that a delegation is easy to maintain is to make its structure and purpose explicit. One way to do this is to make the delegation through an interface using the Interface pattern.

CONSEQUENCES

Delegation can be used without the problems that accompany inheritance. Delegation allows behavior to be easily composed at runtime.

The main disadvantage is that delegation is less structured than inheritance. Relationships between classes built by using delegation are less obvious than those built by using inheritance. The following are some strategies for improving the clarity of delegation-based relationships:

- Use consistent naming schemes to refer to objects in a particular role. For example, if multiple classes delegate the creation of widget objects, the role of the delegatee object becomes more obvious if all of the classes delegating that operation refer to delegatee objects through a variable called `widgetFactory`.
- You can clarify the purpose of a delegation by writing comments.
- Follow the Law of Demeter pattern (described in *Patterns in Java, Volume 2*), which says that if without a delegation a class would have only an indirect association with another class, the delegation should be indirect. Do not directly delegate behavior to an indirectly associated class that provides the behavior; instead, delegate it to a directly associated class and have that class delegate the behavior to the class that provides the behavior. Doing so simplifies the overall design by minimizing the number of associations between objects. In extreme cases, however, these indirect delegations can make an intermediate class less coherent by adding methods unrelated to the class's purpose. In such cases, refactor the unrelated words into a separate class by using the Pure Fabrication pattern (also described in *Patterns in Java, Volume 2*).
- Use well-known design and coding patterns. A person reading code that uses delegation will be more likely to understand the role that the objects play if the roles are part of a well-known pattern or a pattern that recurs frequently in your program.

It is not only possible but advantageous to use all three strategies at the same time.

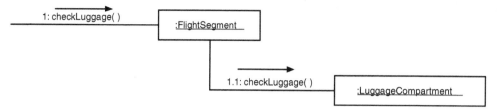

FIGURE 4.5 Check luggage.

JAVA API USAGE

The Java API is full of examples of delegation. It is the basis for Java's delegation event model in which event source objects send events to event listener objects. Event source objects do not generally decide what to do with an event; instead, they delegate the responsibility of processing the event to listener objects.

CODE EXAMPLE

For an example of delegation, we look at another part of the airline reservation system. Suppose that the system is responsible for tracking checked pieces of luggage. We can expect this part of the system to include classes to represent a flight segment,[1] a luggage compartment, and pieces of luggage, as shown in Figure 4.5.

In Figure 4.5, the FlightSegment class has a method called checkLuggage that checks a piece of luggage onto a flight. The flight class delegates that operation to an instance of the LuggageCompartment class.

Another common use for delegation is to implement a collection. Consider the diagram in Figure 4.6.

The LuggageCompartment class maintains a collection of other objects. Problem-domain classes that are responsible for maintaining a collection of other objects normally delegate the responsibility for the collection to another object, such as an instance of java.util.ArrayList. Implementing a collection by delegation is so common that the separate collection class is usually omitted from design drawings.

What follows are code fragments that implement the design shown in Figure 4.6. Shown first is the FlightSegment class that delegates the checkLuggage operation to the LuggageCompartment class:

---

[1] A flight segment is a portion of a trip that you take on an airline without changing planes.

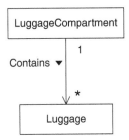

FIGURE 4.6 Luggage compartment.

```
class FlightSegment {
...
    LuggageCompartment luggage;
...
    void checkLuggage(Luggage piece) throws LuggageException {
        luggage.checkLuggage(piece);
    } // checkLuggage(Luggage)
} // class FlightSegment
```

Next, we show the `LuggageCompartment` class that delegates the collection of pieces of luggage to the `ArrayList` class:

```
class LuggageCompartment {
...
    // The pieces of luggage in this LuggageCompartment
    private ArrayList pieces = new ArrayList();
...
    void checkLuggage(Luggage piece) throws LuggageException {
...
        pieces.add(piece);
    } // checkLuggage(Luggage)
} // class LuggageCompartment
```

RELATED PATTERNS

Almost every other pattern uses delegation. Some of the patterns that rely most clearly on delegation are the Decorator pattern and the Proxy pattern.

In addition, the Interface pattern can be useful in making the structure and motivation for a delegation explicit and easier for maintainers to understand.

Interface

SYNOPSIS

Instances of a class provide data and services to instances of other classes. You want to keep client classes independent of specific data-and-service-providing classes so you can substitute another data-and-service-providing class with minimal impact on client classes. You accomplish this by having other classes access the data and services through an interface.

CONTEXT

Suppose you are writing an application to manage the purchase of goods for a business. Among the entities your program needs to know about are vendors, freight companies, receiving locations, and billing locations. One common aspect of these entities is that they all have street addresses. These street addresses appear in different parts of the user interface. You want to have a class for displaying and editing street addresses so that you can reuse it wherever there is a street address in the user interface. We call this class AddressPanel.

You want AddressPanel objects to get and set address information in a separate data object. This raises the question of what the AddressPanel class assumes about the class of data objects with which it will work. Clearly, you will use different classes to represent vendors, freight companies, and the like.

You can solve the problem by creating an address interface. Instances of the AddressPanel class would then simply require the data objects that they work with to implement the address interface. They would call the accessor methods of the interface to get and set the object's address information.

By using the indirection that the interface provides, clients of the AddressPanel interface are able to call the methods of a data object without having to be aware of what class it belongs to. Figure 4.7 is a class diagram showing these relationships.

FORCES

☺ An object relies on another object for data or services. If the object must assume that the other object upon which it relies belongs to a

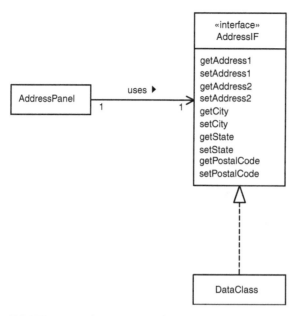

FIGURE 4.7 Indirection through address Interface.

particular class, the reusability of the object's class would be compromised.

☺ You want to vary the kind of object used by other objects for a particular purpose without making the object dependent on any class other than its own.

☹ A class's constructors cannot be accessed through an interface, because Java's interfaces cannot have constructors.

SOLUTION

To avoid classes having to depend on other classes because of a uses/used-by relationship, make the usage indirect through an interface. Figure 4.8 shows this relationship.

The following are the roles that these classes and interfaces play:

Client.   The Client class uses classes that implement the IndirectionIF interface.

IndirectionIF.   The IndirectionIF interface provides indirection that keeps the Client class independent of the class that is playing the Service role. Interfaces in this role are generally public.

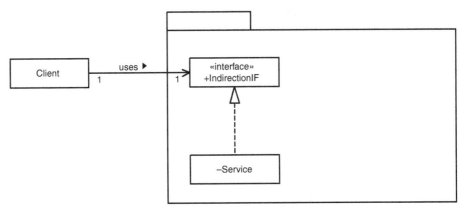

FIGURE 4.8 Interface pattern.

> **Service.** Classes in this role provide a service to classes in the `Client` role. Classes in this role are ideally private to their package. Making `Service` classes private forces classes outside of their package to go through the interface. However, it is common to have implementations of an interface that are in different packages.

IMPLEMENTATION

Implementation of the Interface pattern is straightforward. Define an interface to provide a service, write client classes to access the service through the interface, and write service-providing classes that implement the interface.

Java interfaces cannot have constructors. For this reason, interfaces are not helpful in keeping a class responsible for creating objects independent of the class of objects that it creates. The Java API includes a class called `java.lang.reflect.Constructor` that can be used to construct objects without knowing what class they will be an instance of.

CONSEQUENCES

☺ Applying the Interface pattern keeps a class that needs a service from another class from being coupled to any specific class.

☹ Like any other indirection, the Interface pattern can make a program more difficult to understand.

JAVA API USAGE

The Java API defines the interface `java.io.FilenameFilter`. This interface declares a method called `accept`. The `accept` method takes an argument that is a filename. The method is supposed to return true or false to indicate whether the named file should be included in a collection. The Java API also provides the `java.awt.FileDialog` class that can use a `FilenameFilter` object to filter the files that it displays.

CODE EXAMPLE

The example for the Interface pattern is the `AddressPanel` class. The `AddressIF` interface is discussed under the Context heading. The following is code for the `AddressPanel` class:

```
class AddressPanel extends Panel {
    private AddressIF data;      // Data object
...
    /**
     * Set the data object that this panel will work with.
     */
    public void setData(AddressIF address) {
...
    } // setData(AddressIF)

    /**
     * Save the contents of TextFields into the data object.
     */
    public void save() {
        if (data != null) {
            data.setAddress1(address1Field.getText());
...
            data.setPostalCode(postalCodeField.getText());
        } // if data
    } // save()
} // class AddressPanel
```

Notice that the impact of the Interface pattern on the `AddressPanel` class is very small. The only difference it makes is that the type of its `data` instance variable is an interface type rather than a class.

The heart of the Interface pattern is the interface that provides the indirection between the client class and the service class. What follows is the code for the `AddressIF` interface that provides indirection for the `AddressPanel` class:

```
public interface AddressIF {
    public String getAddress1();
    public void setAddress1(String address1);
...
    public String getPostalCode() ;
    public void setPostalCode(String PostalCode);
} // interface AddressIF
```

The interface simply declares the methods required for the needed service.

What follows is code for the service class. The only impact that the Interface pattern has on the class is that it implements the AddressIF interface.

```
class ReceivingLocation extends Facility implements AddressIF{
    private String address1;
...
    private String postalCode;
...
    public String getAddress1() { return address1; }
    public void setAddress1(String address1) {
        this.address1 = address1;
    } // setAddress1(String)
...
    public String getPostalCode() { return postalCode; }
    public void setPostalCode(String postalCode) {
        this.postalCode = postalCode;
    } // setPostalCode(String)
} // class ReceivingLocation
```

RELATED PATTERNS

Delegation.   The Delegation and Interface patterns are often used together.

Adapter.   The Adapter pattern allows objects that expect another object to implement a particular interface to work with objects that don't implement the expected interface.

Strategy.   The Strategy pattern uses the Interface pattern.

Anonymous Adapter.   The Anonymous Adapter pattern (described in *Patterns in Java, Volume 2*) uses the Interface pattern.

Many other patterns use the Interface pattern.

Abstract Superclass

This pattern was originally described in [Rhiel00].

SYNOPSIS

Ensure consistent behavior of conceptually related classes by giving them a common abstract superclass.

CONTEXT

You want to write classes to provide sequential and read-only access to some data structures. You decide that these classes will implement the interface `java.util.Iterator`.

The `Iterator` interface includes a method called `remove`. The documented purpose of the `remove` method is to remove objects from the source over which an `Iterator` object iterates. However, the description of the `remove` method also says that it is an optional method; an implementation of the method may simply throw an `UnsupportedOperationException`.

Because your intention is to provide read-only access to data structures, you want all of your classes to implement the `remove` method by throwing an `UnsupportedOperationException`. To ensure that these classes implement the `remove` method in the same way, you create a common abstract class for all of your `Iterator` classes to inherit from. The common superclass implements the `remove` method by having it always throw an `UnsupportedOperationException`. This organization is shown in Figure 4.9.

FORCES

- ☺ You want to ensure that logic common to related classes is implemented consistently for each class.
- ☺ You want to avoid the runtime and maintenance overhead of redundant code.
- ☺ You want to make it easy to write related classes.
- ☻ You want to organize common behavior, although in many situations, inheritance is not an appropriate way to accomplish this. The Delegation pattern describes this in detail.

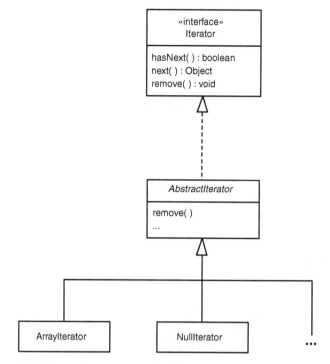

FIGURE 4.9 Iterators with abstract superclass.

SOLUTION

Organize the common behavior of related classes into an abstract superclass.

To the extent possible, organize variant behavior into methods with common signatures.[2] Declare the abstract superclass to have abstract methods with these common signatures. Figure 4.10 shows this organization.

The following are the roles that classes play in the Abstract Superclass pattern:

AbstractSuperclass.   A class in this role is an abstract superclass that encapsulates the common logic for related classes. The related classes extend this class so they can inherit methods from it. Methods whose signature and logic are common to the related classes are put into the superclass so their logic can be inherited by the related classes that extend the superclass.

---

[2] A method's signature is the combination of its name and formal parameters.

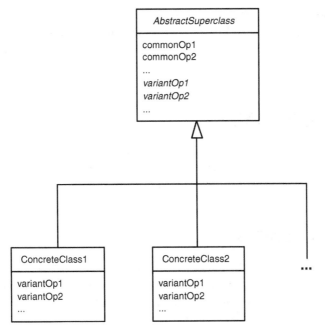

FIGURE 4.10 Abstract Superclass pattern.

Methods with different logic but the same signature are declared in the abstract class as abstract methods, ensuring that each concrete subclass has a method with those signatures.

ConcreteClass1, ConcreteClass2, and so on.   A class in this role is a concrete class whose logic and purpose is related to other concrete classes. Methods common to these related classes are refactored into the abstract superclass.

Common logic that is not encapsulated in common methods is refactored into common methods.

IMPLEMENTATION

If the common method signatures are public, they should, if possible, be organized into a Java interface that the abstract class implements.

CONSEQUENCES

☺ Fewer test cases may be needed to completely test your classes, because there are fewer pieces of code to test.

☹ Using the Abstract Superclass pattern creates dependencies between the superclass and its subclasses. Changes to the superclass may have unintended effects on some subclasses, thus making the program harder to maintain.

JAVA API USAGE

The class `java.awt.AWTEvent` is an abstract class for classes that encapsulate events related to the graphical user interface (GUI). It defines a small number of methods that are common to user-interface event classes.

CODE EXAMPLE

Implementations of the classes discussed under the Context heading are the code example for this pattern. These classes are taken from the ClickBlocks software, which you can find on the Web site for this book in the `org.clickblocks.util` package.

The following is a listing of the `AbstractIterator` class:

```java
/**
 * This abstract class provides the convenience of allowing
 * Iterators to be defined by overriding just the
 * getNextElement single method.
 */
abstract public class AbstractIterator implements Iterator {
    private Object nextElement;

    /**
     * This method must be called by a subclass's constructor.
     */
    protected void init() {
        nextElement = getNextElement();
    } // init()

    /**
     * This method returns the next element in the data
     * structure to be traversed.  If there is no next
     * element, then return this object.
     */
    public abstract Object getNextElement();

    /**
     * Return true if the iteration has more elements.
     */
    public boolean hasNext(){
        return nextElement!=this;
    } // hasNext()
```

```
/**
 * Returns the next element in the iteration.
 *
 * @exception NoSuchElementException iteration has no more elements.
 */
public Object next(){
    if (nextElement==this) {
        throw new NoSuchElementException();
    } // if
    Object previous = nextElement;
    nextElement = getNextElement();
    return previous;
} // next()

/**
 * Remove from the underlying collection the last element
 * returned by the next method.
 *
 * @exception UnsupportedOperationException
 *            if the remove operation is not supported by
 *            this Iterator.
 */
public void remove(){
    throw new UnsupportedOperationException();
} // remove()
} // class AbstractIterator
```

RELATED PATTERNS

Interface and Abstract Class.   The Interface and Abstract Class pattern uses the Abstract Superclass pattern.

Template Method.   The Template Method pattern uses the Abstract Superclass pattern.

Interface and Abstract Class

SYNOPSIS

You need to keep client classes independent of classes that implement a behavior and ensure consistency of behavior between the behavior-implementing classes. Don't choose between using an interface and an abstract class; have the classes implement an interface *and* extend an abstract class.

CONTEXT

You are designing a framework. You want to hide the class or classes that implement some behavior by making the classes private to their package and having them implement a public interface. For the sake of consistency and convenience of implementation, you want the classes to extend a common abstract class. You are not sure how to decide between basing the classes on an interface and an abstract class.

FORCES

☺ Using the Interface pattern, Java interfaces can be used to hide the specific class that implements a behavior from the clients of the class.
☺ Organizing classes that provide related behaviors with a common superclass helps to ensure consistency of implementation. Through reuse, it may also reduce the effort required for implementation.
☹ When people are presented with two different ways to improve the organization of classes, there is a common tendency to choose either one or the other.

SOLUTION

If you are presented with the need to hide from its clients the class of an object that provides a service, then use the Interface pattern. Have the client objects access the service-providing object indirectly through an interface. The indirection allows the clients to access the service-providing object without having to know what kind of objects they are.

If you need to design a set of related classes that provide similar functionality, then organize the common portions of their implementation into an abstract superclass.

If you are presented with both of these needs in the same object design, then use both an interface and an abstract class as shown in Figure 4.11.

When using the combination of an interface and abstract class in this way, the interface is public; the abstract class is package private, if possible.

CONSEQUENCES

☺ Using the Interface and Abstract Class pattern allows an object design to benefit from both an interface and an abstract class.

JAVA API USAGE

The package `javax.swing.table` contains interfaces and classes to support tables in a user interface. For every table that appears in a user interface, a corresponding data model object contains the data values displayed in the table. To be used as the data model for a table, an object must be an

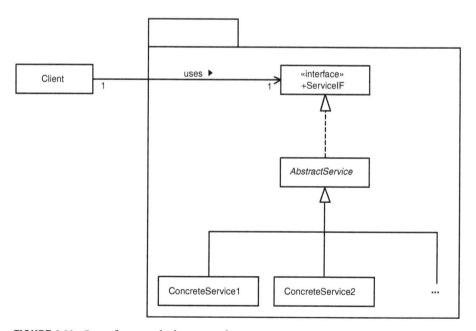

FIGURE 4.11 Interface and abstract class.

instance of a class that implements the `javax.swing.table.TableModel` interface. The package also includes a class named `AbstractTableModel`. `AbstractTableModel` is an abstract class that contains some default logic useful in implementing the methods declared by the `TableModel` interface. Finally, there is a concrete class named `DefaultTableModel` that is the default class used to instantiate a data model for a table. These relationships are shown in Figure 4.12.

CODE EXAMPLE

The code example for the Interface and Abstract Class pattern consists of an interface and classes for managing a data structure called a *doubly linked list*. There is a class called `DoubleLinkedListMgr` that performs various insert and delete operations on the elements of a doubly linked list. The `DoubleLinkedListMgr` class does not require that the objects in the doubly linked list be instances of any particular class. It does require that all of the elements implement an interface called `DoubleLinkIF`. There is an abstract class called `AbstractDoubleLink` that implements the `DoubleLinkIF` interface. Extending the `AbstractDoubleLink` class is a convenient way to write concrete classes that can be manipulated in a doubly linked list.

These classes and the interface are part of `org.clickblocks.dataStructure` package of the ClickBlocks software on the Web site for this book.

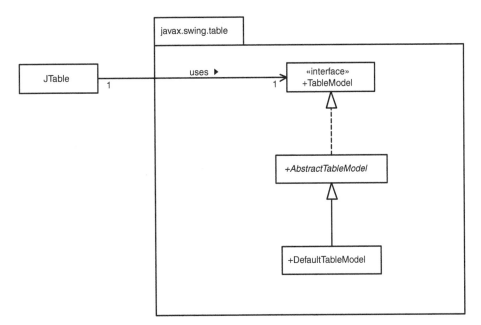

FIGURE 4.12 javax.swing.table relationships.

Doubly Linked List

A doubly linked list is a data structure organized into a sequence so that each element contains a reference to its successor and predecessor. Figure 4.13 shows an example of this structure.

The advantage of a doubly linked list over an array is the amount of work it takes to insert and delete objects. When you insert or delete objects in an array, you must shift everything in the array after the insertion or deletion point. The larger the array, the longer the average insertion and deletion will take. Inserting or deleting objects in a doubly linked list involves adjusting predecessor and successor references.

Inserting or deleting an element in a doubly linked list always takes the same amount of time, no matter how many elements there are. The drawback is that finding the nth element of a doubly linked list requires a search through the first n elements in the list. The larger n is, the longer this takes. Indexing the nth element in an array takes the same amount of time, no matter how large the array is.

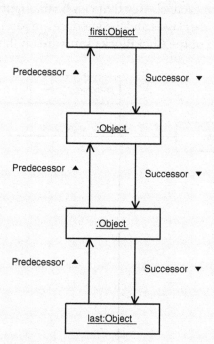

FIGURE 4.13 Doubly linked list.

The following is a listing of the `DoubleLinkIF` interface:

```java
public interface DoubleLinkIF {
    /**
     * Return the node that follows this one in the linked
     * list or null if this is the last node.
     */
    public DoubleLinkIF getNext() ;


    /**
     * Set the node that is to follow this one in the linked
     * list.
     *
     * @param node
     *          The node that is to follow this one in the
     *          linked list or null if this node is to be the
     *          last one in the list.
     */
    public void setNext(DoubleLinkIF newValue) ;


    /**
     * Return the node that precedes this one in the linked
     * list or null if this is the first node.
     */
    public DoubleLinkIF getPrev() ;


    /**
     * Set the node that is to precede this one in the linked
     * list.
     *
     * @param node
     *          The node that is to precede this one in the
     *          linked list or null if this node is to be the
     *          first one in the list.
     */
    public void setPrev(DoubleLinkIF newValue) ;
} // interface DoubleLinkIF
```

The following is a listing of the abstract class `AbstractDoubleLink`
that implements the `DoubleLinkIF` interface:

```java
public abstract class AbstractDoubleLink
                implements DoubleLinkIF {
    private DoubleLinkIF previous;
    private DoubleLinkIF next;


    /**
     * Return the node that follows this one in the linked
     * list or null if this is the last node.
     */
    public DoubleLinkIF getNext() { return next; }
```

```
/**
 * Set the node to follow this one in the linked list.
 *
 * @param node
 *         The node to follow this one or null if this node
 *         is to be the last one in the list.
 */
public void setNext(DoubleLinkIF newValue) {
    next = newValue;
} // setNext(DoubleLinkIF)

/**
 * Return the node that precedes this one or null
 * if this is the first node.
 */
public DoubleLinkIF getPrev() { return previous; }

/**
 * Set the node that is to precede this one.
 *
 * @param node
 *         The node that is to precede this one or
 *         null if this node is to be the first.
 */
public void setPrev(DoubleLinkIF newValue) {
    previous = newValue;
} // setPrev(DoubleLinkIF)
...
} // class AbstractDoubleLink
```

Classes that extend the `AbstractDoubleLink` class generally add additional information of their own.

RELATED PATTERNS

Interface.   The Interface and Abstract Class pattern uses the Interface pattern.

Abstract Class.   The Interface and Abstract Class pattern uses the Abstract Superclass pattern.

Immutable

The Immutable pattern is fundamental in a different sense than other patterns presented in this chapter. The Immutable pattern is considered fundamental because the more appropriate places you use it, the more robust and maintainable your programs will be.

SYNOPSIS

The Immutable pattern increases the robustness of objects that share references to the same object and reduces the overhead of concurrent access to an object. It achieves this by not allowing the shared object's contents to change after the object is constructed. The Immutable pattern also avoids the need to synchronize multiple threads of execution that share an object.

CONTEXT

Value objects are objects whose primary purpose is to encapsulate values rather than to provide behavior. For example, the class `java.awt.Rectangle` encapsulates the position and dimensions of a rectangle.

In situations where multiple objects share access to the same value object, a problem can arise if changes to the shared object are not properly coordinated between the objects that share it. This coordination can require careful programming that is easy to get wrong. If the changes to and fetches of the shared objects' state are done asynchronously, then in addition to the greater likelihood of bugs, correctly functioning code will have the overhead of synchronizing the accesses to the shared objects' state.

The Immutable pattern avoids these problems. It organizes a class so that the state information of its instances never changes after they are constructed.

Suppose you are designing a multiplayer game program that involves the placement and occasional movement of objects on a playing field. In the course of designing classes for the program, you decide to use immutable objects to represent the position of objects on the playing field. An organization of a class for modeling position is shown in Figure 4.14.

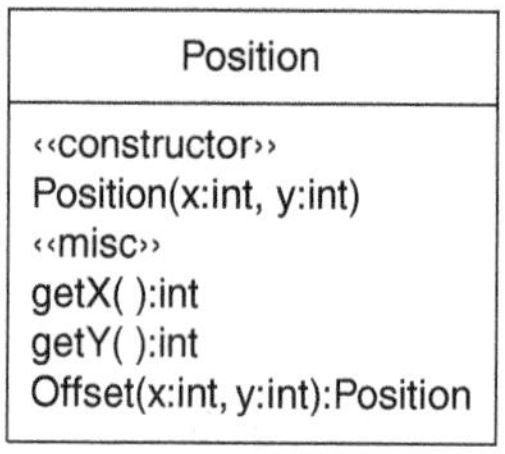

```
┌─────────────────────────────────────┐
│              Position                 │
├─────────────────────────────────────┤
│ ‹‹constructor››                       │
│ Position(x:int, y:int)                │
│ ‹‹misc››                              │
│ getX( ):int                           │
│ getY( ):int                           │
│ Offset(x:int, y:int):Position         │
└─────────────────────────────────────┘
```

FIGURE 4.14 Immutable position.

You have a class called `Position` that has an x and a y value associated with its instances. The class has a constructor that specifies the x and y values. It also has methods to fetch the x and y values associated with its instances, as well as a method that creates a new `Position` object at a given x and y offset from an existing position. It does not have any methods to modify its x or y values. If an object's position changes, it will be made to refer to a new position object.

FORCES

☺ Your program uses instances of a class that is passive in nature. The instances do not ever need to change their own state. The instances of that class are used by multiple other objects.

☺ Coordinating changes to the contents of a value object used by multiple objects can be a source of bugs. When the contents of a value object change, all the objects that use it may need to be informed. Also, when multiple objects use an object, they may attempt to change its state in inconsistent ways.

☺ If multiple threads modify the contents of a value object, the modification operations must be synchronized to ensure the consistency of the contents. The overhead of synchronizing the threads may add an unacceptable overhead to accessing the value object's contents.

☺ An alternative to modifying the contents of a value object is to replace the entire object with another object that has different contents. Doing so avoids the need for synchronization among threads that only fetch the contents of the value object.

☹ If there are multiple threads that update the contents of an object, replacing the object instead of updating its contents will not avoid the need for synchronizing the threads that do the updating.

☹ Replacing a value object with a new value object that contains an updated version of the values in the old object involves copying unchanged values from the old object to the new. If the changes to an object are frequent, or if an object has a large amount of state information associated with it, the cost of replacing value objects may be prohibitive.

SOLUTION

To avoid having to manage the synchronization of changes to value objects used by multiple other objects, make the shared objects immutable, disallowing any changes to their state after they are constructed. You can accomplish this task by not including any methods, other than constructors, in their class that modify state information. The organization of such a class is shown in Figure 4.15.

Notice that the class has accessor methods to get state information but none to set it.

IMPLEMENTATION

There are two concerns when implementing the Immutable pattern:

- No method, other than a constructor, should modify the values of a class's instance variables.
- Any method that computes new state information must store the information in a new instance of the same class rather than modifying the existing object's state.

One possible unexpected detail of implementing the Immutable pattern is that it usually does not involve declaring variables with the `final` modifier. The values of final instance variables are normally provided from within their class. However, the values of an immutable object's instance variables normally are provided by another class that instantiates the object.

CONSEQUENCES

☺ Since the state of immutable objects never changes, there is no need to write code to manage such changes.

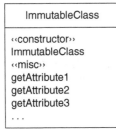

FIGURE 4.15 Immutable pattern.

☺ An immutable object is often used as the value of another object's attribute. If the value of an object's attribute is an immutable object, then it may not be necessary for access to the value's attribute to be synchronized. The reason is that Java guarantees that assigning an object reference to a variable is always done as an atomic operation. If the value of a variable is an object reference and one thread updates its value and another fetches its value, the other thread will fetch either the new or the old object reference.

☹ Operations that would otherwise have changed the state of an object must create a new object. This is an overhead that mutable objects do not incur.

JAVA API USAGE

Instances of the String class are immutable. The sequence of characters that a String object represents is determined when it is constructed. The String class does not provide any methods for changing the sequence of characters that a String object represents. Methods of the String class, such as toLowerCase and substring, compute a new sequence of characters and then return the new sequence of characters in a new String object.

CODE EXAMPLE

The following is what the code for the Position class described in the Context section might look like:

```
class Position {
    private int x;
    private int y;

    public Position(int x, int y) {
        this.x = x;
        this.y = y;
    } // constructor(int, int)

    public int getX() { return x; }

    public int getY() { return y; }

    public Position offset(int xOffset, int yOffset) {
        return new Position(x+xOffset, y+yOffset);
    } // offset(int, int)
} // class Position
```

RELATED PATTERNS

Single Threaded Execution.   The Single Threaded Execution pattern is the pattern most frequently used to coordinate access by multiple threads to a shared object. The Immutable Object pattern can be used to avoid the need for the Single Threaded Execution pattern or any other kind of access coordination.

Read-Only Interface.   The Read-Only Interface pattern is an alternative to the Immutable Object pattern. It allows some objects to modify a value object while other objects can only fetch its values.

Marker Interface

The Marker Interface pattern occurs rarely outside of utility classes. However, it is included in this chapter because it takes advantage of the fundamental nature of class declarations.

SYNOPSIS

The Marker Interface pattern uses the fact that a class implements an interface to indicate semantic Boolean attributes of the class. It works particularly well with utility classes that must determine something about objects without assuming that they are an instance of any particular class.

CONTEXT

Java's `Object` class defines a method called `equals`. The argument to `equals` can be a reference to any object. Since Java's `Object` class is the ultimate superclass of all other classes in Java, all other classes inherit the `equals` method from the `Object` class. The implementation of `equals` provided by the `Object` class is equivalent to the `==` operator. It returns true if the object passed to it is the same object as the object it is associated with. Classes that want their instances to be considered equal if they contain the same values override the `equals` method appropriately.

Container objects, such as `java.util.ArrayList`, call an object's `equals` method when performing a search of their contents to find an object that is equal to a given object. Such searches might call an object's `equals` method for each object in the container objects. This is wasteful in those cases where the object being searched for belongs to a class that does not override the `equals` method. It is faster to use the `==` operator to determine whether two objects are the same object than it is to call the `Object` class's implementation of the `equals` method. If the container class were able to determine that the object being searched for belongs to a class that does not override the `equals` method, then it could use the `==` operator instead of calling `equals`. The problem, however, is that no quick way exists to determine whether an arbitrary object's class has overridden the `equals` method.

It is possible to provide a hint to container classes to let them know that it is correct to use the `==` operator for an equality test on instances of a class. You can define an interface called `EqualByIdentity` that declares no methods or variables. You can then write container classes to assume that if a class implements `EqualByIdentity`, its equality comparison can be done by using the `==` operator.

An interface that does not declare methods or variables and is used to indicate attributes of classes that implement them is said to be a marker interface.

FORCES

- ☺ Utility classes may need to know something about the intended use of an object's class that is either true or false without relying on objects being an instance of a particular class.
- ☺ Classes can implement any number of interfaces.
- ☺ It is possible to determine whether an object's class implements a known interface without relying on the object being an instance of any particular class.
- ☹ Some attributes about the intended use of a class may change during the class's lifetime.

SOLUTION

For instances of a utility class to determine whether another class's instances are included in a classification without the utility class having knowledge of other classes, the utility class can determine whether other classes implement a marker interface. A marker interface is an interface that does not declare any methods or variables. You declare a class to implement a marker interface to indicate that it belongs to the classification associated with the marker interface. Figure 4.16 shows these relationships.

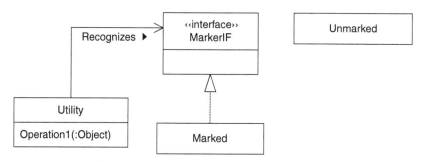

FIGURE 4.16 Marker Interface class diagram.

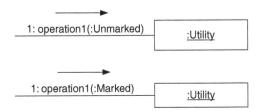

FIGURE 4.17 Marker Interface collaboration.

Figure 4.16 shows a marker interface called `MarkerIF`. Figure 4.16 also shows a class called `Marked` that implements `MarkerIF` and a class called `Unmarked` that doesn't. There is also a utility class called `Utility` that is aware of the `MarkerIF` interface. The collaboration between these classes is shown in Figure 4.17.

Instances of `UtilityClass` receive calls to their `operation1` method. The parameter passed to that method can be an object that implements or does not implement `MarkerIF`.

IMPLEMENTATION

The essence of the Marker Interface pattern is that an object that either does or does not implement a marker interface is passed to a method of a utility class. The formal parameter that corresponds to the object is typically declared as `Object`. If appropriate, it is reasonable to declare that formal parameter to be a more specialized class.

It is also possible to use an interface that declares methods in the Marker Interface pattern. In such cases, the interface used as a marker interface usually extends a pure marker interface.

Declaring that a class implements a marker interface implies that the class is included in the classification implied by the interface. It also implies that all subclasses of that class are included in the classification. If there is any possibility that someone will declare a subclass that does not fit the classification, then you should take measures to prevent that from happening. Such measures might include declaring the class final to prevent it from being subclassed or declaring its `equals` method final to prevent it from being overridden.

CONSEQUENCES

☺ Instances of utility classes are able to make inferences about objects passed to their methods without depending on the objects to be instances of any particular class.

● The relationship between the utility class and the marker interface is transparent to all other classes except those that implement the interface.

JAVA API USAGE

A class indicates that its instances may be serialized by implementing the Serializable interface. Instances of the ObjectOutputStream class write objects as a stream of bytes. An instance of the ObjectInputStream class can read the stream of bytes and turn it back into an object. The conversion of an object to a stream of bytes is called *serialization*. There are many reasons why instances of some classes should not be serialized. The ObjectOutputStream class refuses to serialize objects unless their class implements the Serializable interface to indicate that its serialization is allowed.

CODE EXAMPLE

For an example of an application of the Marker Interface pattern, see the following class that implements a linked-list data structure. At the bottom of the listing are methods called find, findEq, and findEquals. The purpose of all three methods is to find a LinkedList node that refers to a specified object. The find method is the only one of the three that is public. The findEq method performs the necessary equality tests by using the == operator. The findEquals method performs the necessary equality tests by using the equals method of the object being searched for. The find method decides whether to call the findEq method or the findEquals method by determining whether the object to search for implements the marker interface EqualByIdentity.

```java
public class LinkedList implements Cloneable, java.io.Serializable {
...
    /**
     * Find an object in a linked list that is equal to the given
     * object. Equality is normally determined by calling the given
     * object's equals method.  However, if the given object implements
     * the EqualByIdentity interface, then equality will be determined
     * by the == operator.
     */
    public LinkedList find(Object target) {
        if (target == null || target instanceof EqualByIdentity)
            return findEq(target);
        else
            return findEquals(target);
    } // find(Object)
```

```
    /**
     * Find an object in a linked list that is equal to the given
     * object. Equality is determined by the == operator.
     */
    private synchronized LinkedList findEq(Object target) {
...
    } // find(Object)

    /**
     * Find an object in a linked list that is equal to the given
     * object. Equality is determined by calling the given
     * object's equals method.
     */
    private synchronized LinkedList findEquals(Object target) {
...
    } // find(Object)
} // class LinkedList
```

RELATED PATTERNS

Snapshot.   The Marker Interface pattern is used as part of the
    Snapshot pattern to allow serialization of objects.

Polymorphism.   The Polymorphism pattern (described in *Patterns
    in Java, Volume 2*) describes the alternative way to vary the
    behavior of a method call.

Proxy

Proxy is a very general pattern that occurs in many other patterns but never by itself in its pure form. The Proxy pattern was described previously in [GoF95].

SYNOPSIS

The Proxy pattern forces method calls to an object to occur indirectly through a proxy object that acts as a surrogate for the other object, delegating method calls to that object. Classes for proxy objects are declared in a way that usually eliminates the client object's awareness that it is dealing with a proxy.

CONTEXT

A proxy object is an object that receives method calls on behalf of another object. Client objects call the proxy object's method. The proxy object's methods do not directly provide the service that its clients expect; instead, they call the methods of the object that provides the actual service. Figure 4.18 shows this structure.

Although a proxy object's methods do not directly provide the service its clients expect, the proxy object provides some management of those services. Proxy objects share a common interface with the service-providing object. Whether client objects directly access a service-providing object or a proxy object, they access it through the common interface rather than an instance of a particular class. Doing so allows client objects to be unaware that they call the methods of a proxy object rather than the methods of the actual service-providing object. Transparent management of another object's services is the basic reason for using a proxy object.

A proxy object can be used to provide many types of service management. Some of the more important types are documented elsewhere in this

FIGURE 4.18 Method calls through a proxy object.

work as patterns in their own right. The following are some of the more common uses for proxies:

- Create the appearance that a method that takes a long time to complete returns immediately.
- Create the illusion that an object on a different machine is an ordinary local object. This kind of proxy—called a *remote proxy*, or *stub*—is used by RMI, CORBA and other ORBs (object request brokers). Stub classes are described as part of the discussion of ORBs in *Patterns in Java, Volume 3*.
- Control access to a service-providing object based on a security policy. This use of proxies is described as the Protection Proxy pattern in *Patterns in Java, Volume 3*.
- Create the illusion that a service object exists before it actually does. Doing so can be useful if a service object is expensive to create and its services may not be needed. This use of proxies is documented as the Virtual Proxy pattern.

FORCES

- ☺ It is not possible for a service-providing object to provide a service at a convenient time or place.
- ☺ Gaining visibility to an object is complex and you want to hide that complexity.
- ☺ Access to a service-providing object must be controlled without adding complexity to the service-providing object or coupling the service to the access control policy.
- ☺ The management of a service should be provided in a way that is transparent to the clients of that service.
- ☺ The clients of a service-providing object do not care about the identity of the object's class or which instance of its class they are working with.

SOLUTION

Transparent management of a service-providing object can be accomplished by forcing all access to the service-providing object to be accomplished through a proxy object. For the management to be transparent, both the proxy object and the service-providing object must either implement a common interface or be instances of a common superclass.

Figure 4.19 shows the organization of the Proxy pattern but not details for implementing any particular access management policy. The

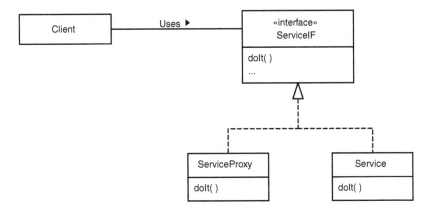

FIGURE 4.19 Proxy class diagram.

Proxy pattern is not very useful unless it implements some particular access management policy. The Proxy pattern is so commonly used with some access management policies that these combinations are described elsewhere as patterns in their own right.

IMPLEMENTATION

Without any specific management policy, the implementation of the Proxy pattern simply involves creating a class that shares a common superclass or interface with a service-providing class and delegates operations to instances of the service-providing class.

CONSEQUENCES

☺ The service provided by a service-providing object is managed in a manner transparent to the object and its clients.

☺ Unless the use of proxies introduces new failure modes, there is normally no need for the code of client classes to reflect the use of proxies.

CODE EXAMPLE

The Proxy pattern is not useful in its pure form; it must be combined with a service management behavior to accomplish anything useful. This example of the Proxy pattern uses proxies to defer an expensive operation until it is actually needed. If the operation is not needed, the operation is never performed.

The example is a proxy for instances of classes such as `java.util.HashMap` that implement both the `java.util.Map` and the `java.long.Cloneable` interfaces. The purpose of the proxy is to delay cloning the underlying `Map` object until it is known that this expensive operation is actually needed.

Clone()

All Java classes inherit the `clone` method from the class `java.lang.Object`. An object's `clone` method returns a shallow copy of the object. The object that the `clone` method returns is an instance of the same class as the original object. Its instance values all have the same values as in the original object. The instance variables of the copy refer to the same objects as the original object.

Since it is a security hole to be able to copy an object that contains sensitive information, the `clone` method inherited from the `Object` class throws an exception unless the class of the object permits cloning. A class permits its instances to be cloned if it implements the `java.lang.Cloneable` interface.

Many classes that permit their instances to be cloned override the `clone` method to avoid situations where their instances are sharing objects that they should not share.

One reason for cloning a `Map` object is to avoid holding a lock on the object for a long time when all that is desired is to fetch multiple key-value pairs. In a multi-threaded program, to ensure that a `Map` object is in a consistent state while fetching key-value pairs from it, you can use a synchronized method to obtain exclusive access to the `Map` object. While that is happening, other threads wait to gain access to the same `Map` object. Such waiting may be unacceptable

Not every class that implements the `Map` interface permits its instances to be cloned. However, many `Map` classes, such as `java.util.HashMap` and `java.util.TreeMap`, do permit their instances to be cloned.

Cloning a `Map` object prior to fetching values out of it is a defensive measure. Cloning the `Map` object avoids the need to obtain a synchronization lock on a `Hashtable` beyond the time it takes for the clone operation to complete. When you have a freshly cloned copy of a `Map` object, you can be sure that no other thread has access to the copy. Because no other thread has access to the copy, you will be able to fetch key-value pairs from the copy without any interference from other threads.

If after you clone a `Map` object no subsequent modification to the original `Map` object occurs, the time and memory spent in creating the clone was wasted. The point of this example is to avoid waste. It accomplishes this by delaying the cloning of a `Map` object until a modification to it actually occurs.

The name of the proxy class is `LazyCloneMap`. Instances of `LazyCloneMap` are a copy-on-write proxy for a `Map` object. When a proxy's clone method is called, it returns a copy of the proxy but does not copy the underlying `Map` object. At this point, both the original and the copy of the proxy refer to the same underlying `Map` object. When one of the proxies is asked to modify the underlying `Map` object, it will recognize that it uses a shared underlying `Map` object; it will clone the underlying `Map` object before it makes the modification. Figure 4.20 shows the structure of the `LazyCloneMap` class.

What follows is the beginning of a listing of the `LazyCloneMap` class.

```
public class LazyCloneMap implements Map, Cloneable {
    /**
     * The Map object that this object is a proxy for.
     */
    private Map underlyingMap;
```

Proxy classes have a way for a proxy object to refer to the object it is a proxy for. This proxy class has an instance variable that refers to the underlying `Map` object. `LazyCloneMap` objects know when they share their underlying `Map` object with other `LazyCloneMap` objects by keeping a count of how many refer to the same underlying `Map` object. They keep this count in an instance of a class named `MutableInteger`. The `MutableInteger` object is shared or not by the same `LazyCloneMap` objects that share the underlying `Map` object. The listing for `MutableInteger` appears later.

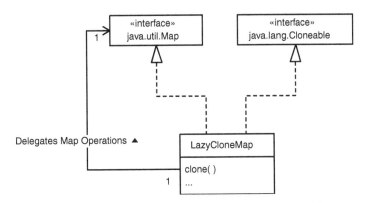

FIGURE 4.20 LazyCloneMap.

```
/**
 * This is the number of proxy objects that share the same
 * underlying map.
 */
private MutableInteger refCount;
```

The clone method that classes inherit from the Object class is protected. There is no interface that declares the public clone method implemented by classes such as HashMap and TreeMap. For this reason, the Lazy-CloneMap class must access the clone method of underlying Map objects through an explicit java.lang.reflect.Method object.

```
/**
 * This is used to invoke the clone method of the
 * underlying Map object.
 */
private Method cloneMethod;

private static Class[] cloneParams = new Class[0];

/**
 * Constructor
 *
 * @param underlyingMap
 *         The Map object that this object should be a
 *         proxy for.
 * @throws NoSuchMethodException
 *          If the underlyingMap object does not have a
 *          public clone() method.
 * @throws InvocationTargetException
 *          The object constructed by this constructor uses
 *          a clone of the given Map object.  If the Map
 *          object's clone method throws an exception, this
 *          constructor throws an InvocationTargetException
 *          whose getCause method returns the original *
 *          exception.
 */
public LazyCloneMap(Map underlyingMap)
                        throws NoSuchMethodException,
                               InvocationTargetException {
    Class mapClass = underlyingMap.getClass();
    cloneMethod = mapClass.getMethod("clone",cloneParams);
    try {
        this.underlyingMap =
            (Map)cloneMethod.invoke(underlyingMap, null);
    } catch (IllegalAccessException e) {
        // This should not happen.
    } // try
    refCount = new MutableInteger(1);
} // constructor(Map)
```

This class's `clone` method does not copy the underlying `Map` object. It does increment the reference count that is also shared by the original `LazyCloneMap` object and the copy. Incrementing the value allows the `LazyCloneMap` objects to know that they share their underlying `Map` object.

```
public Object clone() {
    LazyCloneMap theClone;
    try {
        Cloneable original = (Cloneable)underlyingMap;
        theClone = (LazyCloneMap)super.clone();
    } catch (CloneNotSupportedException e) {
        // this should never happen
        theClone = null;
    } // try
    refCount.setValue(1+refCount.getValue());
    return theClone;
} // clone()
```

The following private method is called by public methods of the `LazyCloneMap` class, such as `put` and `clear`, that modify the underlying `Map` object. The public methods call this private method before modifying the underlying `Map` object to ensure that they are not sharing the underlying `Map` object.

```
private void ensureUnderlyingMapNotShared() {
    if (refCount.getValue()>1) {
        try {
            underlyingMap =
              (Map)cloneMethod.invoke(underlyingMap, null);
            refCount.setValue(refCount.getValue()-1);
            refCount = new MutableInteger(1);
        } catch (IllegalAccessException e) {
            // This should not happen.
        } catch (InvocationTargetException e) {
            Throwable cause = e.getCause();
            throw new RuntimeException("clone failed",
                                       cause);
        } // try
    } // if
} // ensureUnderlyingMapNotShared()
```

The `ensureUnderlyingMapNotShared` method begins by determining whether the value of the reference count is greater than one. If it is greater than one, it will know that this `LazyCloneMap` object shares its underlying `Map` object with other `LazyCloneMap` objects. The `ensureUnderlyingMap-NotShared` method clones the underlying `Map` object so this `LazyCloneMap` object will have its own copy of the underlying `Map` object that it does not share with any other `LazyCloneMap` object. It decrements the reference count so that the other LazyCloneMap objects with which this object shared an underlying Map object will know that they no longer share the same underlying Map object with this object. Also, it creates a new object to contain the reference count of 1 indicating that this LazyCloneMap object does not share its underlying Map object.

The rest of the methods in the LazyCloneMap class delegate their work to the corresponding method of the underlying Map object.

```
public int size(){
    return underlyingMap.size();
}

public boolean isEmpty(){
    return underlyingMap.isEmpty();
}

public boolean containsKey(Object key){
    return underlyingMap.containsKey(key);
}

public boolean containsValue(Object value){
    return underlyingMap.containsValue(value);
}

public Object get(Object key){
    return underlyingMap.get(key);
}
```

Because the next four methods modify the underlying Map object, they call the ensureUnderlyingMapNotShared method before they delegate their work to the underlying Map object.

```
public Object put(Object key, Object value){
    ensureUnderlyingMapNotShared();
    return underlyingMap.put(key, value);
}

public Object remove(Object key){
    ensureUnderlyingMapNotShared();
    return underlyingMap.remove(key);
}

public void putAll(Map m){
    ensureUnderlyingMapNotShared();
    underlyingMap.putAll(m);
}

public void clear(){
    ensureUnderlyingMapNotShared();
    underlyingMap.clear();
}
```

```
public Set keySet(){
    return underlyingMap.keySet();
}

public Collection values(){
    return underlyingMap.values();
  }

public Set entrySet(){
    return underlyingMap.entrySet();
}

public boolean equals(Object that){
    return underlyingMap.equals(that);
}

public int hashCode(){
    return underlyingMap.hashCode();
}
}
```

The following is a listing of the `MutableInteger` class that the `LazyCloneMap` class uses:

```
public class MutableInteger {
    public int val;

    public MutableInteger( int value ) {
        setValue( value );
    }

    public int getValue() {
        return( val );
    }

    public void setValue( int value ) {
        val = value;
    }
    ...
}
```

RELATED PATTERNS

Protection Proxy.   The Protection Proxy pattern (described in *Patterns in Java, Volume 3*) uses a proxy to enforce a security policy on access to a service-providing object.

Façade.   The Façade pattern uses a single object as a front end to a set of interrelated objects rather than as a front end to a single object.

Object Request Broker. The Object Request Broker pattern (described in *Patterns in Java, Volume 3*) uses a proxy to hide the fact that a service object is located on a different machine than the client objects that want to use it.

Virtual Proxy. The Virtual Proxy pattern uses a proxy to create the illusion that a service-providing object exists before it has actually been created. The Virtual Proxy pattern is useful if the object is expensive to create and its services may not be needed. The copy-on-write proxy discussed under the Code Example heading for the Proxy pattern is a kind of virtual proxy.

Decorator. The Decorator pattern is structurally similar to the Proxy pattern in that it forces access to a service-providing object to be done indirectly through another object. The difference is a matter of intent. Instead of trying to manage the service, the indirection object in some way enhances the service.

Creational Patterns

Creational patterns provide guidance on how to create objects when their creation requires making decisions. These decisions will typically involve dynamically deciding which class to instantiate or which objects an object will delegate responsibility to. The value of creational patterns is to tell us how to structure and encapsulate these decisions.

Often, there is more than one creational pattern that you can apply to a situation. Sometimes you can combine multiple patterns advantageously. In other cases, you must choose between competing patterns. For these reasons, it is important to be acquainted with all of the patterns described in this chapter.

If you have time to learn only one pattern in this chapter, the most commonly used one is Factory Method. The Factory Method pattern is a way for an object to initiate the creation of another object without having to know the class of the object created.

The Abstract Factory pattern is a way for objects to initiate the creation of a variety of different kinds of objects without knowing the classes of the objects created, but ensuring that the classes are a correct combination.

The Builder pattern is a way to determine the class of an object created by its contents or context.

The Prototype pattern allows an object to create customized objects without knowing their exact class or the details of how to create them.

The Singleton pattern is a way for multiple objects to share a common object without having to know whether it already exists.

The Object Pool pattern is a way to reuse objects rather than create new objects.

Factory Method

This pattern was previously described in [GoF95].

SYNOPSIS

You need to create an object to represent external data or process an external event. The type of object depends on the contents of the external data or type of event. You want neither the data source, the event source, nor the object's clients to be aware of the actual type of object created. You encapsulate the decision of what class of object to create in its own class.

CONTEXT

Consider the problem of writing a framework for desktop applications. Such applications are typically organized around documents or files. Their operation usually begins with a command to create or edit a word processing document, spreadsheet, time line, or other type of document the application is intended to work with.

A framework to support this type of application will include high-level support for common operations such as creating, opening, or saving documents. Such support will generally include a consistent set of methods to call when the user issues a command. For the purpose of this discussion, we will call the class providing the methods the Application class.

Because the logic to implement most of these commands varies with the type of document, the Application class usually delegates most commands to some sort of document object. The logic in document objects for implementing these commands varies with the type of document. However, some operations, such as displaying the title of a document, will be common to all document objects. This suggests an organization that includes:

- An application-independent document interface
- An abstract class that provides application-independent logic for concrete document classes
- Concrete application-specific classes that implement the interface for specific types of documents

Figure 5.1 shows this organization.

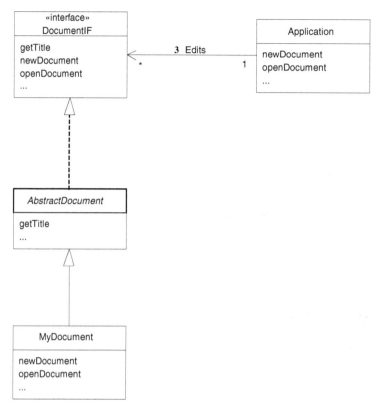

FIGURE 5.1 Application framework.

Neither Figure 5.1 nor the preceding discussion shows how an Application object creates instances of application-specific document classes without itself being application specific.

One way to accomplish this is for the programmer using the framework to provide a class that encapsulates logic for selecting and instantiating application-specific classes. For the Application class to be able to call the programmer-provided class without having any dependencies on it, the framework should provide an interface that the programmer-provided class must implement. Such an interface would declare a method that the programmer-provided class would implement to select and instantiate a class. The Application class works through the framework-provided interface and not with the programmer-provided class. Figure 5.2 shows this organization.

Using the organization shown in Figure 5.2, an Application object calls the createDocument method of an object that implements the DocumentFactoryIF interface. It passes a string to the createDocument method that allows it to infer which subclass of the Document class to

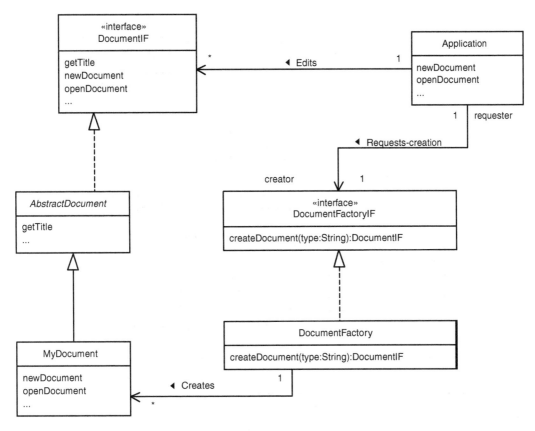

FIGURE 5.2 Application framework with document factory.

instantiate. The `Application` class does not need to know the actual class of the object whose method it calls or which subclass of the `Document` class it instantiated.

FORCES

☺ A class must be able to initiate the creation of objects without having any dependencies on the class of the created object.

☺ The set of classes a class may be expected to instantiate may be dynamic as new classes become available.

SOLUTION

Provide application-independent objects with an application-specific object to which they delegate the creation of other application-specific

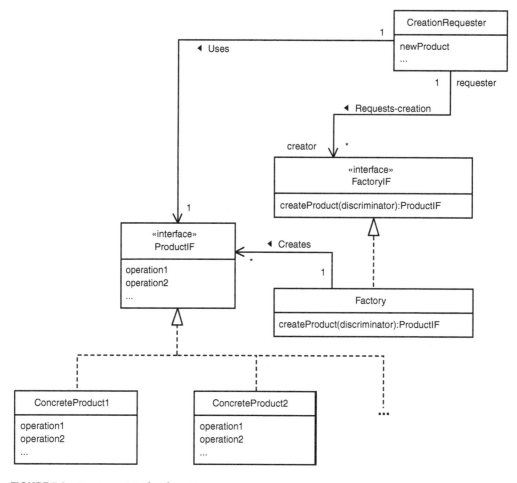

FIGURE 5.3 Factory Method pattern.

objects. Require the application-independent objects that initiate the creation of application-specific objects to assume that the objects implement a common interface.

Figure 5.3 shows the interfaces and classes that typically make up the Factory Method pattern.

The class diagram in Figure 5.3 shows the roles classes and interfaces play in the Factory Method pattern:

ProductIF. The objects created using this pattern must implement an interface in this role.

ConcreteProduct1, ConcreteProduct2, and so on. Classes in this role are instantiated by a `Factory` object. Classes in this role must implement the `ProductIF` interface.

CreationRequester. A class in this role is an application-independent class that needs to create application-specific classes. It does so indirectly through an instance of a class that implements the `FactoryIF` interface.

FactoryIF. This is an application-independent interface. Objects that create `ProductIF` objects on behalf of `CreationRequester` objects must implement this interface. Interfaces of this sort declare a method that can be called by a `CreationRequester` object to create concrete product objects. The arguments this method takes are discussed under the Implementation section for this pattern.

Interfaces filling this role will typically have a name that includes the word *Factory*, such as `DocumentFactoryIF` or `ImageFactoryIF`.

Factory. This is an application-specific class that implements the appropriate `FactoryIF` interface and has a method to create `ConcreteProduct` objects. Classes filling this role will typically have a name, such as `DocumentFactory` or `ImageFactory`, that contains the word *Factory*.

IMPLEMENTATION

In many implementations of the Factory Method pattern the `ConcreteProduct` classes do not directly implement the `ProductIF` interface. Instead, they extend an abstract class that implements the interface. See the Interface and Abstract Class pattern in Chapter 4 for a discussion of the reasons for this.

CLASS DETERMINATION BY CONFIGURATION

There are two main variations on the Factory Method pattern. There is the general case, where the class of the object to create is determined when object creation is initiated. There is also the less common case, where the class of objects that will be created is always the same and is determined before an object's creation is initiated.

A program may use a factory object that always creates an instance of the same class if the class is determined by some configuration information. For example, suppose that a company sells a point-of-sale system that is responsible for communicating with a remote computer to process credit card payments. Its classes expect to send messages to the remote computer and receive responses by using objects that implement a particular interface. The exact format of the messages to send will depend on the company that processes the credit card transactions. For each credit card processing company, there is a corresponding class that implements the required interface and knows how to send the messages that company expects. There is also a corresponding factory class. This organization is shown in Figure 5.4.

Here is an explanation of the design shown in Figure 5.4. When the point-of-sale system starts, it reads its configuration information. The configuration information tells the point of sale that it is to pass credit card transactions either to BancOne or to Wells Fargo for processing. Based on this information, it creates either a `BancOneCCFactory` or a `WellsCCFactory` object. It accesses the object through the `CreditCardProcessorFactoryIF` interface. When it needs an object to process a credit card transaction, it calls the

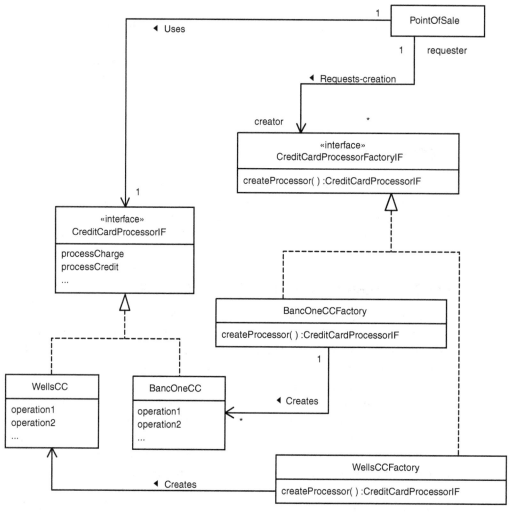

FIGURE 5.4 Credit card processing.

createProcessor method of its CreditCardProcessorFactoryIF, which creates an object that uses the configured credit card processing company.

Note that the factory class's Create method does not need any arguments because it always returns the same type of object.

DATA-DRIVEN CLASS DETERMINATION

Very often, the class of an object created by a factory object is determined by the data that it is intended to encapsulate. The class is determined by the factory object's createProduct method. The determination is usually based on information passed into the method as a parameter. Such createProduct methods often look something like this:

```
Image createImage (String ext) {
    if (ext.equals("gif")
      return new GIFImage();
    if (ext.equals("jpeg"))
      return new JPEGImage();
    ...
} // createImage(String)
```

This sequence of if statements works well for createProduct methods that have a fixed set of product classes to instantiate. To write a createProduct method that handles a variable or a large number of product classes, you can use the Hashed Adapter Objects pattern (described in *Patterns in Java, Volume 2*). Alternatively, you can use the various objects that indicate which class to instantiate as keys in a hash table with java .lang.reflect.Constructor objects for values. Using this technique, you look up an argument value in the hash table and then use the constructor object found in the hash table to instantiate the desired object.

Another point that the preceding example illustrates is that factory methods are a reasonable place to find switch statements or chains of if statements. In many situations, the presence of switch statements or chains of if statements in code indicates that a method should have been implemented as a polymorphic method. Factory methods cannot be implemented using polymorphism, because polymorphism works only after an object has been created.

For many implementations of the Factory Method pattern, the valid arguments to the factory object's createProduct method are a set of predetermined values. It is often convenient for the factory class to define symbolic names for each of those predetermined values. Classes that ask the factory class to create objects can use the constants that define the symbolic names to specify the type of object to be created.

Sometimes, there is more than one layer of data-driven class determination. For example, there may be a top-level factory object that is responsible for creating the factory object that will create the actual product object. For this reason, the data-driven form of the Factory Method pattern is sometimes called *layered initialization*.[1]

CONSEQUENCES

The primary consequences of using the Factory Method pattern are as follows:

- ☺ The creation requester class is independent of the class of concrete product objects actually created.
- ☺ The set of product classes that can be instantiated may be changed dynamically.
- ☻ The indirection between the initiation of object creation and the determination of which class to instantiate can make it more difficult for maintenance programmers to understand.

JAVA API USAGE

The Java API uses the Factory Method pattern in a few different places to allow the integration of the applet environment with its host program. For example, each URL object has associated with it a URLConnection object. You can use URLConnection objects to read the raw bytes of a URL. URLConnection objects also have a method called getContent that returns the content of the URL packaged in an appropriate sort of object. For example, if the URL contains a gif file, then the URLConnection object's getContent method returns an Image object.

The way it works is that URLConnection objects play the role of creation requester in the Factory Method pattern. They delegate the work of the getContent method to a ContentHandler object. ContentHandler is an abstract class that serves as a product class that knows about handling a specific type of content. The way that a URLConnection object gets a ContentHandler object is through a ContentHandlerFactory object. The ContentHandlerFactory class is an abstract class that participates in the Factory Method pattern as a factory interface. The URLConnection class also has a method called setContentHandlerFactory. Programs that host applets call that method to provide a factory object used for all URLConnection objects.

---

[1] In the first edition of this volume, layered initialization was documented as a separate pattern. Reader feedback convinced the author that this point of view was confusing rather than helpful.

CODE EXAMPLE

For our example, suppose you are developing an application to process records in a journal file created by a point-of-sale system.[2] Every line that appears on every register tape has a corresponding record in the journal file. Your application will read all of the records in a journal file and generate summaries of the transactions in the journal file.

Your application will be required to work with point-of-sale systems from multiple manufacturers. Since the journal file produced by each manufacturer's point-of-sale system has a different format, it is especially important to keep the classes responsible for generating the summaries independent of the journal file format.

You notice that all of the journal file formats consist of a sequence of records. The types of records in the journal files are similar. You decide to make the summary-generating classes independent of the journal file formats by representing the journal files internally as a sequence of objects that correspond to the records in the journal file. With this in mind, you design a set of classes that correspond to different types of records that occur in the journal files.

The focus of this example is how your application will create the objects that represent the records in the journal files. This example uses both forms of the Factory Method pattern.

- As the application reads records from a journal file, it uses a factory object to create the objects that correspond to each record in the journal file. Each time the factory object is asked to create an object, it selects the class to instantiate based on information in the record. This is an example of a factory that performs runtime class determination.
- The class of the factory object that creates objects to represent records depends on the type of journal file that the application will be reading. Because the class of this factory object depends on configuration information, it is created by another factory object when the application reads its configuration information.

Figure 5.5 shows the class organization on which this code example is based. Here are descriptions of the classes and interfaces shown in Figure 5.5:

JournalRecordIF. Objects that encapsulate the contents of journal records are an instance of a class that implements this interface.

---

[2] A point-of-sale system is a high-tech cash register.

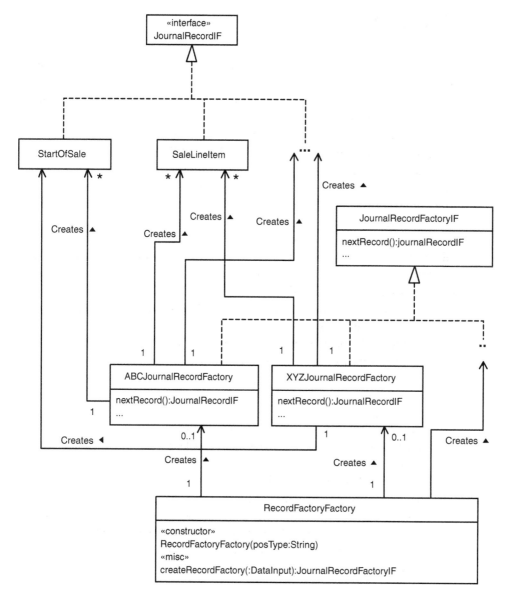

FIGURE 5.5 Journal-file-related factory classes.

Only two such classes are shown in Figure 5.5. However, in the complete application there would be many more.

StartOfSale. Instances of this class represent a journal record that indicates the beginning of a sale transaction.

SaleLineItem. Instances of this class represent a journal record that contains the details of a sale item on a register receipt.

JournalRecordFactoryIF. This interface is implemented by classes responsible for taking the information in journal file records and encapsulating it in objects that implement the `JournalRecordIF` interface. Instances of classes that implement this interface create objects that implement the `JournalRecordIF` interface, such as `StartOfSale` objects and `SaleLineItem` objects.

ABCJournalRecordFactory. Instances of this class are responsible for understanding the format of journal files produced by ABC point-of-sale systems. They read the next journal record from an object that implements `java.io.DataInput` and encapsulate its contents in an instance of a class that implements the `JournalRecordIF` interface.

XYZJournalRecordFactory. Instances of this class are responsible for understanding the format of journal files produced by XYZ point-of-sale systems. They read the next journal record from an object that implements `java.io.DataInput` and encapsulate its contents in an instance of a class that implements the `JournalRecordIF` interface.

RecordFactoryFactory. The name of a type of point-of-sale system is passed to this class's constructor. The constructed object is then used to create instances of the appropriate class that implements the `JournalRecordIF` interface for the specified type of point-of-sale system.

You may notice some structural similarity between this example that uses both forms of the Factory Method pattern and the next pattern in this book, the Abstract Factory pattern. One of the distinguishing characteristics of the Abstract Factory pattern is that the client objects are concerned with the interface implemented by the objects to be created rather than with their content.

Now let's look at the code that implements this design. We will begin with a listing of the `RecordFactoryFactory` class.

```
public class RecordFactoryFactory {
    private Constructor factoryConstructor;
```

When an instance of this class is created, its constructor is passed a string indicating the type of point-of-sale system for which the object will be a factory. It gets a `java.lang.reference.Constructor` object that it will use to construct objects and make the `Constructor` object the value of the `factoryConstructor` instance variable.

```
// POS Types
public static final String ABC = "abc";
//...
```

```
/**
 * Constructor
 *
 * @param posType
 *         The type of point-of-sale system that this object
 *         will be creating JournalRecordFactoryIF object
 *         for.
 * @throws POSException
 *          If there is a problem initializing this object.
 */
public RecordFactoryFactory(String posType)
                                        throws POSException {
    Class[] params = { DataInput.class };
    Class factoryClass;
    if (ABC.equals(posType)) {
        factoryClass = ABCJournalRecordFactory.class;
    ...
    } else {
        String msg = "Unknown POS type: " + posType;
        throw new java.lang.IllegalArgumentException(msg);
    }
    try {
        factoryConstructor
          = factoryClass.getConstructor(params);
    } catch (Exception e) {
        String msg = "Error while constructing factory";
        throw new POSException(msg, e);
    } // try
} // constructor(String)
```

Here is the method that creates JournalRecordFactoryIF objects.

```
public JournalRecordFactoryIF createFactory(DataInput in)
                                        throws POSException {
    Object[] args = {in} ;
    Object factory;
    try {
        factory = factoryConstructor.newInstance(args);
    } catch (Exception e) {
        String msg = "Error creating factory";
        throw new POSException(msg, e);
    } //
    return (JournalRecordFactoryIF)factory;
} // createFactory
} // class RecordFactoryFactory
```

Here is the JournalRecordFactoryIF interface.

```
/**
 * This interface is implemented by classes that are
 * responsible for creating objects that encapsulate the
 * contents of a point-of-sale journal file record.
 */
```

```
public interface JournalRecordFactoryIF {
    /**
     * Return an object that encapsulates the next record in a
     * journal file.
     *
     * @throws EOFException
     *          If there are no more records in the journal
     *          file.
     * @throws IOException
     *          If there is any problem reading the next
     *          record.
     */
    public JournalRecordIF nextRecord() throws EOFException,
                                               IOException;


    ...
} // interface JournalRecordFactoryIF
```

Here is the class `ABCJournalRecordFactory` that implements the `JournalRecordFactoryIF` interface for a type of point-of-sale system named ABC.

```
public class ABCJournalRecordFactory
                      implements JournalRecordFactoryIF {
    // Record Types
    ...
    private static final String SALE_LINE_ITEM = "17";
    private static final String START_OF_SALE = "4";
    ...

    private DataInput in;
    private final SimpleDateFormat dateFormat
      = new SimpleDateFormat("yyyyMMddHHmmss");

    // Counter for sequence number;
    private int sequenceNumber = 0;

    ABCJournalRecordFactory(DataInput input) {
        in = input;
    } // constructor(DataInput)

    /**
     * Return an object that encapsulates the next record in a
     * journal file.
     *
     * @throws EOFException
     *          If there are no more records in the journal
     *          file.
     * @throws IOException
     *          If there is a problem reading the file.
     */
    public JournalRecordIF nextRecord() throws EOFException,
                                               IOException {
```

```
        String record = in.readLine();
        StringTokenizer tokenizer;
        tokenizer = new StringTokenizer(record, ",");
        sequenceNumber++;

        try {
            String recordType = tokenizer.nextToken();
            ...
            if (recordType.equals(START_OF_SALE)) {
                return constructStartOfSale(tokenizer);
            } else if (recordType.equals(SALE_LINE_ITEM)) {
                return constructSaleLineItem(tokenizer);
            ...
            } else {
                String msg = "Unknown record type";
                throw new IOException(msg);
            } // if
        } catch (NoSuchElementException e) {
            // We will treat this exception as an I/O problem
            // since the record does not have all of the
            // expected fields.
            String msg = "record is missing some fields";
            IOException ioe = new IOException(msg);
            ioe.initCause(e);
            throw ioe;
        } // try
    } // nextRecord()

    private
    StartOfSale constructStartOfSale(StringTokenizer tok)
                            throws NoSuchElementException {
        String transactionID = tok.nextToken();
        tok.nextToken();          // Skip mode indicator.
        String timestampString = tok.nextToken();
        Date timestamp = parseTimestamp(timestampString);
        String terminalID = tok.nextToken();

        return new StartOfSale(terminalID,
                               sequenceNumber,
                               timestamp,
                               transactionID);
    } // constructStartOfSale(StringTokenizer)
    ...
} // class ABCJournalRecordFactory
```

RELATED PATTERNS

Hashed Adapter Objects. The Hashed Adapter Objects pattern (described in *Patterns in Java, Volume 2*) can be used in the implementation of the Factory Method pattern. It is useful if the set of classes that a factory object instantiates may change during the running of a program.

Abstract Factory.   The Factory Method pattern is useful for constructing individual objects for a specific purpose without the construction requester knowing the specific classes being instantiated. If you need to create a matched set of such objects, then the Abstract Factory pattern is a more appropriate pattern to use.

Template Method.   When the Factory Method pattern is implemented to determine the type of what will be created using configuration information, the implementation often uses the Template Method pattern.

Prototype.   The Prototype pattern provides an alternate way for an object to work with other objects without knowing the details of their construction.

Strategy.   If you are considering using the Factory Method pattern to vary behavior, the Strategy pattern may be a better alternative.

Abstract Factory

Abstract Factory is also known as Kit or Toolkit.

This pattern was previously described in [GoF95].

SYNOPSIS

Given a set of related interfaces, provide a way to create objects that implement those interfaces from a matched set of concrete classes. The Abstract Factory pattern can be very useful for allowing a program to work with a variety of complex external entities such as different windowing systems with similar functionality.

CONTEXT

Suppose you have the task of building a user-interface framework that works on top of multiple windowing systems, such as Windows, Motif, or MacOS. It must work on each platform with the platform's native look and feel. You organize it by creating an abstract class for each type of widget (text field, pushbutton, list box, etc.) and then writing a concrete subclass of each of those classes for each supported platform. To make this robust, you need to ensure that all the widget objects created are for the desired platform. This is where the abstract factory comes into play.

An abstract factory class defines methods to create an instance of each abstract class that represents a user-interface widget. Concrete factories are concrete subclasses of an abstract factory that implements its methods to create instances of concrete widget classes for the same platform.

In a more general context, an abstract factory class and its concrete subclasses organize sets of concrete classes that work with different but related products. For a broader perspective, consider another situation.

Suppose you are writing a program that performs remote diagnostics on computers made by a manufacturer called Stellar Microsystems. Over time, Stellar has produced computer models having substantially different architectures. Their oldest computers used CPU chips manufactured by Enginola that had a traditional complex instruction set. Since then, they have released multiple generations of computers based on their own reduced instruction set computer (RISC) architectures called ember, super-ember, and ultra-ember. The core components used in these models perform similar functions but involve different sets of components.

In order for your program to know which tests to run and how to interpret the results, it will need to instantiate objects that correspond to each core component in the computer being diagnosed. The class of each object will correspond to the type of component being tested. This means you will have a set of classes for each computer architecture. There will be a class in each set corresponding to the same type of computer component.

Figure 5.6 is a class diagram that shows the organization of the classes that encapsulate diagnostics for different kinds of components. It shows just two kinds of components. The organization for any additional kind of component would be the same. There is an interface for each type of component. For each computer architecture that is supported, there is a class that implements each interface.

The organization shown in Figure 5.6 leads us to the problem that this pattern solves. You need a way to organize the creation of diagnostic objects. You want the classes that use the diagnostic classes to be independent of the specific classes being used. You could use the Factory Method pattern to create diagnostic objects, but there is a problem that the Factory Method pattern does not solve.

You want to ensure that all the objects that you use to diagnose a computer are for that computer's architecture. If you simply use the Factory

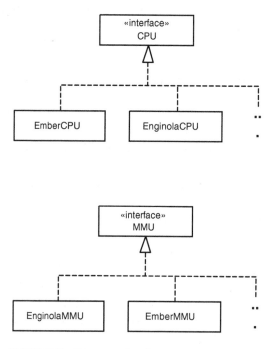

FIGURE 5.6 Diagnostic classes.

Method pattern, the classes that use the diagnostic classes will have the burden of telling each factory which computer architecture the diagnostic objects are for. You want to find a cohesive way of ensuring that all of the diagnostic objects used for a computer are for the correct architecture, without adding any dependencies to the classes that use the objects.

FORCES

☺ A system that works with multiple products should function in a way that is independent of the specific product it is working with.

☺ It should be possible for a system to be configured to work with one or multiple members of a family of products.

☺ Instances of classes intended to interface with a product should be used together and only with the product. This constraint must be enforced.

☺ The rest of a system should work with a product without being aware of the specific classes used to interface with the product.

☺ A system should be extensible so that it can work with additional products by adding additional sets of classes and changing at most only a few lines of code.

☹ The interface that a class implements is not sufficient to distinguish it from other classes that may be instantiated to create an object.

SOLUTION

Figure 5.7 is a class diagram that shows the roles classes play in the Abstract Factory pattern.

Here are descriptions of the roles that the classes and interfaces shown in Figure 5.7 play in the Abstract Factory pattern.

WidgetAIF, WidgetBIF, and so on. Interfaces in this role correspond to a service or feature of a product. Classes that implement one of these interfaces work with the service or feature to which the interface corresponds.

Because of space constraints, only two of these interfaces are shown. Most applications of the Abstract Factory pattern have more than two of these interfaces. There will be as many of these interfaces as there are distinct features or services of the products that are being used.

Product1WidgetA, Product2WidgetA, and so on. Classes in this role correspond to a specific feature of a specific product. You can generically refer to classes in this role as concrete widgets.

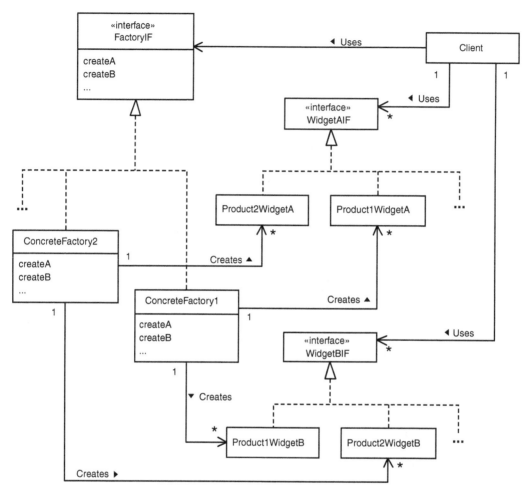

FIGURE 5.7 Abstract Factory.

Client. Classes in this role use concrete widget classes to request or receive services from the product that the client is working with. Client classes interact with concrete widget classes through a `WidgetIF` interface only. They are independent of the actual concrete widget classes they are working with.

FactoryIF. Interfaces in this role declare methods for creating instances of concrete widget classes. Each method returns an instance of a class that implements a different `WidgetIF` interface. Classes that are responsible for creating concrete widget objects implement an interface in this role.

ConcreteFactory1, ConcreteFactory2, and so on. Classes in this role implement a `FactoryIF` interface to create instances of concrete widget classes. Each class in this role corresponds to a different product that a `Client` class may work with. Each method of a `ConcreteFactory` class creates a different kind of concrete widget. However, all of the concrete widgets that its methods create are for working with the product that the `Concrete-Factory` class corresponds to.

Client classes that call these methods should not have any direct knowledge of these concrete factory classes, but instead should access instances of these classes through the `FactoryIF` interface.

IMPLEMENTATION

The main implementation issue for the Abstract Factory pattern is the mechanism that the client classes use to create and access `FactoryIF` objects. The simplest situation is when client objects need to work with only one product during the run of a program. In that case, some class will typically have a static variable set to the `ConcreteFactory` class that is used during the program run. The variable may be public or its value accessed through a public static method.

If the abstract factory object will use information provided by the requesting client to select among multiple concrete factory objects, you can use the Factory Method pattern.

CONSEQUENCES

☺ Client classes are independent of the concrete widget classes that they use.
☺ Adding (as opposed to writing) classes to work with additional products is simple. The class of a concrete factory object usually needs to be referenced in only one place. It is also easy to change the concrete factory used to work with a particular product.
☺ By forcing client classes to go through a `FactoryIF` interface to create concrete widget objects, the Abstract Factory pattern ensures that client objects use a consistent set of objects to work with a product.
☹ The main drawback of the Abstract Factory pattern is that it can be a lot of work to write a new set of classes to interface with a product. It can also take a lot of work to extend the set of features that the existing set of classes is able to exercise in the products that they work with.

Adding support for a new product involves writing a complete set of concrete widget classes to support that product. You must write a concrete widget class for each `WidgetIF` interface. If there are many `WidgetIF` interfaces, then it will be a lot of work to support an additional product.

Adding access to an additional feature of the products interfaced to can also take a lot of work if there are many supported products. It involves writing a new `WidgetIF` interface corresponding to the new feature and a new concrete widget class corresponding to each product.

☹ Client objects may have a need to organize widget classes into a hierarchy that serves the needs of client objects. The basic Abstract Factory pattern does not lend itself to this because it requires concrete widget classes to be organized into a class hierarchy that is independent of client objects. The difficulty can be overcome by mixing the Bridge pattern with the Abstract Factory pattern:

- Create a hierarchy of product-independent widget classes that suits the needs of the client classes. Have each product-independent widget class delegate product-specific logic to a product-specific class that implements a `WidgetIF` interface.
- Java's `java.awt` package contains a number of classes that are implemented using this variation. Classes like `Button` and `TextField` contain logic that is independent of the windowing system being used. These classes provide a native look and feel by delegating windowing system operations to concrete widget classes that implement interfaces defined in the `java.awt.peer` package.

JAVA API USAGE

The Abstract Factory pattern is used in the Java API to implement the `java.awt.Toolkit` class. The `java.awt.Toolkit` class is an abstract factory class used to create objects that work with the native windowing system. The concrete factory class it uses is determined by initialization code, and the singleton concrete factory object is returned by its `getDefaultToolkit` method.

CODE EXAMPLE

For this pattern's code example, we will return to the problem discussed under the Context section. Figure 5.8 shows an expanded class diagram that incorporates the Abstract Factory pattern.

An instance of the `Client` class manages the remote diagnostic process. When it determines the architecture of the machine it has to diagnose, it passes the architecture type to the `createToolkit` method of a `ToolkitFactory` object. The method returns an instance of a class such as `EmberToolkit` or `EnginolaToolkit` that implements the `Architecture-ToolkitIF` interface for the specified computer architecture. The `Client`

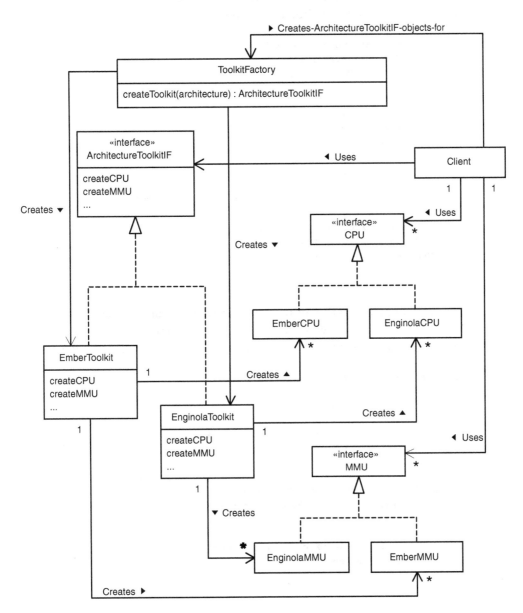

FIGURE 5.8 Diagnostic classes with abstract factory.

object can then use the ArchitectureToolkitIF object to create objects that model central processing units (CPUs), memory management units (MMUs), and other components of the required architecture.

Here is some of the Java code that implements the design for remote computer diagnostics shown in Figure 5.8. The abstract widget classes have the obvious structure.

This code is for a concrete factory class that creates instances of classes to test ember architecture computers:

```
class EmberToolkit implements ArchitectureToolkitIF {
    public CPU createCPU() {
        return new EmberCPU();
    } // createCPU()

    public MMU createMMU() {
        return new EmberMMU();
    } // createMMU()
    ...
} // class EmberFactory
```

The following is the code for the factory interface:

```
public interface ArchitectureToolkitIF {
    public abstract CPU createCPU() ;
    public abstract MMU createMMU() ;
...
} // AbstractFactory
```

This implementation of the Abstract Factory pattern uses the Factory Method pattern to create ArchitectureToolkitIF objects. Here is a listing of the factory class responsible for creating ArchitectureToolkitIF objects.

```
public class ToolkitFactory {
    /**
     * The single instance of this class.
     */
    private static ToolkitFactory myInstance
      = new ToolkitFactory();

    // Symbolic names to identify computer architectures
    public final static int ENGINOLA = 900;
    public final static int EMBER    = 901;
    // ...

    public static ToolkitFactory getInstance() {
        return myInstance;
    } // getInstance()

    /**
     * Return a newly created object that implements the
```

```
 * ArchitectureToolkitIF interface for the given computer
 * architecture.
 */
public
ArchitectureToolkitIF createToolkit(int architecture) {
    switch (architecture) {
      case ENGINOLA:
          return new EnginolaToolkit();

      case EMBER:
          return new EmberToolkit();
    } // switch
    String errMsg = Integer.toString(architecture);
    throw new IllegalArgumentException(errMsg);
  } // createToolkit(int)
} // class ToolkitFactory
```

Client classes typically create concrete widget objects using code that looks something like this:

```
public class Client {
    public void doIt () {
        ToolkitFactory myFactory;
        myFactory = ToolkitFactory.getInstance();
        ArchitectureToolkitIF af;
        af = myFactory.createToolkit(ToolkitFactory.EMBER);
        CPU cpu = af.createCPU();
        ...
    } // doIt
} // class Client
```

RELATED PATTERNS

Factory Method.   In the preceding example, the abstract factory class uses the Factory Method pattern to decide which concrete factory object to give to a client class.

Singleton.   Concrete Factory classes are usually implemented as Singleton classes.

Builder

This pattern was previously described in [GoF95].

SYNOPSIS

The Builder pattern allows a client object to construct a complex object by specifying only its type and content. The client is shielded from the details of the object's construction.

CONTEXT

Consider the problem of writing an email gateway program. The program receives e-mail messages that are in MIME format.[3] It forwards them in a different format for different kinds of e-mail systems. This situation is a good fit for the Builder pattern. It is straightforward to organize this program with an object that parses MIME messages. Each message to parse is paired with a builder object that the parser uses to build a message in the required format. As the parser recognizes each header field and message body part, it calls the corresponding method of the builder object it is working with.

Figure 5.9 shows this structure. In Figure 5.9, the MessageManager class is responsible for collecting MIME formatted e-mail messages and initiating their transmission. The e-mail messages it directly manages are instances of the MIMEMsg class.

Instances of the MIMEMsg class encapsulate MIME formatted e-mail messages. When a MessageManager object wants to transmit a message in a format other than MIME, it must rebuild a message in the desired format. The content of the new message must be the same as the MIME message or as close as the format allows.

The MIMEParser class is a subclass of the MessageParser class that can parse MIME formatted e-mail messages and pass their contents to a builder object.

---

[3] MIME is an acronym for Multipurpose Internet Mail Extensions. It is the standard that most email messages on the Internet conform to. You can find a description of MIME at http://mgrand.home.mindspring.com/mime.html.

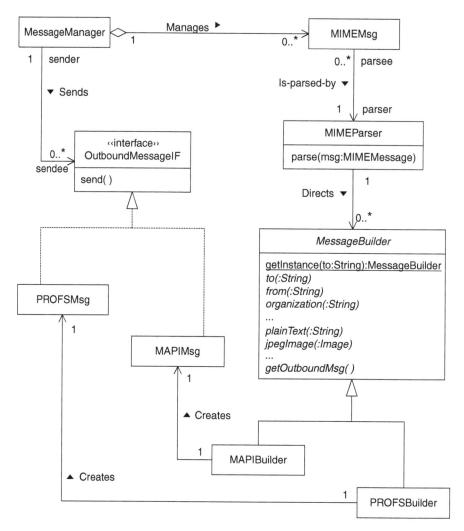

FIGURE 5.9 Builder example.

MessageBuilder is an abstract builder class. It defines methods that correspond to the various header fields and body types that MIME supports. It declares abstract methods that correspond to required header fields and the most common body types. It declares these methods abstract because all concrete subclasses of MessageBuilder should define these methods. However, some of the optional header fields such as organization and fancier body types such as Image/Jpeg may not be supported in all message formats, so the MessageBuilder class provides do-nothing implementations of these methods.

The MessageBuilder class also defines a class method called getInstance. A MIMEParser object passes the getInstance method the destination address of the message it is parsing. From the message's destination address, the getInstance method determines the message format needed for the new message. It returns an instance of the subclass of Message-Builder appropriate for the format of the new message to the MIMEParser object.

The MAPIBuilder and PROFSBuilder classes are concrete builder classes for building Messaging Application Programming Interface (MAPI) and PROFS (a registered trademark of the IBM corporation) messages, respectively.

The builder classes create product objects that implement the OutboundMsgIF interface. This interface defines a method called send that is intended to send the e-mail message wherever it is supposed to go.

Figure 5.10 is a collaboration diagram that shows how these classes work together.

Here is what's happening in Figure 5.10:

1. A MessageManager object receives an e-mail message.

> **1.1** The MessageManager object calls the MIMEParser class's parse method. It will return an OutboundMessageIF object that encapsulates the new message in the needed format.

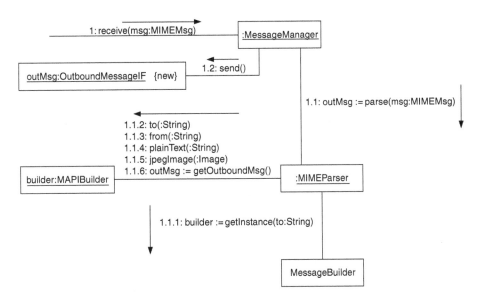

FIGURE 5.10 Builder example collaboration.

1.1.1 The MIMEParser object calls the MessageBuilder class's getInstance method, passing it the destination email address. By analyzing the address, the method selects a concrete subclass of the MessageBuilder class and creates an instance of it.

1.1.2 The MIMEParser object passes the destination email address to the MessageBuilder object's to method.

1.1.3 The MIMEParser object passes the originating email address to the MessageBuilder object's from method.

1.1.4 The MIMEParser object passes the email message's simple content to the MessageBuilder object's plainText method.

1.1.5 The MIMEParser object passes the email message's attached jpeg image to the MessageBuilder object's jpegImage method.

1.1.6 The MIMEParser object calls the MessageBuilder object's getOutboundMsg method to complete and fetch the new message.

1.2 The MessageManager object calls the OutboundMsg object's send method. This sends the message off and completes the message processing.

FORCES

☺ A program must to be able to produce multiple external representations of the same data.

☺ The classes responsible for providing content should be independent of any external data representation and the classes that build them. If content-providing classes have no dependencies on external data representations, then modifications to external data representation classes will not require any maintenance to content-providing classes.

☺ The classes responsible for building external data representations are independent of the classes that provide the content. Their instances can work with any content-providing object without knowing anything about the content-providing object.

SOLUTION

Figure 5.11 is a class diagram showing the participants in the Builder pattern.

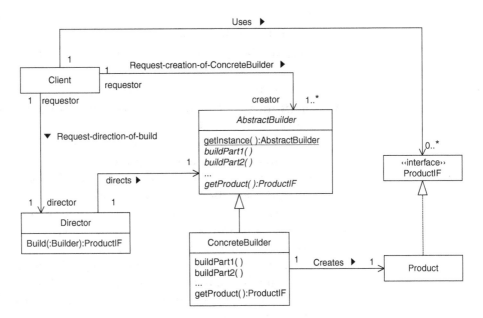

FIGURE 5.11 Builder pattern.

Here are the roles that these classes and interface play in the Builder pattern:

Product.   A class in this role defines a type of data representation. All `Product` classes should implement the `ProductIF` interface so that other classes can refer to `Product` objects through the interface without having to know their class.

ProductIF.   The Builder pattern is used to build a variety of different kinds of `Product` objects for use by `Client` objects. To avoid the need for `Client` objects to know the actual class of `Product` objects built for them, all `Product` classes implement the `ProductIF` interface. `Client` objects refer to `Product` objects built for them through the `ProductIF` interface, so they don't need to know the actual class of the objects built for them.

Client.   An instance of a client class initiates the actions of the Builder pattern. It calls the `AbstractBuilder` class's `getInstance` method. It passes information to `getInstance` telling it what sort of product it wants to have built. The `getInstance` method determines the subclass of `AbstractBuilder` to create and returns it to the `Client` object. The `Client` object then passes the object it got from `getInstance` to a `Director` object's `build` method, which builds the desired object.

ConcreteBuilder. A class in this role is a concrete subclass of the `AbstractBuilder` class that is used to build a specific kind of data representation of a `Director` object.

AbstractBuilder. A class in this role is the abstract superclass of `ConcreteBuilder` classes. An `AbstractBuilder` class defines a static method, typically called `getInstance`, which takes an argument that specifies a data representation. The `getInstance` method returns an instance of a concrete builder class that produces the specified data representation.

An `AbstractBuilder` class also defines methods, shown in the class diagram as `buildPart1`, `buildPart2`, ... A `Director` object calls these methods to tell the object returned by the `getInstance` method what content to put in the created object.

Finally, the builder class defines a method, typically called `getProduct`, which returns the product object created by a concrete builder object.

Director. A `Director` object calls the methods of a concrete builder object to provide the concrete builder with the content for the product object that it builds.

Figure 5.12 is a collaboration diagram showing how these classes work together.

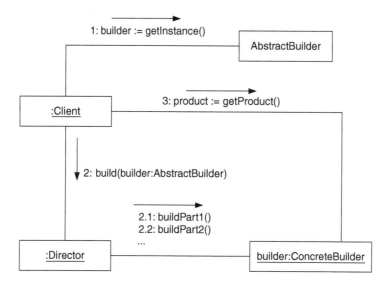

FIGURE 5.12 Builder collaboration.

IMPLEMENTATION

The essential design and implementation issue for the Builder pattern is the set of methods that the builder class defines to provide content to concrete builder objects. These methods can be a major concern because there may be a large number of them. The methods should be general enough to allow all reasonable data representations to be constructed. On the other hand, an excessively general set of methods can be more difficult to implement and to use. The consideration of generality versus difficulty of implementation raises these issues in the implementation phase:

- Each content-providing method declared by the abstract builder class can be abstract or provided with a default do-nothing implementation. Abstract method declarations force concrete builder classes to provide an implementation for that method. Forcing concrete builder classes to provide implementations for methods is good in those cases where the method provides essential information about content. It prevents implementers of those classes from forgetting to implement those methods.

  However, methods that provide optional content or supplementary information about the structure of the content may be unnecessary or even inappropriate for some data representations. Providing a default do-nothing implementation for such methods saves effort in the implementation of concrete builder classes that do not need such methods.

- Organizing concrete builder classes so that calls to content-providing methods simply add data to the product object is often good enough. In some cases, there will be no simple way to tell the builder where in the finished product a particular piece of the product will go. In those situations, it may be simplest to have the content-providing method return an object to the director that encapsulates such a piece of the product. The director object can then pass the object to another content-providing method in a way that implies the position of the piece of the product within the whole product.

CONSEQUENCES

- ☺ Content determination and the construction of a specific data representation are independent of each other. The data representation of the product can change without any impact on the objects that provide the content. Builder objects can work with different content-providing objects without requiring any changes.
- Builder provides finer control over construction than other patterns such as Factory Method by giving the director object step-by-step

control over creation of the product object. Other patterns simply create the entire object in one step.

CODE EXAMPLE

Let's look at some sample code for the classes in this example that collaborate in the Builder pattern. Instances of the `MIMEParser` class fill the role of director objects. Here is the source for the `MIMEParser` class:

```
class MIMEParser {
    private MIMEMessage msg;        // The message being parsed
    private MessageBuilder builder; // The builder object
    ...
    /**
     * Parse a MIME message, calling the builder methods that
     * correspond to message header fields and body parts.
     */
    OutboundMessageIF parse() {
        builder =MessageBuilder.getInstance(getDestination());
        MessagePart hdr = nextHeader();
        while (hdr != null) {
            if (hdr.getName().equals("to"))
              builder.to((String)hdr.getValue());
            else if (hdr.getName().equals("from"))
              builder.from((String)hdr.getValue());
            ...
            hdr = nextHeader();
        } // while hdr
        MessagePart bdy = nextBodyPart();
        while (bdy != null) {
            String name = bdy.getName();
            if (name.equalsIgnoreCase ("text/plain"))
              builder.plainText((String)bdy.getValue());
            ...
            else if (name.equalsIgnoreCase("image/jpeg"))
              builder.jpegImage((Image)bdy.getValue());
            ...
            bdy = nextHeader();
        } // while bdy
        return builder.getOutboundMsg();
    } // parse(Message)
...
    private class MessagePart {
        private String name;
        private Object value;

        MessagePart(String name, Object value) {
            this.name = name;
            this.value = value;
        } // Constructor(String, String)
```

```
    String getName() { return name; }

    Object getValue() { return value; }
} // class MessagePart
} // class MIMEParser
```

The chains of `if` statements that occur in the `parse` method of the preceding class would be rather long if the method were fully fleshed out. MIME supports over 25 different kinds of header fields alone. A less awkward way to organize a chain of tests of object equality that result in a method call is to use the Hashed Adapter Objects pattern described in *Patterns in Java, Volume 2*.

Here is code for the `MessageBuilder` class, which fills the role of abstract builder class:

```
abstract class MessageBuilder {
    /**
     * Return an instance of the subclass appropriate for the
     * email message format implied by the given destination
     * address.
     * @param dest The address to send the email to
     */
    static MessageBuilder getInstance(String dest) {
        MessageBuilder builder = null;
        ...
        return builder;
    } // getInstance(String)

    /**
     * Pass the "to" header field value to this method.
     */
    abstract void to(String value);

    /**
     * Pass the "from" header field value to this method.
     */
    abstract void from(String value);

    /**
     * Pass the "organization" header field value to this
     * method.
     */
    void organization(String value) { }

    /**
     * Pass the content of a plaintext body part to this
     method.
     */
    abstract void plainText(String content);
...

    /**
```

```
            * complete and return the outbound email message.
            */
        abstract OutboundMessageIF getOutboundMsg() ;
} // class MessageBuilder
```

Finally, here is the code for the OutboundMsgIF interface:

```
public interface OutboundMsgIF {
    public void send() ;
} // interface OutboundMsgIF
```

RELATED PATTERNS

Interface.   The Builder pattern uses the Interface pattern to hide the class of a ProductIF object.

Composite.   The object built using the Builder pattern is typically a Composite.

Factory Method.   The Builder pattern uses the Factory Method pattern to decide which concrete builder class to instantiate.

Template Method.   The Abstract Builder class is often implemented using the Template Method pattern.

Null Object.   The Null Object pattern may be used by the Builder pattern to provide do-nothing implementations of methods.

Visitor.   The Visitor pattern allows the client object to be more closely coupled to the construction of the new complex object than the Builder pattern allows. Instead of describing the content of the objects to be built through a series of method calls, the information is presented in bulk as a complex data structure.

Prototype

This pattern was previously described in [GoF95].

SYNOPSIS

The Prototype pattern allows an object to create customized objects without knowing their exact class or the details of how to create them. It works by giving prototypical objects to an object that initiates the creation of objects. The creation-initiating object then creates objects by asking the prototypical objects to make copies of themselves.

CONTEXT

Suppose that you are writing a Computer-Assisted Design (CAD) program that allows its users to draw diagrams from a palette of symbols. The program will have a core set of built-in symbols. However, people with different and specialized interests will use the program. The core set of symbols will not be adequate for people with a specialized interest. These people will want additional symbols that are specific to their interests. Most users of this program will have a specialized interest. It must be possible to provide additional sets of symbols that users can add to the program to suit their needs.

This presents the problem of how to provide these palettes of additional symbols. You can easily organize things so that all symbols, both core and additional, are descended from a common ancestor class. This will give the rest of your diagram-drawing program a consistent way of manipulating symbol objects. It does leave open the question of how the program will create these objects. Creating objects such as these is often more complicated than simply instantiating a class. It may also involve setting values for data attributes or combining objects to form a composite object.

A solution is to provide the drawing program with previously created objects to use as prototypes for creating similar objects. The most important requirement for objects to be used as prototypes is that they have a method, typically called `clone`, that returns a new object that is a copy of the original object. Figure 5.13 shows how this would be organized.

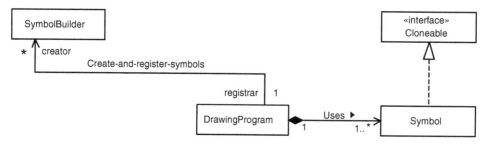

FIGURE 5.13 Symbol prototype.

The drawing program maintains a collection of prototypical Symbol objects. It uses the Symbol objects by cloning them. SymbolBuilder objects create Symbol objects and register them with the drawing program.

All Java classes inherit a method from the Object class called clone. An object's clone method returns a copy of the object. It does this only if the object's class gives permission. A class gives permission for its instances to be cloned if, and only if, it implements the Cloneable interface. Because the Symbol class implements the Cloneable interface, the drawing program is able to clone the Symbol objects that it manages and incorporate those objects into drawings.

FORCES

☺ A system must be able to create objects without knowing their exact class, how they are created, or what data they represent.

☺ Classes to be instantiated are not known by the system until runtime, when they are acquired on the fly by techniques such as dynamic linkage.

☺ The following approaches to allowing the creation of a large variety of objects are undesirable:

● The classes that initiate the creation of objects directly create the objects. This makes them aware of and dependent on a large number of other classes.

● The classes that initiate the creation of objects create the objects indirectly through a factory method class. A factory method that is able to create a large variety of objects may be very large and difficult to maintain.

● The classes that initiate the creation of objects create the objects indirectly through an abstract factory class. In order for an abstract factory to be able to create a large variety of objects, it must have a large variety of concrete factory classes in a hierarchy that parallels the classes to be instantiated.

☺ The different objects that a system must create may be instances of the same class that contain different state information or data content.

SOLUTION

Enable a class to create objects that implement a known interface by giving it a prototypical instance of each kind of object it will create. It is then able to create new objects by cloning a prototypical instance.

Figure 5.14 shows the organization of the Prototype pattern. Here are descriptions of the roles these classes and interfaces play in the Prototype pattern:

Client.   The client class represents the rest of the program for the purposes of the Prototype pattern. The client class needs to create objects that it knows little about. Client classes will have a method that can be called to add a prototypical object to a client object's collection. In Figure 5.14, this method is indicated with the name `registerPrototype`. However, a name that reflects the sort of object being prototyped, such as `registerSymbol`, is more appropriate in an actual implementation.

Prototype.   Classes in this role implement the `PrototypeIF` interface and are instantiated for the purpose of being cloned by the client. Classes in this role are commonly abstract classes with a number of concrete subclasses.

PrototypeIF.   All prototype objects must implement the interface that is in this role. The client class interacts with prototype objects through this interface. Interfaces in this role should extend the `Cloneable` interface so that all objects that implement the interface can be cloned.

PrototypeBuilder.   This corresponds to any class instantiated to supply prototypical objects to the client object. Such classes should have a name that denotes the type of prototypical object that they build, such as `SymbolBuilder`.

A `PrototypeBuilder` object creates `Prototype` objects. It passes each newly created `Prototype` object to a `Client` object's `registerPrototype` method.

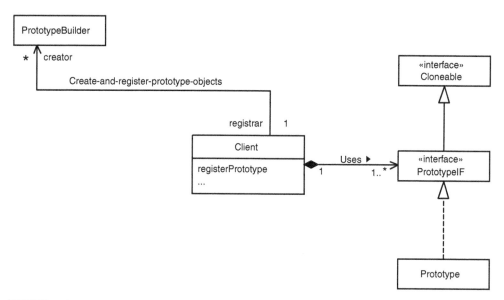

FIGURE 5.14 Prototype pattern.

IMPLEMENTATION

An essential implementation issue is how the PrototypeBuilder objects add objects to a client object's palette of prototypical objects. The simplest strategy is for the client class to provide a method for this purpose, which PrototypeBuilder objects can call. A possible drawback is that the PrototypeBuilder objects will need to know the class of the client object. If that is a problem, the PrototypeBuilder objects can be shielded from knowing the exact class of the client objects by providing an interface or abstract class for the client class to implement or inherit.

How to implement the clone operation for the prototypical objects is another important implementation issue. There are two basic strategies for implementing the clone operation:

- *Shallow copying* means that the variables of the cloned object contain the same values as the variables of the original object and that all object references are to the same objects. In other words, shallow copying copies only the object being cloned, not the objects that it refers to. Both the original and a shallow copy refer to the same objects.
- *Deep copying* means that the variables of the cloned object contain the same values as the variables of the original object, except that variables that refer to objects refer to copies of the objects referred to

by the original object. In other words, deep copying copies the object being cloned and the objects that it refers to. A deep copy refers to copies of the objects that the original refers to.

Implementing deep copying can be tricky. You will need to decide whether you want to make deep or shallow copies of the indirectly copied objects. You will also need to be careful about handling any circular references.

Shallow copying is easier to implement because all classes inherit a `clone` method for the `Object` class that does just that. However, unless an object's class implements the `Cloneable` interface, the `clone` method will refuse to work. If all of the prototypical objects your program uses will be cloning themselves by shallow copying, you can save some time by declaring the `PrototypeIF` interface to extend the `Cloneable` interface. This way, all classes that implement the `PrototypeIF` interface also implement the `Cloneable` interface.

Some objects, such as threads and sockets, cannot be simply copied or shared. Whichever copying strategy is used, if it involves references to such objects, then equivalent objects will need to be constructed for the use of the copied objects.

Unless the `Client` object's palette of prototypical objects consists of a fixed number of objects having fixed purposes, it is inconvenient to use individual variables to refer to each prototypical object. It is easier to use a collection object that can contain a dynamically growing or shrinking palette of prototypical objects. A collection object that plays this role in the Prototype pattern is called a *prototype manager*. Prototype managers can be fancier than just a simple collection. They may allow objects to be retrieved by their attribute values or other keys.

If your program will have multiple client objects, then you have another issue to consider. Will the client objects have their own palette of prototypical objects or will all of them share the same palette? The answer will depend on the needs of your application.

CONSEQUENCES

- ☺ A program can dynamically add and remove prototypical objects at runtime. This is a distinct advantage offered by none of the other creational patterns in this book.
- ☺ A `PrototypeBuilder` object can simply supply a fixed set of prototypical objects.
- ☺ A `PrototypeBuilder` object may provide the additional flexibility of allowing new prototypical objects to be created by object composition and changes to the values of object attributes.

☺ The client object may also be able to create new kinds of prototypical objects. In the drawing program example we looked at previously, the client object could very reasonably allow the user to identify a sub-drawing and then turn the sub-drawing into a new symbol.

☺ The client class is independent of the exact class of the prototypical objects that it uses. Also, the client class does not need to know the details of how to build the prototypical objects.

☺ The `PrototypeBuilder` objects encapsulate the details of constructing prototypical objects.

☺ By insisting that prototypical objects implement an interface such as `PrototypeIF`, the Prototype pattern ensures that the prototypical objects provide a consistent set of methods for the client object to use.

● There is no need to organize prototypical objects into any sort of class hierarchy.

☹ A drawback of the Prototype pattern is the additional time spent writing `PrototypeBuilder` classes.

☹ Programs that use the Prototype pattern rely on dynamic linkage or similar mechanisms. Installation of programs that rely on dynamic linkage or similar mechanisms can be more complicated. They may require information about their environment that may otherwise not be needed.

JAVA API USAGE

The Prototype pattern is the very essence of JavaBeans. JavaBeans are instances of classes that conform to certain naming conventions. The naming conventions allow a bean creation program to know how to customize them. After a bean object has been customized for use in an application, the object is saved to a file to be loaded by the application while it is running. This is a time-delayed way of cloning objects.

CODE EXAMPLE

Suppose that you are writing an interactive role-playing game. That is, a game that allows the user to interact with simulated characters. One of the expectations for this game is that people who play it will grow tired of interacting with the same characters and want to interact with new characters. For this reason, you are also developing an add-on to the game that consists of a few pre-generated characters and a program to generate additional characters.

The characters in the game are instances of a relatively small number of classes such as Hero, Fool, Villain, and Monster. What makes instances of the same class different from each other is the different attribute values that are set for them, such as the images that are used to represent them, height, weight, intelligence, and dexterity.

Figure 5.15 shows some of the classes involved in the game.

Here is the code for the `CharacterIF` interface, the interface that serves the role of `PrototypeIF`.

```
public interface CharacterIF extends Cloneable {
    public String getName() ;
    public void setName(String name) ;
    public Image getImage() ;
    public void setImage(Image image) ;
```

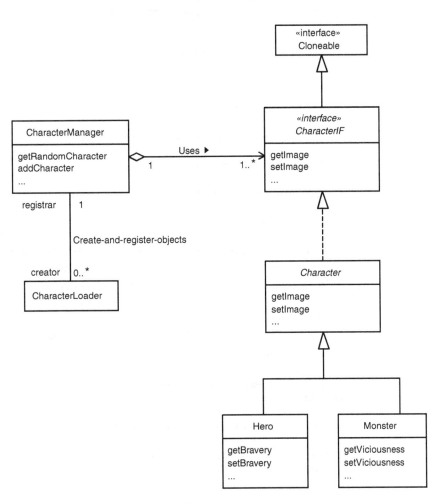

FIGURE 5.15   Prototype example.

```
    public int getStrength() ;
    public void setStrength(int strength) ;
    ...
} // class CharacterIF
```

Here is the code for the `Character` class, the abstract class that serves the role of `Prototype`:

```
public abstract class Character implements CharacterIF {
    ...
    /**
     * Override clone to make it public.
     */
    public Object clone() {
        try {
            return super.clone();
        } catch (CloneNotSupportedException e) {
            // should never happen because this class
            // implements Cloneable.
            throw new InternalError();
        } // try
    } // clone()

    public String getName() { return name; }

    public void setName(String name) { this.name = name; }

    public Image getImage() { return image; }

    public void setImage(Image image) { this.image = image; }
    ...
} // class Character
```

Most of this is just simple accessor methods. The one less-than-obvious method is the `clone` method. All objects inherit a `clone` method from the `Object` class. Because the `clone` method is not public, the `Character` class must override it with a public declaration, just to make it accessible to other classes.

Here is source code for the `Hero` class, one of the classes that serve in the Prototype role:

```
public class Hero extends Character {
    private int bravery;
    ...
    public int getBravery() { return bravery; }

    public void setBravery(int bravery) {
        this.bravery = bravery;
    }
} // class Hero
```

The Monster class is similar to the Hero class.

Following is the code for the `CharacterManager` class that serves in the role of client class:

```
public class CharacterManager {
    private Vector characters = new Vector();
...
    /**
     * Return a copy of random character from the collection.
     */
    Character getRandomCharacter() {
        int i = (int)(characters.size()*Math.random());
        Character c = (Character)characters.elementAt(i);
        return (Character)c.clone();
    } // getRandomCharacter()

    /**
     * Add a prototypical object to the collection.
     */
    void addCharacter(Character character) {
        characters.addElement(character);
    } // addCharacter(Character)
...
} // class CharacterManager
```

Here is the code for the `CharacterLoader` class that fills the role of `PrototypeBuilder`:

```
/**
 * This class loads character objects and adds them to
 * the CharacterManager.
 */
class CharacterLoader {
    private CharacterManager mgr;
    /**
     * Constructor
     * @param cm
     *          The CharacterManager this object will work with.
     */
    CharacterLoader(CharacterManager cm) {
        mgr = cm;
    } // Constructor(CharacterManager)

    /**
     * Load character objects from the specified file.
     * Since failure only affects the rest of the program to
     * the extent that new character objects are not loaded,
     * we need not throw any exceptions.
     */
    int loadCharacters(String fname) {
        int objectCount = 0;    // The number of objects loaded
```

```
        // If construction of InputStream fails, just return
    try {
        InputStream in;
        in = new FileInputStream(fname);
        in = new BufferedInputStream(in);
        ObjectInputStream oIn = new ObjectInputStream(in);
        while(true) {
            Object c = oIn.readObject();
            if (c instanceof Character) {
                mgr.addCharacter((Character)c);
            } // if
        } // while
    } catch (Exception e) {
    } // try
    return objectCount;
    } // loadCharacters(String)
} // class CharacterLoader
```

RELATED PATTERNS

Composite.   The Prototype pattern is often used with the Composite pattern. The composite is used to organize prototype objects.

Abstract Factory.   The Abstract Factory pattern can be a good alternative to the Prototype pattern if the dynamic changes that the Prototype pattern allows to the prototypical object palette are not needed.

   `PrototypeBuilder` classes may use the Abstract Factory pattern to create a set of prototypical objects.

Façade.   The client class commonly acts as a façade that separates the other classes that participate in the Prototype pattern from the rest of the program.

Factory Method.   The Factory Method pattern can be an alternative to the Prototype pattern when the palette of prototypical objects never contains more than one object.

Decorator.   The Prototype pattern is often used with the Decorator pattern to compose prototypical objects.

Singleton

This pattern was previously described in [GoF95].

SYNOPSIS

The Singleton pattern ensures that only one instance of a class is created. All objects that use an instance of that class use the same instance.

CONTEXT

Some classes should have exactly one instance. These classes usually involve the central management of a resource. The resource may be external, as is the case with an object that manages the reuse of database connections. The resource may be internal, such as an object that keeps an error count and other statistics for a compiler.

Suppose you need to write a class that an applet can use to ensure that no more than one audio clip is played at a time. If an applet contains two pieces of code that independently play audio clips, then it is possible for both to be playing at the same time. When two audio clips play at the same time, the results depend on the platform. The results may range from confusing, with users hearing both audio clips together, to terrible, with the platform's sound-producing mechanism unable to cope with playing two different audio clips at once.

To avoid the undesirable situation of two audio clips playing at the same time, the class you write should stop the previous audio clip before starting the next audio clip. A way to design a class to implement this policy while keeping the class simple is to ensure that there is only one instance of the class shared by all objects that use that class. If all requests to play audio clips go through the same object, then it is simple for the object to stop the last audio clip it started before starting the next audio clip. Figure 5.16 shows such a class.

The constructor for the `AudioClipManager` class is private. This prevents another class from directly creating an instance of the `AudioClipManager` class. Instead, to get an instance of the `AudioClip-Manager` class, other classes must call its `getInstance` method. The `getInstance` method is a static method that always returns the same instance of the `AudioClipManager` class. The instance it returns is the instance referred to by its private static variable `instance`.

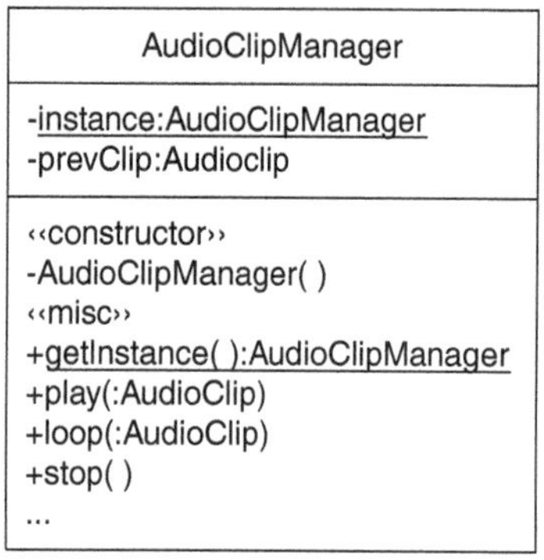

```
┌─────────────────────────────────────────┐
│            AudioClipManager               │
├─────────────────────────────────────────┤
│ -instance:AudioClipManager                │
│ -prevClip:Audioclip                       │
├─────────────────────────────────────────┤
│ ‹‹constructor››                           │
│ -AudioClipManager( )                      │
│ ‹‹misc››                                  │
│ +getInstance( ):AudioClipManager          │
│ +play(:AudioClip)                         │
│ +loop(:AudioClip)                         │
│ +stop( )                                  │
│ ...                                       │
└─────────────────────────────────────────┘
```

FIGURE 5.16 Audio clip manager.

The rest of the `AudioClipManager` class's methods are responsible for controlling the playing of audio clips. The `AudioClipManager` class has a private instance variable named `prevClip`, which is initially null and later refers to the last audio clip played. Before playing a new audio clip, the instance of the `AudioClipManager` class stops the audio clip referred to by the `prevClip`. That ensures that the previously requested audio clip stops before the next audio clip starts.

FORCES

☺ There must be at least one instance of a class. Even if the methods of your class use no instance data or only static data, you may need an instance of the class for a variety of reasons. Some of the more common reasons are that you need an instance to pass a method of another class or that you want to access the class indirectly through an interface.

☺ There should be no more than one instance of a class. This may be the case because you want to have only one source of some information. For example, you may want to have a single object that is responsible for generating a sequence of serial numbers.

☺ The one instance of a class must be accessible to all clients of that class.

☺ An object is cheap to create but takes up a lot of memory or continuously uses other resources during its lifetime.

SOLUTION

The Singleton pattern is relatively simple, since it involves only one class. The organization of this class is shown in Figure 5.17.

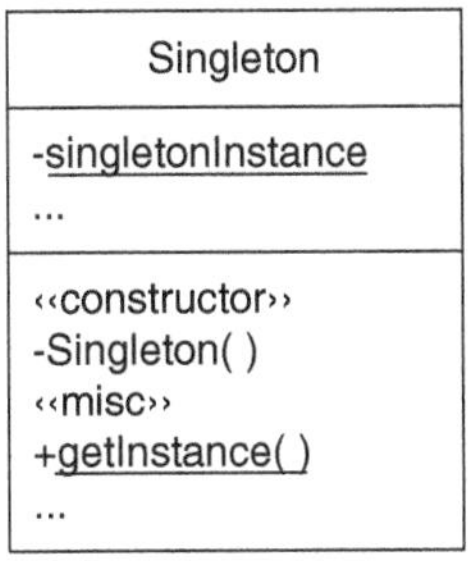

```
┌─────────────────────┐
│      Singleton      │
├─────────────────────┤
│ -singletonInstance  │
│ ...                 │
├─────────────────────┤
│ ‹‹constructor››     │
│ -Singleton( )       │
│ ‹‹misc››            │
│ +getInstance( )     │
│ ...                 │
└─────────────────────┘
```

FIGURE 5.17 Singleton.

A singleton class has a static variable that refers to the one instance of the class you want to use. This instance is created when the class is loaded into memory. You should implement the class in a way that prevents other classes from creating additional instances. That means ensuring that all of the class's constructors are private.

To access the one instance of a singleton class, the class provides a static method, typically called `getInstance` or `getClassname`, which returns a reference to the one instance of the class.

IMPLEMENTATION

Though the Singleton pattern involves a relatively simple solution, there are a surprising number of subtleties in its implementation.

PRIVATE CONSTRUCTOR

To enforce the nature of a singleton class, you must code the class in a way that prevents other classes from directly creating instances of the class. A way to accomplish this is to declare the class's constructors private. Be careful to declare at least one private constructor. If a class does not declare any constructors, then the Java compiler automatically generates a default public constructor.

LAZY INSTANTIATION

A common variation on the Singleton pattern occurs in situations where the instance of a Singleton may not be needed. You do not know whether the program will need to use the singleton instance until the first time that the getInstance method is called. In situations like this, postpone creation of the instance until the first call to `getInstance`.

ALLOWING MORE THAN ONE INSTANCE

Another variation on the Singleton pattern stems from the fact that it has a class's instantiation policy encapsulated in the class itself. Because the instantiation policy is encapsulated in the class's getInstance method, it is possible to vary the creation policy. Some possible policies are to have getInstance alternately return one of two instances or to periodically create a new instance for getInstance to return.

This sort of situation can come up when you are using small, fixed individual objects to represent external resources and you want to balance the load between them. When you generalize this to an arbitrary or variable number of objects, you get the Object Pool pattern.

MAKING COPIES OF A SINGLETON

A singleton object is usually intended to be the only instance of its class. Even in the case in which you allow more than one instance of a singleton object, you generally want to ensure that creation of singleton objects is entirely under the control of the singleton class's getInstance object. This means that you don't want any other classes making copies of a singleton object.

One consequence of this is that a singleton class should not implement the java.lang.Cloneable interface. It should not be possible for another class to make a copy by calling a singleton object's clone method.

Serialization is a mechanism that Java provides for converting the contents of objects into a stream of bytes. *Deserialization* is a mechanism that Java provides for converting a stream of bytes created by serialization to objects that have the same contents as the original objects. There is a detailed description of serialization and deserialization on page 377.

Serialization can be used to copy objects, but copying is not usually the intended use of serialization. These are the two most common uses for serialization:

- Serialization is used to make objects persistent by writing them to a file as a stream of bytes. This allows persisted objects with the same contents to be recreated later on. This is the mechanism by which JavaBeans are saved and reconstituted.
- Serialization is used to support remote procedure calls using RMI. RMI is used by EJB (Enterprise JavaBeans). RMI uses serialization to pass argument values to remote procedure calls and also to pass the return value back to a remote caller.

You will generally not want to perform either of these functions with a singleton object. In general, Singleton objects should not be included in a serialized stream of objects. You can ensure this by never directly serializing a singleton object and by not having any classes save a reference to a singleton object in its instance variables. Instead, have clients of a singleton class call the singleton class's getInstance methods every time they want to access a singleton object.

CONCURRENT GetInstance CALLS

If there is any chance that multiple threads may call a singleton class's getInstance method at the same time, then you will need to make sure that the getInstance method does not create multiple instances of the singleton class. Consider the following code:

```
public class Foo {
    private Foo myInstance;
    ...
    public static Foo getInstance() {
        if (myInstance==null) {
            myInstance = new Foo();
        } // if
        return myInstance;
    } // getInstance()
    ...
} // class Foo
```

If two threads call the getInstance method at the same time and there were no previous calls to the getInstance method, then both calls will see that the value of myInstance is null, and both calls will create an instance of Foo. To avoid this problem, you can declare the getInstance method to be synchronized. This will ensure that only one thread at a time is able to execute the getInstance method.

Declaring the getInstance method to be synchronized does add a small amount of overhead by forcing every call to the getInstance method to get a synchronization lock before it proceeds.

A SUBTLE BUG

There is a rather subtle bug that can occur in implementations of the Singleton pattern. It can cause a singleton class to create and initialize more than one instance of itself over time. The problem occurs in programs that refer to a singleton class only through other classes that are dynamically loaded, as described in the Dynamic Linkage pattern.

Some programs are organized so that they dynamically load a set of classes, use them for a while, and then stop using them. Applets, servlets, and MIDlets are managed this way. When a program stops using classes, the classes it is finished with are garbage-collected. This is normally a good thing. If a program keeps no references to classes after it is finished with them and garbage collection of classes is enabled, the unused classes will eventually be garbage-collected.

This behavior can be a problem for singleton classes. If a singleton class is garbage-collected, it will be loaded again if there is another dynamic reference to it. After the class has been loaded a second time, the next request for its instance will return a new instance! This can produce unexpected results.

Suppose you have a singleton class whose purpose is to maintain performance statistics. Consider what happens if it is garbage-collected and reloaded. The first time its `getInstance` method is called after it is loaded a second time, it will return a new object. Its instance variables will have their initial values, and previously collected statistics will be lost.

If a class is loaded by a `ClassLoader` object, then it will not be garbage-collected until the `ClassLoader` object is eligible to be garbage-collected. If this is not a practical way for you to manage the lifetime of a singleton object, there is a more general way: Ensure that there is a reference, direct or indirect, from a live thread to the object that is not to be garbage-collected. The class in the following listing can be used to do just that.

```
public class ObjectPreserver implements Runnable {
    // This keeps this class and everything it references from
    // being garbage-collected
    private static ObjectPreserver lifeLine
      = new ObjectPreserver();

    // Since this class won't be garbage-collected, neither
    // will this HashSet or the object that it references.
    private static HashSet protectedSet = new HashSet();

    private ObjectPreserver() {
        new Thread(this).start();
    } // constructor()

    public synchronized void run() {
        try {
            wait();
        } catch (InterruptedException e) {
        } // try
    } // run()

    /**
     * Garbage collection of objects passed to this method
     * will be prevented until they are passed to the
     * unpreserveObject method.
     */
    public static void preserveObject(Object o) {
        protectedSet.add(o);
    } // preserveObject()
```

```
/**
 * Objects passed to this method lose the protection
 * from garbage collection.
 */
public static void unpreserveObject(Object o) {
    protectedSet.remove(o);
} // unpreserveObject(Object)
} // class ObjectPreserver
```

If the class object that encapsulates a class or one of a class's instances is passed to the `preserveObject` method of the `ObjectPreserver` class shown in the preceding listing, then that class will not be garbage-collected.

CONSEQUENCES

- ☺ Exactly one instance of a singleton class exists.
- ☺ The singleton class's `getInstance` method encapsulates the creation policy for the singleton class so that classes that use a singleton class do not depend on the details of its instantiation.
- ● Other classes that want a reference to the one instance of the singleton class must get that instance by calling the class's `getInstance` static method, rather than by constructing the instance themselves.
- ☹ Subclassing a singleton class is awkward and results in imperfectly encapsulated classes. In order to subclass a singleton class, you must give it a constructor that is not private. Also, since static functions cannot be overridden, a subclass of a singleton class must leave its superclass's `GetInstance` method exposed.

JAVA API USAGE

The Java API class `java.lang.Runtime` is a singleton class. It has exactly one instance. It has no public constructors. To get a reference to its one instance, other classes must call its static method `getRuntime`.

CODE EXAMPLE

The following listing shows a Java class you can use to avoid playing two audio clips at the same time. The class is a singleton class. You can access its instance by calling its static `getInstance` method. When you play audio clips through that object, it stops the last audio clip it was playing before it starts the newly requested one. If you play all audio clips through the

`AudioClipManager` object, then there will never be more than one audio clip playing at the same time.

```
public class AudioClipManager implements AudioClip{
    private static AudioClipManager instance
      = new AudioClipManager();
    private AudioClip prevClip; // previously requested audio clip

    /**
     * This private constructor is defined so the compiler
     * won't generate a default public constructor.
     */
    private AudioClipManager() { }

    /**
     * Return a reference to the only instance of this class.
     */
    public static AudioClipManager getInstance() {
        return instance;
    } // getInstance()
...
    /**
     * Stop the previously requested audio clip and play the
     * given audio clip.
     * @param clip the new audio clip to play.
     */
    public void play(AudioClip clip) {
        if (prevClip != null)
          prevClip.stop();
        prevClip = clip;
        clip.play();
    } // play(AudioClip)
...
    /**
     * Stop the previously requested audio clip and play the
     * given audio clip in a loop.
     * @param clip the new audio clip to play.
     */
    public void loop(AudioClip clip) {
        if (prevClip != null)
          prevClip.stop();
        prevClip = clip;
        clip.loop();
    } // play(AudioClip)

    /**
     * Stops playing this audio clip.
     */
    public void stop() {
        if (prevClip != null)
          prevClip.stop();
    } // stop()
} // class AudioClipManager
```

RELATED PATTERNS

You can use the Singleton pattern with many other patterns. In particular, it is often used with the Abstract Factory, Builder, and Prototype patterns.

Cache Management.   The Singleton pattern has some similarity to the Cache Management pattern. A Singleton is functionally similar to a Cache that contains only one object.

Object Pool.   The Object Pool pattern is for managing an arbitrarily large collection of similar objects rather than just a single object.

Object Pool

SYNOPSIS

Manage the reuse of objects when a type of object is expensive to create or only a limited number of a kind of object can be created.

CONTEXT

Suppose you have been given the assignment of writing a class library to provide access to a proprietary database. Clients will send queries to the database through a network connection. The database server will receive queries through the network connection and return the results through the same connection.

For a program to query the database, it must have a connection to the database. A convenient way for programmers who will use the library to manage connections is for each part of a program that needs a connection to create its own connection. However, creating database connections that are not needed is bad for a few reasons:

- It can take a few seconds to create each database connection.
- The more connections there are to a database, the longer it takes to create new connections.
- Each database connection uses a network connection. Some platforms limit the number of network connections that they allow.

Your design for the library will have to reconcile these conflicting forces. The need to provide a convenient API for programmers pulls your design in one direction. The high expense of creating database connection objects and a possible limit to the number of concurrent database connections pulls your design in another direction. One way to reconcile these forces is to have the library manage database connections on behalf of the application that uses the library.

The library will use a strategy to manage database connections based on the premise that a program's database connections are interchangeable. So long as a database connection is in a state that allows it to convey a query to the database, it does not matter which of a program's database connections is used. Using this observation, the database access library will be designed to have a two-layer implementation of database connections.

A class called `Connection` will implement the upper layer. Programs that use the database access library will directly create and use `Connection` objects. `Connection` objects will identify a database, but will not directly encapsulate a database connection. Only while a `Connection` object is being used to send a query to a database and fetch the result will it be paired with a `ConnectionImpl` object. `ConnectionImpl` objects encapsulate an actual database connection.

The library will create and manage `ConnectionImpl` objects. It will manage `ConnectionImpl` objects by maintaining a pool of them that are not currently paired up with a `Connection` object. The library will create a `ConnectionImpl` object only when it needs to pair one with a `Connection` object and the pool of `ConnectionImpl` objects is empty. The class diagram in Figure 5.18 shows the classes that will be involved in managing the pool of `ConnectionImpl` objects.

A `Connection` object calls the `ConnectionPool` object's `AcquireImpl` method when it needs a `ConnectionImpl` object, passing it the name of the database it needs to be connected with. If any `ConnectionImpl` objects in the `ConnectionPool` object's collection are connected to the specified database, the `ConnectionPool` object returns one of those objects. If there are no such `ConnectionImpl` objects in the `ConnectionPool` object's collection, then it tries to create one and return it. If it is unable to create a `ConnectionImpl` object, it waits until an existing `ConnectionImpl` object is returned to the pool by a call to the `releaseImpl` method and then it returns that object.

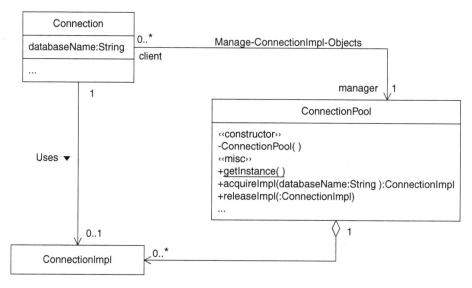

FIGURE 5.18 ConnectionImpl pool management.

The `ConnectionPool` class is a singleton. There should be only one instance of the `ConnectionPool` class. The class's constructor is private. Other classes access the one instance of the `ConnectionPool` class by calling its `getInstance` method, which is static.

There are many reasons a `ConnectionPool` object's `AcquireImpl` method may be unable to create a `ConnectionImpl` object. Among those reasons may be a limit on the number of `ConnectionImpl` objects it can create that connect to the same database. The reason for the limit is to be able to guarantee that a database will be able to support a minimum number of clients. Since there will be a maximum number of connections each database can support, limiting the number of connections to a database that each client can have allows you to guarantee support for a minimum number of client programs.

FORCES

☺ A program may not create more than a limited number of instances of a particular class.

☺ Creating instances of a particular class is sufficiently expensive that creating new instances of that class should be avoided.

☺ A program can avoid creating some objects by reusing objects that it has finished with rather than letting them be garbage-collected.

☺ The instances of a class are interchangeable. If you have multiple instances on hand, you can arbitrarily choose one to use for a purpose. It does not matter which one you choose.

☺ Resources can be managed centrally by a single object or in a decentralized way by multiple objects. It is easier to achieve predictable results by managing resources centrally with a single object.

☺ Some objects consume resources that are in short supply. Some objects may consume a lot of memory. Some objects may periodically check to see whether some condition is true, thereby consuming CPU cycles and perhaps network bandwidth. If the resources that an object consumes are in short supply, then it may be important that the object stop using the resource when the object is not being used.

SOLUTION

If instances of a class can be reused, avoid creating instances of the class by reusing them. The class diagram in Figure 5.19 shows the roles that classes play in the Object Pool pattern.

Here are descriptions of the roles classes play in the Object Pool pattern, as shown in Figure 5.19:

Reusable. Instances of classes in this role collaborate with other objects for a limited amount of time, then they are no longer needed for that collaboration.

Client. Instances of classes in this role use `Reusable` objects.

ReusablePool. Instances of classes in this role manage `Reusable` objects for use by `Client` objects. It is usually desirable to keep all `Reusable` objects that are not currently in use in the same object pool so that they can be managed by one coherent policy. To achieve this, the `ReusablePool` class is designed to be a singleton class. Its constructor(s) are private, which forces other classes to call its `getInstance` method to get the one instance of the `ReusablePool` class.

A `Client` object calls a `ReusablePool` object's `acquireReusable` method when it needs a `Reusable` object. A `ReusablePool` object maintains a collection of `Reusable` objects. It uses the collection of `Reusable` objects to contain a pool of `Reusable` objects that are not currently in use. If there are any `Reusable` objects in the pool when the `acquireReusable` method is called, it removes a `Reusable` object from the pool and returns it. If the pool is empty, then the `acquireReusable` method creates a Reusable object if it can. If the `acquireReusable` method can-

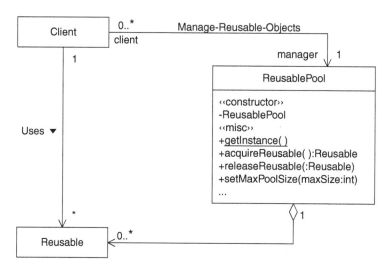

FIGURE 5.19 Object Pool pattern.

not create a new `Reusable` object, then it waits until a `Reusable` object is returned to the collection.

Client objects pass a `Reusable` object to a `ReusablePool` object's `releaseReusable` method when they are finished with the object. The `releaseReusable` method returns a `Reusable` object to the pool of `Reusable` objects that are not in use.

In many applications of the Object Pool pattern, there are reasons for limiting the total number of `Reusable` objects that may exist. In such cases, the `ReusablePool` object that creates `Reusable` objects is responsible for not creating more than a specified maximum number of `Reusable` objects. If `ReusablePool` objects are responsible for limiting the number of objects they will create, then the `ReusablePool` class will have a method for specifying the maximum number of objects to be created. That method is indicated in Figure 5.19 as `setMaxPoolSize`.

IMPLEMENTATION

Here are some of the issues to consider when implementing the Object Pool pattern.

ENSURING A MAXIMUM NUMBER OF INSTANCES

In many cases, the object that manages an object pool is supposed to limit the number of instances of a class that can be created. It is easy for an object to limit the number of objects it creates. However, to robustly enforce a limit on the total number of objects created, the object responsible for managing the object pool must be the only object able to create those objects.

You can ensure that a class is instantiated only by the class that manages the object pool. You can do that by making the managed class's constructor(s) private and implementing the pool management class as a static member class of the managed class. If you do not have control over the structure of the class whose instances are to be managed, you may be able to add that structure to the class through inheritance.

DATA STRUCTURE

When there is a limit on the number of objects that may be created or just a limit on the size of the object pool, using a simple array is usually the best way to implement the object pool. When there is no limit on the size of the object pool, using an `ArrayList` is an appropriate way to implement the object pool.

USING SOFT REFERENCES

The Object Pool pattern keeps objects that are not being used available for reuse. If the program that is using an object pool is running out of memory, then you would like the garbage collector to be able to remove objects from the pool and reclaim the memory that they occupy. You can arrange for the garbage collector to do this by using soft references.

Soft references are implemented in the Java API by the class `java.lang.ref.SoftReference`. A reference to another object is passed to the constructor of a `SoftReference` object. Immediately after a `Soft-Reference` object is constructed, its `get` method returns the object reference that was passed to its constructor. The interesting thing about `SoftReference` objects is that they are special to the garbage collector. If the only live reference to an object is through a `SoftReference` object, then the garbage collector will set the reference in the `SoftReference` object to null so that it can safely reclaim the storage occupied by the referenced object.

If the object pool refers to objects in the pool through soft references, then the garbage collector will reclaim the storage occupied by the objects if there are no other references to the objects and the Java virtual machine (JVM) is running low on memory. This use of the `SoftReference` class is shown in the code example.

LIMITING THE SIZE OF THE POOL

There are some cases where soft references are not a satisfactory solution to limiting the excess resources used by pool-managed objects.

- If the objects being managed use an external resource, you may not always want to wait for the garbage collector to finalize the objects before freeing up the resource.
- If your program needs to run on JVMs older than version 1.2, you cannot use soft references.

An alternative to using soft references is to limit the number of objects that may be in the object pool. If there is a limit on the number of objects in an object pool, it is generally less than the number of objects that the pool will allow to exist at once.

When a pool-managed object is no longer needed, it is released back to the `ReusablePool` object. If the pool already contains its maximum number of objects, then the released object is not added to the pool. If the object is tying up any external resources, it is told to release them. Since the object is not added to the pool, the object may be eligible for garbage collection at this time.

The techniques of limiting the size of a pool and using soft references are generally not used together. Because the garbage collector can clear a soft reference at any time, there is no way of ensuring that a pool always has an accurate count of the number of objects it contains.

MANAGING STATEFUL OBJECTS

One of the assumptions that underlie an object pool is that the objects it manages are interchangeable. When a client acquires an object from a pool, it expects the object to be in a known state. If it is possible for clients to alter the state of pool-managed objects, there has to be a way for the pool to ensure that its objects return to the expected state. These are the most common ways this is done:

- The pool explicitly resets the state of an object before a client acquires the object. This may not be possible in some cases. For example, once a database connection is closed, it may not be possible for the pool to reopen it. Besides, you really don't want clients closing the database connection.
- You can prevent clients from changing the state of pool-managed objects by using the Decorator pattern. For example, to do this with a database connection, you would create a wrapper object that implements the same interface as a real database connect object. The wrapper object would delegate all of its methods to a real database connection object, except for the method that closes the connection. That method would be implemented to do nothing.

CONSEQUENCES

- ☺ Using the Object Pool pattern avoids the creation of objects. It works best when the demand for objects does not vary greatly over time.
- ☺ Keeping the logic to manage the creation and reuse of a class's instances in a separate class from the class whose instances are being managed results in a more cohesive design. It eliminates interactions between the implementation of a creation and reuse policy and the implementation of the managed class's functionality.

CODE EXAMPLE

Implementations of the Object Pool pattern use one of two techniques to ensure that they do not consume an excessive amount of memory with objects awaiting reuse. Either they use soft references to refer to the objects or they limit the number of objects that may be in the pool. Since these two techniques are somewhat different, there is an example of each one in this section. Both classes are generic. They can be used to keep a pool of any kind of objects.

Here is a listing of a class that implements the object pool using soft references.

```
public class SoftObjectPool implements ObjectPoolIF {
    /**
     * This collection contains the objects that are waiting
     * to be reused.
     */
    private ArrayList pool ;
```

Because there is no fixed limit on the number of objects that can be in the pool awaiting reuse, this class uses an `ArrayList` object to contain its collection of objects.

Because this class is generic, it does not know how to create the objects that it manages. Instead, it delegates the responsibility for creating objects to an object that implements an interface named `CreationIF`. The `CreationIF` interface is listed toward the end of this section.

```
    private CreationIF creator ;
```

Instances of this class are responsible for limiting the number of pool-managed objects that may exist at one time. The `instanceCount` variable contains the number of pool-managed objects that currently exist. The `maxInstances` variable contains the maximum number of pool-managed objects that may be under management by this object pool. An object pool will not create a new object unless the value of `instanceCount` is less than the value of `maxInstances`.

```
    private int instanceCount;
    private int maxInstances ;
```

Because this class is a generic object pool, it does not know in advance what kind of objects its clients want it to manage. As an inexpensive sanity check, this class requires that a class be passed as one of the arguments to its constructors. When an object is released to the pool for reuse, the pool checks that the object is an instance of the specified class. The class used for this purpose is the value of the `poolClass` variable.

```
    private Class poolClass;

    /**
     * Constructor
     *
```

```
 * @param poolClass
 *         The Class to instantiate to create Pool Objects.
 * @param creator
 *         The object that the pool will delegate the
 *         responsibility for creating objects that it will
 *         manage.
 */
public SoftObjectPool( Class poolClass,
                       CreationIF creator ) {
    this( poolClass, creator, Integer.MAX_VALUE);
} // constructor(Class, CreationIF, int)

/**
 * Constructor
 *
 * @param poolClass
 *         The Class to instantiate to create Pool Objects.
 * @param creator
 *         The object that the pool will delegate the
 *         responsibility for creating objects that it will
 *         manage.
 * @param maxInstances
 *         The maximum number of instances of the poolClass
 *         class that the pool should allow to exist at one
 *         time.  If the pool is asked to produce an
 *         instance of poolClass when there are no objects
 *         in the pool awaiting reuse and there are this
 *         many pool-managed obects in use, then the pool
 *         will not produce an object until an object is
 *         returned to the pool for reuse.
 */
public SoftObjectPool( Class poolClass,
                       CreationIF creator,
                       int maxInstances ) {
    this.creator = creator;
    this.poolClass = poolClass;
    pool = new ArrayList();
} // constructor(Class, CreationIF, int, int)

/**
 * Return the number of objects in the pool that are
 * awaiting reuse.  The actual number may be less than
 * this because what is returned is the number of soft
 * references in the pool.  Any or all of the soft
 * references may have been cleared by the garbage
 * collector.
 */
public int getSize() {
    synchronized (pool) {
        return pool.size();
    } // synchronized
} // getSize()
```

```
/**
 * Return the number of pool-managed objects that
 * currently exist.
 */
public int getInstanceCount() {
    return instanceCount;
} // getInstanceCount()

/**
 * Return the maximum number of pool-managed objects that
 * this pool will allow to exist at one time.
 */
public int getMaxInstances() {
    return maxInstances;
} // getMaxInstances()

/**
 * Set the maximum number of objects that this pool will
 * allow to exist at one time.
 *
 * If the pool is asked to produce an instance of
 * poolClass when there are no objects in the pool
 * awaiting reuse and there are already this many
 * pool-managed objects in use, then the pool will not
 * produce an object until an object is returned to the
 * pool for reuse.
 *
 * @param newValue
 *          The new value for the maximum number of
 *          pool-managed objects that may exist at one time.
 *          Setting this to a value that is less than the
 *          value returned by the getInstanceCount method
 *          will not cause any objects to be deleted.
 *          It will just prevent any new pool-managed
 *          objects from being created.
 */
public void setMaxInstances(int newValue) {
    maxInstances = newValue;
} // setMaxInstances()

/**
 * Return an object from the pool.  If there is no object
 * in the pool, one will be created unless the number of
 * pool-managed objects is greater than or equal to the
 * value returned by the getMaxInstances method.  If the
 * number of pool-managed objects exceeds this amount,
 * then this method returns null.
 */
public Object getObject() {
    synchronized (pool) {
        Object thisObject = removeObject();
        if (thisObject!=null) {
            return thisObject;
```

```
        } // if thisObject
        if (getInstanceCount() < getMaxInstances()){
            return createObject();
        } else {
            return null;
        } // if
    } // synchronized (pool)
} // getObject()


/**
 * Return an object from the pool.  If there is no object
 * in the pool, one will be created unless the number of
 * pool-managed objects is greater than or equal to the
 * value returned by the getMaxInstances method.  If the
 * number of pool-managed objects exceeds this amount,
 * then this method will wait until an object becomes
 * available for reuse.
 *
 * @throws InterruptedException
 *         If the calling thread is interrupted.
 */
public Object waitForObject() throws InterruptedException {
    synchronized (pool) {
        Object thisObject = removeObject();
        if (thisObject!=null) {
            return thisObject;
        } // if thisObject
        if (getInstanceCount() < getMaxInstances()){
            return createObject();
        } else {
            do {
                // Wait until notified that an object has
                // been put back in the pool.
                pool.wait();
                thisObject = removeObject();
            } while (thisObject==null);
            return thisObject;
        } // if
    } // synchronized (pool)
} // waitForObject()


/**
 * Remove an object from the pool array and return it.
 */
private Object removeObject() {
    while (pool.size()>0) {
        SoftReference thisRef
          = (SoftReference)pool.remove(pool.size()-1);
        Object thisObject = thisRef.get();
        if (thisObject!=null) {
            return thisObject;
        } // if thisObject
        instanceCount-;
```

```
        } // while
        return null;
    } // removeObject()

    /**
     * Create an object to be managed by this pool.
     */
    private Object createObject() {
        Object newObject = creator.create();
        instanceCount++;
        return newObject;
    } // createObject()

    /**
     * Release an object to the Pool for reuse.
     *
     * @param obj
     *         The object that is available for reuse.
     */
    public void release( Object obj ) {
        // no nulls
        if ( obj == null ) {
            throw new NullPointerException();
        } // if null
        if ( !poolClass.isInstance(obj)) {
            String actualClassName = obj.getClass().getName();
            throw new ArrayStoreException(actualClassName);
        } // if isInstance
        synchronized (pool) {
            pool.add(obj);
            // Notify a waiting thread that we have put an
            // object in the pool.
            pool.notify();
        } // synchronized
    } // release()
} // class SoftObjectPool
```

Here is a listing of a class that limits the number of objects that may be awaiting reuse instead of using soft references. The portions of it that are the same as the previous class are left out of this listing.

```
public class ObjectPool implements ObjectPoolIF {
    private int size ;
```

Because there is a definite limit on the number of objects this class will allow to be awaiting reuse, this class can use a simple array to contain them. It uses the instance variable named size to count the number of objects that are actually awaiting reuse.

```
    /**
     * This array contains the objects that are waiting to be
     * reused.  It is managed as a stack.
```

```
    */
    private Object[] pool ;
...
    /**
     * Internal operations are synchronized on this object.
     */
    private Object lockObject = new Object();
```

See the discussion of the Internal Lock Object pattern for a more detailed explanation of lock objects.

```
...
    /**
     * Constructor
     *
     * @param poolClass
     *        The Class to instantiate to create Pool Objects.
     * @param creator
     *        The object that the pool will delegate the
     *        responsibility for creating objects that it will
     *        manage.
     * @param capacity
     *        The number of currently unused objects that this
     *        object pool may contain at once.
     * @param maxInstances
     *        The maximum number of instances of the poolClass
     *        class that the pool should allow to exist at one
     *        time.
     */
    public ObjectPool( Class poolClass,
                       CreationIF creator,
                       int capacity,
                       int maxInstances ) {
        size = 0;
        this.creator = creator;
        this.maxInstances = maxInstances;
        pool = (Object[])Array.newInstance(poolClass,
                                           capacity);
    } // constructor(Class, CreationIF, int, int)

    /**
     * Return the number of objects in the pool that are
     * awaiting reuse.
     */
    public int getSize() {
        return size;
    } // getSize()

    /**
     * Return the maximum number of objects that may be in the
     * pool awaiting reuse.
     */
    public int getCapacity() {
```

```
        return pool.length;
} // getCapacity()


/**
 * Set the maximum number of objects that may be in the
 * pool awaiting reuse.
 *
 * @param newValue
 *         The new value for the maximum number of objects
 *         that may be in the pool awaiting reuse.  This
 *         must be greater than zero.
 */
public void setCapacity(int newValue) {
    if (newValue<=0) {
        String msg = "Capacity must be greater than zero:"
                   + newValue;
        throw new IllegalArgumentException(msg);
    } // if
    synchronized (lockObject) {
        Object[] newPool = new Object[newValue];
        System.arraycopy(pool, 0, newPool, 0, newValue);
        pool = newPool;
    } // synchronized
} // setCapacity(int)


...


/**
 * Return an object from the pool.  If there is no object in
 * the pool, one will be created unless the number of
 * pool-managed objects is greater than or equal to the
 * value returned by the <code>getMaxInstances</code>
 * method.  If the number of pool-managed objects exceeds
 * this amount, then this method returns null.
 */
public Object getObject() {
    synchronized (lockObject) {
        if (size>0) {
            return removeObject();
        } else if (getInstanceCount() < getMaxInstances()){
            return createObject();
        } else {
            return null;
        } // if
    } // synchronized (lockObject)
} // getObject()


/**
 * Return an object from the pool.  If there is no object in
 * the pool, one will be created unless the number of
 * pool-managed objects is greater than or equal to the
 * value returned by the <code>getMaxInstances</code>
 * method.  If the number of pool-managed objects exceeds
```

```
 * this amount, then this method will wait until an object
 * becomes available for reuse.
 *
 * @throws InterruptedException
 *          If the calling thread is interrupted.
 */
public Object waitForObject() throws InterruptedException {
    synchronized (lockObject) {
        if (size>0) {
            return removeObject();
        } else if (getInstanceCount() < getMaxInstances()){
            return createObject();
        } else {
            do {
                // Wait until notified that an object has
                // been put back in the pool.
                wait();
            } while(size<=0);
            return removeObject();
        } // if
    } // synchronized (lockObject)
} // waitForObject()

/**
 * Remove an object from the pool array and return it.
 */
private Object removeObject() {
    size—;
    return pool[size];
} // removeObject()
```

. . .

```
/**
 * Release an object to the Pool for reuse.
 *
 * @param obj
 *          The object that is available for reuse.
 * @throws ArrayStoreException
 *          If the given object is not an instance of the
 *          class passed to this pool object's constructor.
 * @throws NullPointerException
 *          If the given object is null.
 */
public void release( Object obj ) {
    // no nulls
    if ( obj == null ) {
        throw new NullPointerException();
    } // if null
    synchronized (lockObject) {
        if (getSize() < getCapacity()) {
            pool[size] = obj;
            size++;
```

```
            // Notify a waiting thread that we have put an
            // object in the pool.
            lockObject.notify();
      } // if
   } // synchronized
  } // release()
} // class ObjectPool
```

Here is a listing of the `CreationIF` interface.

```
public interface CreationIF {
   /**
    * Return a newly created object.
    */
   public Object create() ;
} // interface creationIF
```

RELATED PATTERNS

Cache Management.   The Cache Management pattern manages the reuse of specific instances of a class. The Pool pattern manages and creates instances of a class that can be used interchangeably.

Factory Method.   The Factory Method pattern can be used to encapsulate the creation logic for objects. However, it does not manage them after their creation.

Singleton.   Objects that manage object pools are usually singletons.

Thread Pool.   The Thread Pool pattern (discussed in *Patterns in Java, Volume 3*) is a specialized form of the Object Pool pattern.

Lock Object.   The Lock Object pattern may be used in the implementation of the Object Pool pattern.

Partitioning Patterns

A common problem-solving strategy is called *divide and conquer.* It involves dividing a complex problem that is difficult to solve into simpler problems that are easier to solve. The patterns in this chapter provide guidance on how to partition classes and interfaces in ways that make it easier to arrive at a good design.

The Filter pattern describes how to organize computations on a data stream in a flexible way that allows you to mix and match different computations on the same data stream.

The Composite pattern provides guidance on how to organize a hierarchy of objects.

The Read-Only Interface pattern describes how to partition the classes that use an object so that those that should be allowed to modify it can do so, and those that shouldn't be allowed to modify it can't.

Filter

This pattern was previously described in [BMRSS96].

SYNOPSIS

Objects that have compatible interfaces but perform different transformations and computations on data streams can be dynamically connected to perform arbitrary operations.

CONTEXT

The purpose of many programs is to perform computations on a stream of data. An example of a program that performs simple transformations on the contents of a data stream is the UNIX uniq program. The uniq program organizes its input into lines. The uniq program normally copies all the lines it reads to its output. However, when it finds consecutive lines that contain identical characters, it copies only the first such line to its output. UNIX also comes with a program called wc that does a simple analysis of a data stream. It produces a count of the number of characters, words, and lines that were in the data stream. Compilers perform a complex series of transformations and analyses on their source code input to produce their binary output.

Since many programs perform transformations and analyses on data streams, it would clearly be beneficial to define classes that perform the more common transformations and analyses. Such classes will get a lot of reuse.

Classes that perform simple transformations and analyses on data streams tend to be very generic in nature. When writing such classes, you cannot anticipate all the ways they will be used. Some applications will want to apply transformations and analyses to only selected parts of a data stream. Clearly, these classes should be written in a way that allows great flexibility in how their instances can be connected. One way to accomplish this flexibility is to define a common interface for all of these classes so an instance of one can use an instance of another without having to take into account which class the object is an instance of. Figure 6.1 shows this organization.

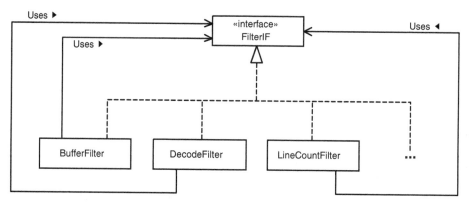

FIGURE 6.1 File filters.

FORCES

☺ Classes that implement common data transformations and analyses can be used in a great variety of programs.

☺ You can dynamically combine data analysis and transformation objects by connecting them together.

☺ The use of transformation/analysis objects should be transparent to other objects.

SOLUTION

Base a solution on common interfaces and delegation. The Filter pattern organizes the classes that participate in it as data sources, data sinks, and data filters. The data filter classes perform the transformation and analysis operations. There are two basic forms of the Filter pattern. In one, data flows as a result of a data sink object calling a method in a data source object. In the other, data flows when a data source object passes data to a method of a data sink object.

Figure 6.2 is a class diagram for the form of Filter where data sink objects get data by calling methods in data sources. This form of Filter is sometimes called a *pull filter*.

Here are descriptions of how the classes in Figure 6.2 participate in the pull form of the Filter pattern:

SourceIF.   An interface in this role declares one or more methods that return data when it is called. In Figure 6.2, one such method is indicated in the diagram as getData.

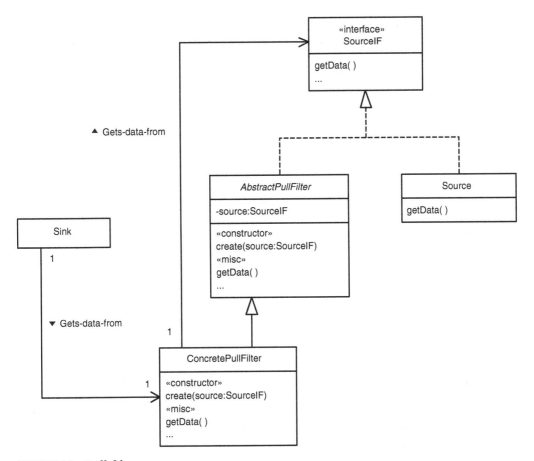

FIGURE 6.2 Pull filter.

Source. A class in this role is responsible primarily for providing data rather than transforming or analyzing data. Classes in this role are also required to implement the SourceIF interface.

AbstractPullFilter. A class in this role is an abstract superclass of classes that transform and analyze data. It has a constructor that takes an argument that is a SourceIF object. Instances of this class delegate the fetching of data to the SourceIF object that was passed to their constructor. Because subclasses of this class inherit the fact that it implements the SourceIF interface, their instances can provide data to other AbstractPullFilter objects.

AbstractPullFilter classes typically have an instance variable that is set by their constructor and refers to the SourceIF object passed to their constructor. However, to ensure that their subclasses do not depend on this instance variable, the instance variable should be private. `AbstractPullFilter` classes typically define a `getData` method that simply calls the `getData` method of the `SourceIF` object referred to by the instance variable.

ConcretePullFilter. Classes in this role are a concrete subclass of an `AbstractPullFilter` class. They override the `getData` method that they inherit to perform the appropriate transformation or analysis operations.

Sink. Instances of classes in this role call the `getData` method of a `SourceIF` object. Unlike `ConcretePullFilter` objects, instances of `Sink` classes use data without passing it on to another `AbstractPullFilter` object.

Figure 6.3 is a class diagram for the form of Filter where data source objects pass data to methods of data sink objects. This form of Filter is sometimes called a *push filter.*

SinkIF. An interface in this role declares one or more methods that take data through one of its parameters. In Figure 6.3, one such method is indicated in the diagram as `putData`.

Sink. A class in this role is responsible primarily for receiving and processing data rather than transforming or analyzing data. Classes in this role are also required to implement the `SinkIF` interface. Data is passed to `Sink` objects by passing the data to the `Sink` object's `putData` method.

AbstractPushFilter. A class in this role is an abstract superclass of classes that transform and analyze data. It has a constructor that takes an argument that is a `SinkIF` object. Instances of this class pass data to the `SinkIF` object that was passed to their constructor. Because subclasses of this class inherit the fact that it implements the `SinkIF` interface, their instances can accept data from other objects that pass data to `SinkIF` objects.

AbstractPushFilter classes typically have an instance variable that is set by their constructor and refers to the `SinkIF` object passed to their constructor. However, to ensure that their subclasses do not depend on this instance variable, the instance variable should be private. `AbstractPushFilter` classes typically define a `putData` method that simply calls the `putData` method of the `SinkIF` object referred to by the instance variable.

ConcretePushFilter. Classes in this role are a concrete subclass of an `AbstractPushFilter` class. They override the `putData` method that they inherit to perform the appropriate transformation or analysis operations.

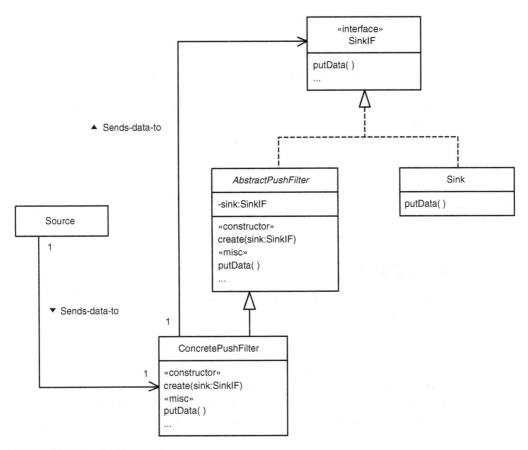

FIGURE 6.3 Push filter.

Source. Instances of classes in this role call the `putData` method of a `SinkIF` object.

IMPLEMENTATION

Filter classes should be implemented in a way that does not assume anything about the programs that they will be used in or with which other filter classes they will be used. Because of that, it follows that filter objects should not have side effects and should communicate with each other only through the data that they exchange.

Making filter classes independent of the programs that they are used in increases their reusability. However, in some cases there can be performance penalties if a filter object is not allowed to use context-specific information. The best design is sometimes a compromise between these considerations.

For example, you could define one or more interfaces that declare methods for providing context-specific information to a filter object. If a program detects that a filter object implements one of those interfaces, it can use the interface to provide additional information to the filter.

Forcing the filter class's getData or putData methods to go through their superclass's getData or putData method can add a small amount of additional overhead. It is easy to eliminate this overhead. If your classes are running on a JVM that uses Sun's HotSpot technology, then the HotSpot optimization will remove most of the overhead. If your classes are running in an environment that does not do this sort of optimization, there are compilers that can optimize out the overhead by in-lining the call to the superclass's getData or putData method.

CONSEQUENCES

- ☺ The portion of a program that follows the Filter pattern can be structured as a set of sources, sinks, and filters.
- ☺ Filter objects that do not maintain internal state can be dynamically replaced while a program is running. This property of stateless filters allows dynamic change of behavior and adaptation to different requirements at runtime.
- ● It is quite reasonable for a program to incorporate both forms of the Filter pattern. However, it is unusual for the same class to participate in both forms.
- ☹ If your design calls for filters to be dynamically added to or removed while processing a data stream, then you will need to design a mechanism to manage this change in a predictable way.

JAVA API USAGE

The java.io package includes the FilterReader class, which participates in the Filter pattern as an abstract source filter class. The corresponding abstract source class is Reader. Concrete subclasses of the FilterReader class include BufferedReader, FileReader, and LineNumberReader. There is no separate interface that fills the SourceIF role. The Reader class also fills the SourceIF role.

The java.io package includes the FilterWriter class, which participates in the Filter pattern as an abstract sink filter class. The corresponding abstract sink class is Writer. Concrete subclasses of the FilterWriter class include BufferedWriter, FileWriter, and PrintWriter. The Writer class also fills the SinkIF role.

Here is a common arrangement of `FilterReader` objects for a program that reads lines of text as commands and needs to track line numbers for producing error messages:

```
LineNumberReader in;
void init(String fName) {
    FileReader fin;
        try {
            fin = new FileReader(fName);
            in =new LineNumberReader(new BufferedReader(fin));
        } catch (FileNotFoundException e) {
            System.out.println("Unable to open "+fName);
            ...
        }
    ...
```

CODE EXAMPLE

For an example of classes that implement the pull form of the Filter pattern, here are classes that read and filter a stream of bytes. First, here is a class that participates in the Filter pattern as an abstract source:

```
public interface InStreamIF {
    /**
     * Read bytes and fill an array with those bytes.
     * @param array The array of bytes to fill.
     * @return If not enough bytes are available to fill the
     *         array then this method returns after having
     *         only put that many bytes in the array.  This
     *         method returns -1 if the end of the data
     *         stream is encountered.
     * @throws IOException  if an I/O error occurs.
     */
    public int read(byte[] array) throws IOException;
} // interface InStreamIF
```

Next is a class that implements the `InStreamIF` interface and participates in the Filter pattern as a source:

```
/**
 * This class reads a stream of bytes from a file.
 */
public class FileInStream implements InStreamIF {
    private RandomAccessFile file;

    /**
     * Constructor
     * @param fName The name of the file to read
     */
    public FileInStream(String fName) throws IOException {
```

```
        file = new RandomAccessFile(fName, "r");
    } // Constructor(String)

    /**
     * Read bytes from a file and fill an array with those
     * bytes.
     */
    public int read(byte[] array) throws IOException {
        return file.read(array);
    } // read(byte[])
} // class FileInStream
```

The following class participates in the Filter pattern as an abstract source filter:

```
public abstract class FilterInStream implements InStreamIF {
    private InStreamIF inStream;
    /**
     * Constructor
     * @param inStream
     *          The InStreamIF object that this object should
     *          delegate read operations to.
     */
    public FilterInStream(InStreamIF inStream)
                                        throws IOException {
        this.inStream = inStream;
    } // Constructor(InStreamIF)

    /**
     * Read bytes from a stream of bytes and fill an array
     * with those bytes.
     */
    public int read(byte[] array) throws IOException {
        return inStream.read(array);
    } // read(byte[])
} // class FilterInStream
```

Now we look at some classes that participate in the Filter pattern as a concrete source filter. The first of these performs the simple analysis of counting the number of bytes it has read:

```
public class ByteCountInStream extends FilterInStream {
    private long byteCount = 0;

    /**
     * Constructor
     * @param inStream
     *          The InStream that this object should delegate
     *          read operations to.
     */
    public ByteCountInStream(InStreamIF inStream)
                                        throws IOException {
```

```
    super(inStream);
} // Constructor(InStream)


/**
 * Read bytes from a stream of bytes into an array.
 */
public int read(byte[] array) throws IOException {
    int count;
    count = super.read(array);
    if (count >0)
      byteCount += count;
    return count;
} // read(byte[])


/**
 * Return the number of bytes that have been read by
 * this object.
 */
public long getByteCount() {
    return byteCount;
} // getByteCount()
} // class ByteCountInStream
```

Finally, here is a filter class that performs character code translations of a stream of bytes:

```
/**
 * This class treats the bytes in a byte stream as eight bit
 * character codes and translates them to other character
 * codes using a translation table.
 */
public class TranslateInStream extends FilterInStream {
    private byte[] translationTable;
    private final static int TRANS_TBL_LENGTH = 256;

    /**
     * Constructor
     * @param inStream
     *        The InStreamIF object that this object should
     * delegate read operations to.
     * @param table
     *        An array of bytes used to determine
     *        translation values for character codes.  The
     *        value to replace character code n with is at
     *        index n of the translation table.  If the array
     *        is longer than TRANS_TBL_LENGTH elements, the
     *        additional elements are ignored.  If the array
     *        is shorter than TRANS_TBL_LENGTH elements, then
     *        no translation is done on character codes
     *        greater than or equal to the length of the
     *        array.
     */
    public TranslateInStream(InStreamIF inStream,
```

```
                              byte[] table) throws IOException{
      super(inStream);
      // Copy translation data to create translation table.
      translationTable = new byte[TRANS_TBL_LENGTH];
      System.arraycopy(table, 0, translationTable, 0,
                    Math.min(TRANS_TBL_LENGTH,
                              table.length));
      for (int i = table.length; i < TRANS_TBL_LENGTH; i++){
         translationTable[i] = (byte)i;
      } // for
   } // Constructor(InStream)

   public int read(byte[] array) throws IOException {
      int count;
      count = super.read(array);
      for (int i = 0; i < count; i++) {
         array[i] = translationTable[array[i]];
      } // for
      return count;
   } // read(byte[])
} // class ByteCountInStream
```

RELATED PATTERNS

Composite.   The Composite pattern can be an alternative to the Filter pattern. It allows for the possibility of routing data through branches of a tree.

Pipe.   The Pipe pattern is sometimes an alternative to the Filter pattern and is sometimes used with the Filter pattern.

  This book does not contain a chapter for the Pipe pattern. It is described in [BMRSS96]. Like the Filter pattern, the Pipe pattern allows an object that is a data source to send a stream of data to an object that is a data sink. Instead of the movement of data being initiated by the source or the sink object, they operate asynchronously of each other. The data source object puts data in a buffer when it wants to. The data sink gets data from the buffer when it wants to. If the buffer is empty when the data sink tries to get data from it, the data sink waits until there is data in the buffer.

  The Java API includes the classes java.io.PipedReader and java.io.PipedWriter that together form an implementation of the Pipe pattern.

Decorator.   The Filter pattern is a special case of the Decorator pattern, where a data source or data sink object is wrapped to add logic to the handling of a data stream.

Composite

The Composite pattern is also known as the Recursive Composition pattern. The Composite pattern was previously described in [GoF95].

SYNOPSIS

The Composite pattern allows you to build complex objects by recursively composing similar objects in a tree-like manner. The Composite pattern also allows the objects in the tree to be manipulated in a consistent manner, by requiring all of the objects in the tree to have a common interface or superclass.

The following description of the Composite pattern describes it in terms of recursively building a composite object from other objects. The reason it appears in this partitioning patterns chapter is that during the design process the Composite pattern is often used to recursively decompose a complex object into simpler objects.

CONTEXT

Suppose that you are writing a document formatting program. It formats characters into lines of text organized into columns that are organized into pages. However, a document may contain other elements. Columns and pages can contain frames that can contain columns. Columns, frames, and lines of text can contain images. Figure 6.4 is a class diagram that shows these relationships.

As you can see, there is a fair amount of complexity here. Page and Frame objects must know how to handle and combine two kinds of elements. Column objects must know how to handle and combine three kinds of elements. The Composite pattern removes that complexity by allowing these objects to know how to handle only one kind of element. It accomplishes this by insisting that all document element classes implement a common interface. Figure 6.5 shows how you can simplify the document element class relationships by using the Composite pattern.

By applying the Composite pattern, you have introduced a common interface for all document elements and a common superclass for all container classes. Doing this reduces the number of aggregation relationships to one. Management of the aggregation is now the responsibility of the

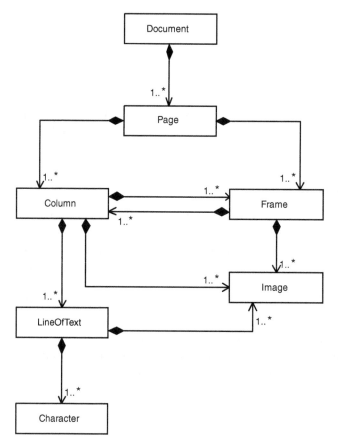

FIGURE 6.4 Document container relationships.

CompositeDocumentElement class. The concrete container classes (Document, Page, Column, etc.) only need to understand how to combine one kind of element.

FORCES

☺ You have a complex object you want to decompose into a part-whole hierarchy of objects.

☺ You want to minimize the complexity of the part-whole hierarchy by minimizing the number of different kinds of child objects that objects in the tree need to be aware of.

☺ There is no requirement to distinguish between most of the part-whole relationships.

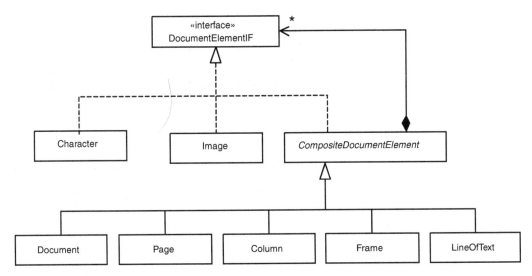

FIGURE 6.5 Document composite.

SOLUTION

Minimize the complexity of a composite object organized into part-whole hierarchies by providing an interface to be implemented by all objects in the hierarchy and an abstract superclass for all composites in the hierarchy. The generalized class relationships for such an organization are shown in Figure 6.6.

Here are descriptions of the interface and classes that participate in the Composite pattern:

ComponentIF.   An interface in the `ComponentIF` role is implemented by all the objects in the hierarchy of objects that make up a composite object. Composite objects normally treat the objects that they contain as instances of classes that implement the `ComponentIF` interface rather than as instances of their actual class.

Component1, Component2, and so on.   Instances of these classes are used as leaves in the tree organization.

AbstractComposite.   A class in this role is the abstract superclass of all composite objects that participate in the Composite pattern. `AbstractComposite` defines and provides default implementations of methods for managing a composite object's components. The `add` method adds a component to a composite object. The `remove` method removes a component from a composite

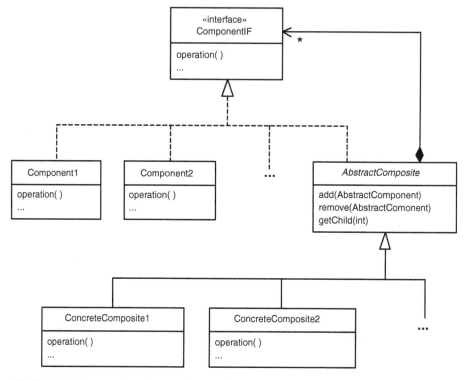

FIGURE 6.6 Composite class relationships.

object. The `getChild` method returns a reference to a component object of a composite object.

ConcreteComposite1, ConcreteComposite2, and so on. Instances of these are composite objects that use other instances of `AbstractComponent`.

Instances of these classes can be assembled in a treelike manner, as shown in Figure 6.7.

Note that you don't need to have an abstract composite class if there is only one concrete composite class.

IMPLEMENTATION

If classes that participate in the Composite pattern implement any operations by delegating them to their parent object, then the best way to preserve speed and simplicity is to have each instance of `AbstractComponent` contain a reference to its parent. It is important to implement the parent

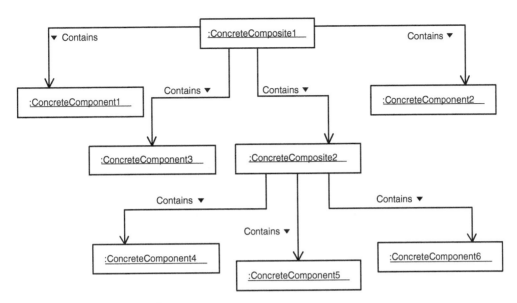

FIGURE 6.7 Composite object.

pointer in a way that ensures consistency between parent and child. It must always be true that a `ComponentIF` object identifies an `AbstractComposite` object as its parent if, and only if, the `AbstractComposite` identifies it as one of its children. The best way to enforce this is to modify parent and child references only in the `AbstractComposite` class's add and remove methods.

Sharing components among multiple parents using the Flyweight pattern is a way to conserve memory. However, shared components cannot easily maintain parent references.

The `AbstractComposite` class may provide a default implementation of child management for composite objects. However, it is very common for concrete composite classes to override the default implementation.

If a concrete composite object delegates an operation to the objects that constitute it, then caching the result of the operation may improve performance. If a concrete composite object caches the result of an operation, it is important that the objects that constitute the composite notify the composite object to invalidate its cached values.

CONSEQUENCES

☺ You can access a tree-structured composite object and the objects that constitute it through the `ComponentIF` interface, whether they are simple objects or composite. The structure of the composite does not force other objects to make this distinction.

☺ Client objects of an `AbstractComponent` can simply treat it as an `AbstractComponent`, without having to be aware of any subclasses of `AbstractComponent`.

☺ If a client invokes a method of a `ComponentIF` object that is supposed to perform an operation and the `ComponentIF` object is an `AbstractComposite` object, then it may delegate the operation to the `ComponentIF` objects that constitute it. Similarly, if a client object calls a method of a `ComponentIF` object that is *not* an `AbstractComposite` and the method requires some contextual information, then the `ComponentIF` object delegates the request for contextual information to its parent.

● Some components may implement operations that are unique to that component. For example, under the Context heading of this pattern is a design for the recursive composition of a document. At the lowest level, it has a document consisting of character and image elements. It is very reasonable for the character elements of a document to have a `getFont` method. A document's image elements have no need for a `getFont` method. The main benefit of the Composite pattern is to allow the clients of a composite object and the objects that constitute it to be unaware of the specific class of the objects they deal with. To allow other classes to call `getFont` without being aware of the specific class they are dealing with, all the objects that can constitute a document can inherit the `getFont` method from `DocumentElementIF`. In general, when applying the Composite pattern, the interface in the `ComponentIF` role declares specialized methods if they are needed by any `ConcreteComponent` class.

A principle of object-oriented design is that specialized methods should appear only in classes that need them. Normally, a class should have methods that provide related functionality and form a cohesive set. This principle is essential to the Low Coupling/High Cohesion pattern described in *Patterns in Java, Volume 2*. Putting a specialized method in a general-purpose class rather than in the specialized class that needs the method is contrary to the principle of high cohesion. It is contrary to that principle because it adds a method unrelated to the other methods of the general-purpose class. The unrelated method is inherited by subclasses of the general-purpose class that are unrelated to the method.

Because simplicity through ignorance of class is the basis of the Composite pattern, when applying the Composite pattern it is okay to sacrifice high cohesion for simplicity. This exception to a widely accepted rule is based on experience rather than theory.

☹ The Composite pattern allows any `ComponentIF` object to be a child of an `AbstractComposite`. If you need to enforce a more restrictive relationship, then you will have to add type-aware code to `AbstractComposite` or its subclasses. That reduces some of the value of the Composite pattern.

JAVA API USAGE

The `java.awt` package contains an example of the Composite pattern. Its `Component` class fills the `ComponentIF` role. Its `Container` class fills the `AbstractComposite` role. It has a number of classes in the `ConcreteComponent` role, including `Label`, `TextField`, and `Button`. The classes in the `ConcreteComposite` role include `Panel`, `Frame`, and `Dialog`.

CODE EXAMPLE

The example of applying the Composite pattern is a more detailed version of the document-related classes that appeared under the Context heading. Figure 6.8 is a more detailed class diagram.

Figure 6.8 shows some methods that were left out of Figure 6.6. As you look through the following code, you will see that the `setFont` method is an example of a method that consults an object's parent object. The `getCharLength` method gathers information from an object's children and caches it for later use. The `changeNotification` method is used to invalidate cached information.

There is also an abstract class named `AbstractDocumentElement`. This abstract class contains common logic for managing fonts and parents.

Here is code for the `DocumentElementIF` interface that all classes that make up a document must implement:

```
public interface DocumentElementIF {
    ...

    /**
     * Return this object's parent or null if parentless.
     */
    public CompositeDocumentElement getParent() ;

    /**
     * Return the Font associated with this object.
     */
    public Font getFont() ;

    /**
     * Associate a Font with this object.
```

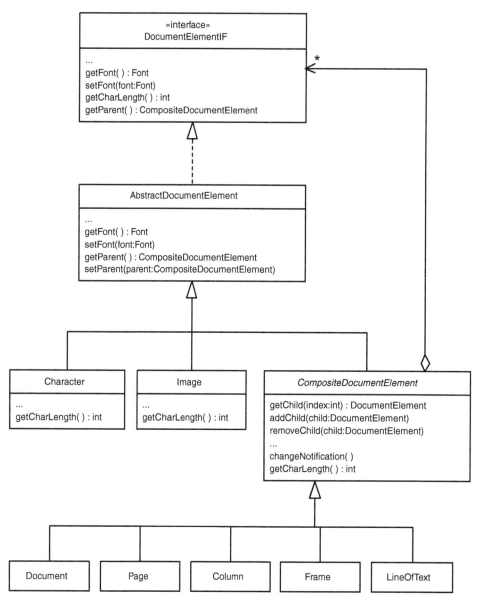

FIGURE 6.8 Detailed document composite.

```
 * @param font The font to associate with this object.
 */
public void setFont(Font font) ;

/**
 * Return the number of characters that this object
 * contains.
```

```
  */
    public int getCharLength() ;
} // interface DocumentElementIF
```

Here is a listing of the AbstractDocumentElement class that contains the common logic for managing fonts and parents:

```
abstract class AbstractDocumentElement
                                implements DocumentElementIF {
  /**
   * This is the font associated with this object.  If the
   * font variable is null, then this object's font will be
   * inherited through the container hierarchy from an
   * enclosing object.
   */
  private Font font;

  /**
   * This object's container
   */
  private CompositeDocumentElement parent;

  ...

  /**
   * Return this object's parent or null if it has no parent.
   */
  public CompositeDocumentElement getParent() {
      return parent;
  } // getParent()

  /**
   * Set this object's parent.
   */
  protected void setParent(CompositeDocumentElement parent) {
      this.parent = parent;
  } // setParent(AbstractDocumentElement)

  /**
   * Return the Font associated with this object.  If
   * there is no Font associated with this object, then
   * return the Font associated with this object's parent.
   * If there is no Font associated with this object's
   * parent then return null.
   */
  public Font getFont() {
      if (font != null)
        return font;
      else if (parent != null)
        return parent.getFont();
      else
        return null;
  } // getFont()
```

```
    /**
     * Associate a Font with this object.
     * @param font
     *          The font to associate with this object
     */
    public void setFont(Font font) {
        this.font = font;
    } // setFont(Font)

    /**
     * Return the number of characters that this object
     * contains.
     */
    public abstract int getCharLength() ;
} // class AbstractDocumentElement
```

Here is the code for the CompositeDocumentElement class, which is the abstract superclass of all document elements that contain other document elements.

```
public abstract class CompositeDocumentElement
                        extends AbstractDocumentElement {
    // Collection of this object's children
    private Vector children = new Vector();

    /**
     * The cached value from the previous call to getCharLength
     * or -1 to indicate that charLength does not contain a
     * cached value.
     */
    private int cachedCharLength = -1;

    /**
     * Return the child object of this object that is at the
     * given position.
     * @param index
     *          The index of the child.
     */
    public DocumentElementIF getChild(int index) {
        return (DocumentElementIF)children.elementAt(index);
    } // getChild(int)

    /**
     * Make the given DocumentElementIF a child of this object.
     */
    public
    synchronized void addChild(DocumentElementIF child) {
        synchronized (child) {
            children.addElement(child);
            ((AbstractDocumentElement)child).setParent(this);
            changeNotification();
        } // synchronized
    } // addChild(DocumentElementIF)
```

The addChild and removeChild methods are both synchronized and also contain a synchronized statement to get a lock on the given child. This is because these methods modify both the container and its child.

```
/**
 * Make the given DocumentElementIF NOT a child of this
 * object.
 */
public synchronized
void removeChild(AbstractDocumentElement child) {
    synchronized (child) {
        if (this == child.getParent()) {
            child.setParent(null);
        } // if
        children.removeElement(child);
        changeNotification();
    } // synchronized
} // removeChild(AbstractDocumentElement)

...

/**
 * A call to this method means that one of this object's
 * children has changed in a way that invalidates whatever
 * data this object may be caching about its children.
 */
public void changeNotification() {
    cachedCharLength = -1;
    if (getParent() != null)
      getParent().changeNotification();
} // changeNotification()

/**
 * Return the number of characters that this object
 * contains.
 */
public int getCharLength() {
    int len = 0;
    for (int i = 0; i < children.size(); i++) {
        AbstractDocumentElement thisChild;
        thisChild
          = (AbstractDocumentElement)children.elementAt(i);
        len += thisChild.getCharLength();
    } // for
    cachedCharLength = len;
    return len;
} // getCharLength()
} // class CompositeDocumentElement
```

The Image class is an example of a class that implements a method so that the other classes that constitute a document do not need to be aware of the Image class as requiring any special treatment. Its getCharLength method always returns 1, so that an image can be treated as just a big character.

```
class Image extends Abstract DocumentElement {
...
    public int getCharLength() {
        return 1;
    } // getCharLength()
} // class Image
```

The other classes in the class diagram that are subclasses of CompositeDocumentElement do not have any features that are interesting with respect to the Composite pattern. In the interest of brevity, just one of them is shown as follows.

```
class Page extends CompositeDocumentElement {
...
} // class Page
```

RELATED PATTERNS

Chain of Responsibility. The Chain of Responsibility pattern can be combined with the Composite pattern by adding child to parent links so that children can get information from an ancestor without having to know which ancestor the information came from.

Low Coupling/High Cohesion. The Low Coupling/High Cohesion pattern (described in *Patterns in Java, Volume 2*) discourages putting specialized methods in general-purpose classes, which is something that the Composite pattern encourages.

Visitor. You can use the Visitor pattern to encapsulate operations in a single class that would otherwise be spread across multiple classes.

Read-Only Interface

The idea behind this pattern was briefly mentioned in the first edition of this book as a read-only object. The Read-Only Interface pattern was first described as a pattern in [LL01].

SYNOPSIS

An object is supposed to be modified by some of its clients and not by others. Ensure that clients that are not supposed to modify an object don't modify an object by forcing them to access the object through an interface that does not include any methods that modify the object.

CONTEXT

You are designing software that will be part of a building security system. Part of its job is to monitor the state of physical sensors that detect the opening and closing of doors, the temperature of rooms, and other such things. The sensors send messages to a computer running the security software. The security software may update a screen or take other actions as a result of receiving a message. Figure 6.9 shows these interactions.

Figure 6.9 shows two top-level interactions. Both interactions begin with a sensor whose software implements an interface named `SensorIF`. In the first interaction, a temperature sensor delivers a temperature to a `SensorController` object in the monitoring software. In the second interaction, a sensor transmits a change in the state of a door (open, closed, locked, etc.). All sensors send data to the `SensorController` object. The `SensorController` object is responsible for determining the identity and type of the sensor that sent data. It passes the data to the object in the monitoring program that corresponds to the sensor that sent the data.

Each data object, such as the `DoorData` and `TemperatureData` objects shown in Figure 6.9, corresponds to a sensor. Each contains data that reflects the data most recently received from the sensor to which it corresponds. When a data object receives new data, it notifies listener objects that have previously registered to be notified when there is a change in the

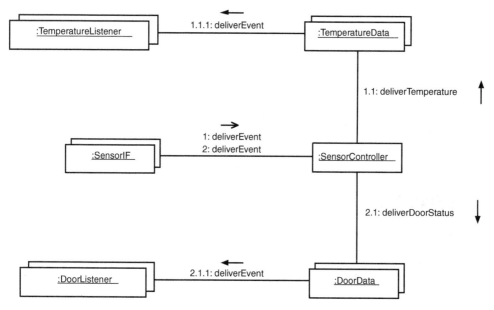

FIGURE 6.9 Security controller collaborations.

content of the data object. Any object can be a listener object if it implements the appropriate interface. Typical listener objects are responsible for displaying the most current information received from a sensor or alerting objects that are responsible for notifying other objects if the values in some data objects meet specified conditions.

This collaboration requires the SensorController object to update the contents of data objects. However, you don't want listener objects to update the contents of data objects.

One way to ensure that no programmer makes the mistake of coding a listener object to update a data object is to insist that listener objects access data objects through an interface that does not include methods to modify the contents of a data object. Figure 6.10 shows a relevant part of this organization.

In Figure 6.10, the SensorController class uses the TemperatureData class directly. It is able to set the temperature value in TemperatureData objects by calling their setTemperature method. Objects that implement the TemperatureListener interface are able to get the temperature value from a TemperatureData object because the getTemperature method is declared in the TemperatureIF interface. However, TemperatureListener objects cannot modify the temperature value in a TemperatureData object because they access TemperatureData objects through the TemperatureIF interface, and the TemperatureIF interface does not declare the setTemperature method.

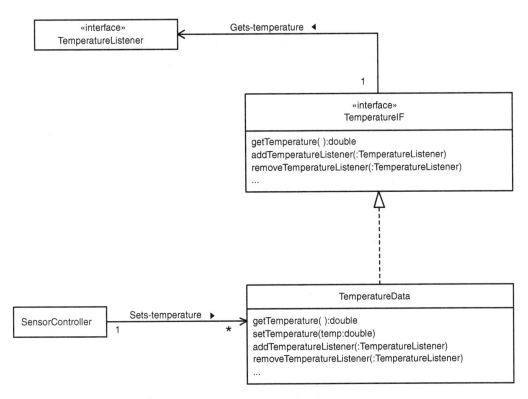

FIGURE 6.10 Data interface.

FORCES

☺ There is a class whose instances you want some other classes to be able to modify but not others.

☺ You want the instances of a class to be modified by instances of classes that are in a different package. This means that making the methods that modify the class's instances package private will not be a useful way to limit which classes can call them.

☹ You are in a position to force clients of a class to access the class through an interface you specify. This will generally be the case if you are designing the class and its clients. It may not be practical in a number of situations. The client classes may be third-party software or you may be in a maintenance situation where you don't want to change the interface that the client classes use.

☹ This pattern is useful to protect against programming mistakes. However, it is not helpful in protecting against malicious programming practices.

SOLUTION

Provide read-only access to a mutable object by requiring objects to access the mutable object through an interface that does not include any methods for modifying the object. This organization is shown in Figure 6.11.

Here are descriptions of the roles that classes and interfaces play in the Read-Only Interface pattern:

Mutable. A class in this role has methods to get and set the values of its attributes. It also implements the ReadOnlyIF interface.

ReadOnlyIF. An interface in this role has the same get methods as the Mutable class, which implements the interface. However, this interface does not include any methods that would cause a Mutable object to modify its contents.

MutatorClient. Classes in this role use the Mutable class directly and may call its methods that modify the state of a Mutable object.

ReadOnlyClient. Classes in this role access the Mutable class through the ReadOnlyIF interface. Classes that access the Mutable class through the ReadOnlyIF interface are not able to access methods that modify Mutable objects.

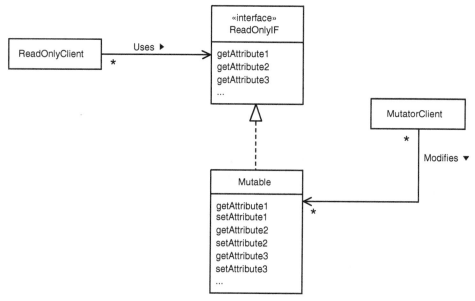

FIGURE 6.11 Read-only interface.

IMPLEMENTATION

If the `Mutable` class is intended to be used as a JavaBean, then there is a different set of considerations that must be addressed to provide a read-only view of a mutable object.

If a class is being used as a JavaBean, then the fact that it implements the `ReadOnlyIF` interface will not be helpful in preventing programmers from improperly updating its instances. This is because JavaBeans do not rely on the interfaces a class implements to determine which of its methods may be called. Instead, they use a mechanism called *introspection* for this purpose.

To determine which methods of a bean object can be called, introspection relies on the BeanInfo associated with the bean object's class. If there is no BeanInfo associated with the class, introspection creates a default BeanInfo that offers the programmer access to every public method that introspection finds.

To prevent introspection from making available to the programmer public methods that will modify a bean object, you must provide its class with an explicit BeanInfo. The BeanInfo must describe all the bean's properties as read-only. It must also not provide any explicit access to methods that modify the contents of the bean.

CONSEQUENCES

- ☺ Using the Read-Only Interface pattern prevents programming mistakes that would result in classes being able to modify objects that they should not be able to modify.
- ☹ The Read-Only Interface pattern does not prevent objects from being improperly modified as a result of malicious programming. Use the Protection Proxy pattern described in *Patterns in Java, Volume 3* to safeguard against malicious programming.

CODE EXAMPLE

The code example for this pattern is some code that implements part of the design shown under the Context heading. Here is a listing of the `TemperatureData` class.

```
public class TemperatureData implements Tempe  ratureIF {
    private double temperature;
    private ArrayList listeners = new ArrayList();
```

```
/**
 * Set the temperature value stored in this object.
 */
public void setTemperature(double temperature) {
    this.temperature = temperature;
    fireTemperature();
} // setTemperature

/**
 * Return the temperature reading encapsulated in this
 * object.
 */
public double getTemperature() {
    return temperature;
} // getTemperature()

/**
 * Add a listener to this object.
 */
public void addListener(TemperatureIF listener) {
    listeners.add(listener);
} // addListener(TemperatureIF)

/**
 * Remove a listener from this object;
 */
public void removeListener(TemperatureIF listener) {
    listeners.remove(listener);
} // removeListener(TemperatureIF)

/**
 * Send a TemperatureEvent to all registered
 * TemperatureListener objects.
 */
private void fireTemperature() {
    int count = listeners.size();
    TemperatureEvent evt;
    evt = new TemperatureEvent(this, temperature);
    for (int i = 0; i<count; i++) {
        TemperatureListener thisListener
          = (TemperatureListener)listeners.get(i);
        thisListener.temperatureChanged(evt) ;
    } // for
} // fireTemperature()

...
} // class TemperatureData
```

SensorController objects set the temperature in a TemperatureData object by calling its setTemperature method. No other class is supposed to call the setTemperature method. To enforce this, other classes access TemperatureData objects through the TemperatureIF interface:

```
public interface TemperatureIF {
    /**
     * Return the temperature reading encapsulated in this
     * object.
     */
    public double getTemperature() ;

    /**
     * Add a listener to this object.
     */
    public void addListener(TemperatureIF listener) ;

    /**
     * Remove a listener from this object;
     */
    public void removeListener(TemperatureIF listener) ;

    ...
} // interface TemperatureIF
```

Notice that the `TemperatureIF` interface does not have the `setTemperature` method.

RELATED PATTERNS

Interface. The Read-Only Interface pattern uses the Interface pattern.

Protection Proxy. The Read-Only Interface pattern is not helpful in protecting against malicious programming practices. The Protection Proxy pattern described in *Patterns in Java, Volume 3* can be used to enforce read-only access to a mutable object in the face of malicious programming. It does that at the expense of additional programming complexity and runtime overhead.

Structural Patterns

The patterns in this chapter describe common ways that different types of objects can be organized to work with each other.

The Adapter pattern describes how an object can have a client that expects it to implement a particular interface, even though it does not implement the interface.

The Iterator pattern describes how an object can access the contents of a collection of objects without knowing the structure or class of the collection.

The Bridge pattern describes how to manage parallel hierarchies of abstractions and implementations.

The Façade pattern describes how to hide the complexity of using a group of related objects behind a single object.

The Flyweight pattern describes how to avoid multiple instances of an object consuming memory by sharing instances that contain common values.

The Dynamic Linkage pattern describes how to dynamically add classes to a program at runtime.

The Virtual Proxy pattern describes how to postpone the creation of objects in a way that is transparent to their clients.

The Decorator pattern describes how to dynamically augment or modify the behavior of existing objects.

The Cache Management pattern describes how to avoid creating similar objects multiple times by reusing the object that was previously created.

Adapter

This pattern was previously described in [GoF95].

SYNOPSIS

An adapter class implements an interface known to its clients and provides access to an instance of a class not known to its clients. An adapter object provides the functionality promised by an interface without having to assume what class is used to implement that interface.

CONTEXT

Suppose that you are writing a method that copies an array of objects. The method is supposed to filter out objects that do not meet certain criteria, so that the copied array may not contain all of the elements in the original array. To promote reuse, you want the method to be independent of the filtering criteria being used. You can do this by defining an interface that declares a method the array copier can call to find out whether it should include a given object in the new array, as shown in Figure 7.1

In Figure 7.1, an `ArrayCopier` class delegates to the `CopyFilterIF` interface the decision to copy an element from the old array to the new array. If the `isCopyable` method returns true for an object, then the object is copied to the new array.

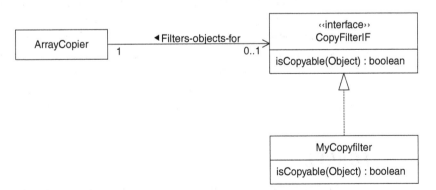

FIGURE 7.1 Simple copy filter.

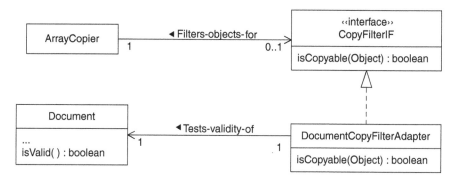

FIGURE 7.2 Copy filter adapter.

This solution solves the immediate problem of allowing the copy criteria used by ArrayCopier objects to be encapsulated in a separate object without having to be concerned about what the object's class is. This solution presents another problem. Sometimes the logic needed for filtering is in a method of the objects being filtered. If these objects do not implement the CopyFilterIF interface, then the ArrayCopier object cannot directly ask these objects whether they should be copied. However, the ArrayCopier object can indirectly ask the filtered objects whether they should be copied, even if they do not implement the CopyFilterIF interface.

Suppose a class called Document has a method called isValid that returns a boolean result. You want an ArrayCopier object to use the result of isValid to filter a copy operation. Because Document does not implement the CopyFilterIF interface, an ArrayCopier object cannot directly use a Document object for filtering. Another object that does implement the CopyFilterIF interface cannot independently determine whether a Document object should be copied to a new array. It does not work because it has no way to get the necessary information without calling the Document object's isValid method. The answer is for that object to call the Document object's isValid method, resulting in the solution shown in Figure 7.2.

In this solution, the ArrayCopier object, as always, calls the isCopyable method of an object that implements the CopyFilterIF interface. In this case, the object is an instance of the DocumentCopyFilterAdapter class. The DocumentCopyFilterAdapter class implements the isCopyable method by delegating the call to the Document object's isValid method.

FORCES

☺ You want to use a class that calls a method through an interface, but you want to use it with a class that does not implement the interface.

Modifying the class to implement the interface is not an option either because

● You do not have the source code for the class.
● The class is a general-purpose class and it would be inappropriate for it to implement an interface for a specialized purpose.

☺ You want to dynamically determine which of another object's methods an object calls without the object having knowledge of the other object's class.

SOLUTION

Suppose you have a class that calls a method through an interface. You want an instance of this class to call a method of an object that does not implement the interface. You can arrange for the instance to make the call through an adapter object that implements the interface by delegating the calls to a method of the object that doesn't implement the interface. The diagram in Figure 7.3 shows how this works.

Here are the roles that the classes and interface play in Figure 7.3:

Client.   A class in this role calls a method of another class through an interface to avoid assuming the actual class that implements the method.

TargetIF.   An interface in this role declares a method that the client class calls.

Adapter.   A class in this role implements the TargetIF interface. It implements the method that the Client calls by delegating the call to a method of the Adaptee class, which does not implement the TargetIF interface.

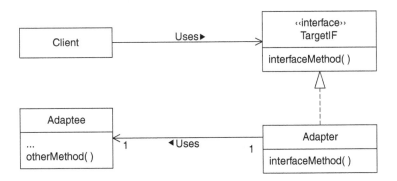

FIGURE 7.3 Adapter.

Adaptee. A class in this role does not implement the `TargetIF` method but has a method that the `Client` class wants to call.

It is possible for an `Adapter` class to do more than simply delegate a method call. It may perform some transformation on the arguments. It may provide additional logic to hide differences between the intended semantics of the interface's method and the actual semantics of the `Adaptee` class's method. There is no limit to how complex an adapter class can be. So long as the essential purpose of the class is as an intermediary for method calls to one other object, you can consider it to be an adapter class.

IMPLEMENTATION

Implementation of the adapter class is rather straightforward. However, an issue you should consider when implementing the Adapter pattern is how the `Adapter` objects will know which instance of the `Adaptee` class to call. There are two approaches.

- Pass a reference to the `Adaptee` object as a parameter to the adapter object's constructor or one of its methods. This allows the `Adapter` object to be used with any instance or possibly multiple instances of the `Adaptee` class. This approach is illustrated in the following example:

```
class CustomerBillToAdapter implements AddressIF {
    private Customer myCustomer;

    public CustomerBillToAdapter(Customer customer) {
        myCustomer = customer;
    } // constructor

    public String getAddress1() {
        return myCustomer.getBillToAddress1();
    }

    public void setAddress1(String address1) {
        myCustomer.setBillToAddress1(address1);
    } // setAddress1(String)
    . . .
} // class CustomerBillToAdapter
```

- Make the adapter class an inner class of the `Adaptee` class. This simplifies the association between the adapter object and the `Adaptee` object by making it automatic. It also makes the association inflexible. This approach is illustrated in the following example:

```
MenuItem exit = new MenuItem(caption);
exit.addActionListener(new ActionListener() {
    public void actionPerformed(ActionEvent evt) {
        close();
    } // actionPerformed(ActionEvent)
} );
```

Inner Classes

Java allows class declarations to be nested, like this:

```
public class Foo {
    private int x;
    ...
    class Bar {
        void increment() {
            x = x+1;
        } // increment()
        ...
    } // class bar
} // class foo
```

Because the Bar class is defined inside of the Foo class, it is considered to be part of the Foo class. Because it is part of the Foo class, it can refer to the Foo class's private instance variables. When an instance of the Foo class creates an instance of the Bar class, the instance of Foo that created the Bar object is called the Bar object's *enclosing instance*. Any references in the Bar class to one of the Foo class's instance variables will refer to the variables of the enclosing instance.

Inner classes may be private. A private class is accessible to its enclosing class but not to any classes outside of its enclosing class. If a class is needed only to support another class, then the best way to organize the supporting class may be as a private inner class of the class that it supports.

If an object needs to have another object call one of its methods and to do so it passes an adapter object to the other object, then it is appropriate for the adapter object to be an instance of a private inner class.

An inner class may be declared inside of a method. If an inner class is declared inside of a method, then it can access the enclosing class's instance variables and the enclosing method's local variables.

Inner classes declared in a method can be anonymous. The second bullet under the Implementation heading shows an example of this. The syntax combines the creation of the class's instance with the class's definition. It consists of the word new followed by the name of the class to be extended or an interface to be implemented, the constructor arguments, and then the class body in curly braces.

The example shown in the second bullet under the Implementation heading defines an anonymous inner class that implements the `ActionListener` interface. It creates an instance of the anonymous class and passes it to the `MenuItem` object's `addActionListener` method.

For more information about inner classes, see Section 8.1.2 of the Java Language Specification at http://java.sun.com/docs/books/jls/second_edition/html/.

CONSEQUENCES

☺ The `Client` and `Adaptee` classes remain independent of each other.

☺ You can use an adapter class to determine which of an object's methods another object calls. For example, you may have a class whose instances are GUI widgets that allow telephone numbers to be displayed and edited. This class fetches and stores telephone numbers by calling methods defined by an interface. To make use of the interface you define adapter classes. You may have an adapter class to fetch and store a fax number from instances of a class and another adapter class to fetch and store pager numbers from instances of the same class. The difference between the two adapter classes would be that they call different methods of the `Adaptee` class. Here is an example.

Suppose there is a class named `PhoneNumberEditor` that is responsible for allowing a user to edit a phone number. An object is passed to the constructor of a `PhoneNumberEditor` that implements this interface.

```
public interface PhoneNumberIF {
    public String getPhoneNumber() ;

    public void setPhoneNumber(String newValue) ;
} // interface PhoneNumberIF
```

If you want to create two `PhoneNumberEditor` objects to edit the office and fax numbers of a person, you might write some code that looks like this:

```
PhoneNumberEditor voiceNumber;
voiceNumber = new PhoneNumberEditor(new PhoneNumberIF() {
    public String getPhoneNumber() {
        return person.getOfficeNumber();
    } // getPhoneNumber
```

```
    public void setPhoneNumber(String newValue) {
        person.setOfficeNumber(newValue);
    } // setPhoneNumber(String)
}) ;
```

```
PhoneNumberEditor faxNumber;
faxNumber = new PhoneNumberEditor(new PhoneNumberIF() {
    public String getPhoneNumber() {
        return person.getFAXNumber();
    } // getPhoneNumber

    public void setPhoneNumber(String newValue) {
        person.setFAXNumber(newValue);
    } // setPhoneNumber(String)
}) ;
```

Each `PhoneNumberEditor` object is created with a different adapter. Each adapter calls different methods of the same object.

☹ The Adapter pattern adds indirection to a program. Like any other indirection, it contributes to the difficulty involved in understanding the program.

JAVA API USAGE AND EXAMPLE

A very common way to use adapter classes with the Java API is for event handling, like this:

```
Button ok = new Button("OK");
ok.addActionListener(new ActionListener() {
    public void actionPerformed(ActionEvent evt) {
        doIt();
    } // actionPerformed(ActionEvent)
  } );
add(ok);
```

The previous example creates an instance of an anonymous class that implements the `ActionListener` interface. The class's `actionPerformed` method is called when the `Button` object is pressed. This coding pattern is very common for code that handles events.

The Java API does not include any public adapter classes that are ready to use. It does include classes such as `java.awt.event.WindowAdapter` that are intended to be subclassed rather than used directly. The idea is that some event listener interfaces, such as `WindowListener`, declare multiple methods that may not all need to be implemented in many cases. The `WindowListener` interface declares eight methods that are called to provide notification about different kinds of window events. Often only one or two of those event types are of interest. The methods corresponding to events that are not of interest will typically be given do-nothing implementations. The `WindowAdapter` class implements the `WindowListener` interface and implements all eight of its methods with do-nothing implementations. An adapter class that subclasses the `WindowAdapter` class needs to implement only those methods corresponding to events that are of interest. It inherits do-nothing implementations for the rest. For example:

```
addWindowListener(new WindowAdapter() {
   public void windowClosing(WindowEvent e) {
      System.exit();
   } // windowClosing(WindowEvent)
 } );
```

In the preceding example, the anonymous adapter class is a subclass of the `WindowAdapter` class. It only implements the `windowClosing` method. It inherits do-nothing implementations for the other seven methods from the `WindowAdapter` class.

RELATED PATTERNS

Façade. The `Adapter` class provides an object that acts as an intermediary for method calls between a client object and **one other** object not known to the client objects. The Façade pattern provides an object that acts as an intermediary for method calls between its client object and **multiple** objects not known to the client objects.

Iterator. The Iterator pattern is a specialized form of the Adapter pattern for sequentially accessing the contents of a collection of objects.

Proxy. The Proxy pattern, like the Adapter pattern, uses an object that is a surrogate for another object. However, a Proxy object has the same interface as the object for which it is a surrogate.

Strategy. The Strategy pattern is structurally similar to the Adapter pattern. The difference is in the intent. The Adapter pattern allows a `Client` object to carry out its originally intended function by calling methods of objects that implement a particular interface. The Strategy pattern provides objects that implement a particular interface for the purpose of altering or determining the behavior of a `Client` object.

Anonymous Adapter. The Anonymous Adapter pattern (described in *Patterns in Java, Volume 2*) is a coding pattern that uses anonymous `Adapter` objects to handle events.

Iterator

This pattern was described previously in [GoF95].

SYNOPSIS

The Iterator pattern defines an interface that declares methods for sequentially accessing the objects in a collection. A class that accesses a collection only through such an interface is independent of the class that implements the interface and the class of the collection.

CONTEXT

Suppose you are writing classes to browse inventory in a warehouse. There will be a user interface that allows a user to see the description, quantity on hand, location, and other information about each inventory item.

The inventory browsing classes will be part of a customizable application. For this reason, they must be independent of the actual class that provides collections of inventory items. To provide this independence, you design an interface to allow the user interface to sequentially access a collection of inventory items without having to be aware of the actual collection class being used. The class diagram in Figure 7.4 shows the relevant part of the design.

In Figure 7.4, the user-interface classes that constitute the inventory browser are shown as the composite class InventoryBrowser. An instance of the InventoryBrowser class is asked to display InventoryItem objects in the collection encapsulated by an InventoryCollection object. The InventoryBrowser object does not directly access the InventoryCollection object. Instead, it is given an object that implements the InventoryIteratorIF interface. The InventoryIteratorIF interface defines methods to allow an object to sequentially fetch the contents of a collection of InventoryItem objects.

FORCES

☺ A class needs access to the contents of a collection without becoming dependent on the class that is used to implement the collection.

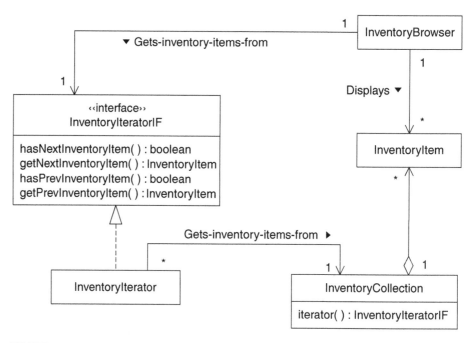

FIGURE 7.4 Inventory iterator.

☺ A class needs a uniform way of accessing the contents of multiple collections.

SOLUTION

The class diagram in Figure 7.5 shows the organization of the classes and interfaces that participate in the Iterator pattern.

Here are descriptions of the roles that classes and interfaces play in the organization shown in Figure 7.5:

Collection.   A class in this role encapsulates a collection of objects or values.

IteratorIF.   An interface in this role defines methods to sequentially access the objects that are encapsulated by a Collection object.

Iterator.   A class in this role implements an IteratorIF interface. Its instances provide sequential access to the contents of the Collection object associated with Iterator object.

CollectionIF.   Collection classes normally take responsibility for creating their own iterator objects. It is convenient to have a consistent way to ask a Collection object to create an Iterator

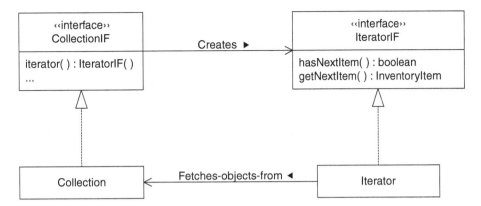

FIGURE 7.5 Iterator pattern.

object for itself. To provide that consistency, all `Collection` classes implement a `CollectionIF` interface that declares a method for creating `Iterator` objects.

IMPLEMENTATION

ADDITIONAL METHODS

The iterator interface shown under the "Solution" heading has a minimal set of methods. It is common for iterator interfaces to define additional methods when they are useful and the underlying collection classes support them. In addition to methods for testing the existence of and fetching the next collection element, the following sorts of methods are common:

- Test for the existence of and fetch the previous collection element.
- Move to the first or last collection element.
- Get the number of elements in the traversal.

INNER CLASS

In many cases, an iterator class's traversal algorithm requires access to a collection class's internal data structure. For this reason, iterator classes are often implemented as a private inner class of a collection class.

NULL ITERATOR

A *null iterator* is an iterator that returns no objects. Its `hasNext` method always returns false. Null iterators are usually implemented as a simple class that implements the appropriate iterator interface. The use of null iterators can simplify the implementation of collection classes and other iterator classes by removing the need for some code to handle the special case of a null traversal.

MODIFICATION TO THE UNDERLYING COLLECTION

Modifying a collection object while an iterator is traversing its contents can cause problems. If no provisions are made for dealing with such modifications, an iterator may return an inconsistent set of results. The potential inconsistencies include skipping objects or returning the same object twice.

A simple way to handle this is to consider an iterator to be invalid after its underlying collection is modified. You can implement this by having a collection class's methods increment a counter when they modify the collection. Iterator objects can detect changes to their underlying collection by noticing a difference in its change count. If an iterator object's method notices that the underlying collection has changed, then it can throw an exception.

A more robust way of handling modifications to an underlying collection is to ensure that the iterator does return a consistent set of results. There are a number of ways to accomplish this. Though making a full copy of the underlying collection works in most cases, it is usually the least desirable technique because it is the most expensive in both time and memory.

CONSEQUENCES

- ☺ It is possible to access a collection of objects without knowing the source of the objects.
- ☺ By using multiple iterator objects, it is simple to have and manage multiple traversals at the same time.
- ☺ A collection class may provide different kinds of iterator objects to traverse the collection in different ways. For example, a collection class that maintains an association between key objects and value objects may have a different method for creating iterators that traverse just the key objects and for creating iterators that traverse just the value objects.

JAVA API USAGE

The collection classes in the `java.util` package follow the Iterator pattern. The interface `java.util.Collection` plays the `ConnectionIF` role. The package includes a number of classes that implement `java.util.Collection`.

The `java.util.Iterator` interface plays the `IteratorIF` role. The classes in the package that implement `java.util.Collection` define private inner classes that implement `java.util.Iterator` and play the Iterator role.

CODE EXAMPLE

For a code example, we will look at some skeletal code that implements the design discussed under the Context heading. The following is a listing of the `InventoryIteratorIF` interface.

```
public interface InventoryIteratorIF {
    public boolean hasNextInventoryItem() ;
    public InventoryItem getNextInventoryItem() ;
    public boolean hasPrevInventoryItem() ;
    public InventoryItem getPrevInventoryItem() ;
} // interface InventoryIterator
```

The following is a skeletal listing of the `InventoryCollection` class. The listing includes the `iterator` method that other classes will use to get an object to iterate over the contents of an `InventoryCollection` object. It also includes the private class that the `iterator` method instantiates.

```
public class InventoryCollection {
    ...
    public InventoryIteratorIF iterator() {
        return new InventoryIterator();
    } // iterator()

    private class InventoryIterator
                    implements InventoryIteratorIF {
        public boolean hasNextInventoryItem() {
            ...
        } // hasNextInventoryItem()

        public InventoryItem getNextInventoryItem() {
            ...
        } // getNextInventoryItem()

        public boolean hasPrevInventoryItem() {
            ...
        } // hasPrevInventoryItem()

        public InventoryItem getPrevInventoryItem() {
            ...
        } // getPrevInventoryItem()
    } // class InventoryIterator
    ...
} // class InventoryCollection
```

RELATED PATTERNS

Adapter.   The Iterator pattern is a specialized form of the Adapter pattern for sequentially accessing the contents of collection objects.

Factory Method.   Some collection classes may use the Factory Method pattern to determine what kind of iterator to instantiate.

Null Object.   Null iterators are sometimes used to implement the Null Object pattern.

Bridge

This pattern was previously described in [GoF95].

SYNOPSIS

The Bridge pattern is useful when there is a hierarchy of abstractions and a corresponding hierarchy of implementations. Rather than combining the abstractions and implementations into many distinct classes, the Bridge pattern implements the abstractions and implementations as independent classes that can be combined dynamically.

CONTEXT

Suppose you need to provide Java classes that access physical sensors for control applications. These are devices such as scales, speed-measuring devices, and location-sensing devices. What these devices have in common is that they perform a physical measurement and produce a number. One way that these devices differ is in the type of measurement that they produce.

- The scale produces a single number based on a measurement at a single point in time.
- The speed-measuring device produces a single measurement that is an average over a period of time.
- The location-sensing device produces a stream of measurements.

This suggests that these devices can be supported by three classes, shown in Figure 7.6, that support these different measurement techniques.

These three classes provide clean abstractions that apply to many more types of sensors than the three that inspired them. Since there are other kinds of sensors that produce simple measurements, time-averaged measurements, and streams of measurements, you would like to be able to reuse these classes with other kinds of sensors. A difficulty in achieving such reuse is that the details of communicating with sensors from different manufacturers vary. Suppose the software that you are writing will need to work with sensors from multiple manufacturers called Eagle and Hawk. You could handle that problem by having manufacturer-specific classes, as shown in Figure 7.7.

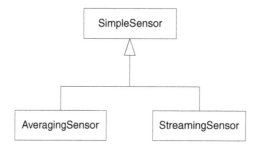

FIGURE 7.6 Sensor classes.

The problem with this solution is not just that it does not reuse classes for simple, averaging, and streaming sensors. Because it exposes differences between manufacturers to other classes, it forces other classes to recognize differences between manufacturers and therefore be less reusable. The challenge here is to represent a hierarchy of abstractions in a way that keeps the abstractions independent of their implementations.

A way to accomplish that is to add some indirection that shields a hierarchy of classes that support abstractions from classes that implement those abstractions. Have the abstraction classes access implementation classes through a hierarchy of implementation interfaces that parallels the abstraction hierarchy.

The solution shown in Figure 7.8 divides the problem into three hierarchies that are separated by horizontal gray lines:

- On the top, there is a hierarchy of manufacturer-independent sensor classes.
- On the bottom, there are parallel hierarchies of manufacturer-specific classes.
- In the middle, there is a parallel hierarchy of interfaces that are used to allow the manufacturer-independent classes to be independent of any manufacturer-specific classes.

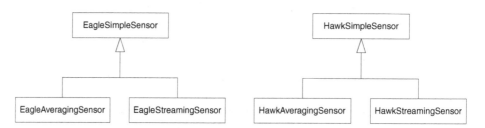

FIGURE 7.7 Manufacturer-specific sensor classes.

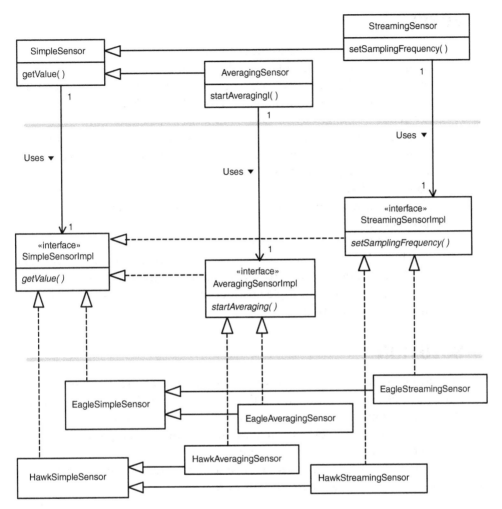

FIGURE 7.8 Independent sensor and sensor manufacturer classes.

Any logic that is common to the type of sensor will go in a manufacturer-independent class. Logic that is specific to a manufacturer will go in a manufacturer-specific class.

Most of the logic that we are talking about in this example is for handling exceptional conditions. An example of such a condition is that a simple sensor detects an out-of-range value that is too large for it to measure. Manufacturer-independent handling for that condition could be to translate that to a predetermined maximum value for the application. Manufacturer-specific handling for that condition might require not considering any readings from the sensor to be valid until a certain amount of time has elapsed after the end of the out-of-range condition.

FORCES

☺ When you combine hierarchies of abstractions and hierarchies of their implementations into a single class hierarchy, classes that use those classes become tied to a specific implementation of the abstraction. Changing the implementation used for an abstraction should not require changes to the classes that use the abstraction.

☺ You would like to reuse logic common to different implementations of an abstraction. The usual way to make logic reusable is to encapsulate it in a separate class.

☺ You would like to be able to create a new implementation of an abstraction without having to re-implement the common logic of the abstraction.

☺ You would like to be able to extend the common logic of an abstraction by writing one new class rather than writing a new class for each combination of the base abstraction and its implementation.

☺ When appropriate, multiple abstractions should be able to share the same implementation.

SOLUTION

The Bridge pattern allows classes corresponding to abstractions to be separate from classes that implement those abstractions. You can maintain a clean separation by having the abstraction classes access the implementation classes through interfaces that are in a hierarchy that parallels the inheritance hierarchy of the abstraction classes.

Figure 7.9 shows the roles that classes and interfaces play in the Bridge pattern. Here are descriptions of these roles:

Abstraction.   This class represents the top-level abstraction. It is responsible for maintaining a reference to an object that implements the AbstractionImpl interface, so that it can delegate operations to its implementation. If an instance of the Abstraction class is also an instance of a subclass of the Abstraction class, then the instance will refer to an object that implements the corresponding sub-interface of the AbstractionImpl interface.

SpecializedAbstraction.   This role corresponds to any subclass of the Abstraction class. For each such subclass of the Abstraction class there is a corresponding sub-interface of the AbstractionImpl interface. Each SpecializedAbstraction class delegates its operations to an implementation object that

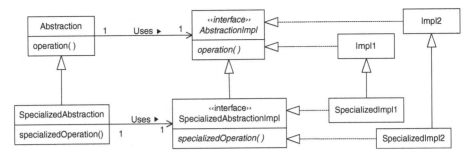

FIGURE 7.9 Bridge pattern.

implements the `SpecializedAbstractionImpl` interface that corresponds to the `SpecializedAbstraction` class.

AbstractionImpl. This interface declares methods for all of the low-level operations that an implementation for the `Abstraction` class must provide.

SpecializedAbstractionImpl. This corresponds to a sub-interface of `AbstractionImpl`. Each `SpecializedAbstractionImpl` interface corresponds to a `SpecializedAbstraction` class and declares methods for the low-level operations needed for an implementation of that class.

Impl1, Impl2. These classes implement the `AbstractionImpl` interface and provide different implementations for the `Abstraction` class.

SpecializedImpl1, SpecializedImpl2. These classes implement one of the `SpecializedAbstractionImpl` interfaces and provide different implementations for a `SpecializedAbstraction` class.

Figure 7.9 shows the abstraction implementation interfaces having the same methods as the corresponding abstraction classes. This is a presentational convenience. It is possible for abstraction implementation interfaces to have different methods than the corresponding abstraction classes.

IMPLEMENTATION

One issue that always must be decided when implementing the Bridge pattern is how to create implementation objects for each abstraction object. The most basic decision to make is whether abstraction objects will create their own implementation objects or delegate the creation of their implementation objects to another object.

Having the abstraction objects delegate the creation of implementation objects is usually the best choice. It preserves the independence of the abstraction and implementation classes. If abstraction classes are designed to delegate the creation of implementation objects, then the design usually uses the Abstract Factory pattern to create the implementation objects.

However, if there are only a small number of implementation classes for an abstract class and the set of implementation classes is not expected to change, then having the abstraction classes create their own implementation objects is a reasonable optimization.

A related decision is whether an abstraction object will use the same implementation object throughout its lifetime. As usage patterns or other conditions change, it may be appropriate to change the implementation object that an abstraction object uses. If an abstraction class directly creates its own implementation objects, then it is reasonable to directly embed the logic for changing the implementation object in the abstraction class. Otherwise, you can use the Decorator pattern to encapsulate the logic for switching implementation objects in a wrapper class.

CONSEQUENCES

The Bridge pattern keeps classes that represent an abstraction independent of the classes that supply an implementation for the abstraction. The abstraction and its implementations are organized into separate class hierarchies. You can extend each class hierarchy without directly impacting another class hierarchy. It is also possible to have multiple implementation classes for an abstraction class or multiple abstraction classes using the same implementation class.

Classes that are clients of the abstraction classes do not have any knowledge of the implementation classes, so an abstraction object can change its implementation without any impact on its clients.

JAVA API USAGE

The Java API includes the package `java.awt`. This package contains the `Component` class. The `Component` class is an abstract class that encapsulates logic common to all GUI components. The `Component` class has subclasses such as `Button`, `List`, and `TextField` that encapsulate the logic for those GUI components that is platform independent. The package `java.awt.peer` contains interfaces such as `ComponentPeer`, `ButtonPeer`, `ListPeer`, and `TextFieldPeer` that declare methods required for implementation classes that provide platform-specific support for the subclasses of the `Component` class.

The subclasses of the `Component` class use the Abstract Factory pattern to create their implementation objects. The `java.awt.Toolkit` class is an abstract class that plays the role of abstract factory. The platform supplies the implementation classes and the concrete factory class used to instantiate the implementation classes.

CODE EXAMPLE

For an example of the Bridge pattern, we will look at some code to implement the sensor-related classes that were discussed under the Context heading. We will assume that the objects that represent sensors and their implementation are created by a Factory Method. The Factory Method object will know what sensors are available and what objects to create to provide access to a sensor, and it will create those objects when access to a sensor is first requested.

Here is the code for the `SimpleSensor` class that plays the role of abstraction class:

```java
public class SimpleSensor {
    // A reference to the object that implements operations
    // specific to the actual sensor device that this object
    // represents.
    private SimpleSensorImpl impl;
    /**
     * @param impl
     *          Object that implements sensor type-specific
     *          operations.
     */
    SimpleSensor(SimpleSensorImpl impl) {
        this.impl = impl;
    } // constructor(SimpleSensorImpl)

    protected SimpleSensorImpl getImpl() {
        return impl;
    } // getImpl()
...
    /**
     * Return the value of the sensor's current measurement.
     */
    public int getValue() throws SensorException {
        return impl.getValue();
    } // getValue()
} // class SimpleSensor
```

As you can see, the `SimpleSensor` class is simple. It does little more than delegate its operations to an object that implements the `SimpleSensorImpl` interface. Here is the `SimpleSensorImpl` interface:

```
interface SimpleSensorImpl {
    /**
     * Return the value of the sensor's current measurement.
     */
    public int getValue() throws SensorException;
} // interface SimpleSensorImpl
```

Some subclasses of the SimpleSensor class maintain the same simple structure. The following is code for the AveragingSensor class. Instances of the AveragingSensor class represent sensors that produce values that are the average of measurements made over a period of time.

```
public class AveragingSensor extends SimpleSensor {
    /**
     * @param impl
     *         Object that implements sensor type-specific
     *         operations.
     */
    AveragingSensor(AveragingSensorImpl impl) {
        super(impl);
    } // constructor(AveragingSensorImpl)
...
    /**
     * Averaging sensors produce a value that is the average
     * of measurements made over a period of time.  That
     * period of time begins when this method is called.
     */
    public void beginAverage() throws SensorException {
        ((AveragingSensorImpl)getImpl()).beginAverage();
    } // beginAverage()
} // class AveragingSensor
```

As you can see, the AveragingSensor class is also very simple, delegating its operations to the implementation objects that it is using. Here is its corresponding implementation interface:

```
interface AveragingSensorImpl extends SimpleSensorImpl {
    /**
     * Averaging sensors produce a value that is the average
     * of measurements made over a period of time.  That
     * period of time begins when this method is called.
     */
    public void beginAverage() throws SensorException;
} // interface AveragingSensorImpl
```

It is reasonable for subclasses of the SimpleSensor class to be more complex and provide additional services of their own. The StreamingSensor class delivers a stream of measurements to objects registered to receive the measurements. It delivers each measurement by passing the measurement to a method of the object to which it is delivering the measurement. It does not place any requirements on how long that method may take before it returns. There is merely an expectation that the method will return in a reasonable amount of time. On the other hand, the implementation objects used with instances of the StreamingSensor class may need to deliver measurements at a steady rate or lose them. In order to avoid losing measurements, instances of the StreamingSensor class buffer measurements that are delivered to it, while it asynchronously delivers those measurements to other objects. Here is code for the StreamingSensor class:

```java
public class StreamingSensor extends SimpleSensor
                implements StreamingSensorListener, Runnable {
    // These objects are used to provide a buffer that allows
    // the implementation object to asynchronously deliver
    // measurement values while this object is delivering
    // value it has already received to its listeners.
    private DataInputStream consumer;
    private DataOutputStream producer;

    // collection of listeners
    private Vector listeners = new Vector();

    /**
     * @param impl
     *        The object that implements the sensor type-
     *        specific operations this object will provide.
     */
    StreamingSensor(StreamingSensorImpl impl)
                                        throws SensorException {
        super(impl);

        // Create pipe stream that will support this object's
        // ability to deliver measurement values at the same
        // time it is receiving them.
        PipedInputStream pipedInput = new PipedInputStream();
        consumer = new DataInputStream(pipedInput);
        PipedOutputStream pipedOutput;
        try {
            pipedOutput = new PipedOutputStream(pipedInput);
        } catch (IOException e) {
            throw new SensorException("pipe creation failed");
        } // try
        producer = new DataOutputStream(pipedOutput);

        // start a thread to deliver measurement values
        new Thread(this).start();
    } // constructor(StreamingSensorImpl)
    ...
    /**
     * Streaming sensors produce a stream of measurement
     * values.  The stream of values is produced with a
     * frequency no greater than the given number of times
```

```
 * per minute.
 * @param freq
 *         The maximum number of times per minute that this
 *         streaming sensor will produce a measurement
 *         value.
 */
public void setSamplingFrequency(int freq)
                                  throws SensorException {
    // delegate this to the implementation object
    StreamingSensorImpl impl;
    impl = (StreamingSensorImpl)getImpl();
    impl.setSamplingFrequency(freq);
} // setSamplingFrequency(int)


/**
 * StreamingSensor objects deliver a stream of values to
 * interested objects by passing each value to the
 * object's processMeasurement method.  The delivery of
 * values is done using its own thread and is asynchronous
 * of everything else.
 * @param value The measurement value being delivered.
 */
public void processMeasurement(int value) {
    try {
        producer.writeInt(value);
    } catch (IOException e) {
        // Cannot deliver value, just discard it.
    } // try
} // processMeasurement(int)


/**
 * This method registers its argument as a recipient of future
 * measurement values from this sensor.
 */
public void addStreamingSensorListener(
                    StreamingSensorListener listener) {
    listeners.addElement(listener);
} // addStreamingSensorListener(StreamingSensorListener)


/**
 * This method unregisters its argument as a recipient of
 * future measurement values from this sensor.
 */
public void removeStreamingSensorListener(
                    StreamingSensorListener listener) {
    listeners.removeElement(listener);
} // addStreamingSensorListener(StreamingSensorListener)


/**
 * This method asynchronously removes measurement values
 * from the pipe and delivers them to registered
 * listeners.
```

```
    */
    public void run() {
        while (true) {
            int value;
            try {
                value = consumer.readInt();
            } catch (IOException e) {
                // Pipe is broken so return from this method
                // letting this thread die.
                return;
            } // try
            for (int i=0; i < listeners.size(); i++) {
                StreamingSensorListener listener;
                listener
                  = (StreamingSensorListener)listeners.elementAt(i);
                listener.processMeasurement(value);
            } // for
        } // while
    } // run()
} // class StreamingSensor
```

In order for the StreamingSensor class to deliver a measurement to an object, the object must implement the StreamingSensorListener interface. It delivers measurements by passing them to the processMeasurement method that the StreamingSensorListener interface declares. The StreamingSensor class also implements the StreamingSensorListener interface. Implementation objects deliver measurements to instances of the StreamingSensor class by calling its processMeasurement method.

Finally, here is the implementation interface that corresponds to the StreamingSensor class:

```
interface StreamingSensorImpl extends SimpleSensorImpl {
    /**
     * Streaming sensors produce a stream of measurement
     * values.  The stream of values is produced with a
     * frequency no greater than the given number of times per
     * minute.
     * @param freq
     *        The maximum number of times per minute that this
     *        streaming sensor will produce a measurement
     *        value.
     */
    public void setSamplingFrequency(int freq)
      throws SensorException;

    /**
     * This method is called by an object that represents the
     * streaming sensor abstraction so that this object can
     * perform a call-back to that object to deliver
     * measurement values to it.
```

```
 * @param abstraction The abstraction object to deliver
 *                          measurement values to.
 */
public void setStreamingSensorListener(
                        StreamingSensorListener listener);
} // interface StreamingSensorImpl
```

RELATED PATTERNS

Layered Architecture.   The Bridge design pattern is a way of organizing the entities identified using the Layered Architecture pattern (described in [BMRSS96]) into classes.

Abstract Factory.   The Abstract Factory pattern can be used by the Bridge pattern to decide which implementation class to instantiate for an abstraction object.

Decorator.   The Decorator pattern can be used to dynamically select the implementation object that an abstraction object delegates an operation to.

Façade

This pattern was previously described in [GoF95].

SYNOPSIS

The Façade pattern simplifies access to a related set of objects by providing one object that all objects outside the set use to communicate with the set.

CONTEXT

Consider the organization of classes to support the creation and sending of email messages. The classes may include the following:

- A `MessageBody` class whose instances will contain message bodies
- An `Attachment` class whose instances will contain message attachments that can be attached to a `MessageBody` object
- A `MessageHeader` class whose instances will contain header information (to, from, subject, etc.) for an email message
- A `Message` class whose instances will tie together a `MessageHeader` object and a `MessageBody` object
- A `Security` class whose instances can be used to add a digital signature to a message
- A `MessageSender` class whose instances are responsible for sending `Message` objects to a server that is responsible for delivering the email to its destination or to another server

Figure 7.10 is a class diagram showing the relationships between these classes and a client class.

As you can see, working with these email classes adds complexity to a client class. To use these classes, a client must know of at least these six of them, the relationships between them, and the order in which it must create instances of the classes. If every client of these classes must take on this additional complexity, it makes the email classes more difficult to reuse.

The Façade pattern is a way to shield clients of classes like these email classes from their complexity. It works by providing an additional

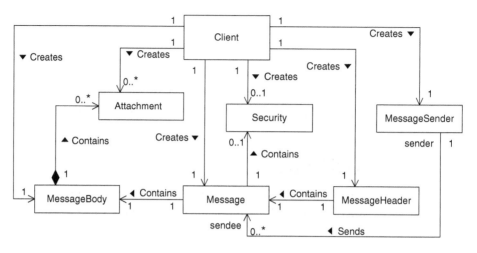

FIGURE 7.10 Email creation.

reusable object that hides most of the complexity of working with the other classes from client classes. Figure 7.11 is a class diagram showing this more reusable organization.

In this new scheme, the portion of the Client class that was responsible for interacting with the email classes has been refactored into a separate reusable class. Client classes now need only be aware of the

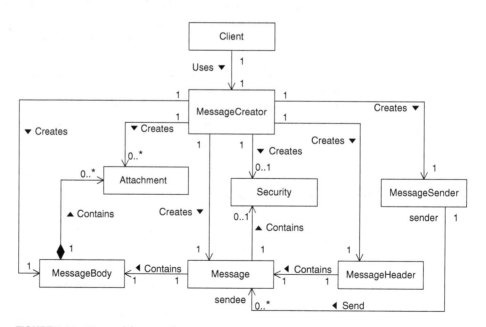

FIGURE 7.11 Reusable email creation.

`MessageCreator` class. Furthermore, the internal logic of the `MessageCreator` class can shield client classes from having to create the parts of an email message in any particular order.

FORCES

- ☺ There are many dependencies between classes that implement an abstraction and their client classes. The dependencies add noticeable complexity to clients.
- ☺ You want to simplify the client classes, because simpler classes result in fewer bugs. Simpler clients also mean that less work is required to reuse the classes that implement the abstraction.
- ☺ You are designing classes to function in cleanly separated layers. You want to minimize the number of classes that are visible from one layer to the next.

SOLUTION

Figure 7.12 is a class diagram showing the general structure of the Façade pattern. The client object interacts with a `Façade` object that provides necessary functionality by interacting with the rest of the objects. If there is some additional functionality that is needed by only some clients, then instead of providing it directly, the `Façade` object may provide a method to access another object that does provide the functionality.

It is not necessary for a `Façade` class to act as an impenetrable barrier separating client classes from the classes that implement an abstraction. It is sufficient, and sometimes better, for a `Façade` class to merely be a default way of accessing the functionality of the classes that implement an abstraction. If some clients need to directly access abstraction-implementing classes, then the `Façade` class should facilitate this with a method that returns a reference to the appropriate implementation object.

The point of the `Façade` class is to *allow* simple clients, not *require* them.

IMPLEMENTATION

A `Façade` class should provide a way for client objects to obtain a direct reference to an instance of abstraction-implementing classes that client objects may need to know about. However, there may be some abstraction-implementing classes that client classes have no legitimate reason to know about. The `Façade` class should hide these classes from client classes. One

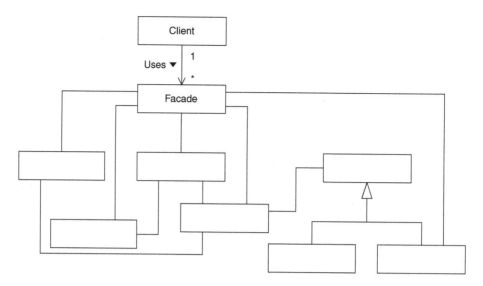

FIGURE 7.12 Façade pattern.

way to do that is to make these classes private inner classes of the Façade class.

Sometimes you want to vary the implementation classes that a façade object uses to accommodate variations on the abstraction being implemented. For example, returning to the email example under the Context heading, you may need a different set of classes to create MIME-, MAPI-, or Notes-compliant messages. Different sets of implementation classes usually require different Façade classes. You can hide the use of different Façade classes from client classes by applying the Interface pattern. Define an interface that all Façade classes for email creation must implement. Have client classes access the Façade class through an interface rather than directly.

CONSEQUENCES

☺ Interposing a façade class between the classes that implement an abstraction and their clients simplifies client classes by moving dependencies from client classes to the façade class. Clients of façade objects do not need to know about any of the classes behind the façade.

☺ Because the Façade pattern reduces or eliminates the coupling between a client class and the classes that implement an abstraction, it may be possible to change the classes that implement the abstraction without any impact on the client class.

JAVA API USAGE

The `java.net` `URL` class is an example of the Façade pattern. It provides access to the contents of URLs. A class can be a client of the `URL` class and use it to get the contents of a URL without being aware of the many classes that operate behind the façade provided by the `URL` class. On the other hand, to send data to a URL, the client of a `URL` object may call its `openConnection` method, which returns the `URLConnection` object that the `URL` object uses.

CODE EXAMPLE

The following is code for the `MessageCreator` class shown in the class diagram under the Context heading. Instances of the `MessageCreator` class are used to create and send email messages. It is shown here as a typical example of a `Façade` class.

```
public class MessageCreator {
    // Constants to indicate the type of message to create
    public final static int MIME = 1;
    public final static int MAPI = 2;
...
    private Hashtable headerFields = new Hashtable();
    private RichText messageBody;
    private Vector attachments = new Vector();
    private boolean signMessage;

    public MessageCreator(String to,
                          String from,
                          String subject) {
      this(to, from , subject, inferMessageType(to));
    } // Constructor(String, String, String)

    public MessageCreator(String to, String from,
                          String subject, int type) {
      headerFields.put("to", to);
      headerFields.put("from", from);
      headerFields.put("subject", subject);
      ...
    } // Constructor(String, String, String, int)

    /**
     * Set the contents of the message body.
     */
    public void setMessageBody(String messageBody) {
        setMessageBody(new RichTextString(messageBody));
    } // setMessageBody(String)

    /**
```

```
 * Set the contents of the message body.
 */
public void setMessageBody(RichText messageBody) {
    this.messageBody = messageBody;
} // setMessageBody(RichText)

/**
 * Add an attachment to the message
 */
public void addAttachment(Object attachment) {
    attachments.addElement(attachment);
} // addAttachment(Object)

/**
 * Set whether this message should be signed.  The default
 * is false.
 */
public void setSignMessage(boolean signFlag) {
    signMessage = signFlag;
} // setSignMessage(boolean)

/**
 * Set the value of a header field.
 */
public void setHeaderField(String name, String value) {
    headerFields.put(name.toLowerCase(), value);
} // setHeaderField(String, String)

/**
 * Send the message.
 */
public void send() {
    ...
} // send()

/**
 * Infer a message type from a destination email address.
 */
private static int inferMessageType(String address) {
    int type = 0;
...
    return type;
} // inferMessageType(String)

/**
 * Create a Security object appropriate for signing this
 * message.
 */
private Security createSecurity() {
    Security s = null;
    ...
    return s;
} // createSecurity()
```

```
/**
 * Create a MessageSender object appropriate for the type
 * of message being sent.
 */
private void createMessageSender(Message msg) {
   ...
} // createMessageSender(Message)
...
} // class MessageCreator
```

The Façade pattern places no demands on the classes that the Façade class uses. Since they contain nothing that contributes to the Façade pattern, their code is not shown.

RELATED PATTERNS

Interface.   The Interface pattern can be used with the Façade pattern to allow different façade classes to be used without client classes being aware of the different classes.

Law of Demeter.   A conceptual model that uses the Law of Demeter pattern (described in *Patterns in Java, Volume 2*) often gives rise to a design that follows the Façade pattern.

Adapter.   The Adapter pattern is used to allow client classes to treat a single object that does not implement an interface as an object that does implement the interface. The Façade pattern can be used to allow client classes to treat a group of objects as a single object that implements a particular interface.

Pure Fabrication.   The design of a façade class is an application of the Pure Fabrication pattern described in *Patterns in Java, Volume 2*.

Flyweight

This pattern was previously described in [GoF95].

SYNOPSIS

If instances of a class that contain the same information can be used inter-changeably, the Flyweight pattern allows a program to avoid the expense of multiple instances that contain the same information by sharing one instance.

CONTEXT

Suppose that you are writing a word processor. Figure 7.13 is a class diagram showing some basic classes you might use to represent a document.

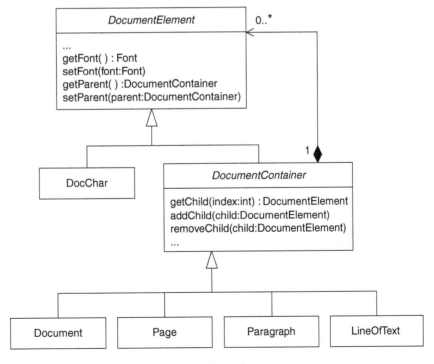

FIGURE 7.13 Document representation classes.

Figure 7.13's class organization includes the following classes:

- The `DocumentElement` class is the ultimate superclass of all classes used to represent a document. All subclasses of the `DocumentElement` class inherit methods to set and fetch their font.
- An instance of the `DocChar` class is used to represent each character in a document.
- The `DocumentContainer` class is the superclass of container classes `Document`, `Page`, `Paragraph`, and `LineOfText`.

You can specify the font of each character by calling the `setFont` method of the `DocChar` object that represents it. If the character's font is unspecified, then it uses its container's font. If its container's font has not been set, then the container uses *its* container's font, and so on.

Given this structure, one document that is a few pages long might contain tens of `Paragraph` objects that contain a few hundred `LineOfText` objects and thousands or tens of thousands of `DocChar` objects. Clearly, using this design will result in a program that uses a lot of memory to store characters.

It is possible to avoid the memory overhead of those many `DocChar` objects by having only one instance of each distinct `DocChar` object. The classes in Figure 7.13 use a `DocChar` object to represent each character in a document. To represent, "She saw her father," a `LineOfText` object uses `DocChar` objects, as shown in Figure 7.14.

As you can see, the characters "h," "e," " ," "a,"and "r" are used multiple times. In an entire document, all of the characters typically occur many times. It is possible to reorganize the objects so that one `DocChar` object is used to represent all occurrences of the same character. Figure 7.15 shows this organization.

To make the sharing of `DocChar` objects work, the `DocChar` objects cannot have any intrinsic attributes that are not common to every place the object is referenced. An intrinsic attribute is one whose value is stored with the object. This is distinct from an extrinsic attribute, whose value is stored outside of the object it applies to.

The class organization shown in Figure 7.13 shows a `DocChar` class whose instances can have an intrinsic font attribute. Those `Character` objects that do not have a font stored intrinsically use the font of their paragraph.

To make the sharing of `DocChar` objects work, the classes need to be reorganized so that `DocChar` objects that have their own font store them extrinsically. The class diagram in Figure 7.16 includes a `CharacterContext` class whose instances store extrinsic attributes for a range of characters.

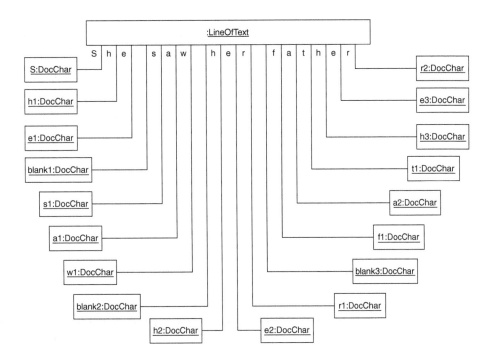

FIGURE 7.14 Unshared character objects.

In this organization, the DocCharFactory class is responsible for providing a DocChar object that represents a given character. Given the same character to represent, a DocCharFactory object's getDocChar method will always return the same DocChar object. Also, the DocumentContainer class defines the font methods rather than the DocumentElement class. All the concrete classes are subclasses of the DocumentContainer class, except for the DocChar class. This means that the DocChar class does not have an intrinsic font attribute. If the user wants to associate a font with a character or range of characters, then the program creates a CharacterContext object, as shown in Figure 7.17.

FORCES

☺ You have an application that uses a large number of similar objects.
☺ You want to reduce the memory overhead of having a large number of similar objects.
☺ The program does not rely on the object identity of any of the objects that you want it to share. When a program uses different objects in different contexts, it is possible to distinguish between the contexts

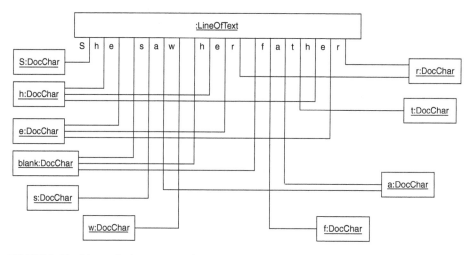

FIGURE 7.15 Shared character objects.

by the object identities of the objects. When different contexts share objects, then their object identities are no longer useful for distinguishing between contexts.

☺ Representing similar things with similar objects to represent each thing takes more memory than representing similar things with the

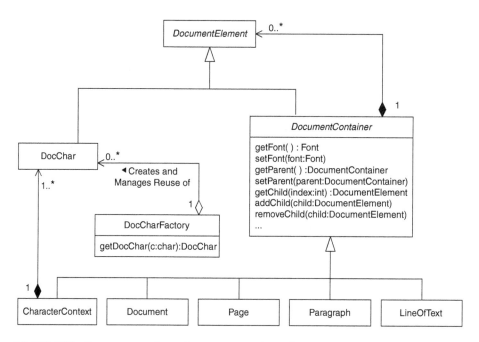

FIGURE 7.16 Document shared representation classes.

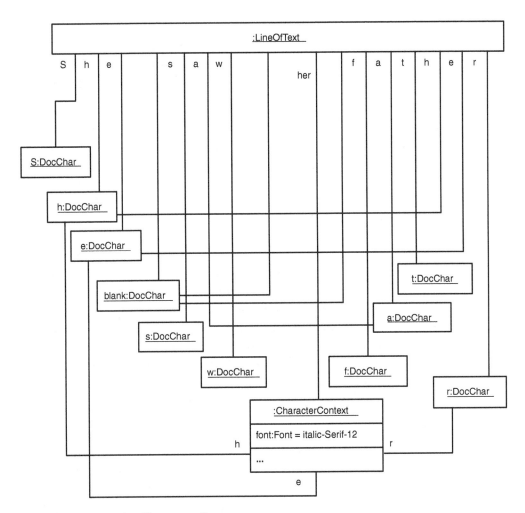

FIGURE 7.17 Font in CharacterContext.

same object. The more things that can be represented with the same object, the greater the memory savings.

SOLUTION

Figure 7.18 shows the general organization of classes for the Flyweight pattern.

Here are descriptions of the roles the classes that participate in the Flyweight pattern play:

AbstractFlyweight. The AbtractFlyweight class is the superclass of all other flyweight classes. It defines the methods common to

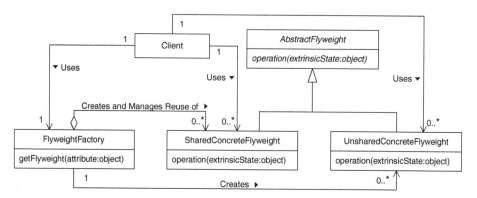

FIGURE 7.18 Flyweight pattern.

flyweight classes. These methods require access to extrinsic state information. These methods typically access extrinsic state information through parameters.

SharedConcreteFlyweight. Instances of classes in this role are sharable objects. If they contain any intrinsic state, it must be common to all of the entities that they represent. For example, the sharable DocChar objects from the example under the Context heading have the character that they represent as their intrinsic state.

UnsharedConcreteFlyweight. Instances of classes that participate in the UnsharedConcreteFlyweight role are not sharable. The Flyweight pattern does not require the sharing of objects. It simply allows the sharing of objects. If there are unsharable objects that are instances of the AbstractFlyweight class, then they will be instances of different subclasses of the AbstractFlyweight class than objects that are sharable.

FlyweightFactory. Instances of FlyweightFactory classes provide instances of the AbstractFlyweight class to client objects. If a client object asks a FlyweightFactory object to provide an instance of an UnsharedConcreteFlyweight class, then it simply creates the instance. However, if a client object asks a FlyweightFactory object to provide an instance of a SharedConcreteFlyweight class, it first checks to see if it previously created a similar object. If it did, then it provides the previously created object to the client. Otherwise, it creates a new object and provides that to the client.

Client. Instances of classes in this role use flyweight objects.

If there is only one class in the `SharedConcreteFlyweight` role, then it may be unnecessary to have any classes in the role of `AbstractFlyweight` or `UnsharedConcreteFlyweight`.

IMPLEMENTATION

There is a trade-off to make between the number of attributes you make extrinsic and the number of flyweight objects needed at runtime. The more attributes you make extrinsic, the fewer flyweight objects will be needed. The more attributes you make intrinsic, the less time it will take objects to access their attributes.

For example, in the document representation example, if the user makes a range of characters italic, the program creates a separate `CharacterContext` object to contain the extrinsic font attribute for the `DocChar` objects that represent those characters. An alternative would be to allow the font attribute to be intrinsic to `DocChar` objects. If the font attribute is intrinsic, then `DocChar` objects will spend less time accessing their font attribute. Letting the font attribute be intrinsic also means that the program will need a `DocChar` object for each combination of character and font that it has to represent.

CONSEQUENCES

☺ Using shared flyweight objects can drastically reduce the number of objects in memory. There is a price to pay for the reduced memory consumption:

The Flyweight pattern makes a program more complex. The major sources of additional complexity are providing flyweight objects with their extrinsic state and managing the reuse of flyweight objects.

The Flyweight pattern can increase the runtime of a program because it takes more effort for an object to access extrinsic state than intrinsic state.

☹ Usually it is possible to distinguish between entities by the objects that represent them. The Flyweight pattern makes that impossible, because it results in multiple entities being represented by the same object.

☹ Shared flyweight objects cannot contain parent pointers.

☹ Because of the complexity that the Flyweight pattern adds and the constraints it places on the organization of classes, the Flyweight pattern should be considered an optimization to be used after the rest of a design is worked out.

JAVA API USAGE

Java uses the Flyweight pattern to manage the String objects used to represent string literals. If there is more than one string literal in a program that consists of the same sequence of characters, Java uses the same String object to represent all of those string literals.

The String class's intern method is responsible for managing the String objects used to represent string literals.

CODE EXAMPLE

The following is some of the code that implements the class diagram in Figure 7.16. Some of the classes don't contain any code that is of interest with respect to the Flyweight pattern, so code for those classes is not presented. For example, there is no code of interest in the DocumentElement class. On the other hand, the DocumentContainer class defines some methods inherited by all of the container classes that are used to represent a document.

```java
abstract class DocumentContainer extends DocumentElement {
    // Collection of this object's children
    private Vector children = new Vector();

    // This is the font associated with this object.  If the
    // font variable is null, then this object's font will
    // be inherited through the container hierarchy from an
    // enclosing object.
    private Font font;

    DocumentContainer parent; // this object's container

    /**
     * Return the child of this object at the given position.
     */
    public DocumentElement getChild(int index) {
       return (DocumentElement)children.elementAt(index);
    } // getChild(int)

    /**
     * Make the given DocumentElement a child of this object.
     */
    public synchronized void addChild(DocumentElement child) {
       synchronized (child) {
           children.addElement(child);
           if (child instanceof DocumentContainer)
             ((DocumentContainer)child).parent = this;
       } // synchronized
    } // addChild(DocumentElement)
```

```
/**
 * Make the given DocumentElement NOT a child of this
 * object.
 */
public
synchronized void removeChild(DocumentElement child) {
    synchronized (child) {
        if (child instanceof DocumentContainer
            && this == ((DocumentContainer)child).parent)
          ((DocumentContainer)child).parent = null;
        children.removeElement(child);
    } // synchronized
} // removeChild(DocumentElement)

/**
 * Return this object's parent or null if it has no parent.
 */
public DocumentContainer getParent() {
    return parent;
} // getParent()

/**
 * Return the Font associated with this object.  If no
 * Font is associated with this object, return its
 * parent's Font. If no Font is associated with this
 * object's parent, then return null.
 */
public Font getFont() {
    if (font != null)
      return font;
    else if (parent != null)
      return parent.getFont();
    else
      return null;
} // getFont()

/**
 * Associate a Font with this object.
 */
public void setFont(Font font) {
    this.font = font;
} // setFont(Font)
...
} // class DocumentContainer
```

The methods shown for the DocumentContainer class manage the state of all the document container classes including the CharacterContext class. Using these inherited methods, the CharacterContext class is able to manage the extrinsic state of DocChar objects even though it doesn't declare any of its own methods for that purpose. The following is the code for the DocChar class that represents characters in a document.

```
class DocChar extends DocumentElement {
    private char character;

    DocChar (char c) {
        character = c;
    } // Constructor(char)
...
    /**
     * Return the character that this object represents
     */
    public char getChar() {
        return character;
    } // getChar()

    /**
     * This method returns a unique value that determines
     * where it is stored internally in a hash table.
     */
    public int hashCode() {
        return getChar();
    } // hashCode()

    /**
     * Redefine equals so that two DocChar objects are
     * considered equal if they represent the same character.
     */
    public boolean equals(Object o) {
        // Call getChar rather than access character directly
        // so that this method will respect any alternate way
        // a subclass has of providing the character it
        // represents.
        return (o instanceof DocChar
                && ((DocChar)o).getChar() == getChar());
    } // equals(Object)
} // class DocChar
```

Finally, here is the code for the DocCharFactory class, which is responsible for the sharing of DocChar objects:

```
class DocCharFactory {
    private MutableDocChar myChar = new MutableDocChar();

    /**
     * Collection of previously created DocChar objects.
     */
    private HashMap docCharPool = new HashMap();

    /**
     * Return a DocChar object that represents the given character.
     */
    synchronized DocChar getDocChar(char c) {
        myChar.setChar(c);
```

```
        DocChar thisChar = (DocChar)docCharPool.get(myChar);
        if (thisChar == null) {
            thisChar = new DocChar(c);
            docCharPool.put(thisChar, thisChar);
        } // if
        return thisChar;
    } // getDocChar(char)
```

To allow lookups of DocChar objects in a HashMap or similar collection, you need a DocChar object that represents the same character as the DocChar object you want to find in the collection. Creating a DocChar object to perform each lookup would mean that we are still creating a DocChar object for each character in the document. Though these DocChar objects would get garbage-collected because they are not referenced after being used to do the lookup, it would be better to avoid creating them in the first place.

An alternative to creating a DocChar object for each lookup is to reuse the same DocChar object, changing the character that it represents for each lookup. The problem with changing the character a DocChar object represents is that DocChar objects are immutable. There is no way to change the character that a DocChar object represents.

The DocCharFactory class gets around this problem by using this private subclass of DocChar that does provide a way to change the character that it represents:

```
    private static class MutableDocChar extends DocChar {
        private char character;

        MutableDocChar() {
            // It doesn't matter what we pass to super.
            super('\u0000');
        } // Constructor(char)

        /**
         * Return the character that this object represents.
         */
        public char getChar() {
            return character;
        } // getChar()

        /**
         * Set the character that this object represents.
         */
        public void setChar(char c) {
            character = c;
        } // setChar(char)
    } // class MutableDocChar
} // class DocCharFactory
```

RELATED PATTERNS

Composite.   The Flyweight pattern is often combined with the Composite pattern to represent the leaf nodes of a hierarchical structure with shared objects.

Factory Method.   The Flyweight pattern uses the Factory Method pattern to create new flyweight objects.

Cache Management.   The implementation of a `FlyweightFactory` class may use a cache.

Immutable.   Shared flyweight objects are often immutable.

Dynamic Linkage

SYNOPSIS

Allow a program, upon request, to load and use arbitrary classes that implement a known interface.

CONTEXT

Suppose you are writing software for a new kind of smart food processor that can be fed raw ingredients and by slicing, dicing, mixing, boiling, baking, frying, and stirring is able to produce cooked, ready-to-eat food. On a mechanical level, the new food processor is a very sophisticated piece of equipment. However, a crucial part of the food processor is a selection of programs to prepare different kinds of foods. A program that can turn flour, water, yeast, and other ingredients into different kinds of bread is very different from a program that can stir-fry shrimp to exactly the right texture. The food processor will be required to run a great variety of programs that allow it to produce a great variety of foods. Because of the large variety of programs that will be required, it is not possible to build them all into the food processor. Instead, the food processor will load its programs from a CD-ROM or similar medium.

In order for these dynamically loaded programs and the food processor's operating environment to work with each other, they will need a way to call each other's methods. The class diagram in Figure 7.19 shows an arrangement of classes and interfaces to allow this.

The organization shown in Figure 7.19 allows an object in the food processor environment to call methods of the top-level object in a food processor program by calling the methods of its superclass. It also allows the top-level object to call the methods of the food processor environment object through the `FoodProcessorEnvironmentIF` interface that it implements. Figure 7.20 is a collaboration diagram showing these classes working together.

Figure 7.20 shows the initial steps that occur when the food processor's operating environment is asked to run a program:

1.1 The environment calls the `forName` method of the class named `Class`, passing it the name of the program to run. The `forName` method finds the `Class` object having the same name as the

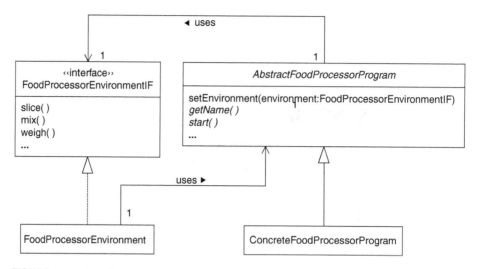

FIGURE 7.19 Food processor program class diagram.

program. If necessary, it loads the class from the CD-ROM. The `forName` method concludes by returning the `Class` object that encapsulates the top-level class of the program.

1.2 The environment creates an instance of the top-level class of the program. The diagram names that instance `program`.

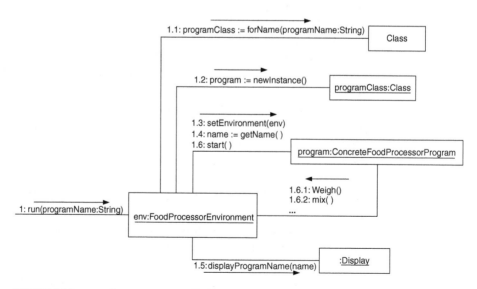

FIGURE 7.20 Food processor collaboration.

1.3 The environment passes a reference to itself to the `program` object's `setEnvironment` method. Passing this reference to the program allows the program to call the environment's methods.

1.4 The environment gets the program's name from the program.

1.5 The environment displays the program's name.

1.6 The environment starts the program running.

1.6.1 The program weighs its ingredients.

1.6.2 The program mixes its ingredients.

The program continues executing additional steps that are beyond the scope of the drawing.

FORCES

☺ A program must be able to load and use arbitrary classes that it has no prior knowledge of.

☺ Instances of a loaded class must be able to call back to the program that loaded it.

☹ Adding classes to a program that the program was not distributed with poses a security risk. There is also a risk of a version mismatch between the class and the program.

SOLUTION

Figure 7.21 is a class diagram showing the roles of interfaces and classes that participate in the Dynamic Linkage pattern.

Here are descriptions of the roles classes and interfaces play in the Dynamic Linkage pattern.

EnvironmentIF.   An interface in this role declares the environment's methods that a loaded class can call.

Environment.   A class in this role is part of the environment that loads a `ConcreteLoadableClass` class. It implements the `EnvironmentIF` interface. A reference to an instance of this class is passed to instances of the `ConcreteLoadableClass` class, so that they can call the methods of the `Environment` object declared by the `EnvironmentIF` interface.

AbstractLoadableClass.   Any class that is the top-level class of a food processor program must be a subclass of a class in the `AbstractLoadableClass` role. A class in this role is expected to

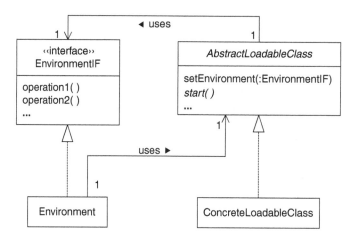

FIGURE 7.21 Dynamic linkage pattern.

declare a number of other, usually abstract, methods in addition to the two that are shown. Here is a description of these methods:

- There should be a method with a name like `setEnvironment`, which allows instances of subclasses of `AbstractLoadableClass` to be passed a reference to an instance of a class that implements the `EnvironmentIF` interface. The purpose of this method is to allow `AbstractLoadableClass` objects to call the methods of an `Environment` object.

- The environment calls another method, typically named `start`, to tell an instance of a loaded class to start doing whatever it is supposed to be doing.

ConcreteLoadableClass.   Classes in this role are subclasses of `AbstractLoadableClass` that can be dynamically loaded.

IMPLEMENTATION

The Dynamic Linkage pattern, as presented, requires the environment to know about the `AbstractLoadableClass` class and that the loaded class knows about the `EnvironmentIF` interface. In cases where less structure is needed, other mechanisms for interoperation are possible. For example, JavaBeans uses a combination of reflection classes and naming conventions to allow other classes to infer how to interact with a bean.

Another requirement of the Dynamic Linkage pattern is that the `Environment` class somehow knows the name of a class that it wants to load. The mechanism for discovering the name varies with the application.

In some cases, names may be hardwired. For the food processor example, a reasonable mechanism would be for a CD or other distribution medium to contain a directory of programs. The food processor would display the directory of programs as a menu, allowing the user to pick one.

INCOMPATIBLE CLASSES

Some implementations of the Dynamic Linkage pattern may need to deal with the possibility of incompatible versions of the same class being used by different dynamically loaded classes. For example, suppose that programs for making lasagna sheets and wonton wrappers come on different CDs and both use a helper class named Fu. However, the two classes named Fu are incompatible. Suppose the food processor first runs the lasagna program and then tries to run the wonton wrapper program. If the wonton wrapper class is given the lasagna Fu class when it is loaded, it will not work.

A strategy for avoiding this problem is to ensure that all of the supporting classes that are implicitly dynamically loaded along with an explicitly dynamically loaded class are not used by any other explicitly dynamically loaded class. You can implement that strategy by using a different ClassLoader object for each dynamically loaded class. For example, some browsers use a different class loader for loading different applets. This prevents classes loaded as part of one applet from being used as part of another.

SECURITY RISK

A program that dynamically loads classes and calls their methods poses some security risks. You would like to assume that the loaded classes will behave as intended and be generally well behaved. However, there is a possibility that this will not be the case. Here are some of the potential risks:

- The class may do something that denies the use of the environment for other purposes. One of its methods that is supposed to return in a reasonable amount of time may never return. If the environment is multithreaded, the class may consume CPU cycles, memory, or other resources that are needed for other purposes.
- The class may do something that violates the integrity of its environment. This can take many forms.

A detailed description of how to deal with these issues is beyond the scope of this book. Here are a few high-level remarks to get you started in the right direction.

The first issue to resolve is the magnitude of the security risk in question. If the likelihood of anything going wrong is sufficiently low or the consequences are sufficiently low, then it is not worth taking any measures to lessen the likelihood or consequences of a security problem. On the other hand, if the likelihood or consequences are sufficiently great, then it is worth taking all possible measures.

The next issue is how likely it is that a particular class will cause a security problem. This is often referred to as *trust*. The first question related to trust is whether or not a class will be allowed into an environment. Java's class loading mechanism is organized so that the loading of classes is the responsibility of a subclass of the abstract class `java.lang` `.ClassLoader`. The documentation supplied for this class describes the class loading mechanism in some detail.

A common strategy for determining the level of trust given to a class is to base it on the level of trust granted to the entity that created the class. You can determine where a class came from if it is accompanied by a certificate containing the digital signature of the entity that created the class. Typically, classes are distributed in `.jar` files that are digitally signed by their creator.

Java has an elaborate mechanism for controlling access to methods based on trust and permissions. It is described in a document called "Java 2 Platform Security Architecture." This document is part of the documentation that Sun provides for the Java 2 SDK.

Correctly using the mechanisms provided by the security architecture will make it unlikely that classes from sources that you do not trust will be able to do things that they are not supposed to do. An additional measure you can take to ensure that even trusted classes are able to access only those things that they are supposed to is to use the protection proxy class described in *Patterns in Java, Volume 3*.

CONSEQUENCES

- ☺ Subclasses of the `AbstractLoadableClass` class can be dynamically loaded.
- ☺ The operating environment and the loaded classes do not need any specific foreknowledge of each other.
- ● Dynamic linkage increases the total amount of time it takes for a program to load all of the classes that it uses. However, it does have the effect of spreading out, over time, the overhead of loading classes. This can make an interactive program seem more responsive. The Virtual Proxy pattern can be used for that purpose.
- ☹ Using the Dynamic Linkage pattern poses a security risk.

JAVA API USAGE

Web browsers use the Dynamic Linkage pattern to run applets. Figure 7.22 is a class diagram showing the relationship between applet and browser.

The browser environment accesses a subclass of `Applet` that it loads as an instance of the `Applet` class. Loaded applet subclasses access the browser environment through the `AppletStub` interface.

CODE EXAMPLE

The example is the code that implements the food processor design shown under the Context heading. First, here is the interface for the food processor environment:

```
public interface FoodProcessorEnvironmentIF {
    /**
     * Make a slice of food of the given width.
     */
    public void slice(int width) ;

    /**
     * Mix food at the given speed.
     */
    public void mix(int speed) ;

    /**
     * Weigh food.
     * @return the weight in ounces.
     */
    public double weight() ;
...
} // interface FoodProcessorEnvironmentIF
```

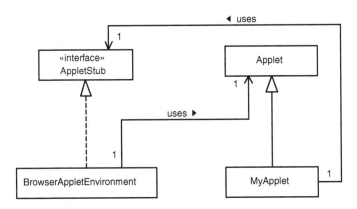

FIGURE 7.22 Applets and browsers.

Here is the abstract class that is the superclass for all top-level program classes:

```
public abstract class AbstractFoodProcessorProgram {
    private FoodProcessorEnvironmentIF environment;

    /**
     * The food processor environment passes a reference to
     * itself to this method. That allows instances of
     * subclasses of this class to call the methods of the
     * food processor environment object that implements the
     * FoodProcessorEnvironmentIF interface.
     */
    public void setEnvironment(
                    FoodProcessorEnvironmentIF environment) {
        this.environment = environment;
    } // setEnvironment(FoodProcessorEnvironmentIF)

    /**
     * Allow subclasses to fetch the reference to the
     * environment.
     */
    protected FoodProcessorEnvironmentIF getEnvironment() {
        return environment;
    } // getEnvironment()

    /**
     * Return the name of this food processing program object.
     */
    public abstract String getName() ;

    /**
     * A call to this method tells a food processing program
     * to start doing whatever it is supposed to be doing.
     */
    public abstract void start() ;
...
} // class AbstractFoodProcessorProgram
```

Here is the class that is responsible for the food processor environment being able to run programs; it uses a ClassLoader object to manage the classes that it loads.

```
public class FoodProcessorEnvironment
                    implements FoodProcessorEnvironmentIF {
    private static final URL[] classPath; // URL for programs.
    static {
        try {
            classPath = new URL[]{new URL("file:///bin")};
        } catch (java.net.MalformedURLException e) {
            throw new ExceptionInInitializerError(e);
        } // try
```

```
        } // static

        /**
         * Make a slice of food of the given width.
         */
        public void slice(int width) {
...
        } // slice(int)

        /**
         * Mix food at the given speed.
         */
        public void mix(int speed) {
...
        } // mix(int)

        /**
         * Weigh food.
         * @return the weight in ounces.
         */
        public double weigh() {
            double weight = 0.0;
...
            return weight;
        } // weight()
...
        /**
         * Run the named program.
         */
        void run(String programName) {
            // Create a ClassLoader to load the program classes.
            // When those classes are no longer used, they can be
            // garbage-collected when their ClassLoader is garbage-
            // collected.
            URLClassLoader classLoader;
            classLoader = new URLClassLoader(classPath);
            Class programClass;
            try {
                programClass = classLoader.loadClass(programName);
            } catch (ClassNotFoundException e) {
                // Not found
...
                return;
            } // try
            AbstractFoodProcessorProgram program;
            try {
                program = (AbstractFoodProcessorProgram)
                                    programClass.newInstance();
            } catch (Exception e) {
                // Unable to run
                ...
                return;
            } // try
```

```
        program.setEnvironment(this);
        display(program.getName());
        program.start();
    } // run(String)
    ...
} // class FoodProcessorEnvironment
```

Finally, here is sample code for a top-level program class:

```
public class ConcreteFoodProcessorProgram
            extends AbstractFoodProcessorProgram {
    /**
     * Return the name of this food processing program object.
     */
    public String getName() { return "Chocolate Milk"; }

    /**
     * A call to this method tells a food processing program
     * to start doing whatever it is supposed to be doing.
     */
    public void start() {
        double weight = getEnvironment().weigh();
        if (weight > 120.0 && weight < 160.0)
          getEnvironment().mix(4);
        ...
    } // start()
    ...
} // class ConcreteFoodProcessorProgram
```

RELATED PATTERNS

Virtual Proxy.   Implementations of the Virtual Proxy pattern sometimes use the Dynamic Linkage pattern to load the class that it needs to create its underlying object.

Protection Proxy.   The Protection Proxy pattern (described in *Patterns in Java, Volume 3*) is sometimes used with the Dynamic Linkage pattern to minimize security risks.

Virtual Proxy

This pattern was previously described in [Larman98].

SYNOPSIS

If an object is expensive to instantiate and may not be needed, it may be advantageous to postpone its instantiation until it is clear the object is needed. The Virtual Proxy pattern hides from its clients the fact that an object may not yet exist, by having them access the object indirectly through a proxy object that implements the same interface as the object that may not exist. The technique of delaying the instantiation of an object until it is actually needed is sometimes called *lazy instantiation*.

CONTEXT

Suppose you are part of a team that has written a large Java applet for a company that operates a chain of home improvement warehouses. The applet allows people to buy everything that the warehouses sell through a Web page. In addition to offering a catalog, it includes a variety of assistants to allow customers to decide just what they need. These assistants include:

- A kitchen cabinet assistant that allows a customer to design a set of kitchen cabinets and then automatically order all of the pieces necessary to assemble the cabinets.
- An assistant to determine how much lumber a customer needs to build a wood deck.
- An assistant to determine the quantity of broadloom carpet needed for a particular floor plan and the best way to cut it.

There are more assistants, but they are not the point of this discussion. The point is that the applet is very large. Due to its size, it takes an unacceptably long amount of time for a browser to download the applet over a modem connection.

One way to reduce the time needed to download the applet is not to download any of the assistants until they are needed. The Virtual Proxy pattern provides a way to postpone downloading part of an applet in a way that is transparent to the rest of the applet. The idea is that instead of having the rest of the applet directly access the classes that constitute an assistant, they will access those classes indirectly through a proxy class. The proxy classes are specially coded so that they don't contain any static references[1] to the class they are a proxy for. This means that when the proxy classes are loaded, there are no references to the class they are a proxy for. If the rest of the applet refers only to the proxies and not to the classes that implement assistants, Java will not automatically load the assistants.

When a method of a proxy is called, it first ensures that the classes that implement the assistant are loaded and instantiated. It then calls the corresponding method through an interface. Figure 7.23 is a class diagram showing this organization.

Figure 7.23 shows the main portion of the applet referring to a CabinetAssistantProxy class that implements the CabinetAssistantIF interface. The main portion of the applet contains no references to the classes that implement the cabinet assistant. When they are needed, the CabinetAssistantProxy class ensures that the classes that implement the cabinet assistant are loaded and instantiated. The code that accomplishes this is listed under the Code Example heading.

FORCES

☺ There is a class that is very time consuming to instantiate.

☺ It may not always be necessary to instantiate the class.

☺ If there are a number of classes whose instances will not be needed until an indefinite amount of time has passed, instantiating them all at once may introduce a noticeable delay in the program's response. Postponing their instantiation until they are needed may spread out the time that the program spends instantiating them and appears to make the program more responsive.

☺ Managing the delayed instantiation of classes should not be a burden placed on the class's clients. Therefore, the delayed instantiation of a class should be transparent to its clients.

---

[1] By static reference, I mean a reference to a class that a compiler will recognize at compile time. For example

```
Foo myFoo;
```

is an example of a static reference to a class named Foo. Contrast this static reference to Foo with this example:

```
Class clazz = Class.forName("Foo");
```

In this example the compiler sees a string that happens to contain the name of a class. The string is not recognized as the name of a class until runtime, when the forName method is called.

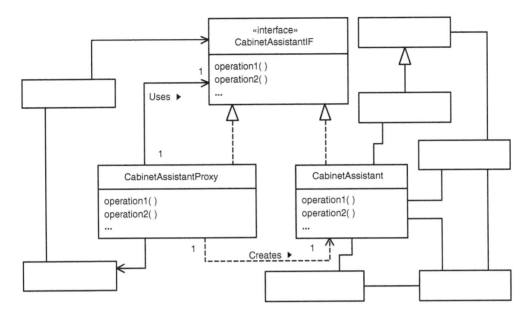

FIGURE 7.23 Cabinet assistant proxy.

☹ Sometimes the best way to ensure the good performance of a program is to prolong its initialization, so that all objects that are expensive to instantiate are created when the program starts. This can prevent having to spend time initializing things later on.

SOLUTION

Figure 7.24 is a class diagram showing the organization of classes that participate in the Virtual Proxy pattern.

Here is an explanation of the roles played by the interface and classes of the Virtual Proxy pattern:

Service.   A Service class supplies the top-level logic for a service that it provides. When you create an instance of it, it creates the other objects that it needs. These classes are indicated in the diagram as ServiceHelper1, ServiceHelper2, and so on.

Client.   A class in this role uses the service provided by the Service class. Client classes never directly use a Service class. Instead, they use a ServiceProxy class that provides the functionality of the Service class. Not directly using a Service class keeps client classes insensitive to whether the instance of the Service class that Client objects indirectly use already exists.

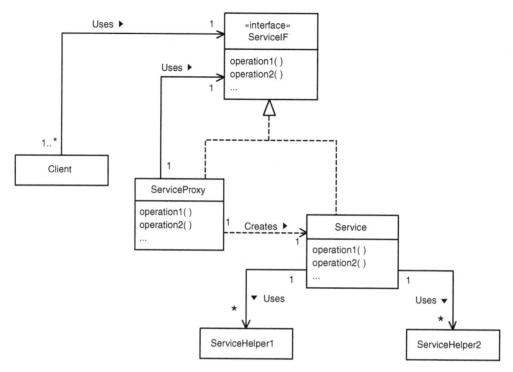

FIGURE 7.24 Virtual Proxy pattern.

ServiceProxy. The purpose of the ServiceProxy class is to delay creating instances of the Service class until they are actually needed.

A ServiceProxy class provides indirection between Client classes and a Service class. The indirection hides from Client objects the fact that when a ServiceProxy object is created, the corresponding Service object does not exist and the Service class may not even have been loaded.

A ServiceProxy object is responsible for creating the corresponding Service object. A ServiceProxy object creates the corresponding Service object the first time it is asked to perform an operation that requires the existence of the Service object.

A ServiceProxy class is specially coded to obtain access to the Service class through a dynamic reference. Usually, classes reference other classes through static references. A static reference simply consists of the name of a class appearing in an appropriate place in some source code. When a compiler sees that kind of reference, it generates output that causes the other class to automatically be loaded along with the class that contains the reference.

The Virtual Proxy pattern prevents the loading of the `Service` class and related classes along with the rest of the program by ensuring that the rest of the program does not contain any static references to the `Service` class. Instead, the rest of the program refers to the `Service` class through the `ServiceProxy` class and the `ServiceProxy` class refers to the `Service` class through a dynamic reference.

A dynamic reference consists of a method call that passes a string, containing the name of a class, to a method that loads the class if it isn't loaded and returns a reference to the class. Typically, the method call is to the static method `java.lang.class.forName`. Because the name of the class only appears inside of a string, compilers are not aware that the class will be referenced and so they do not generate any output that causes that class to be loaded.

ServiceIF.   A `ServiceProxy` class creates an instance of the `Service` class through method calls that do not require static references to the `Service` class. A `ServiceProxy` class also calls methods of the `Service` class without having any static references to the `Service` class. It calls methods of the `Service` class by taking advantage of the fact that the `Service` class implements the `ServiceIF` interface.

The `ServiceIF` interface is an interface that declares all methods that the `Service` class implements and are needed by the `ServiceProxy` class. A `ServiceProxy` object treats the reference to the `Service` object that it creates as a reference to a `ServiceIF` object. That `Service` class uses static references to the `ServiceIF` interface to call methods of `Service` objects. No static references to the `Service` class are required.

IMPLEMENTATION

SHARED SERVICE OBJECTS

The solution assumes that when a `ServiceProxy` object is first asked to perform an operation, it creates a `Service` object and will then continuously have a `Service` object associated with it. However, if the `Service` object consumes a lot of memory or some other resource while it exists, it may be a bad thing to have as many `Service` objects as you have `ServiceProxy` objects.

If the Service objects are not stateful and are interchangeable, then consider using the Object Pool pattern to minimize the number of Service objects that you create. The idea is that when a ServiceProxy object needs a Service object to perform an operation, it gets the Service object from an object pool. When the Service object finishes the requested operation, the ServiceProxy object returns it to the object pool. This allows you to have many ServiceProxy objects but only a few Service objects.

DEFERRED CLASS LOADING

In many cases, the class accessed through a virtual proxy uses other classes that the rest of the program does not use. Because of this relationship, these classes are not loaded until after the class accessed by the virtual proxy is loaded. If it is important that these classes are not loaded until the class accessed by the virtual proxy is loaded, then a problem may occur when the program is in the maintenance phase of its life cycle. A maintenance programmer may add a direct reference to one of these classes without realizing the performance implications. Unless the quality control testing for the program includes performance tests, the problem is likely to go unnoticed until the program's users complain.

You can lessen the likelihood of this happening by making the relationship between the classes explicit. You can make the relationship explicit by putting the classes in question in a package with only the class used by the proxy being visible outside the package. Figure 7.25 shows this organization.

CONSEQUENCES

- ☺ Classes accessed by the rest of a program exclusively through a virtual proxy are not loaded until they are needed.
- ☺ Objects accessed through a virtual proxy are not created until they are needed.
- ☺ Classes that use the proxy do not need to be aware of whether the Service class is loaded, of whether an instance of it exists, or that the class even exists.
- ● All classes other than the proxy class must access the services of the Service class indirectly through the proxy. This is critical. If just one class accesses the Service class directly, then the Service class will be loaded before it is needed. This is a quiet sort of bug. It generally affects performance but not function, so it is hard to track down.

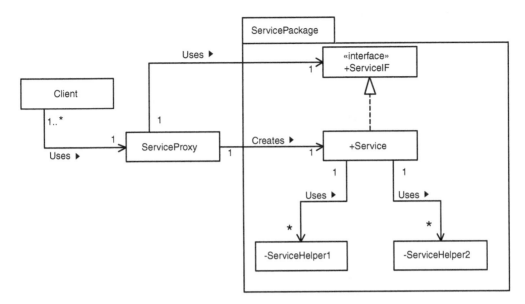

FIGURE 7.25 Relationship made explicit by using a package.

CODE EXAMPLE

To conclude the example begun under the Context heading, here is some of the code that implements the cabinet assistant and its proxy. First, the relevant code for the CabinetAssistant class:

```
/**
 * This is a service class that is used by a virtual proxy.
 * The noteworthy aspect of this class is that it implements an
 * interface written to declare the methods of this class
 * rather than the other way around.
 */
public class CabinetAssistant implements CabinetAssistantIF {
    public CabinetAssistant(String s) {
...
    } // Constructor(String)
...
    public void operation1() {
...
    } // operation1()

    public void operation2() {
...
    } // operation2()
} // class CabinetAssistant
```

The CabinetAssistantIF interface simply declares the methods defined by the CabinetAssistant class:

```
public interface CabinetAssistantIF {
    public void operation1();
    public void operation2();
...
} // interface CabinetAssistantIF
```

Finally, here is the code for the CabinetAssistantProxy class, where all of the interesting things happen:

```
public class CabinetAssistantProxy
                                implements CabinetAssistantIF {
    private CabinetAssistantIF assistant = null;

    // for assistant object's constructor
    private String myParam;

    public CabinetAssistantProxy(String s) {
        myParam = s;
    } // constructor(String)

    /**
     * Get the CabinetAssistant object that is used to
     * implement operations.  This method creates it if it did
     * not exist.
     */
    private CabinetAssistantIF getCabinetAssistant() {
        if (assistant == null) {
            try {
                // Get the class object that represents
                // the Assistant class.
                Class clazz;
                clazz = Class.forName("CabinetAssistant");

                // Get a constructor object to access the
                // CabinetAssistant class's constructor that
                // takes a single string argument.
                Constructor constructor;

                // Get the constructor object to create the
                // CabinetAssistant object.
                Class[] formalArgs;
                params = new Class [] { String.class };
                constructor = clazz.getConstructor(params);

                // Use the constructor object.
                Object[] actuals = new Object[] { myParam };
                Assistant = (CabinetAssistantIF)
                            constructor.newInstance(actuals);
            } catch (Exception e) {
            } // try
            if (assistant == null) {
                // Deal with failure to create
                // CabinetAssistant object
```

```
                    throw new RuntimeException();
              } // if
        } // if
        return assistant;
   } // getCabinetAssistant()

   public void operation1() {
        getCabinetAssistant().operation1();
   } // operation1()

   public void operation2() {
        getCabinetAssistant().operation2();
   } // operation2()
...
} // class CabinetAssistantProxy
```

RELATED PATTERNS

Façade. The Façade pattern can be used with the Virtual Proxy pattern to minimize the number of proxy classes that are needed.

Proxy. The Virtual Proxy pattern is a specialized version of the Proxy pattern.

Object Pool. You can use the Object Pool pattern to allow many ServiceProxy objects to share and reuse a small number of Service objects.

Decorator

The Decorator pattern is also known as the Wrapper pattern. This pattern was previously described in [GoF95].

SYNOPSIS

The Decorator pattern extends the functionality of an object in a way that is transparent to its clients, by implementing the same interface as the original class and delegating operations to the original class.

CONTEXT

Suppose you are responsible for maintaining the software of a security system that controls physical access to a building. Its basic architecture is that a card reader or other data entry device captures some identifying information and passes the information to the object that controls a door. If the object that controls the door is satisfied with the information, it unlocks the door. Figure 7.26 is a collaboration diagram showing this.

Suppose that you need to integrate this access control mechanism with a surveillance system. A surveillance system typically has more cameras connected to it than it has TV monitors. Most of the TV monitors cycle through the images from different cameras. They show a picture from each camera for a few seconds and then move on to the next camera for which the monitor is responsible. There are rules about how the surveillance system is supposed to be set up to ensure its effectiveness. For this discussion, the relevant rules are:

- At least one camera covers each doorway connected to the access control system.
- Each monitor is responsible for not more than one camera that covers an access-controlled doorway. The reason for this is that if there are

FIGURE 7.26 Basic physical access control.

multiple cameras viewing a doorway, then the failure of a single monitor should not prevent the images from all of the cameras on that doorway from being seen.

The specific integration requirement is that when an object that controls a door receives a request for the door to open, the monitors responsible for the cameras pointed at the doorway display that doorway. Your first thought about satisfying this requirement is that you will enhance a class or write some subclasses. Then you discover the relationships shown in Figure 7.27.

There are three different kinds of doors installed and two different kinds of surveillance monitors in use. You could resolve the situation by writing two subclasses of each of the door controller classes, but you would rather not have to write six classes. Instead, you use the Decorator pattern to solve the problem by delegation rather than inheritance.

You write two new classes called `DoorControllerWrapperA` and `DoorControllerWrapperB`. The organization of these classes is shown in Figure 7.28. Both these classes implement the `DoorControllerIF` interface. They inherit the implementation of the `DoorControllerIF` interface from their abstract superclass `AbstractDoorControllerWrapper`.

The `AbstractDoorControllerWrapper` class implements all the methods of the `DoorController` interface with implementations that simply call the corresponding method of another object that implements the `DoorController` interface. The `DoorControllerA` and `DoorControllerB` classes are concrete wrapper classes. They extend the behavior of the `requestOpen` implementation that they inherit to also ask a surveillance monitor to display its view of that doorway. Figure 7.29 is a collaboration diagram that shows this.

This approach allows doorways viewed by multiple cameras to be handled by simply putting multiple wrappers in front of the `DoorControllerIF` object.

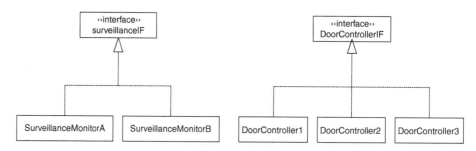

FIGURE 7.27 Security system classes.

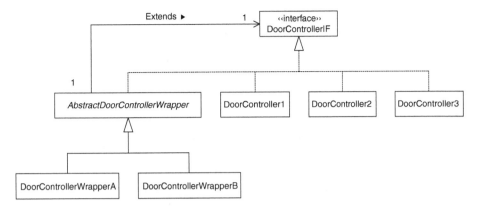

FIGURE 7.28 Door controller classes.

FORCES

☺ There is a need to extend the functionality of a class, but there are reasons not to extend it through inheritance.

☺ There is the need to dynamically extend the functionality of an object and possibly also to withdraw the extended functionality.

SOLUTION

Figure 7.30 is a class diagram showing the general structure of the Decorator pattern.

Here are descriptions of the roles that classes and interfaces play in the Decorator pattern.

AbstractServiceIF. An interface in this role is implemented by all service objects that may potentially be extended through the

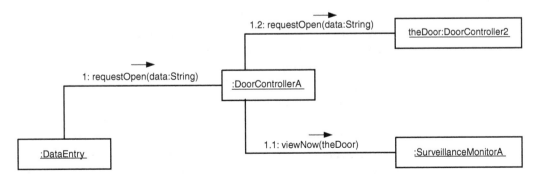

FIGURE 7.29 Door surveillance collaboration.

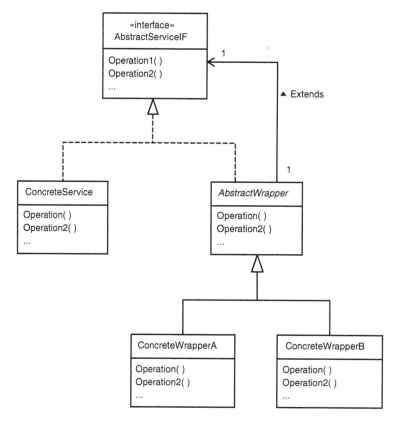

FIGURE 7.30 Decorator pattern.

Decorator pattern. Classes whose instances can be used to dynamically extend classes that implement the `AbstractServiceIF` interface must also implement the `AbstractServiceIF` interface.

ConcreteService. Classes in this role provide the basic functionality that is extended by the Decorator pattern.

AbstractWrapper. The abstract class in this role is the common superclass for wrapper classes. Instances of this class take responsibility for maintaining a reference to the `AbstractServiceIF` object that `ConcreteWrapper` objects delegate to.

This class also normally implements all methods declared by the `AbstractServiceIF` interface, so they simply call the like-named method of the `AbstractServiceIF` object that the wrapper object delegates to. This default implementation provides exactly the behavior needed for methods whose behavior is not being extended.

ConcreteWrapperA, ConcreteWrapperB, and so on. These concrete wrapper classes extend the behavior of the methods they inherit from the `AbstractWrapper` class in whatever way is needed.

IMPLEMENTATION

Most implementations of the Decorator pattern are simpler than the general case. Here are some of the common simplifications:

- If there is only one `ConcreteService` class and no `AbstractService` class, then the `AbstractWrapper` class may be a subclass of the `ConcreteService` class.
- If there will be only one concrete wrapper class, then there is no need for a separate `AbstractWrapper` class. You can merge the `Abstract-Wrapper` class's responsibilities with the concrete wrapper class. It may also be reasonable to dispense with the `AbstractWrapper` class if there will be two concrete wrapper classes, but no more than that.

CONSEQUENCES

- ☺ The Decorator pattern provides more flexibility than inheritance. It allows you to dynamically alter the behavior of individual objects by adding and removing wrappers. Inheritance, on the other hand, determines the nature of all instances of a class statically.
- ☺ By using different combinations of a few different kinds of wrapper objects, you can create many different combinations of behavior. To create many different kinds of behavior with inheritance requires that you define that many different classes.
- ● Using the Decorator pattern generally results in fewer classes than using inheritance. Having fewer classes simplifies the design and implementation of programs. On the other hand, using the Decorator pattern usually results in more objects. The larger number of objects can make debugging more difficult, especially since the objects tend to look mostly alike.
- ☹ The flexibility of wrapper objects makes them more error prone than inheritance. For example, it is possible to combine wrapper objects in ways that do not work or to create circular references between wrapper objects.
- ☹ One last difficulty associated with using the Decorator pattern is that it makes using object identity to identify service objects difficult, since it hides service objects behind wrapper objects.

CODE EXAMPLE

The code example for the Decorator pattern is code that implements some of the door controller classes shown in diagrams under the Context heading. Here is an implementation of the DoorControllerIF interface:

```
interface DoorControllerIF {
    /**
     * Ask the door to open if the given key is acceptable.
     */
    public void requestOpen(String key);

    /**
     * close the door
     */
    public void close();
    ...
} // interface DoorControllerIF
```

Here is the AbstractDoorControllerWrapper class that provides default implementations to its subclasses for the methods declared by the DoorControllerIF interface:

```
abstract class AbstractDoorControllerWrapper
                              implements DoorControllerIF {
    private DoorControllerIF wrappee;
    /**
     * Constructor
     * @param wrappee The object this object will delegate to.
     */
    AbstractDoorControllerWrapper(DoorControllerIF wrappee) {
        this.wrappee = wrappee;
    } // constructor(wrappee)

    /**
     * Ask the door to open if the given key is acceptable.
     */
    public void requestOpen(String key) {
        wrappee.requestOpen(key);
    } // requestOpen(String)

    /**
     * close the door
     */
    public void close() {
        wrappee.close();
    } // close()
...
} // class AbstractDoorControllerWrapper
```

Finally, here is a subclass of the `AbstractDoorControllerWrapper` class that extends the default behavior by asking a monitor to display the image from a named camera:

```
class DoorControllerWrapperA
                    extends AbstractDoorControllerWrapper {
    private String camera; // name of camera viewing this door
    private SurveillanceMonitorIF monitor; // camera's monitor

    /**
     * Constructor
     * @param wrappee The DoorController object that this
     *                object will delegate to.
     * @param camera The name of a camera that views this door
     * @param monitor The monitor to ask to view camera's image.
     */
    DoorControllerWrapperA(DoorControllerIF wrappee,
                           String camera,
                           SurveillanceMonitorIF monitor) {
        super(wrappee);
        this.camera = camera;
        this.monitor = monitor;
    } // constructor(wrappee)

    /**
     * Ask the door to open if the given key is acceptable.
     */
    public void requestOpen(String key) {
        monitor.viewNow(camera);
        super.requestOpen(key);
    } // requestOpen(String)
} // class DoorControllerWrapperA
```

RELATED PATTERNS

Delegation. The Decorator pattern is a structured way of applying the Delegation pattern.

Filter. The Filter pattern is a specialized version of the Decorator pattern that focuses on manipulating a data stream.

Strategy. The Decorator pattern can be used to arrange for things to happen before or after the methods of another object are called. If you want to arrange for things to happen in the middle of calls to a method, consider using the Strategy pattern.

Template Method. The Template Method pattern is another alternative to the Decorator pattern that allows variable behavior in the middle of a method call instead of before or after it.

Cache Management

SYNOPSIS

The Cache Management pattern allows fast access to objects that would otherwise take a long time to access. It involves keeping a copy of objects that are expensive to construct. The object may be expensive to construct for any number of reasons, such as requiring a lengthy computation or being fetched from a database.

CONTEXT

Suppose you are writing a program that allows people to fetch information about products in a catalog. Fetching all of a product's information can take a few seconds because it may have to be gathered from multiple sources. Keeping a product's information in the program's memory allows the next request for the product's information to be satisfied more quickly, since it is not necessary to spend the time to gather the information.

Keeping information in memory that takes a relatively long time to fetch into memory for quick access the next time it is needed is called *caching*. The large number of products in the catalog makes it infeasible to cache information for all the products in memory. What can be done is to keep information for as many products as feasible in memory. Products guessed to be the most likely to be used are kept in memory so they are there when needed. Products guessed to be less likely to be used are not kept in memory. Deciding which and how many objects to keep in memory is called *cache management*.

Figure 7.31 shows how cache management would work for the product information example.

1. A product ID is passed to a `ProductCacheManager` object's `getProductInfo` method.

   1.1. The `ProductCacheManager` object's `getProductInfo` method attempts to retrieve the product description object from a `Cache` object. If it successfully retrieves the object from the cache, it returns the object.

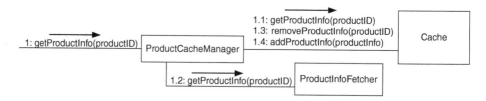

FIGURE 7.31 Product cache management collaboration.

1.2. If it was unable to retrieve the product description object from the cache, it calls a `ProductInfoFetcher` object's `getProductInfo` method to fetch the product description.

1.3. Many cache managers implement a policy to limit the number of objects in a cache because keeping too many objects in the cache can be wasteful or even counterproductive. If the cache manager decides that the retrieved object should be stored in the cache but the cache already contains as many objects as it should, the cache manager will avoid increasing the number of objects in the cache. It does this by picking a product description object to remove from the cache and passes its product ID to the `Cache` object's `removeProductInfo` method.

1.4. Finally, if the cache manager had decided that the fetched object should be stored in the cache, it calls the `Cache` object's `addProductInfo` method.

FORCES

☺ There is a need to access an object that takes a long time to construct or fetch. Typical reasons for the construction of an object being expensive are that its contents must be fetched from external sources or that it requires a lengthy computation. The point is that it takes substantially longer to construct the object than to access the object once it is cached in internal memory.

☺ When the number of objects that are expensive to construct is small enough that all of them can fit comfortably in local memory, then keeping all of the objects in local memory will provide the best results. This guarantees that if access to one of these objects is needed again, it will not be necessary to incur the expense of constructing the object again.

☺ If very many expensive-to-construct objects will be constructed, then all of them may not fit in memory at the same time. If they do fit in memory, they may use memory that will later be needed for other purposes. Therefore, it may be necessary to set an upper bound on the number of objects cached in local memory.

☺ An upper bound on the number of objects in a cache requires an enforcement policy. The enforcement policy will determine which fetched objects to cache and which to discard when the number of objects in the cache reaches the upper bound. Such a policy should attempt to predict which objects are most and least likely to be used in the near future.

☻ Some objects reflect the state of something outside of the program's own memory. The contents of such objects may not be valid after the time that such objects are created.

SOLUTION

Figure 7.32 shows the general structure of the Cache Management pattern.

Here are descriptions of the classes that participate in the Cache Management pattern and the roles that they play:

Client. Instances of classes in this role delegate the responsibility of obtaining access to specified objects to a `CacheManager` object.

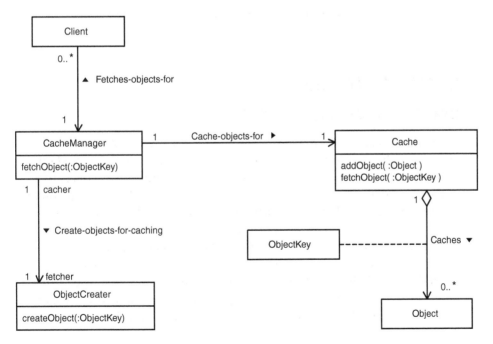

FIGURE 7.32 Cache Management pattern.

ObjectKey. Instances of the `ObjectKey` class identify the object to be fetched or created.

CacheManager. `Client` objects request objects from a `CacheManager` object by calling its `fetchObject` method. The argument to the `fetchObject` method is an `ObjectKey` object that identifies the object to fetch. The `fetchObject` method works by first calling the `Cache` object's `fetchObject` method. If that fails, it calls the `ObjectCreater` object's `createObject` method.

ObjectCreater. `ObjectCreater` objects are responsible for creating objects that are not in the cache.

Cache. A `Cache` object is responsible for managing a collection of cached objects. Given an `ObjectKey` object, a `Cache` object quickly finds the corresponding cached object. The `Cache-Manager` object passes an `ObjectKey` object to the `Cache` object's `fetchObject` method to get a cached object from the cache. If the `fetchObject` method does not return the requested object, the `CacheManager` object asks the `ObjectCreater` object to create it. If the `ObjectCreater` object returns the requested object, the `Cache` object passes the returned object to this object's `add-Object` method. The `addObject` method adds the object to the cache if this is consistent with its cache management policy. The `addObject` method may remove an object from the cache to make room for the object it is adding to the cache.

IMPLEMENTATION

STRUCTURAL CONSIDERATIONS

If you are designing both the `CacheManager` class and the `ObjectCreator` class, they should implement a common interface. `Client` objects should access `CacheManager` objects through the common interface. This is to make the use of a cache transparent to `Client` objects. If they implement a common interface, then `Client` objects are using an object that implements the same interface whether caching is being used or not.

The reason that such an interface is not indicated in the Solution section as part of this pattern is that classes in the `ObjectCreator` role are often designed before caching becomes a consideration. Because of this, `ObjectCreator` objects often do not implement any suitable interface and the effort required to have them implement such an interface is generally not expended.

IMPLEMENTATION OF THE CACHE

Implementing the Cache Management pattern involves making some potentially complex choices. Making optimal choices can involve much statistical analysis, queuing theory, and other sorts of mathematical analysis. However, it is usually possible to produce a reasonable implementation by being aware of what the choices are and experimenting with different solutions.

The most basic decision to make when implementing the Cache Management pattern is how to implement the cache itself. The considerations for picking a data structure for the cache are as follows:

- It must be able to quickly find objects when given their `ObjectKey`.
- Since search operations will be done more frequently than addition or removal, searching should be as fast as or faster than those operations.
- Since we expect frequent additions and removal of objects, the data structure must not make these operations a lot more expensive than search operations.

A hash table satisfies these needs. When implementing in Java, a cache is usually implemented using an instance of the `java.util.HashMap` or `java.util.Hashtable` class.

PERFORMANCE-TUNING A CACHE

The remaining implementation issues relate to performance tuning. Performance tuning is not something to spend time on until after your program is functioning correctly. In the design and initial coding stages of your development effort, make some initial decisions about how to deal with these issues and then ignore them until you are ready to deal with performance-related issues.

The simplest way of measuring the effectiveness of caching is to compute a statistic called its *hit rate*. The hit rate is the percentage of object fetch requests that the cache manager satisfies with objects stored in the cache. If every request is satisfied with an object from the cache, then the hit rate is 100 percent. If no request is satisfied, then the hit rate is 0 percent. The hit rate depends largely on how well the implementation of the Cache Management pattern matches the way that objects are requested.

There is always a maximum amount of memory that you can afford to devote to a cache. This means that you will have to set a limit on the objects that can be in the cache. If the potential set of objects available for collection in a cache is small, you don't have to impose an explicit limit. Most problems are not so conveniently self-limiting.

Specifying in advance a maximum amount of memory to devote to a cache is difficult since you may not know in advance how much memory will be available or how much memory the rest of your program will need. Enforcing a limit on the amount of memory a cache can use is especially difficult in Java because there is no definite relationship between an object and the amount of physical memory that it occupies.

An alternative to specifying and enforcing a limit that measures memory is simply to count objects. Object counting is a workable alternative to measuring actual memory usage if the average memory usage for each object is a reasonable approximation of the memory usage for each object. Counting objects is very straightforward, so you can simplify things by limiting the contents of a cache to a certain number of objects. Of course, the existence of a limit on the size of a cache raises the question of what should happen when the size of the cache reaches the maximum number of objects and another object is created. At that point, there is one more object than the cache is supposed to hold. The cache manager must then discard an object.

The selection of which object to discard is important because it directly affects the hit rate. If the discarded object is always the next one requested, then the hit rate will be 0 percent. On the other hand, if the object discarded will not be requested before any other object in the cache, then discarding that object has the least negative impact on the hit rate. Clearly, making a good choice about which object to discard requires a forecast of future object requests.

In some cases, it is possible to make an educated guess about which objects a program will need in the near future, based on knowledge of the application domain. In the most fortunate cases, it is possible to predict with high probability that a specific object will be the next one requested. In those cases, if the object is not already in the cache, it may be advantageous to asynchronously create it immediately rather than wait for the program to request it. This technique is called *prefetching* the object.

In most cases, the application domain will not provide enough clues to make such precise forecasts. However, there is a usage pattern that turns up in so many cases that it is the basis for a good default strategy for deciding which object to discard: The more recently a program has requested an object, the more likely it is to request the object again. The strategy based on this observation is always to discard the least recently used object in the cache. People often abbreviate this "least recently used" strategy as LRU.

Now let's take a look at setting a numeric limit on the number of objects in a cache. A mathematical analysis can give a precise value to use for the maximum number of objects that may be placed in a cache. It is unusual to do such an analysis for two reasons. The first is that the mathematical analysis involves probability and queuing theory that is beyond the knowledge of most programmers. The other reason is that such an analysis can be prohibitively time consuming. The number of details that need to be gathered about the program and its environment can be prohibitively large. However, you can usually arrive at a reasonable cache size empirically.

Begin by adding code to your `CacheManager` class to measure the hit rate as the number of object requests satisfied from the cache divided by the total number of object requests. You can then try running with different limits on the object size. As you do that, you will be looking for two things. The most important thing to look out for is that if the cache is too large it can cause the rest of your program to fail or slow down. The program can fail by running out of memory. If the program is garbage-collected, as most Java programs are, it can slow down waiting for the garbage collector to finish scavenging memory for new objects. If the program is running in a virtual memory environment, a large cache can cause excessive paging.

Suppose that you want to tune a program that uses a cache. You run the program, under otherwise identical conditions, with different maximum cache sizes set. Let's say that you try values as large as 6000. At 6000 you find that the program takes three times as long to run as at 4000. This means that 6000 is too large. Look at the possible hit rates you could receive at the other values, as shown in Table 7.1.

Clearly, there is no need to allow the cache to be larger than 4000 objects since that achieves a 100 percent hit rate. Under the conditions in which you ran the program, the ideal cache size is 4000. If the program will be run only under those exact conditions, then no further tuning may

TABLE 7.1 Cache Size and
Hit Rates

Max Cache Size	Hit Rate, %
250	20
500	60
1000	80
2000	90
3000	98
4000	100
5000	100

be needed. Many programs will be run under other conditions. If you are concerned that your program will be run under other conditions, you may want to use a smaller cache size to avoid problems under conditions where less memory is available. The number you pick will be a compromise between wanting a high hit rate and a small cache size. Since lowering the cache size to 3000 only reduces the hit rate to 98 percent, then 3000 might be an acceptable cache size. If a 90 percent hit rate is good enough, then 2000 is an acceptable cache size.

If it is not possible to achieve a high hit rate with available memory and creating the objects is sufficiently expensive, then you should consider using a secondary cache. A secondary cache is typically a disk file that is used as a cache. The secondary cache takes longer to access than the primary cache that is in memory. However, if it takes sufficiently less time to fetch objects out of a local disk file than it would to create them again from their original source, then it can be advantageous to use a secondary cache.

The way that you use a secondary cache is to move objects from the primary cache to the secondary cache instead of discarding the objects when the primary cache is full.

INTERACTION WITH THE GARBAGE COLLECTOR

Putting a fixed limit on the number of objects that may be in a cache can be an effective way to ensure that the cache will not consume an excessive amount of memory. The downside is that by having to pick a number that you are sure is low enough not to interfere with other uses of memory, you may be sizing the cache for the worst case. By sizing the cache for the worst case you may be reducing the performance that you get in the average case. It would be nice if there were a way to size the cache for the average case and then remove objects from the cache if the memory were needed for another purpose.

It turns out that there is a way. It involves working with the garbage collector so that the garbage collector can arrange for the removal of objects from the cache when the JVM is running out of memory.

The garbage collector has a special relationship with the class `java.lang.ref.SoftReference`. A reference to another object is passed to the constructor of a `SoftReference` object. Immediately after a `Soft-Reference` object is constructed, its `get` method returns the object reference that was passed to its constructor. If the only live reference to an object is through a `SoftReference` object and the storage occupied by the object is needed for other purposes, then the garbage collector will set the reference in the `SoftReference` object to null so that it can safely reclaim the storage occupied by the referenced object.

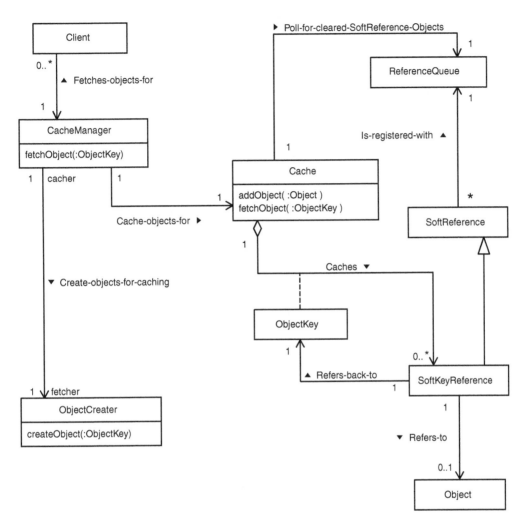

FIGURE 7.33 Cache Management with soft references.

Figure 7.33 shows how the `SoftReference` class and the related class `java.lang.ref.ReferenceQueue` fit into the organization of the Cache Management pattern. The `Cache` object does not refer directly to the objects that it contains. Instead, it associates each `ObjectKey` object with a `SoftKeyReference` object that initially contains a reference to the object identified by the `ObjectKey` object.

The `SoftKeyReference` object class is a subclass of `java.lang.ref` `.SoftReference`. When a `SoftKeyReference` object is created, it contains a reference to a cached object and a reference to the `ObjectKey` object that identifies the cached object. At some point, if the garbage collector decides that it needs the storage occupied by a cached object and there is no normal reference to the cached object, then the garbage collector will clear the reference (set it to null) to the cached object in the `SoftKeyReference` object. Clearing the reference is something that the garbage collector must do before reclaiming the object's storage.

When the `Cache` object tries to get a cached object from a `SoftKeyReference` object after it has been cleared, it gets a null. Since the `Cache` object produces null to indicate that no cached object corresponds to a given `ObjectKey` object, clearing the `SoftKeyReference` object has the effect of removing the cached object from the cache even though the `ObjectKey` object is still in the cache. There is a mechanism that eventually does remove the `ObjectKey` object for the cache.

When a `SoftKeyReference` object is created, it is registered with the `Cache` object's `ReferenceQueue` object. If the garbage collector clears the reference in a `SoftKeyReference` object, because it is registered with the `Cache` object's `ReferenceQueue` object, the `SoftKeyReference` object is enqueued in the `ReferenceQueue` object. Each time the `CacheManager` object is asked to produce an object, it polls the `ReferenceQueue` object to check for enqueued `SoftKeyReference` objects.

There is an `ObjectKey` object associated with each `SoftKeyReference` object. When the `CacheManager` object gets a `SoftKeyReference` object from its `ReferenceQueue` object, it removes the `ObjectKey` object associated with the `SoftKeyReference` object from the `Cache` object.

CONSEQUENCES

Sometimes applications of the Cache Management pattern are added to the design of a program after the need for a performance optimization has been discovered. This is usually not a problem because the impact of the Cache Management pattern on the rest of a program is minimal. If access to the objects in question is already implemented using the Virtual Proxy pattern, an implementation of the Cache Management pattern can be inserted into the proxy class with no modification to other classes.

☺ The primary consequence of using the Cache Management pattern is that a program spends less time fetching objects from expensive sources.

☹ When objects are created with data from an external source, another consequence of using the Cache Management pattern is that the cache may become inconsistent with the original data source. The consistency problem breaks down into two separate problems that can be solved independently of each other. Those problems are *read consistency* and *write consistency*.

Read consistency means that the cache always reflects updates to information in the original object source. If the objects being cached are stock prices, then the prices in the object source can change and the prices in the cache will no longer be current.

Write consistency means that the original object source always reflects updates to the cache.

To achieve absolute read or write consistency for objects in a cache with the original object source requires a mechanism to keep them synchronized. Such mechanisms can be complicated to implement and add considerable execution time. They generally involve techniques such as locking and optimistic concurrency, which are beyond the scope of this volume. Some patterns in *Patterns in Java, Volume 3* deal with these issues. They are mentioned under the Related Patterns heading at the end of this pattern.

If it is not feasible to achieve absolute read or write consistency, you may be able to settle for relative consistency. Relative consistency does not guarantee that the contents of a cache always appear to match the original object source. Instead, the guarantee is that if an update occurs in the cache or the original data source, the other will reflect the update within some specified amount of time. The Ephemeral Cache Item pattern (described in *Patterns in Java, Volume 3*) discusses this approach in greater detail.

CODE EXAMPLE

Suppose you are writing software for an employee timekeeping system. The system consists of timekeeping terminals and a timekeeping server. The terminals are small boxes mounted on the walls of a place of business. When an employee arrives at work or leaves work, the employee notifies the timekeeping system by running his or her ID card through a timekeeping terminal. The terminal reads the employee's ID on the card and acknowledges the card by displaying the employee's name and options. The employee then selects an option to indicate that he or she is starting work, ending work, going on break, or other options. The timekeeping terminals transmit these timekeeping events to the timekeeping server. At the end of each pay period, the business's payroll system gets the number of hours each employee worked from the timekeeping system and prepares paychecks.

The exact details an employee sees will depend on an employee profile that a terminal receives from the timekeeping server. The employee profile will include the employee's name, the language in which to display prompts for the employee, and any special options that apply to the employee.

Most businesses assign their employees a fixed location in the business place to do their work. Employees with a fixed work location will normally use the timekeeping terminal nearest to their work location. To avoid long lines in front of timekeeping terminals, it is recommended that the terminals be positioned so that fewer than 70 employees with fixed work locations will use the same timekeeping terminal.

A substantial portion of the acquisition cost of the timekeeping system will be the cost of the terminals. To keep their cost down, the timekeeping terminals will have a minimal amount of memory. However, to keep response time down, we will want the terminals to cache employee profiles so that most of the time they will be able to respond immediately when presented with an employee's ID card. This means that you will have to impose a maximum cache size that is rather modest. A reasonable basis for an initial maximum cache size is the recommendation that the terminals be positioned so that no more than 70 employees with fixed work locations use the same terminal. Based on this, we come up with an initial cache size of up to 80 employee profiles.

The reason for picking a number larger than 70 is that under some situations more than 70 employees may use the same timekeeping terminal. Sometimes one part of a business will borrow employees from another part of a business when they experience a peak workload. Also, there will be employees, such as maintenance staff, that float from one location to another.

Figure 7.34 is a class diagram that shows how the Cache Management pattern is applied to this problem.

Here is the code that implements the timekeeping terminal's cache management. First, here is the code for the `EmployeeProfileManager` class:

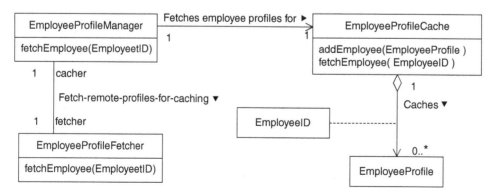

FIGURE 7.34 Timekeeping Cache Management.

```
class EmployeeProfileManager {
    private EmployeeCache cache = new EmployeeCache();
    private EmployeeProfileFetcher server
      = new EmployeeProfileFetcher();

    /**
     * Fetch an employee profile for the given employee id
     * from the internal cache or timekeeping server if not in
     * the internal cache.
     * @return employee's profile or null if employee profile
     *          not found.
     */
    EmployeeProfile fetchEmployee(EmployeeID id) {
        EmployeeProfile profile = cache.fetchEmployee(id);
        if (profile == null) {    // if not in cache try server
            profile = server.fetchEmployee(id);
            if (profile != null) { // Got profile from server
                // put profile in the cache
                cache.addEmployee(profile);
            } // if != null
        } // if == null
        return profile;
    } // fetchEmployee(EmployeeID)
} // class EmployeeProfileManager
```

The logic in the EmployeeProfileManager class is straightforward conditional logic. The logic of the EmployeeCache class is more intricate, since it manipulates a data structure to determine which employee profile to remove from the cache before adding an employee profile to a full cache. It also uses soft references in the way discussed under the Implementation heading.

```
class EmployeeCache {
    /**
     * We use a linked list to determine the least recently
     * used employee profile.  The cache itself is implemented
     * by a Hashtable object. The Hashtable values are linked
     * list objects that refer to the actual EmployeeProfile
     * object.
     */
    private Hashtable cache = new Hashtable();

    /**
     * This is the head of the linked list that refers to the
     * most recently used EmployeeProfile.
     */
    LinkedList mru = null;

    /**
     * This is the end of the linked list that refers to the
     * least recently used EmployeeProfile.
```

```
    */
    LinkedList lru = null;

    /**
     * The maximum number of EmployeeProfile objects that may
     * be in the cache.
     */
    private final int MAX_CACHE_SIZE = 80;

    /**
     * The number of EmployeeProfile objects currently in the
     * cache.
     */
    private int currentCacheSize = 0;

    /**
     * This object manages the cleanup after the garbage
     * collector decides it is time to reclaim the storage
     * used by an EmployeeProfile.
     */
    private CleanupQueue myCleanup = new CleanupQueue();

    /**
     * Objects are passed to this method for addition to the
     * cache.  However, this method is not required to actually
     * add an object to the cache if that is contrary to its
     * policy for what object should be added.  This method
     * may also remove objects already in the cache to make
     * room for new objects.
     */
    public void addEmployee(EmployeeProfile emp) {
        EmployeeID id = emp.getID();
        if (cache.get(id) == null) { // if not in cache
            // Add profile to cache,
            // making it the most recently used.
            if (currentCacheSize == 0) {
                // treat empty cache as a special case
                lru = mru = new LinkedList(emp);
            } else {                // currentCacheSize > 0
                LinkedList newLink;
                if (currentCacheSize >= MAX_CACHE_SIZE) {
                    // remove least recently used
                    // EmployeeProfile from the cache
                    newLink = lru;
                    lru = newLink.previous;
                    cache.remove(id);
                    currentCacheSize—;
                    lru.next = null;
                    newLink.setProfile(emp);
                } else {
                    newLink = new LinkedList(emp);
                } // if >= MAX_CACHE_SIZE
                newLink.next = mru;
                mru.previous = newLink;
```

```
                    newLink.previous = null;
                    mru = newLink;
                } // if 0
                // Put the most recently used profile in cache.
                cache.put(id, mru);
                currentCacheSize++;
            } else {                  // profile already in cache
                // addEmployee shouldn't be called when the object
                // is already in the cache.  Since that has
                // happened, do a fetch so that object becomes
                // the most recently used.
                fetchEmployee(id);
            } // if cache.get(id)
    } // addEmployee(EmployeeProfile)


    /**
     * Return the EmployeeProfile associated with the given
     * EmployeeID in the cache or null if no EmployeeProfile is
     * associated with the given EmployeeID.
     */
    EmployeeProfile fetchEmployee(EmployeeID id) {
        // Remove any EmployeeID from cache whose corresponding
        // EmployeeProfile has been removed by the garbage
        // collector.
        myCleanup.cleanup();

        LinkedList foundLink = (LinkedList)cache.get(id);
        if (foundLink == null)
          return null;             // Not in cache
        if (mru != foundLink) {
            if ( foundLink == lru ) {
                lru = foundLink.previous;
                lru.next = null;
            } // if lru
            if (foundLink.previous != null)
              foundLink.previous.next = foundLink.next;
            if (foundLink.next != null)
              foundLink.next.previous = foundLink.previous;
            mru.previous = foundLink;
            foundLink.previous = null;
            foundLink.next = mru;
            mru = foundLink;
        } // if currentCacheSize > 1
        return foundLink.getProfile();
    } // fetchEmployee(EmployeeID)


    /**
     * Remove the EmployeeProfile associated with the given
     * EmployeeID in the cache.
     */
    void removeEmployee(EmployeeID id) {
        LinkedList foundLink = (LinkedList)cache.get(id);
        if (foundLink != null) {
```

```
                    if (mru == foundLink) {
                        mru = foundLink.next;
                    } // if mru
                    if ( foundLink == lru ) {
                        lru = foundLink.previous;
                    } // if lru
                    if (foundLink.previous != null) {
                        foundLink.previous.next = foundLink.next;
                    } // if foundLink.previous
                    if (foundLink.next != null) {
                        foundLink.next.previous = foundLink.previous;
                    } // if foundLink.next
                } // if !null
        } // removeEmployee(EmployeeID)


        /**
         * Private doubly linked list class for managing list of
         * most recently used employee profiles.  This class
         * implements the CleanupIF interface so that its instances
         * can be notified after the garbage collector decides to
         * remove an EmployeeProfile.
         */
        private class LinkedList implements CleanupIF {
            SoftReference profileReference;
            LinkedList previous;
            LinkedList next;

            LinkedList(EmployeeProfile profile) {
                setProfile(profile);
            } // constructor(EmployeeProfile)

            void setProfile(EmployeeProfile profile) {
                profileReference =
                  myCleanup.createSoftReference(profile,this);
            } // setProfile(EmployeeProfile, EmployeeID)

            EmployeeProfile getProfile() {
                return (EmployeeProfile)profileReference.get();
            } // getProfile()


            /**
             * When this method is called, the object that
             * implements it is expected to remove itself from
             * whatever data structures it is part of.
             */
            public void extricate() {
                EmployeeProfile profile;
                profile = (EmployeeProfile)profileReference.get();
                removeEmployee(profile.getID());
            } // extricate()
        } // class LinkedList
    } // class EmployeeCache
```

Here are the `EmployeeProfile` and `EmployeeID` classes:

```java
class EmployeeProfile {
    private EmployeeID id;        // Employee Id
    private Locale locale;        // Language Preference
    private boolean supervisor;
    private String name;          // Employee name

    public EmployeeProfile(EmployeeID id,
                           Locale locale,
                           boolean supervisor,
                           String name) {
        this.id = id;
        this.locale = locale;
        this.supervisor = supervisor;
        this.name = name;
    } // Constructor(EmployeeID, Locale, boolean, String)

    public EmployeeID getID() { return id; }

    public Locale getLocale() { return locale; }

    public boolean isSupervisor() { return supervisor; }
} // class EmployeeProfile

class EmployeeID {
    private String id;

    /**
     * constructor
     * @param id A string containing the employee ID.
     */
    public EmployeeID(String id) {
        this.id = id;
    } // constructor(String)

    /**
     * Returns a hash code value for this object.
     */
    public int hashCode() { return id.hashCode(); }

    /**
     * Return true if the given object is an EmployeeId equal
     * to this one.
     */
    public boolean equals(Object obj) {
        return ( obj instanceof EmployeeID
                && id.equals(((EmployeeID)obj).id) );
    } // equals(Object)

    /**
     * Return the string representation of this EmployeeID.
     */
```

```
      public String toString() { return id; }
} // class EmployeeID
```

Here is the class org.clickblocks.dataStructure.CleanupQueue that the EmployeeCache class uses to manage reclamation of EmployeeProfile objects by the garbage collector.

```
/**
 * The class encapsulates a ReferenceQueue.  It ensures
 * that the only kind of Reference objects that will be
 * enqueued to the ReferenceQueue are SoftCleanupReference
 * objects.  It also encapsulates logic to tell CleanupIF
 * objects enqueued to the ReferenceQueue to remove
 * themselves from whatever data structure they are part of.
 */
public class CleanupQueue {
    /**
     * The ReferenceQueue encapsulated by this object.
     */
    private ReferenceQueue refQueue = new ReferenceQueue();

    /**
     * This is true while a call to cleanup is pending.
     */
    private boolean cleaning;

    /**
     * Return a soft reference registered to be enqueued to
     * the reference queue encapsulated by this object.
     *
     * @param obj
     *        The object that the reference will refer to.
     * @param cleanup
     *        The CleanupIF object whose extricate method is
     *        to be called after the soft reference is
     *        enqueued.
     */
    public SoftReference createSoftReference(Object obj,
                                    CleanupIF cleanup) {
       return new SoftCleanupReference(obj, refQueue, cleanup);
    } // createReference(Object, CleanupIF)

    /**
     * Call the extricate method of all enqueued CleanupIF
     * objects.  If there is currently a call in progress,
     * then just return.
     */
    public void cleanup() {
        synchronized (this) {
            if (cleaning) {
                return;
            } // if
```

```
            cleaning = true;
    } // synchronized
    try {
        while (refQueue.poll()!=null) {
            SoftCleanupReference r;
            r = (SoftCleanupReference)refQueue.remove();
            r.extricate();
        } // while
    } catch (InterruptedException e) {
    } finally {
        cleaning = false;
    } // try
  } // cleanup()
} // class CleanupQueue
```

Finally, here is the `CleanupIF` interface that the `CleanupQueue` class uses to notify other objects that a soft reference has been cleared.

```
public interface CleanupIF {
    /**
     * When this method is called, the object that implements it is
     * expected to remove itself from whatever data structures it is
     * part of.
     */
    public void extricate() ;
} // interface CleanupIF
```

RELATED PATTERNS

Façade.   The Cache Management pattern uses the Façade pattern.

Template Method.   The Cache Management pattern uses the Template Method pattern to keep its `Cache` class reusable across application domains.

Virtual Proxy.   The Cache Management pattern is often used with a variant of the Virtual Proxy pattern to make the cache transparent to objects that access objects in the cache.

Object Replication.   The Object Replication pattern (described in *Patterns in Java, Volume 3*) describes some issues related to maintaining cache consistency.

Optimistic Concurrency.   The Optimistic Concurrency pattern (described in *Patterns in Java, Volume 3*) describes a technique that can sometimes be used to manage cache consistency with superior performance.

Ephemeral Cache Item.   The Ephemeral Cache Item pattern (described in *Patterns in Java, Volume 3*) describes the management of caches with relative consistency.

C H A P T E R

Behavioral Patterns

Chain of Responsibility (305)
Command (317)
Little Language (329)
Mediator (355)
Snapshot (369)
Observer (387)
State (397)
Null Object (407)
Strategy (413)
Template Method (419)
Visitor (427)

The patterns in this chapter are used to organize, manage, and combine behavior.

Chain of Responsibility

This pattern was previously described in [GoF95].

SYNOPSIS

The Chain of Responsibility pattern allows an object to send a command without knowing what object or objects will receive it. It accomplishes this by passing the command to a chain of objects that is typically part of a larger structure. Each object in the chain may handle the command, pass the command on to the next object in the chain, or do both.

CONTEXT

Suppose that you are writing software to monitor a security system. Physically, the security system consists of sensing devices (motion detectors, smoke detectors, etc.) that transmit status information to a computer. The computer's job is to log all status information, maintain a display showing current status information, and transmit alarms in the event of an emergency.

One of the goals for the monitoring software is that it should be highly scalable. It should be able to work for a small retail store, an office building, a warehouse, or a multi-building complex. That goal has implications for the way that you design the monitoring software.

To keep things simple, your monitoring program should instantiate an object for every sensor it is to monitor. This provides a simple way to model each sensor's state. To ensure scalability, an object responsible for an individual sensor should not assume anything about its environment, except that it is at the bottom level of a hierarchical organization.

The organization will include objects corresponding to real-world things such as rooms, areas, floors, and buildings. Directly modeling the real world provides a straightforward way to display the status of different parts of buildings. It also allows the interpretation of a sensor's state to be based on its environment. For example, if the temperature of a closed room exceeds 180°F, then you may want the fire sprinklers in just that room to turn on. If the temperature in an open area of a warehouse exceeds 150°F, you may want to turn on the fire sprinklers over that area and the adjacent areas. On the other hand, if the temperature in a freezer exceeds 30°F, you may want to sound an alarm to let people know that that freezer is getting too warm.

In all these cases, the object that models a sensor does not decide what to do with the state of the sensor. Instead, it delegates that decision to an object at a higher level of the hierarchy that has more contextual knowledge. Such objects either decide what to do about a notification or pass it on to the object that is organizationally above it.

Figure 8.1 shows an example of objects organized in this hierarchical way.

For example, when a `TemperatureSensor` object contained in an area of a warehouse receives a notification of the current temperature from the physical sensor, it passes that notification to the `Area` object that contains it. Rather than decide the significance of the temperature, it passes the notification to the `Warehouse` object that contains the `Area` object. The `Warehouse` object determines the meaning of the temperature. If the temperature is above 150°F, the `Warehouse` object decides that there is a fire. It turns on the sprinklers in the area that notified it and the surrounding areas. The `Warehouse` object does not pass on the temperature notification.

FORCES

☺ You want an object to be able to send a command to another object without specifying the receiver. The sending object does not care

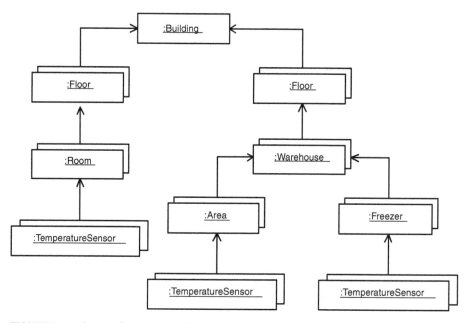

FIGURE 8.1 Physical security object organization.

which object handles the command, only that an object will receive the command and handle it.

☺ You want the receivers of a command to be able to handle the command without having to know anything about the object that sent the command.

☺ More than one object may be able to receive and handle a command, so you need a way to prioritize among the receivers without the sending object knowing anything about them.

☺ The objects you may want to potentially handle commands are organized into a structure that can serve to prioritize among the potential handlers of a command.

SOLUTION

Figure 8.2 presents a class diagram that shows the organization of the Chain of Responsibility pattern. Following are explanations of the roles these classes play in the Chain of Responsibility pattern:

CommandSender. Instances of a class in this role send commands to the first object in a chain of objects that may handle the

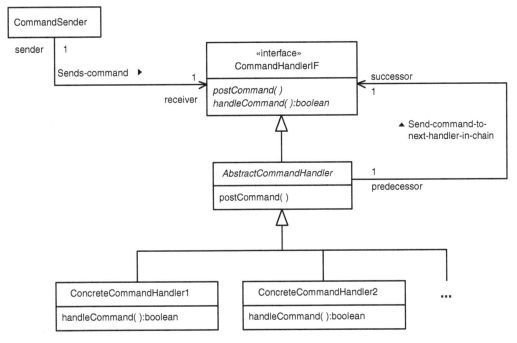

FIGURE 8.2 Chain of Responsibility pattern.

command. They send a command by calling the first CommandHandlerIF object's postCommand method.

CommandHandlerIF.   All objects in a chain of objects that may handle a command must implement an interface in this role. It defines two methods.

1. It defines a handleCommand method to handle whatever commands an implementing class is expected to handle. The handleCommand method returns true if it handled a command or false if it did not.
2. It defines a postCommand method that calls the handleCommand method. If the handleCommand method returns false and there is a next object in the chain, it calls the object's postCommand method. If the handleCommand method returns true, it means there is no need to pass the command on to the next object in the chain.

AbstractCommandHandler.   Classes in this role are abstract classes that implement the postCommand method. The purpose of this is to provide the convenience of a common implementation of postCommand for classes in the ConcreteCommandHandler role. It is very unusual for classes to want anything other than the default logic for the postCommand method. Classes in the CommandSender role should refer to objects in a chain of responsibility only through the CommandHandlerIF interface and not as instances of the AbstractCommandHandler class. The AbstractCommandHandler class is an implementation detail. Though unusual, it is possible to have classes that implement the CommandHandlerIF interface that are not subclasses of the AbstractCommandHandler class.

ConcreteCommandHandler1, ConcreteCommandHandler2, and so on.   Instances of classes in this role are objects in a chain of objects that can handle commands.

Typically, CommandHandler objects are part of a larger structure. This is the case in the example shown in Figure 8.1.

IMPLEMENTATION

In many cases, the objects that constitute a chain of responsibility are part of a larger structure, and the chain of responsibility is formed through some links of that larger structure. When links to form a chain of responsibility do not already exist, you must add instance variables and access methods to the classes to create links that form a chain of responsibility.

A decision to make, whenever implementing the Chain of Responsibility pattern, is how you will pass commands to and through the chain of objects. There are two basic ways to do it. One way is to encapsulate each kind of command in a single object that can be passed to a single `postCommand` method. The other way is to have as many different types of `postCommand` and `handleCommand` methods as there are different types of information associated with commands.

Passing commands in a single object is often the better choice. It incurs the cost of object creation but minimizes the cost of passing parameters to the methods of the next object in the chain. That minimizes the cost of propagating a command through a chain of objects. Passing commands in a single object usually results in less code.

On the other hand, passing the information that constitutes a command through separate parameters saves the cost of object creation at the cost of additional parameter passing. If you know that the chain of objects will be short, passing a command as multiple parameters can be the better choice.

CONSEQUENCES

- ☺ The Chain of Responsibility pattern reduces coupling between the object that sends a command and the object that handles the command. The sender of a command does not need to know what object will actually handle the command. It merely needs to be able to send the command to the object that is at the head of the chain of responsibility.
- ☺ The Chain of Responsibility pattern allows flexibility in deciding how to handle commands. Decisions about which object will handle a command can be varied by changing which objects are in the chain of responsibility or changing the order of the objects in the chain of responsibility.
- ● The Chain of Responsibility pattern does not guarantee that every command will be handled. Commands that are not handled are ignored.
- ☺ If the number of objects in a chain becomes large, there can be efficiency concerns about the amount of time that it takes a command to propagate through the chain. A high percentage of commands that are not handled exacerbates the problem because commands that are not handled are propagated through the full length of the chain.

JAVA API USAGE

Version 1.0 of Java used the Chain of Command pattern to handle user-interface events. That event-handling scheme used a user interface's container hierarchy as a chain of responsibility. When an event was posted to a button or other GUI component, it would either handle the event or post it to its container. Though it was usable, there were enough problems that the creators of Java took the drastic step of changing Java's event model. The two most serious problems related to efficiency and flexibility are as follows:

- Some platforms generate many events that most GUIs do not handle or have any interest in. One such event is MOUSE_MOVE. It may be generated every time a mouse moves just one pixel. Some programs that were built using the original event model visibly slowed down whenever there was rapid mouse movement because they spent so much time passing MOUSE_MOVE events that were never handled through the container hierarchy.
- The Chain of Responsibility pattern assumes that all the objects that can handle a command are instances of a common superclass or implement a common interface. This limits a program to posting commands to instances of that common superclass or interface. Java's original event model required that every object that could handle an event was an instance of the common superclass Component. This meant that it was impossible to deliver events directly to non-GUI objects, since only GUI objects are instances of Component.

This second problem is actually an advantage for some applications. The Chain of Responsibility pattern makes it less convenient to deliver commands to objects that are not part of the chain of handlers. For some applications, delivering a command to an object outside the chain of handlers is most likely a bug. The physical security example discussed under the Context heading is an example of such an application. For applications such as this, using the Chain of Responsibility pattern will result in fewer opportunities to introduce bugs into the application than will be using the delegation event model.

Another advantage that the Chain of Responsibility has over the delegation event model is that it allows you to explicitly control the order in which commands are delivered to handlers.

CODE EXAMPLE

Continuing the physical security example, Figure 8.3 shows the classes used in the physical security example.

In Figure 8.3, the classes that extend the Sensor class call the notify method they inherit from it to report a measurement to the object that is responsible for handling its measurements. Classes that extend the

Delegation Event Model

The delegation event model involves three kinds of objects:

- Event sources are objects that are a source of information about the occurrence of some sort of event.
- Event listeners are objects that want to be informed that some particular sort of event has occurred.
- Events are objects that encapsulate information about the occurrence of an event.

Event source objects pass event objects to event listener objects. Event objects are an instance of a subclass of the `java.util.EventObject` class.

There is a naming convention that gives structure to the delegation event model. We will illustrate the naming convention using action events.

`Action` events are represented using the `ActionEvent` class. In order for instances of a class to be able to receive action events, the class must implement the `ActionListener` interface. Interfaces such as `ActionListener` declare one or more void methods that will be passed the appropriate event type. Classes that are sources of action events define methods called `addActionListener` and `removeActionListener`. These methods allow `ActionListener` objects to be registered and unregistered to receive action events from an object that is a source of action events.

For more information about the delegation event model, see the JavaBeans specification, which you can find at http://java/sun.com/products/javabeans/docs/spec.html.

`AbstractSecurityZone` class are responsible for handling measurements from the appropriate kind of `Sensor` object.

The following is some code for the classes shown in Figure 8.3. First, here is code for the `TemperatureSensor` class. Notice that the `TemperatureSensor` class does nothing with a reading from a temperature sensor but pass it on.

```
class TemperatureSensor extends Sensor {
    private SecurityZone zone;
...
    /**
     * When the temperature sensor associated with this object
     * observes a different temperature this method is called.
```

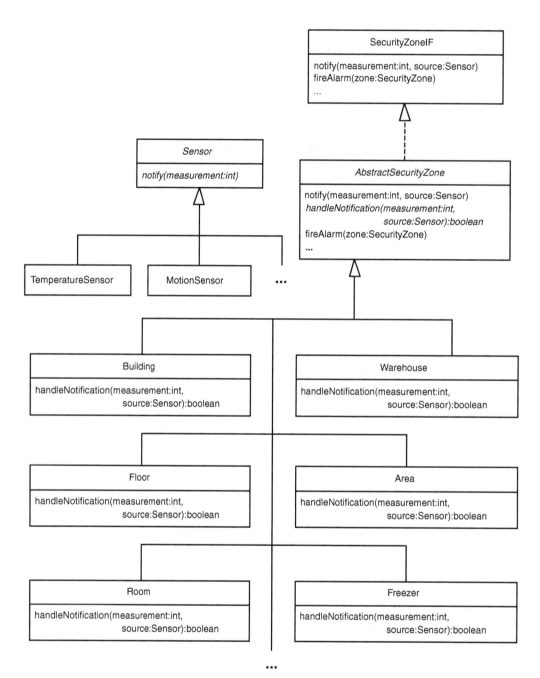

FIGURE 8.3 Physical security classes.

```
    */
    void notify(int measurement) {
        zone.notify(measurement, this);
    } // notify(int)
} // class TemperatureSensor
```

All of the classes that model security zones implement that `SecurityZoneIF` interface:

```
public interface SecurityZoneIF {
    /**
     * This method is called to notify this security zone of a
     * change in a sensor measurement.
     */
    public void notify(int measurement, Sensor source) ;

    /**
     * This method is called by a child zone to report a fire.
     */
    public void fireAlarm(SecurityZone zone) ;
} // interface SecurityZoneIF
```

Here is the code for the `SecurityZone` class, which is the superclass of all of the classes that form the chains of responsibility in this example:

```
abstract class SecurityZone implements SecurityZoneIF {
    private SecurityZone parent;
...
    /**
     * Return this object's parent zone.
     */
    SecurityZone getParent() {
        return parent;
    } // getParent()

    /**
     * Call this method to notify this zone of a new sensor
     * measurement.
     */
    public void notify(int measurement, Sensor sensor) {
        if (!handleNotification(measurement, sensor)
                && parent != null) {
            parent.notify(measurement, sensor);
        } // if
    } // notify(int, Sensor)

    /**
     * This method is called by the notify method so that
     * this object can have a chance to handle measurements.
     */
    protected
    abstract boolean handleNotification(int measurement,
                                        Sensor sensor);
```

```
    /**
     * This method is called by a child zone to report a fire.
     * It is expected that the child zone has turned on
     * sprinklers or taken other measures to control the fire
     * within the child zone. The purpose of this method is to
     * be overridden by subclasses so it can take any
     * necessary actions outside of the child zone.
     */
    public void fireAlarm(SecurityZone zone) {
        // Turn on sprinklers
...
        if (parent != null)
            parent.fireAlarm(zone);
    } // fireAlarm(SecurityZone)
} // class SecurityZone
```

Here are the subclasses of SecurityZone that were discussed under the Context heading:

```
class Area extends SecurityZone {
...
    /**
     * This method is called by the notify method so that this
     * object can have a chance to handle measurements.
     */
    boolean handleNotification(int measurement, Sensor sensor){
        if (sensor instanceof TemperatureSensor) {
            if (measurement > 150) {
                fireAlarm(this);
                return true;
            } // if
        } // if
...
        return false;
    } // handleNotification(int, Sensor)
} // class Area

class Warehouse extends SecurityZone {
    ...
    /**
     * This method is called by the notify method so this
     * object can have a chance to handle measurements.
     */
    protected
    boolean handleNotification(int measurement, Sensor sensor){
...
        return false;
    } // handleNotification(int, Sensor)

    public void fireAlarm(SecurityZone zone) {
        if (zone instanceof Area) {
            // Turn on sprinklers in surrounding areas
            ...
```

```
              // Don't call super.fireAlarm because that will
              // turn on sprinklers for the whole warehouse.
              if (getParent() != null)
                getParent().fireAlarm(zone);
              return;
          } // if
...
          super.fireAlarm(zone);
      } // fireAlarm(SecurityZone)
} // class Warehouse
```

RELATED PATTERNS

Composite.   When the chain of objects used by the Chain of
Responsibility pattern is part of a larger structure, the larger
structure is usually built using the Composite pattern.

Command.   The Chain of Responsibility pattern makes the particular object that executes a command indefinite. The Command
pattern makes the object that executes a command explicit and
specific.

Template Method.   When the objects that make up a chain of
responsibility are part of a larger organization built using the
Composite pattern, the Template Method pattern is often used
to organize the behavior of individual objects.

Command

This pattern was previously described in [GoF95].

SYNOPSIS

Encapsulate commands in objects so that you can control their selection and sequencing, queue them, undo them, and otherwise manipulate them.

CONTEXT

Suppose you want to design a word processing program so that it can undo and redo commands. A way to accomplish this is to materialize each command as an object with do and undo methods. The class diagram for this is shown in Figure 8.4.

When you tell the word processor to do something, instead of directly performing the command, it creates an instance of the subclass of AbstractCommand corresponding to the command. It passes all necessary information to the instance's constructor. For example, when commanded to insert one or more characters, it creates an InsertStringCommand object. It passes, to the object's constructor, the position in the document to make the insertion and the string to insert at that position.

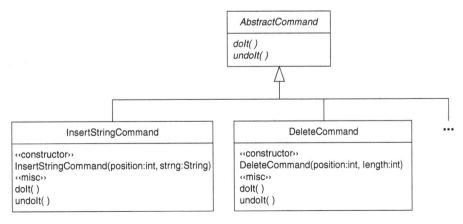

FIGURE 8.4 Do and undo class diagram.

Once the word processor has materialized a command as an object, it calls the object's doIt method to execute the command. The word processor also puts the command object in a data structure that allows the word processor to maintain a history of the commands that have been executed. Maintaining a command history allows the word processor to undo commands in the reverse order that they were issued by calling their undo methods.

FORCES

- ☺ You need to control the sequencing, selection, or timing of command execution.
- ☺ You need to manage the undo and redo of commands.
- ☺ You need to maintain a persistent log of commands executed. You can generate such a log by enhancing command objects so that their doIt and undoIt methods generate log entries. Since you can use a persistent log to back out the effects of previously executed commands, a persistent log can be incorporated into a transaction management mechanism to allow commands to be undone if a transaction is aborted.

SOLUTION

Figure 8.5 presents a class diagram that shows classes that participate in the Command pattern.

Here are explanations of the roles that classes play in the Command pattern:

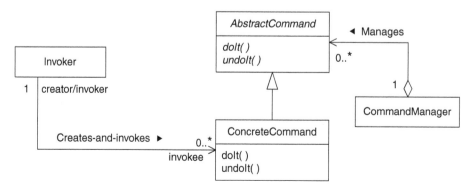

FIGURE 8.5 Command pattern.

AbstractCommand.   A class in this role is the superclass of other classes that encapsulate commands. It minimally defines an abstract doIt method that other classes call to execute the command encapsulated by its subclasses. If undo support is required, an AbstractCommand class also defines an undoIt method that undoes the effects of the last call to the doIt method.

ConcreteCommand.   Classes in this role are concrete classes that encapsulate a specific command. Other classes invoke the command through a call to the class's doIt method. The undo logic for the command is invoked through a call to the class's undoIt method.

   The object's constructor normally supplies any parameters that the command requires. Most commands require at least one parameter, which is the object that the command acts on. For example, a command to save an object to disk normally requires that the object to be saved be passed to the command object's constructor.

Invoker.   A class in this role creates concrete command objects if it needs to invoke a command. It may call a command object's doIt method or leave that for the CommandManager object to do.

CommandManager.   A CommandManager class is responsible for managing a collection of command objects created by an Invoker object. The specific responsibilities of a CommandManager class can include managing the undo and redo of commands, sequencing commands, and scheduling commands.

   CommandManager classes are usually independent of the applications in which they are used and can be very reusable.

IMPLEMENTATION

There are a few issues to consider when implementing the Command pattern. The first and possibly most important is to decide what commands will be. If the commands are issued by a user interface that provides user-level commands, then a very natural way to identify concrete command classes is to have a concrete command class for each user-level command. If you stick with this strategy and there are any particularly complex user commands, then there will be equally complex command classes. To avoid putting too much complexity in one class, you may want to implement more complex user-level commands with multiple command classes.

   If the number of external or user-level commands is very large, then you might follow the strategy of implementing external or user-level commands with combinations of command objects. This strategy may allow you to implement a large number of external commands with a smaller number of command classes.

UNDO/REDO

Another implementation issue to consider is the capture of state information necessary to undo commands. In order to be able to undo the effects of a command, it is necessary to save enough of the state of the objects it operates on to be able to restore that state.

There may be commands that cannot be undone because they involve saving an excessive amount of state information. For example, a global search-and-replace command may sometimes involve changing so much information that keeping all of the original information would take up a prohibitive amount of storage. There may be commands that can never be undone because it is not possible to restore the state that those commands change. Commands that involve the deletion of files often fall into this category.

The CommandManager object should be aware when a command is executed that is not undoable. There are a number of reasons for this:

- Suppose that a CommandManager object is responsible for the initial execution of commands. If it is aware that a command will be undoable before it is executed, then it can provide a common mechanism for warning a user that an undoable command is about to be executed. When it warns a user, it can also offer the user the option of not executing the command.
- Keeping a command history for undo purposes consumes memory and sometimes other resources. After executing a command that cannot be undone, any command history that is available can be disposed of. Keeping the command history after executing a command that is not undoable is a waste of resources.
- Most user interfaces for programs that have an undo command have a menu item for users to issue an undo command. A good user interface avoids surprising users. Responding to an undo command with a notification that the last command was not undoable surprises a user who expected an undo command to be carried out. A way to avoid this surprise is for the command manager object to enable or disable the undo menu item to reflect whether the last executed command was undoable or not undoable.

You can simplify the pattern if you do not need to support undo operations. If no undo support is required, then the AbstractCommand class does not need to define an undoIt method.

AVOIDING USER-INTERFACE DEPENDENCIES

There is a common extension to the Command pattern used when commands are issued by a user interface. The purpose of the extension is to avoid tying user-interface components to a specific command object or even requiring user-interface components to know about any concrete command classes. The extension consists of embedding the name of a command in user-interface components and using a factory method object to create the command objects, as shown in Figure 8.6.

In the organization shown in Figure 8.6, GUI component classes refer to the name of the command that they invoke, rather than the command class that implements that command or an instance of it. They invoke commands indirectly by passing the name of the command to a factory object that creates an instance of the appropriate concrete command class.

Invoking commands through a command factory provides a layer of indirection that can be very useful. The indirection allows multiple command-issuing objects to transparently share the same command object. More importantly, the indirection makes it easier to have user-customizable menus and toolbars.

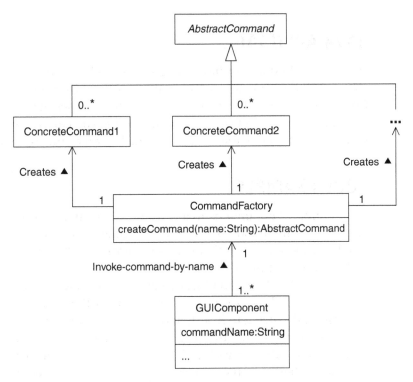

FIGURE 8.6 Command factory.

Programs commonly create commands in response to events such as keystrokes or selecting a menu item. Some programs use events to represent commands. This is usually not a good idea, since changes to the user interface can imply changes to the commands that the user interface invokes.

CONSEQUENCES

☺ The object that invokes a command is not the same object that executes a command. This separation provides flexibility in the timing and sequencing of commands. Materializing commands as objects means that they can be collected, delegated to, and otherwise manipulated like any other kind of object.

☺ Being able to collect and control the sequencing of commands means that you can use the Command pattern as the basis of a mechanism that supports keyboard macros. This is a mechanism that records a sequence of commands and allows them to be replayed later. The Command pattern can also be used to create other kinds of composite patterns.

☺ Adding new commands is usually easy because it does not break any dependencies.

JAVA API USAGE

Java's core API does not have any good examples of the Command pattern. However, it does contain some support for the GUI extension to the Command pattern. Its button and menu item classes have methods called `getActionCommand` and `setActionCommand` that you can use to get and set the name of a command associated with the button or menu item.

CODE EXAMPLE

The example of commands in a word processor that can be undone and redone, presented under the Context heading, continues here. Figure 8.7 is a collaboration diagram that shows the normal collaboration that creates and executes commands.

Figure 8.7 shows an object creating an instance of the `Insert-StringCommand` class, passing to its constructor the document to insert a string into, the string to insert, and the position in which to insert the string. After initializing the `InsertStringCommand` object, the constructor calls the `CommandManager` object's `invokeCommand` method. The `invoke-Command` method calls the `InsertStringCommand` object's `doIt` method, which does the actual string insertion. If the `doIt` method returns true, indicating

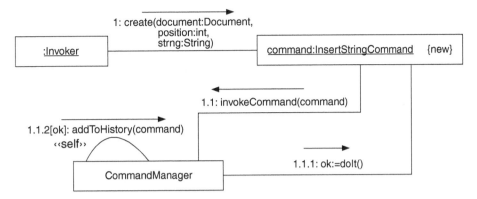

FIGURE 8.7 Word processor command collaboration.

that the command was successful and can be undone, then the Command-
Manager object adds the InsertStringCommand object to its command history.

Here is some code that implements this. First is the AbstractCommand
class, which is the superclass of all of the concrete command classes in
this example:

```
public abstract class AbstractCommand {
    public final static CommandManager manager
      = new CommandManager();

    /**
     * Perform the command encapsulated by this object.
     * @return true if successful and can be undone.
     */
    public abstract boolean doIt();

    /**
     * Undo the last invocation of doIt.
     * @return true if the undo was successful
     */
    public abstract boolean undoIt();
} // class AbstractCommand
```

The AbstractCommand class creates the instance of CommandManager
used to manage all instances of AbstractCommand. Concrete subclasses of
AbstractCommand are able to access the CommandManager object through the
AbstractCommand class's manager variable.

Here is source code for a concrete subclass of the AbstractCommand
class:

```
class InsertStringCommand extends AbstractCommand {
    ...
    /**
```

```
     * Constructor
     */
    InsertStringCommand(Document document,
                        int position,
                        String strng) {
        this.document = document;
        this.position = position;
        this.strng = strng;
        manager.invokeCommand(this);
    } // Constructor(Document, int, String)

    /**
     * Perform the command encapsulated by this object.
     * @return true if this call to doCommand was successful
     *         and can be undone.
     */
    public boolean doIt() {
        try {
            document.insertStringCommand(position, strng);
        } catch (Exception e) {
            return false;
        } // try
        return true;
    } // doIt()

    /**
     * Undo the command encapsulated by this object.
     * @return true if undo was successful
     */
    public boolean undoIt() {
        try {
            document.deleteCommand(position, strng.length());
        } catch (Exception e) {
            return false;
        } // try
        return true;
    } // undoIt()
} // class InsertStringCommand
```

The basic structure of most other subclasses of the `AbstractCommand` class is similar. Notable exceptions are the classes for undo and redo commands, which are shown later in this section.

The following listing is of the `CommandManager` class, which is responsible for managing the execution of commands. More specifically, for the purposes of the word processing program, instances of this class are responsible for maintaining a command history for undo and redo. Notice the special handling for undo and redo.

```
class CommandManager {
    // The maximum number of commands to keep in the history
    private int maxHistoryLength = 100;
```

```java
private LinkedList history = new LinkedList();
private LinkedList redoList = new LinkedList();


/**
 * Invoke a command and add it to the history,
 */
public void invokeCommand(AbstractCommand command) {
    if (command instanceof Undo) {
        undo();
        return;
    } // if undo
    if (command instanceof Redo) {
        redo();
        return;
    } // if redo
    if (command.doIt()) {
        // doIt returned true, which means it can be undone
        addToHistory(command);
    } else { // cannot be undone, so clear command history
        history.clear();
    } // if
    // After command that isn't undo/redo, ensure redo
    // list is empty.
    if (redoList.size() > 0)
      redoList.clear();
} // invokeCommand(AbstractCommand)

private void undo() {
    if (history.size() > 0) { // If history not empty
        AbstractCommand undoCmd;
        undoCmd = (AbstractCommand)history.removeFirst();
        undoCmd.undoIt();
        redoList.addFirst(undoCmd);
    } // if
} // undo()

private void redo() {
    if (redoList.size() > 0) { // If redo list not empty
        AbstractCommand redoCommand;
        redoCmd = (AbstractCommand)redoList.removeFirst();
        redoCmd.doIt();
        history.addFirst(redoCmd);
    } // if
} // redo()


/**
 * Add a command to the command history.
 */
private void addToHistory(AbstractCommand command) {
    history.addFirst(command);
    // If size of history has exceeded maxHistoryLength,
    // remove the oldest command from the history
    if (history.size() > maxHistoryLength)
```

```
                history.removeLast();
        } // addToHistory(AbstractCommand)
} // class CommandManager
```

You will notice that the `CommandManager` class does not actually use the command classes that represent the undo and redo classes. It just checks whether their instances implement the `Undo` or `Redo` interfaces. These interfaces are purely marker interfaces. They do not declare any members. Here is the listing for the Undo interface:

```
interface Undo {
} // interface Undo
```

The source code for the `Redo` interface is similar.

The reason for using these marker interfaces is to keep the `CommandManager` class independent of specific subclasses of the `AbstractCommand` class. Because the `CommandManager` class is responsible for managing undo and redo, all that classes representing undo and redo need to do is let a `CommandManager` object know that it should undo or redo the last command. It is preferable for it to do this in a way that does not require the `CommandManager` class to expose any of its special logic. This implies a mechanism that allows a `CommandManager` object to ask whether it needs to perform an undo or redo, rather than being told. Being able to determine whether an object implements the `Undo` or `Redo` interface allows a `CommandManager` object to ask whether it should perform an undo or redo without having to know anything about the class that implements the interface.

Finally, here is source code for the `UndoCommand` class. The `RedoCommand` class source code is very similar.

```
class UndoCommand extends AbstractCommand implements Undo {
    /**
     * This implementation of doIt does not actually do
     * anything.  The logic for undo is in the CommandManager
     * class.
     */
    public boolean doIt() {
        // This method should never be called
        throw new NoSuchMethodError();
    } // doIt()

    /**
     * This implementation of undoIt does not actually do
     * anything.  Undo commands are not undone.  Instead, a
     * redo command is issued.
     */
    public boolean undoIt() {
        // This method should never be called
```

```
        throw new NoSuchMethodError();
    } // undoIt()
} // class UndoCommand
```

Because there should never be a reason to call the methods of this class, the methods always throw an exception.

RELATED PATTERNS

Factory Method.   The Factory Method pattern is sometimes used to provide a layer of indirection between a user interface and command classes.

Little Language.   You can use the Command pattern to help implement the Little Language pattern. You can also use the Little Language pattern to implement commands.

Marker Interface.   You can use the Marker Interface pattern with the Command pattern to implement undo/redo processing.

Snapshot.   If you want to provide a coarse-grained undo mechanism that saves the entire state of an object rather than a command-by-command account of how to reconstruct previous states, you can use the Snapshot pattern.

Template Method.   The Template Method pattern can be used to implement the top-level undo logic of the Command pattern.

Little Language

The Little Language pattern is based on the Interpreter pattern documented in [GoF95] and the notion of little languages popularized by Jon Bentley [Bentley86]. You can find more sophisticated techniques for designing and implementing languages in [ASU86].

SYNOPSIS

Suppose you need to solve many similar problems and you notice that the solutions to these problems can be expressed as different combinations of a small number of elements or operations. The simplest way to express solutions to these problems may be to define a little language. Common types of problems you can solve with little languages are searches of common data structures, creation of complex data structures, and formatting of data.

CONTEXT

Suppose that you need to write a program that searches a collection of files to find files that contain a given combination or combinations of words. You don't want to have to write a separate program for each search. Instead, you can define a little language that allows users to describe combinations of words and then write one program that finds files that contains a combination of words specified in the little language.

The definition of a language usually consists of two parts. The *syntax* of a language defines the words and symbols that make up the language and how they may be combined. The *semantics* of a language defines the meaning of the words, symbols and their combinations that make up the language.

You usually define the syntax of a language by writing a grammar. A grammar is a set of rules that define the sequences of characters that make up the words and symbols of the language. A grammar also contains rules that define how you can combine the words and symbols of the language to form larger constructs.

The precise definition of the semantics of a large language can be very complicated and lengthy. However, for a little language a few simple paragraphs of explanation may be good enough.

Let's return to the idea of defining a little language to define combinations of words. One way to define a little language is to first create a few examples of what the language should look like. Then you can generalize from the examples to a complete definition.

Following this plan, consider some things that will be useful to say in a little language for specifying combinations of words. The most basic thing is to be able to specify a combination that consists of just a single word. The most obvious way to specify that is by simply writing the word, like this:

```
bottle
```

You will also want to be able to specify combinations of words that don't contain a word. A simple way of doing that is to precede the word you don't want in combinations by the word *not*, like this:

```
not box
```

This specifies all combinations of words that do not contain the word *box*.

Using words like *not* to mean something other than a word that can be part of a combination makes those words special. Words like that are called *reserved words* because they are reserved for a special purpose and cannot be used the way that other words can be used. If you treat the word *not* as a reserved word, then that means that you cannot specify a combination of words that contains the word *not* by just writing the word *not*. As you read further in this discussion, you will see that there are reasons to treat other words as reserved words. This suggests that it will be useful to have a way to indicate a combination of words that contains any arbitrary word, sequence of words, or punctuation. A way of indicating a combination of arbitrary words and punctuation is to enclose the sequence of words in quotation marks, like this:

```
"Yes, not the"
```

The next level of complexity is to specify combinations of two words. Obviously, the syntax for a combination of two words must allow you to specify which words are in the combination. Since there are different ways to combine words, the syntax for specifying combinations of two words must also provide for specifying how the words are combined. One way to do that is to write one word of the combination, followed by a special word that indicates how the words are combined, followed by the second word of the combination. For example, you could write

```
bottle or jar
```

to indicate combinations of words that contain at least one of the words *bottle* or *jar*.

You will need additional words to indicate other ways to combine two words:

- Use the word *and* to indicate combinations of words that contain both words.
- Use the word *near* to indicate combinations that include the two words occurring within 25 words of each other.

If you wanted to combine the reserved word *and* with the reserved word *not* to indicate a combination of words that contains *garlic* but not *onions* it would be reasonable to write

```
garlic and not onions
```

These examples cover most of the things you will need to describe combinations involving two words. When you go beyond two words, you will need to deal with additional issues. It seems clear that

```
red and "pickup truck" and broken
```

means combinations of words that contain all three of the words *red*, the phrase *pickup truck*, and the word *broken*. When you mix different ways of combining words, the meaning becomes ambiguous. Does

```
turkey or chicken and soup
```

mean combinations of words that contain the word *turkey* or both of the words *chicken* and *soup*? Does it mean combinations of words that contain the word *soup* and at least one of the words *chicken* or *turkey*? One way to resolve this ambiguity is to require the use of parentheses to specify the order in which the logical connectors in a combination are used. To specify the first interpretation you could write:

```
turkey or (chicken and soup)
```

To specify the second interpretation, you could write

```
(turkey or chicken) and soup
```

Most people don't like being forced to write parentheses, so a rule that resolves the ambiguity without parentheses is desirable. A common type of rule used in language definitions to resolve this sort of ambiguity is called a *precedence rule*.

A precedence rule is a rule that assigns a different precedence to the different operations that occur in a language. Its use is to provide a way of deciding the order of operations. Operations with a higher precedence are done before operations with a lower precedence. Suppose that you assign the following precedence values:

near	3
and	2
or	1

Given those precedence values, the meaning of

```
mansion or big near house and rich
```

would be combinations of words that include the word *mansion* or both the words *rich* and *big,* with the word *big* occurring within 25 words of the word *house.*

Before you try to design any classes to make sense out of this little language, it is important to write a grammar that defines the syntax of the language. This will provide a clear specification from which to code. There are a few different strategies for organizing a grammar. The strategy used in this example is a *top-down* strategy. This means starting with the top-level construct in the language, a combination, and deciding all of the lower-level constructs that can constitute it, until the grammar is complete.

Above the level of individual characters, the constructs that make up a grammar are called *tokens.* The tokens in a grammar are classified as either terminal tokens or nonterminal tokens. Terminal tokens correspond to a contiguous sequence of characters. The word in a combination such as

```
fence
```

is a terminal token, as are parentheses and quoted strings. Higher-level constructs that are defined in terms of terminal tokens are called nonterminal tokens. A combination is a nonterminal token.

In most little languages, including this word combination language, terminal tokens may be separated by white-space characters that do not contribute to the meaning of the language.

The rules that determine how to recognize sequences of characters as terminal tokens are called *lexical analysis rules.* The rules that determine how to recognize nonterminal tokens as sequences of terminal and nonterminal tokens are called *productions.*

The notation used here for writing productions is called *Backus-Naur Form,* or, more commonly, BNF. In BNF, terminal tokens and nonterminal tokens are written using different fonts to distinguish them. This book indicates terminal tokens like this:

quoted_string

This book indicates nonterminal tokens like this:

combination

A production consists of a nonterminal token and a sequence of terminal and nonterminal tokens that can be recognized as that first nonterminal. Here is an example of a production:

combination → **word**

This production says that a combination nonterminal token can consist of just a word terminal token.

If there are multiple sequences of tokens that can be recognized as a nonterminal, then there will be multiple productions for that nonterminal. There will be one production for each sequence that can be recognized as that nonterminal. For example, the following set of productions specifies the syntax for combinations that do or don't contain a particular word:

combination → **word**
combination → **not word**

The technique that you use to specify that a nonterminal token should be recognized from an indefinitely long sequence of tokens is *recursion*. Here is a set of productions that captures most of the syntax of the preceding examples:

combination → **(** *combination* **)**
combination → *simpleCombination*
combination → *simpleCombination* **or** *combination*
combination → *simpleCombination* **and** *combination*
combination → *simpleCombination* **near** *combination*
simpleCombination → **word**
simpleCombination → **not word**

Notice that four of the five productions for *combination* are recursive. Three of those four productions could have been written with *combination* as the first nonterminal token and *simpleCombination* as the second nonterminal token. Either way, they would match the same sequences of tokens. However, for the implementation technique shown later in this section for turning productions into code, it makes a difference. For the technique we will discuss, it is always best to write productions as shown, in a right-recursive way. What we mean by *right-recursive* is that where there is a choice about where to put a recursion in a production, we choose to put the recursion as far to the right as we can.

Though this set of productions does not capture all the details of this word combination language, it captures enough that we can work through an example. We will examine how to use these productions to recognize this string as a combination:

```
fox and not brown
```

Looking at the productions for *combination*, we see that *combination* can begin with a left parenthesis or a *simpleCombination*. The string begins with a word token. Since the string we are trying to recognize as a *combination* does not begin with a left parenthesis, we try to recognize the beginning of the string as a *simpleCombination*. This matches the production

```
simpleCombination → word
```

This leaves us having recognized this much of the string:

```
‾‾‾
fox and not brown
```

The line over the string shows how much of the string has been recognized. This is what we have recognized:

```
simpleCombination
       |
     word
       |
      fox
```

In other words, what we have recognized is a *simpleCombination* token that consists of a word token that is the word *fox*. What we want to recognize is *combination*. Four productions for combination begin with *simpleCombination*. One of these productions is

```
combination → simpleCombination
```

This gives us a choice of matching this production with what we have already recognized or trying to match a longer production for *combination*. When faced with this type of choice, we always try to match a longer production. If we are unable to match a longer production, then we back up and match the shorter production.

The next token in the string is an **and** token. There is one production for *combination* that begins with *simpleCombination* followed by and:

```
combination → simpleCombination and combination
```

In order to finish matching the string to this production, we will need to recognize the rest of the string as a *combination*.

The next token in the string is a **not** token. Looking at the productions for *combination*, we see that *combination* can begin with a left parenthesis or a *simpleCombination*. Since the string we are trying to recognize as a *combination* does not begin with a left parenthesis, we try to recognize the beginning of the string as a *simpleCombination*. There is a production for *simpleCombination* that begins with a **not** token. Now we are trying to finish matching the production

```
simpleCombination → not word
```

so that we can finish matching

```
combination → simpleCombination and combination
```

Because we have matched half of the *simpleCombination* production, we expect the next token in the string to be a word token. We have recognized this much of the string:

```
fox and not brown
```

The next token is a **word** token. This means we have successfully matched the productions that we were tying to match. Since it also exhausts the content of the string, we have recognized the entire string as a combination with this internal structure:

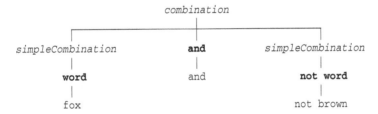

This tree structure that was constructed while parsing the string is called a *parse tree*. For most languages, the implementation is simpler and faster if it first builds a parse tree data structure and then uses the parse tree to drive subsequent actions.

As mentioned before, the set of productions we used to work through the preceding example does not capture all the details of the word combination language. It does not allow a combination to include quoted strings. It also doesn't capture precedence rules for **and**, **near**, or **or**.

There is another nuance that will be helpful to add to the productions. The previous set of productions uses the same nonterminal token to match the token sequences **word** and **not word**. This means that after we have built the parse tree, the same type of object will represent both kinds of sequences. It will simplify the interpretation of the parse tree and make it faster if it is possible to determine which type of sequence an object represents just by looking at its type. You can accomplish this by having productions that recognize those sequences as two different nonterminals.

Here is the final set of productions with those improvements added:

```
combination    → orCombination
orCombination  → andCombination or orCombination
orCombination  → andCombination
andCombination → nearCombination and andCombination
andCombination → nearCombination
nearCombination → simpleCombination near nearCombination
nearCombination → simpleCombination
simpleCombination → ( orCombination )
simpleCombination → wordCombination
simpleCombination → notWordCombination
wordCombination → word
wordCombination → quoted_string
notWordCombination → not word
notWordCombination → not quoted_string
```

You may notice that if you use these productions to parse a string, creating a parse tree node object for each nonterminal, you will have more parse tree node objects than were produced by the previous set of productions. Here is the parse tree that would be produced by parsing the same string as in the previous example

```
fox and not brown
```

and using the preceding productions to create a parse tree node object for each nonterminal:

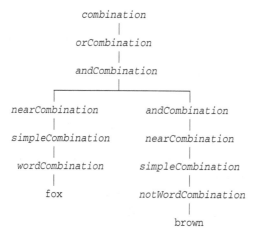

Notice that this parse tree contains many nodes that do not add anything useful to the tree. Without losing any information, this parse tree could be simplified to this:

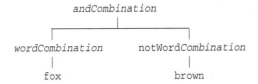

Before you write any code, you should decide which productions are purely organizational in nature and which productions provide useful information. A parser should produce only those parse tree nodes that provide information.

The preceding discussion covers the basics of writing productions to recognize tokens. Now let's consider how to define lexical rules that determine how to recognize terminal tokens from sequences of characters.

In many little languages, the lexical rules are sometimes simple enough that you can adequately define them by a natural language set of descriptions like this:

- White space consists of one or more consecutive space, tab, new-line, or carriage-return characters. White space can be used to separate terminal tokens. It has no other significance and is discarded.
- An **and** token consists of this sequence of three letters: **a**, **n**, **d**
- . . .

Where this approach does not seem adequate, you may prefer a more precise approach based on regular expressions. Regular expressions are a way of specifying how to match a sequence of characters. For example, the regular expression

```
[0-9]+
```

matches a sequence of one or more digits. There are a variety of regular expression notations you can use. The regular expression notation used in this section to define the lexical rules for the word combination language is explained in Table 8.1. It should be sufficiently expressive for most little languages.

Table 8.2 shows a set of lexical rules for the word combination language. In the first column is a regular expression. The second column contains the name of the terminal token, if any, that is recognized when the regular expression is matched. When a parser needs to find the next terminal token in its input, it will try the regular expressions in the order they appear until it finds one that matches the input. If no regular expression matches the input, then the parser knows that something is wrong with the input.

TABLE 8.1 Word Combination Language

Regular Expression	What it Matches
c	Matches the character *c* if *c* is not one of the special characters described in the following.
\	If a \ is followed by one of the escape sequences that Java allows in strings, then it means the same thing as that escape. If a \ is followed by any of the characters that are considered special in regular expressions, then the pair of characters is treated as the second character without it being special. For example, \\ matches a backslash character.
.	Matches any character.
^	Matches the beginning of a line or a string.
$	Matches the end of a line or string.
[s]	Matches a character that is in a set of characters and character ranges. For example, [aeiou] matches a lowercase vowel. [A-Za-z_] matches an uppercase or lowercase letter or an underscore.
[^s]	Matches a character that is *not* in a set of characters and character ranges. For example, [^0-9] matches a character that is not a digit. The ^ is treated specially only right after the [. For example, [+^] matches a plus sign or a circumflex.
r*	Matches zero or more occurrences of the regular expression *r*.
r+	Matches one or more occurrences of the regular expression *r*.
r?	Matches zero or one occurrences of the regular expression *r*.
rx	Matches what the regular expression *r* matches, followed by what the regular expression *x* matches.
(r)	Matches what the regular expression *r* matches. For example, (xyz)* matches zero or more occurrences of the sequence xyz.
r|x	Matches any string that matches the regular expression *r* or the regular expression *x*. For example, (abc)|(xyz) matches the sequence abc or the sequence xyz.
r{m,n}	Matches at least *m* occurrences but no more than *n* occurrences of regular expression *r*.

When a regular expression matches the input, if there is a terminal token in the second column, then the parser recognizes that token and processes it according to whatever production it is trying to match. If there is no terminal token in the second column, then the input that the regular expression matches is discarded and the parser begins again with the first regular expression.

Now we have specified the syntax of the word combination language. In the process of specifying the syntax, we have also discussed the seman-

TABLE 8.2 Lexical Rules for the Word Combination Language

`[\u0000-\u0020]+`	
`[Oo][Rr]`	**or**
`[Aa][Nn][Dd]`	**and**
`[Nn][Ee][Aa][Rr]`	**near**
`[Nn][Oo][Tt]`	**not**
`[a-zA-Z0-9]+`	**word**
`\(`	**(**
`\)`	**)**
`"([^"]*(\\")*)*"`	**quoted_string**

tics of the language sufficiently. The next thing to do is to design the classes. Figure 8.8 shows the classes necessary to implement the word combination language.

Figure 8.8 shows an `InputStream` class. Instances of the `LexicalAnalyzer` class read characters of a word combination from an instance of the `InputStream` class. An instance of the `Parser` class reads tokens from an instance of the `LexicalAnalyzer` class by calling its `nextToken` method. The diagram indicates that the `nextToken` method returns a `TerminalToken` object. However, the diagram does not include any `TerminalToken` class. If it did, the `TerminalToken` class would be an abstract class that defines no methods or variables. Each subclass of the `TerminalToken` class would correspond to a different terminal token. The subclasses of the `TerminalToken` class would define no methods and either no variables or one variable containing the string recognized as that terminal token. These would be very lightweight objects, encapsulating only the type of terminal token that the object represents and in some cases a string. Implementations of the Little Language pattern do not usually bother to encapsulate these pieces of information. Implementations of the `LexicalAnalyzer` class usually provide these pieces of information as unencapsulated pieces of information.

As a `Parser` object gets tokens from a `LexicalAnalyzer` object, it creates instances of subclasses of the `Combination` class, organizing them into a parse tree.

The `Combination` class is the abstract superclass of all the classes that are instantiated to create parse tree nodes. The `Combination` class defines an abstract method called `contains`. The `contains` method takes a string as its argument and returns an array of `int`. Subclasses of `Combination` override the `contains` method to determine whether it meets the requirements of the particular subclass for containing the desired combination of words. If the string does contain the required combination of words, it passes back an array of `int` values that are the offsets in the string of the words

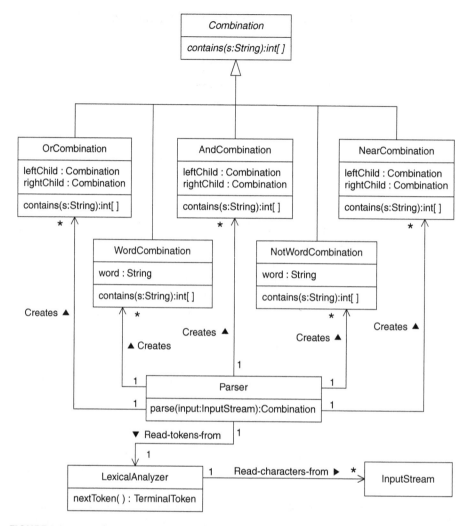

FIGURE 8.8 Word combination language classes.

that satisfied the combination. If the string does not contain the required combination of words, then the `contains` method returns null.

FORCES

☺ You need to identify, create, or format similar kinds of data using many different combinations of a moderate number of operations.
☺ A straightforward representation of combinations of operations can provide adequate performance.

SOLUTION

The Little Language pattern begins with the design of a little language that can specify combinations of operations needed to solve a specific type of problem. The design of a little language specifies its syntax using productions and lexical rules as described under the Context heading. The semantics of a little language are usually specified informally by describing what the constructs of the language do using English or another natural language.

Once you have defined a little language, the next step is to design the classes that you will use to implement the language. Figure 8.9 is a class diagram showing the organization of classes that participate in the Little Language pattern.

Here are explanations of the roles that these classes play in the Little Language pattern:

> **Client.** An instance of a class in this role runs a little language program, feeding it whatever data it needs and using the results that the program produces. It creates an instance of the `Parser`

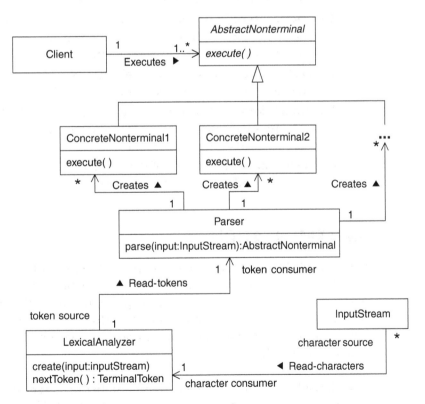

FIGURE 8.9 Little Language pattern classes.

class to parse programs that it supplies through InputStream objects. The Parser object's parse method returns an instance of the AbstractNonterminal class to the Client object. This object is the root of a parse tree. The Client object calls the AbstractNonterminal object's execute method to run the program.

LexicalAnalyzer.   When a Parser object's parse method is called, it creates a LexicalAnalyzer object to read characters from the same InputStream object that was passed to it. The LexicalAnalyzer object reads characters from the InputStream object, recognizes terminal tokens it finds using the lexical rules, and returns these tokens to the Parser class when it calls the LexicalAnalyzer object's nextToken method. The nextToken method returns the next terminal token that it finds in the input.

Parser.   A Client object creates an instance of the Parser class and then calls the Parser object's parse method to parse input from InputStream objects by matching the tokens in the input against the productions of the grammar. The parse method builds a parse tree as it matches the productions and returns a reference to the parse tree's root to the Client object.

AbstractNonterminal.   A class in this role is the abstract superclass of all the classes whose instances can be parse tree nodes. A Client object calls its abstract execute method to execute the program.

ConcreteNonterminal1, ConcreteNonterminal2, and so on.   Instances of classes in these roles are used as parse tree nodes.

TerminalToken.   This abstract class defines no variables or methods. Its subclasses correspond to the terminal tokens that the LexicalAnalyzer class recognizes.

InputStream.   An instance of the java.io.InputStream class can be used to read a stream of characters.

IMPLEMENTATION

Some people feel that it is better to implement a parser by spreading most of its logic through multiple classes that correspond to nonterminal tokens or even productions. A common reason given to explain this organization is that it is somehow more object-oriented. However, it is a less maintainable organization for parsers than the one described previously. There are two reasons for this:

● Spreading the parsing logic over a number of classes results in less cohesive classes that are difficult to understand. The parser for little languages is usually small enough that people can understand it in its entirety. Spreading the parsing logic over multiple classes makes it much more difficult to understand in its entirety.

● If a parser is too big to understand in its entirety, then it is big enough that its implementation would be worth changing so that it uses a tool that automatically generates the parser from productions. All available tools that are known to the author of this book generate a parser as a single class or as one main class with some helper classes. If there are other tools that generate a parser as multiple classes, it is very likely that the organization of those classes will be different than any manually generated organization. This means that if a parser is manually organized as many classes, switching to an automatically generated parser will involve fixing any classes that break because they refer to a defunct class of the manually generated parser. Manually generating a parser as multiple classes can make it more difficult to migrate to an automatically generated parser.

Most subclasses of `TerminalToken` do not contain any methods or variables. Those subclasses of `TerminalToken` that do contain variables usually contain just one variable whose value is the substring of the input that the class's instances match. Because subclasses of `TerminalToken` contain so little information, most implementations of the Little Language pattern do not bother using `TerminalToken` or its subclasses. Instead, they pass the type of token that the lexical analyzer recognized and the corresponding string from the lexical analyzer to the parser without encapsulating them in an object.

Parsers build parse trees from the bottom up. The root of a parse tree corresponds to at least as much of the program source as all of its children put together. As a parser parses its input, it creates small parse trees. It joins the small parse trees into larger parse trees with a common root as it recognizes larger and larger constructs. When the parser is done, there is just one big parse tree.

Many optimizations and design subtleties that are important to full-service languages are not important to little languages. The point is that the techniques described in this pattern are not sufficient for designing or implementing larger languages like Java.

CONSEQUENCES

● The Little Language pattern allows users to specify different combinations of operations. It is almost always easier to design and implement a little language than it is to design and implement a GUI that

provides as much flexibility and expressiveness as a little language. On the other hand, most users find the GUI easier to use.
- A language is a form of user interface. Like any user interface, you learn what it makes easy and not so easy to use by using it and watching other people use it.
- A Parser class is usually implemented by writing private methods that mostly correspond to nonterminal tokens. This organization is easy to understand and grammar changes are easy to implement, so long as the grammar remains relatively small. If the language gets too large, this organization becomes unmanageable.

For larger and full-service languages, there are different and more sophisticated design and implementation techniques. Tools exist that can automatically generate Parser and LexicalAnalyzer classes from productions and lexical rules. There are other tools that assist in the building and simplification of parse trees.

JAVA API USAGE

Subclasses of java.text.Format use the Little Language pattern. The constructors of these classes are passed, explicitly or implicitly, a string that contains a description of a format in a little language. Each subclass has its own little language for such things as substituting text in messages (MessageFormat), formatting date and time information (DateFormat), and formatting decimal numbers (DecimalFormat).

Because of the flat structure of these little languages, their parsers do not generate a parse tree but rather an array of objects.

CODE EXAMPLE

The first code example is the lexical analyzer. Because the word combination language's lexical rules are sufficiently similar to Java's lexical rules, the java.io.StreamTokenizer class can do much of the work. This is the same class that Sun's Java compiler uses for its lexical analysis.

```
class LexicalAnalyzer {
    private StreamTokenizer input;
    private int lastToken;

    // constants to identify the type of the last token.
    static final int INVALID_CHAR = -1;// unexpected character.
    static final int NO_TOKEN = 0;// No tokens recognized yet.
```

```
static final int OR = 1;
static final int AND = 2;
static final int NEAR = 3;
static final int NOT = 4;
static final int WORD = 5;
static final int LEFT_PAREN = 6;
static final int RIGHT_PAREN = 7;
static final int QUOTED_STRING = 8;
static final int EOF = 9;

/**
 * Constructor
 * @param input The input stream to read.
 */
LexicalAnalyzer(InputStream in) {
    input = new StreamTokenizer(in);
    input.resetSyntax();
    input.eolIsSignificant(false);
    input.wordChars('a', 'z');
    input.wordChars('A','Z');
    input.wordChars('0','9');
    input.wordChars('\u0000',' ');
    input.ordinaryChar('(');
    input.ordinaryChar(')');
    input.quoteChar('"');
} // constructor(InputStream)

/**
 * Return the string recognized as word token or the body
 * of a quoted string.
 */
String getString() {
    return input.sval;
} // getString()

/**
 * Return the type of the next token.  For word and quoted
 * string tokens, the string that the token represents can
 * be fetched by calling the getString method.
 */
int nextToken() {
    int token;
    try {
        switch (input.nextToken()) {
          case StreamTokenizer.TT_EOF:
              token = EOF;
              break;
          case StreamTokenizer.TT_WORD:
              if (input.sval.equalsIgnoreCase("or"))
                token = OR;
              else if (input.sval.equalsIgnoreCase("and"))
                token = AND;
              else if (input.sval.equalsIgnoreCase("near"))
```

```
                  token = NEAR;
              else if (input.sval.equalsIgnoreCase("not"))
                  token = NOT;
              else
                  token = WORD;
              break;
          case '"':
              token = QUOTED_STRING;
              break;
          case '(':
              token = LEFT_PAREN;
              break;
          case ')':
              token = RIGHT_PAREN;
              break;
          default:
              token = INVALID_CHAR;
              break;
          } // switch
      } catch (IOException e) {
          // Treat an IOException as an end of file
          token = EOF;
      } // try
      return token;
    } // nextToken()
} // class LexicalAnalyzer
```

Although the `LexicalAnalyzer` class uses the `StringTokenizer` class to do much of the lexical analysis, it provides its own codes to indicate the type of token that it recognized. This allows the implementation of the `LexicalAnalyzer` class to change without any impact on classes that use the `LexicalAnalyzer` class.

The parser implementation uses a technique called *recursive descent*. A recursive descent parser has methods that correspond to nonterminal tokens defined by grammar productions. The methods call each other in roughly the same pattern in which the corresponding grammar productions refer to each other. Where there is recursion in the grammar productions, there is generally recursion in the methods. One important exception is when the recursion is a self-recursion through the rightmost token in a production, like this:

orCombination → *andCombination* **or** *orCombination*

Translating this in the obvious way into a self-recursive method produces a method that performs a self-recursion as the last thing it does before it returns. That type of recursion is a special case called *tail recursion*. Tail recursion is special because you can always change a tail recursion into a loop. In the following code for the `Parser` class, you will see that methods corresponding to nonterminals defined in a self-recursive way implement the self-recursion using a loop.

```java
public class Parser {
    private LexicalAnalyzer lexer; // lexical analyzer
    private int token;

    /**
     * Parse a word combination from the given input stream.
     * @param input
     *        Read word combinations from this InputStream.
     * @return A combination object that is the root of the
     *         parse tree.
     */
    public Combination parse(InputStream input)
                                        throws SyntaxException{
        lexer = new LexicalAnalyzer(input);
        Combination c = orCombination();
        expect(LexicalAnalyzer.EOF);
        return c;
    } // parse(InputStream)

    private Combination orCombination()
                            throws SyntaxException {
        Combination c = andCombination();
        while (token == LexicalAnalyzer.OR) {
            c = new OrCombination(c, andCombination());
        } // while
        return c;
    } // orCombination()

    private Combination andCombination()
                                throws SyntaxException {
        Combination c = nearCombination();
        while (token == LexicalAnalyzer.AND) {
            c = new AndCombination(c, nearCombination());
        } // while
        return c;
    } // andCombination

    private Combination nearCombination()
                                throws SyntaxException {
        Combination c = simpleCombination();
        while (token == LexicalAnalyzer.NEAR) {
            c = new NearCombination(c, simpleCombination());
        } // while
        return c;
    } // nearCombination()

    private Combination simpleCombination()
                                throws SyntaxException {
        if (token == LexicalAnalyzer.LEFT_PAREN) {
            nextToken();
            Combination c = orCombination();
            expect(LexicalAnalyzer.RIGHT_PAREN);
            return c;
```

```
                    } // if '('
                    if (token == LexicalAnalyzer.NOT)
                      return notWordCombination();
                    else
                      return wordCombination();
            } // simpleCombination()

            private Combination wordCombination()
                                              throws SyntaxException {
                    if (token != LexicalAnalyzer.WORD
                        && token != LexicalAnalyzer.QUOTED_STRING) {
                        // print error message and throw SyntaxException
                        expect(LexicalAnalyzer.WORD);
                    } // if
                    Combination c = new WordCombination(lexer.getString());
                    nextToken();
                    return c;
            } // wordCombination()

            private Combination notWordCombination()
                                              throws SyntaxException {
                    expect(LexicalAnalyzer.NOT);
                    if (token != LexicalAnalyzer.WORD
                        && token != LexicalAnalyzer.QUOTED_STRING) {
                        // print error message and throw SyntaxException
                        expect(LexicalAnalyzer.WORD);
                    } // if
                    Combination c;
                    c = new NotWordCombination(lexer.getString());
                    nextToken();
                    return c;
            } // notWordCombination()

            // Get the next token from the lexer.
            private void nextToken() {
                token = lexer.nextToken();
            } // nextToken()
```

The remainder of the `Parser` class is a method called `expect` and a helper method for `expect` called `tokenName`. The `expect` method issues an error message if the current terminal token is not the type of token passed to the `expect` method. If the token is the expected kind of token, then the `expect` method reads the next token from the lexical analyzer.

Most recursive descent parsers have a method similar to `expect`, and it is often called `expect`.

```
            // Complain if the current token is not the specified kind
            // of token.
            private void expect(int t) throws SyntaxException {
                if (token != t) {
                    String msg = "found " + tokenName(token)
                        + " when expecting " + tokenName(t);
```

```
            throw new SyntaxException(msg);
        } // if
        nextToken();
    } // expect(int)

    private String tokenName(int t) {
        String tname;
        switch (t) {
          case LexicalAnalyzer.OR:
            tname = "OR";
            break;
          case LexicalAnalyzer.AND:
            tname = "AND";
            break;
          case LexicalAnalyzer.NEAR:
            tname = "NEAR";
            break;
          case LexicalAnalyzer.NOT:
            tname = "NOT";
            break;
          case LexicalAnalyzer.WORD:
            tname = "word";
            break;
          case LexicalAnalyzer.LEFT_PAREN:
            tname = "(";
            break;
          case LexicalAnalyzer.RIGHT_PAREN:
            tname = ")";
            break;
          case LexicalAnalyzer.QUOTED_STRING:
            tname = "quoted string";
            break;
          case LexicalAnalyzer.EOF:
            tname = "end of file";
            break;
          default:
            tname = "???";
            break;
        } // switch
        return tname;
    } // tokenName(int)
} // class Parser
```

There is an obvious relationship between the productions of the formal grammar and the preceding code for the Parser class. Because the relationship between the two is so obvious, you may feel tempted to skip writing the formal grammar and just define your little language with code. Skipping the formal grammar is usually a bad idea for the following reasons:

● Without a formal grammar, there is no precise way to communicate the definition of your language to other people without having them read your source code.

- As the syntax for languages becomes larger or more complex, so does the parser for the language. As the parser becomes more complex, the code becomes cluttered with necessary details and the relationship between the code and the grammar it implements becomes less obvious.
- Over time, languages often evolve, gaining new features. When trying to make changes to a language that has no formal grammar, you may find it difficult to distinguish between changes to the language's grammar and changes to its implementation.

The next piece of code in this example is the `Combination` class, which is the abstract superclass of all parse tree objects:

```
abstract class Combination {
    /**
     * If the given string contains the words that this
     * Combination object requires, this method returns an
     * array of ints.  In most cases, the array contains the
     * offsets of the words in the string that are required by
     * this combination.  However, if the array is empty, then
     * all the words in the string satisfy the combination.
     * If the given string does not contain the words that this
     * Combination object requires, then this method returns
     * null.
     */
    abstract int[] contains(String s) ;
} // class Combination
```

You will notice that the methods of `Combination` and its subclasses relate almost exclusively to the execution of combinations. There is almost no code related to the manipulation of the objects in the parse tree. Some larger languages require additional analysis of a program after it is parsed, in order to turn it into an executable form. For such languages, a parse tree is an intermediate form for a program, distinct from its executable form. The Little Language pattern assumes that a language is simple enough that you can use a parse tree for both purposes.

Here is the source for `NotWordCombination`, which is the simplest subclass of `Combination`:

```
class NotWordCombination extends Combination {
    private String word;

    /**
     * constructor
     * @param word The word that this combination requires in
     *             a string
     */
    NotWordCombination(String word) {
```

```
        this.word = word;
    } // constructor(String)

    /**
     * If the given string contains the word that this
     * NotWordCombination object requires, this method returns
     * an array of the offsets where the word occurs in the
     * string.  Otherwise this method returns null.
     */
    int[] contains(String s) {
        if (s.indexOf(word) >= 0)
          return null;
        return new int[0];
    } // contains(String)
} // class NotWordCombination
```

The `WordCombination` class is similar. The main difference is that it contains logic to return a vector of the offsets of all of the occurrences in a given string of the word associated with a `WordCombination` object.

The subclasses of `Combination` that represent logical operators, `OrCombination`, `AndCombination`, and `NearCombination` are more complex. They are responsible for combining the results of two child `Combination` objects. Here is source code for `AndCombination` and `OrCombination`:

```
class AndCombination extends Combination {
    private Combination leftChild, rightChild;

    AndCombination(Combination leftChild,
                   Combination rightChild) {
        this.leftChild = leftChild;
        this.rightChild = rightChild;
    } // constructor(Combination, Combination)

    int[] contains(String s) {
        int[] leftResult = leftChild.contains(s);
        int[] rightResult = rightChild.contains(s);
        if (leftResult == null ||rightResult == null)
          return null;
        if (leftResult.length == 0)
          return rightResult;
        if (rightResult.length == 0)
          return leftResult;

        // Sort results so that they can be compared and merged
        Sorter.sort(leftResult);
        Sorter.sort(rightResult);

        // Count common offsets to find out if there are common
        // offsets and how many there will be.
        int commonCount = 0;
        for (int l=0,r=0;
            l<leftResult.length && r<rightResult.length;){
```

```
                if (leftResult[l] < rightResult[r]) {
                    l++;
                } else if (leftResult[l] > rightResult[r]) {
                    r++;
                } else {
                    commonCount++;
                    l++;
                    r++;
                } // if
            } // for
        if (commonCount == 0)
          return null;                // There are no common results

        // merge common results
        int[] myResult = new int[commonCount];
        commonCount = 0;
        for (int l=0,r=0;
                l<leftResult.length && r<rightResult.length;){
                if (leftResult[l] < rightResult[r]) {
                    l++;
                } else if (leftResult[l] > rightResult[r]) {
                    r++;
                } else {
                    myResult[commonCount] = leftResult[l];
                    commonCount++;
                    l++;
                    r++;
                } // if
            } // for
        return myResult;
    } // contains(String)
} // class AndCombination

class OrCombination extends Combination {
    private Combination leftChild, rightChild;

    /**
     * constructor
     * @param left This object's left child.
     * @param right This object's right child.
     */
    OrCombination(Combination left, Combination right) {
        leftChild = left;
        rightChild = right;
    } // constructor(Combination, Combination)

    int[] contains(String s) {
        int[] leftResult = leftChild.contains(s);
        int[] rightResult = rightChild.contains(s);
        if (leftResult == null)
          return rightResult;
        if (rightResult == null)
          return leftResult;
```

```
      if (leftResult.length == 0)
        return leftResult;
      if (rightResult.length == 0)
        return rightResult;
      // create array of combined results
      int[] myResult
        = new int[leftResult.length + rightResult.length];
      System.arraycopy(leftResult, 0, myResult, 0,
                       leftResult.length);
      System.arraycopy(rightResult, 0, myResult,
                       leftResult.length,
                       rightResult.length);
      return myResult;
    } // contains(String)
} // class OrCombination
```

RELATED PATTERNS

Composite.   A parse tree is organized with the Composite pattern.

Visitor.   The Visitor pattern allows you to encapsulate the logic for simple manipulations of a parse tree in a single class.

Mediator

This pattern was previously described in [GoF95]

SYNOPSIS

The Mediator pattern uses one object to coordinate state changes between other objects. It puts the logic to manage state changes of other objects in one class, instead of distributing the logic over the other classes. This results in a more cohesive implementation of the logic and decreased coupling between the other classes.

CONTEXT

The Mediator pattern addresses a problem that commonly occurs in dialog boxes. Suppose you have to implement a dialog box that looks like the one in Figure 8.10, in order to specify information to reserve a banquet room in a hotel.

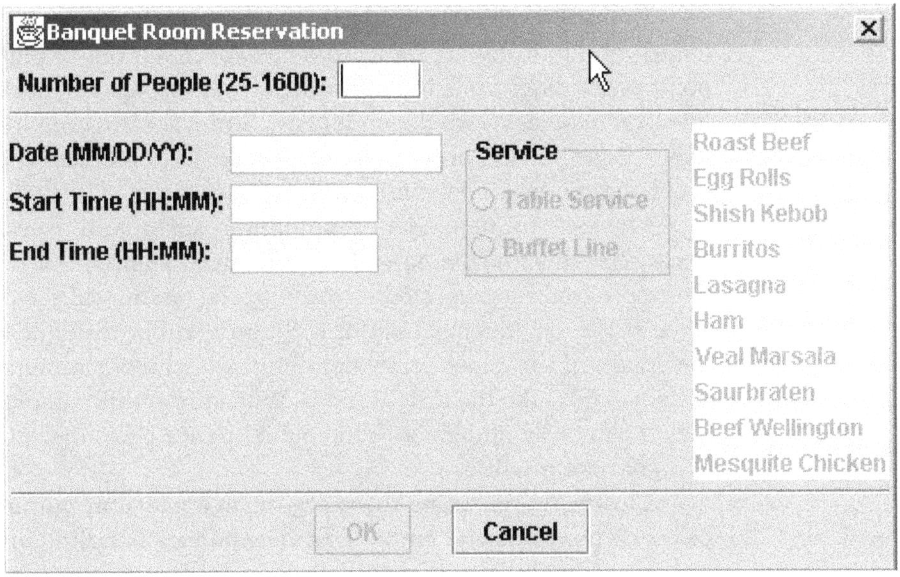

FIGURE 8.10 Banquet room dialog.

The purpose of the dialog in Figure 8.10 is to provide information to reserve a banquet room in a hotel. The requirements of the dialog give rise to a number of dependencies among the dialog's objects.

- When the dialog first comes up, only the fields labeled "Number of People" and the Cancel button are enabled. The rest of the dialog is disabled until a number in the range of 25 to 1000 is entered into the Number of People field. At that point, the fields labeled "Date," "Start Time," and "End Time" become enabled but only allow times that a room of an appropriate size is available. The radio buttons are also enabled. Subsequent changes to the Number of People field clear the other fields and the radio buttons.
- The start time must be earlier than the end time.
- When a user fills in the Time and Date fields and selects a radio button, then the list of foods becomes enabled. The date, time, and type of service requested determine the foods that appear in the list. Some foods are seasonal. The hotel offers these only between certain dates. Breakfast foods are on the list only for morning banquets. Some foods suitable for table service are not suitable for buffets.
- When at least one food is selected and the text fields contain valid data, the OK button is enabled.

If each object in the dialog takes responsibility for the dependencies it is associated with, the result is a highly coupled set of objects with low cohesion. Figure 8.11 shows the relationships between the objects.

In the interest of simplifying the diagram, the association names, role names, and multiplicity indicators have been left out of Figure 8.11. The point of the diagram is the number of links. As you can see, each object is involved in at least two dependencies. Some are involved in as many as five. A large portion of the time it will take to implement the dialog will be spent coding the 15 dependency links.

The logic for dependency handling is spread out over eight objects. Because of this, the dialog will be difficult to maintain. When a maintenance programmer works on the dialog, he or she will see only a small piece of the dependency handling. Since it will be difficult to understand the details of the dependency handling as a whole, maintenance programmers will not take the time to do it. When programmers maintain code they do not fully understand, the maintenance takes more time and is often of poor quality.

Clearly, reorganizing these objects in a way that minimizes the number of connections and gathers the dependency handling into one cohesive object is a good thing. It is an improvement that will save programmer time and produce more robust code. This is what the Mediator pattern is

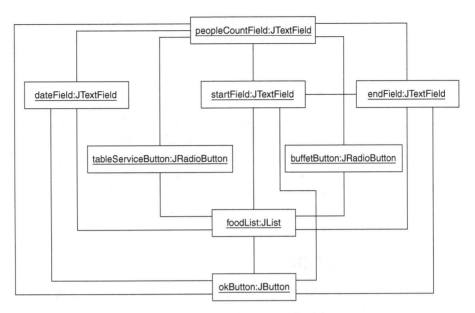

FIGURE 8.11 Decentralized dependency management.

about. Instead of each object individually managing the dependencies it has with other objects, you use another object that consolidates all of the dependency handling. In this arrangement, each of the other objects has only one dependency connection.

Figure 8.12 shows the dialog's objects organized with an additional object to centrally manage dependencies.

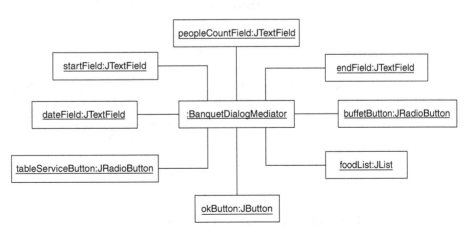

FIGURE 8.12 Centralized dependency management.

In addition to making the implementation easier to code and maintain, the design shown in Figure 8.12 is easier to understand.

FORCES

☺ You have a set of related objects and most of the objects are involved in multiple dependency relationships.

☺ You find yourself defining subclasses so that individual objects will be able to participate in dependency relationships.

☺ Classes are difficult to reuse because their basic function is entwined with dependency relationships.

SOLUTION

Figure 8.13 shows how classes and interfaces participate in the Mediator pattern in the general case.

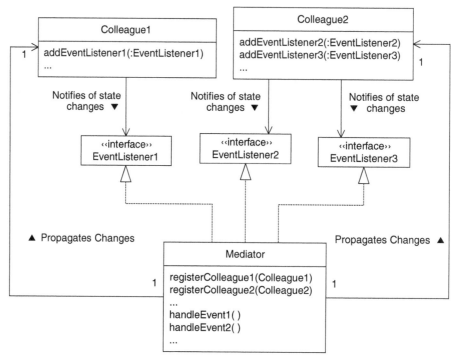

FIGURE 8.13 Mediator pattern classes.

Here are explanations of the roles that these classes and interfaces play in the Mediator pattern:

Colleague1, Colleague2, and so on. Instances of classes in these roles have state-related dependencies. There are two types of dependencies.

- One type of dependency requires an object to get approval from other objects before making specific types of state changes.
- The other type of dependency requires an object to notify other objects after it has made specific types of state changes.

Both types of dependencies are handled in a similar way. Instances of `Colleague1`, `Colleague2`, and so on, are associated with a `Mediator` object. When they need to notify other objects about a state change, they call a method of the `Mediator` object. The `Mediator` object's method takes care of the rest.

EventListener1, EventListener2, and so on. Interfaces in this role allow the `Colleague1`, `Colleague2`, and so on, classes to achieve a higher level of reuse. They do this by allowing these classes to be unaware that they are working with a `Mediator` object. Each of these interfaces defines methods related to a particular kind of event. To provide state notifications, Colleague objects call the appropriate method of the appropriate interface without knowing the class of the Mediator object that implements the method.

Mediator. Instances of classes in the `Mediator` role have logic to process state notifications from `Colleague1`, `Colleague2`, and so on, objects. `Mediator` classes implement one or more `EventListener` interfaces. `Colleague1`, `Colleague2`, and so on, objects call methods declared by `EventListener` interfaces to inform a `Mediator` object of state changes. The `Mediator` object then performs whatever logic is appropriate. For notifications of proposed state changes, this will typically include indicating approval or disapproval of the change. For notification of completed state changes, this will typically include propagating the notification to other objects.

    `Mediator` classes have methods that can be called to associate them with `Colleague1`, `Colleague2`, and so on, objects. These methods are indicated in the diagram as `registerColleague1`, `registerColleague2`, and so on. They are passed an appropriate `Colleague` object and generally call one or more of its `add...Listener` methods to inform the `Colleague` object that it should inform the `Mediator` object of state changes.

The facilities that `Colleague1`, `Colleague2`, and so on, objects provide to allow other objects to express their interest in state changes and the mechanism for providing notifications of those state changes normally conforms to Java's delegation event model.

IMPLEMENTATION

In many cases, one object is responsible for creating all of the `Colleague` objects and their `Mediator` object. That object acts as a container for the objects that it creates. When there is a single object responsible for creating all of the `Colleague` objects and their `Mediator` object, the `Mediator` class is usually declared as a private member of that class. Limiting the visibility of a `Mediator` class increases the robustness of the program.

There are some decisions that you will have to make when you implement the `Mediator` pattern. One such decision is whether mediator objects will maintain their own internal model of the state of `Colleague` objects or fetch the state of each object when it needs to know the object's state.

If you take the first approach, then the Mediator object begins by assuming the initial state of the `Colleague` objects that it is responsible for. It will have an instance variable for each `Colleague` object. A `Mediator` object sets the initial value of each of those instance variables to be what it expects the initial state of the corresponding `Colleague` object to be. When a `Colleague` object notifies the `Mediator` object that its state has changed, the `Mediator` object changes the values of its instance variables to match the new state. After the `Mediator` object updates its instance variable, it uses the values of its instance variables to make whatever decisions it needs to make.

If you take the second approach, the `Mediator` object does not try to model the state of `Colleague` objects with its instance variables. Instead, when a `Colleague` object notifies it of a state change, the `Mediator` object makes whatever decisions it needs to make by fetching the state of each `Colleague` object it must base its decisions on.

When most people initially try to implement the Mediator pattern, they think of the first approach. However, in most cases the second approach is the better choice.

The disadvantage of the first approach is that it is possible for the `Mediator` object to be wrong about the state of a `Colleague` object. To get a `Mediator` object to correctly model the state of `Colleague` objects may require it to have additional code to mimic the logic of the `Colleague` objects. If a maintenance programmer later modifies one of the `Colleague` classes, the modification may mysteriously break the `Mediator` class.

The advantage of the second approach is its simplicity. The `Mediator` object can never be wrong about the state of a `Colleague` object. That makes it easier to implement and maintain. However, if fetching the complete state of `Colleague` objects is too time consuming, then the approach of having the `Mediator` object model the state of `Colleague` objects may be more practical.

CONSEQUENCES

- ☺ Most of the complexity involved in managing dependencies is shifted from other objects to the `Mediator` object. This makes the other objects easier to implement and maintain.
- ☺ Putting dependency logic for other classes in one mediator class makes it easier for maintenance programmers to find the dependencies.
- ☺ Using a `Mediator` object usually results in fewer execution paths through the code. This means that less effort is required for exhaustive testing since there are fewer cases to test. The impact of fewer code paths on testing is described in more detail in the discussion of the White Box Testing pattern in *Patterns in Java, Volume 2*.
- ☺ Using a `Mediator` object usually means that there is no need to subclass `Colleague` classes just to implement their dependency handling.
- ☺ Colleague classes are more reusable because their core functionality is not entwined with dependency-handling code. Dependency-handling code tends to be specific to an application.
- ● Putting all the dependency logic for a set of related objects in one place can make understanding the dependency logic easier, up to a point. If a Mediator class gets to be too large, then breaking it into smaller pieces can make it more understandable.
- ☹ Because dependency-handling code is usually application specific, Mediator classes are not usually reusable.

JAVA API USAGE

The examples of the Mediator pattern that occur in the Java API are a little different from the Mediators you are likely to code. This is because Mediator classes usually contain application-specific code, and the classes of the Java API are application independent.

Java-based GUIs can be built mostly from objects that are instances of subclasses of `java.awt.swing.JComponent`. `JComponent` objects use an instance of a subclass of `java.awt.swing.FocusManager` as a mediator. If `JComponent` objects are associated with a `FocusManager` object (they usually are), then they call its `processKeyEvent` method when they receive a

KeyEvent. The purpose of a FocusManager object is to recognize keystrokes that should cause a different JComponent object to receive the focus and make it so.

The way that JComponent objects use a FocusManager object differs from the Mediator pattern described in this chapter in two ways:

- JComponent objects pass key events only to FocusManager objects. Most Mediator classes that you write will have to handle more than one kind of event.
- JComponent objects do not access FocusManager objects through an interface. They directly refer to the FocusManager class. Having JComponent objects refer to FocusManager objects through an interface would provide a more flexible organization. Apparently, the designers of the Java API felt that because the interaction between JComponent objects and FocusManager objects is at a low level, there is no need for this flexibility.

CODE EXAMPLE

The code example for the Mediator pattern is the code for a mediator object for the dialog discussed under the Context heading. One thing that you may notice about this example is that it is more complex than most of the other examples. This reflects the nature of the Mediator pattern, which is to make all the complexity of event handling the responsibility of Mediator classes.

The mediator class is implemented as a private inner class of the dialog's class called BanquetMediator:

```
private class BanquetMediator {
    private JButton okButton;
    private JTextComponent dateField;
    private JTextComponent startField;
...
```

As shown here, the BanquetMediator class has private instance variables that it uses to refer to the GUI objects that the dialog registers with it. The BanquetMediator class does not implement any EventListener interfaces to allow it to receive events from its registered GUI objects. Instead, it uses adapter objects to receive those events. There are two main reasons for the BanquetMediator class to use adapters to receive events:

- The BanquetMediator class is able to ensure that only the GUI objects that are supposed to be sending events to a BanquetMediator object are able to do so. This makes the `BanquetMediator` class more robust. `BanquetMediator` objects achieve that by making their event-handling methods accessible only to the registered GUI objects. All of the `BanquetMediator` class's event-handling methods are private. The adapter objects are instances of private or anonymous inner classes that are able to call the `BanquetMediator` class's inner methods. Because the adapter classes are private or anonymous, only the `BanquetMediator` class can create instances of them. Instances of the adapter classes are provided only to registered GUI objects.

● Using a different adapter object to process events from each GUI object relieves the `BanquetMediator` class of the burden of having to determine which GUI object an event came from. The `Banquet-Mediator` class declares private or anonymous adapter classes that it uses to receive events only from objects in a specific role. By declaring additional classes, the `BanquetMediator` class relieves its adapter classes of the burden of selecting a behavior based on the source of an event.

You will see examples of these adapter classes later in the code listing. Anonymous adapter classes are used for processing types of events that must be processed differently for each event source. Private named adapter classes are used to process types of events that do not require different behavior for different event sources. The `BanquetMediator` class declares instance variables to refer to the single instance that it creates of its private adapter classes.

```
private ItemAdapter itemAdapter = new ItemAdapter();
```
...

The `BanquetMediator` class's constructor declares and instantiates an anonymous adapter class that processes events that the enclosing dialog object sends when it is opened. The adapter calls the `BanquetMediator` method responsible for setting the registered GUI components to their initial state.

```
BanquetMediator() {
    WindowAdapter windowAdapter = new WindowAdapter() {
        public void windowOpened(WindowEvent e) {
            initialState();
        } // windowOpened(WindowEvent)
    };
    BanquetReservationDialog enclosingDialog;
    enclosingDialog = BanquetReservationDialog.this;
    enclosingDialog.addWindowListener(windowAdapter);
} // Constructor()
```
...

The `ItemAdapter` class is a private adapter class defined and used by the `BanquetMediator` class to process events from both radio buttons in the dialog. When an `ItemAdapter` object receives an `ItemEvent`, it calls the `BanquetMediator` class's `enforceInvariants` method. This method is central to the purpose of the `BanquetMediator` class. The `enforceInvariants` method enforces all of the invariant relationships between the components of the dialog. It is called in response to events from all of the dialog's GUI components.

```
private class ItemAdapter implements ItemListener {
    public void itemStateChanged(ItemEvent e) {
        enforceInvariants();
    } // itemStateChanged(ItemEvent)
} // class ItemAdapter
```

The method responsible for registering a button object in the OK role is very simple because the `BanquetMediator` class is not responsible for processing events from that button. It is only responsible for determining whether the OK button should be enabled or disabled.

```
public void registerOkButton(JButton ok) {
    okButton = ok;
} // registerOkButton(JButton)
```

The registration methods for other GUI objects are more complex because they are concerned with custom event handling for objects registered in a particular role. The motivation for the custom event handling will be to verify the contents of individual GUI objects. The following registration method is more typical. It registers the field for entering the number of people that will be attending a banquet.

```
public
void registerPeopleCountField(final JTextComponent field) {
    peopleCountField = field;
    DocumentAdapter docAdapter
      = new DocumentAdapter() {
          protected void parseDocument() {
              int count = PEOPLE_COUNT_DEFAULT;
              try {
                  String countText = field.getText();
                  count = Integer.parseInt(countText);
              } catch (NumberFormatException e) {
              }
              if (MIN_PEOPLE<=count
                  && count<=MAX_PEOPLE )
                peopleCount =  count;
              else
                peopleCount = PEOPLE_COUNT_DEFAULT;
          } // parseDocument()
```

```
        };
    Document doc = field.getDocument();
    doc.addDocumentListener(docAdapter);
} // registerPeopleCountField(JTextComponent)
```

This registration method provides an anonymous adapter object that goes beyond just calling the `enforceInvariants` method. The anonymous adapter's superclass takes care of that. Before the superclass's code calls the `BanquetMediator` object's `enforceInvariants` method, it calls its own `parseDocument` method. The anonymous adapter class overrides `parseDocument` so that it sets the `BanquetMediator` object's `peopleCount` instance variable. If the field contains a valid value for the number of people who will attend the banquet, then it sets `peopleCount` to be that value. Otherwise, it sets `peopleCount` to a special value that will tell the `enforceInvariants` method that no valid value has been entered for the number of people who will be attending the banquet.

The registration methods for the other text fields are similar. They provide an adapter object that validates the value in the field, sets an instance variable, and then calls the `enforceInvariants` method.

The `enforceInvariants` method may change the state of some GUI components in order to force them to comply with some of the invariant relationships. When it changes the state of some of those GUI components, they produce events. The `BanquetMediator` object, through its adapters, is listening for some of those events. When a GUI component responds to one of the `enforceInvariants` method's state changes by delivering an event to one of the `BanquetMediator` object's adapters, it recursively calls the `enforceInvariants` method. To avoid an infinite recursion, the `BanquetMediator` class uses a flag to recognize when to recognize recursive calls to the `enforceInvariants` method.

```
private boolean busy = false;
...

    private void enforceInvariants() {
        if (busy)
          return;
        busy = true;
        protectedEnforceInvariants();
        busy = false;
    } // enforceInvariants()
```

As you can see from the preceding piece of code, the `enforceInvariants` method does not directly do the work of enforcing invariant relationships. What it does do is immediately return if it is called recursively; otherwise, it calls the `protectedEnforceInvariants` method.

The `enforceInvariants` method detects recursive calls by first testing and then setting the value of the `busy` variable. Because the Java event model guarantees synchronous delivery of events, the enforceInvariants method is not written to deal with being called to handle one event while it is still processing another. In such a situation, the method would have to be synchronized in a manner appropriate for the semantics of the events it has to process.

Here are the invariant relationships that the protectedEnforce-Invariants method enforces:

- The Date, Start Time, and End Time fields are enabled if, and only if, the Number of People field contains a valid value.
- If the radio buttons are disabled, then they are in an unselected state.
- The food list is enabled if and only if the Date, Start Time, and End Time fields are enabled, and the buffet button or table button is selected. To be considered valid, the end time must be at least one hour later than the start time.
- The OK button is enabled if, and only if, the food list is enabled and one or more foods on the list have been selected.

```
private void protectedEnforceInvariants() {
    // set enable to true if number of people is set.
    boolean enable
      = (peopleCount != PEOPLE_COUNT_DEFAULT);

    // Date, start, end, buffet button and table button
    // are enabled if, and only if, a valid value is in
    // the number of people field.
    dateField.setEnabled(enable);
    startField.setEnabled(enable);
    endField.setEnabled(enable);
    buffetButton.setEnabled(enable);
    tableServiceButton.setEnabled(enable);
    if (enable) {
        // Food list is enabled if and only if date or
        // time fields or radio buttons are enabled and
        // end time is at least one hour later than
        // start time and the buffet button or table
        // button is selected.
        enable = (buffetButton.isSelected()
                  || tableServiceButton.isSelected());
        foodList.setEnabled(enable
                    && endAtLeastOneHourAfterStart());
    } else {
        // if date or time fields or radio buttons are
        // disabled, food list must also be disabled.
        foodList.setEnabled(false);
        // radio buttons not enabled must deselect.
        buffetButton.setSelected(false);
        tableServiceButton.setSelected(false);
    } // if enable
```

```
        okButton.setEnabled(foodList.isEnabled()
                    && foodList.getMinSelectionIndex()>-1);
    } // protectedEnforceInvariants()
```

Mediator classes often have internal auxiliary methods that supplement the logic of the primary invariant enforcing method. Putting some of the logic in auxiliary methods helps keep the primary invariant enforcing method down to a manageable size. The following method returns true if the Date, Start Time, and End Time fields contain valid values and the time in the End Time field is at least one hour after the end field.

```
    private boolean endAtLeastOneHourAfterStart() {
        Calendar startCalendar = getStartCalendar();
        if (startCalendar == null)
          return false;
        Calendar endCalendar = getEndCalendar();
        if (endCalendar == null)
          return false;
        startCalendar.add(Calendar.MINUTE, 59);
        return getEndCalendar().after(startCalendar);
    } // endAtLeastOneHourAfterStart()
```

RELATED PATTERNS

Adapter. Mediator classes often use adapter objects to receive notifications of state changes.

Interface. The Mediator pattern uses the Interface pattern to keep the `Colleague` classes independent of the `Mediator` class.

Low Coupling/High Cohesion. The Mediator pattern is a good example of an exception to the advice of the Low Coupling/High Cohesion pattern (described in *Patterns in Java, Volume 2*).

Observer. The Observer pattern is a large portion of Java's delegation event model. If you want to use the Mediator pattern in a context that you feel Java's event model is inappropriate for, you can substitute the Observer pattern.

Controller. The Controller pattern (described in *Patterns in Java, Volume 2*) is used to determine what object will handle an external event. The Mediator pattern is used to help implement the handling of events.

White Box Testing. Using the Mediator pattern usually results in fewer execution paths through the code. This means that less effort is required to test a program using the White Box Testing pattern described in *Patterns in Java, Volume 2*.

Snapshot

This pattern is based partially on the Memento pattern documented in [GoF95].

SYNOPSIS

Capture a snapshot of an object's state so that the object's state can be restored later. The object that initiates the capture or restoration of the state does not need to know anything about the state information. It only needs to know that the object whose state it is restoring or capturing implements a particular interface.

CONTEXT

Suppose that you are writing a program to a play a role-playing game. For the purposes of this discussion, the details of the games are not important. What is important is that it is a single-player game. To play the game, a player directs a character to interact with various computer-controlled characters and simulated objects. One way that a game can end is for the character under the player's control to die. Players of the game will not consider this a desirable outcome.

Among the many features planned for the game are two features that involve saving and restoring the state of the game. The program needs these features because playing one of these games to its conclusion can take a few days of nonstop play.

- To allow a player to play the game over multiple short intervals, it must be possible to save the state of the game to a file so that it can be continued later.
- To arrive at the game's conclusion, a player must successfully guide his or her character through many adventures. If the player's character dies before the game is over, the player will have the option of starting the game over from the very beginning. That may be an unattractive option because the player may be well into the game and have played through the earlier portions of the game a number of times. The program will also offer the player the option of resuming the game at an earlier point than when the character died.

It will do this by saving part of the game's state, including credit for the character's previous experiences and a record of some of the character's possessions. It will perform a partial state save when the player's character has accomplished a major task. As the game proceeds, these checkpoints become part of the game's overall state, needing to be saved when the rest of the state is saved to disk.

Though the game will involve many classes, there are only a few that will share the responsibility for creating these snapshots of the game's state:

The classes in Figure 8.14 participate in two distinct state-saving mechanisms:

● There is a mechanism for saving part of a game's state when the player's character achieves a milestone.
● There is a mechanism for saving and restoring an entire game.

There are two classes in Figure 8.14 that participate in both mechanisms:

UserInterface. All player-initiated actions come through the UserInterface class. The UserInterface class delivers most of the actions that a player initiates to an instance of the GameModel class. However, player-initiated snapshots of the game follow different routes, which are discussed subsequently.

GameModel. The GameModel class is responsible for maintaining the state of the game during play. The UserInterface class notifies an instance of the GameModel class when the player does something related to the game. The instance of the GameModel class determines what the consequences of that action are, modifies the state of the game accordingly, and notifies the user interface. An instance of the GameModel class may also initiate some actions. It will always report the consequences of any action it initiates to the user interface but will not always report the action itself.

The UserInterface class's involvement in making snapshots is to initiate one kind of snapshot and both kinds of restores. Because the GameModel class is the top-level class responsible for the state of the game, it is involved in any operation that manipulates the game's state.

These are the other classes and interfaces involved in performing partial state saves and restores:

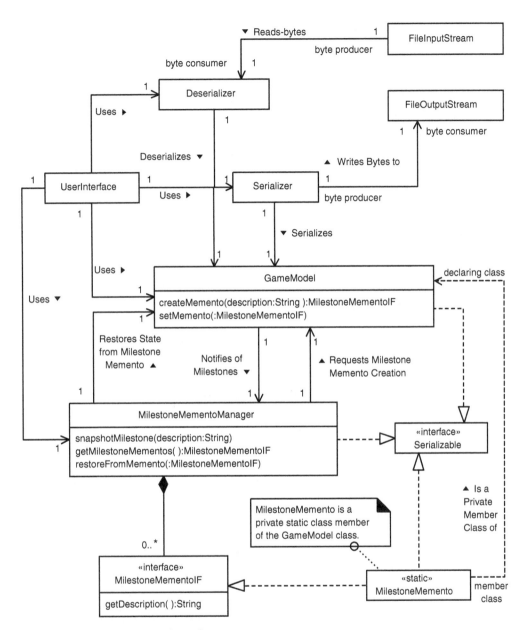

FIGURE 8.14 Game snapshot classes.

MilestoneMemento. MilestoneMemento is a private class defined by the GameModel class. A GameModel object creates instances of MilestoneMemento that contain copies of the values that make up the partial state to be saved. Given a MilestoneMemento object, a GameModel object can restore itself to the previous state contained in the MilestoneMemento object.

MilestoneMementoIF. The `MilestoneMemento` class implements this interface. This interface is public. Outside of the `GameModel` class, instances of the `MilestoneMemento` class can be accessed only as instances of the `Object` class or through the `MilestoneMementoIF` interface. Neither mode of access allows an object to access the state information encapsulated in `MilestoneMemento` objects.

MilestoneMementoManager. The `MilestoneMementoManager` class contributes to the decision to create `MilestoneMemento` objects. It also manages their use after they are created.

Here is how the capture of a game's partial state happens after the player's character has achieved a milestone:

1. A `GameModel` object enters a state indicating that the player's character has achieved one of the game's major milestones.
2. There is a `MilestoneMementoManager` object associated with each `GameModel` object. When the `GameModel` object enters a milestone state, it calls the associated `MilestoneMementoManager` object's `snapshotMilestone` method. It passes to the method a string that is a description of the milestone. The player's character may previously have achieved this milestone, died, and then returned to an earlier milestone. If a `MilestoneMemento` object already exists for a milestone, then another `MilestoneMemento` object is not created for the milestone.
3. A `MilestoneMementoManager` object determines whether a `MilestoneMemento` object already exists for a milestone by comparing the description string passed to its `snapshotMilestone` method to the descriptions of the `MilestoneMemento` objects that already exist. If a `MilestoneMemento` object already exists with the given description, then the `snapshotMilestone` method takes no additional action.
4. If the `MilestoneMementoManager` object determines that no `MilestoneMemento` object already exists for the milestone, then the `MilestoneMementoManager` object initiates the creation of a `MilestoneMemento` object to capture the game's partial state at that time. It does this by calling the `GameModel` object's `createMemento` method, passing it the same description that was passed to the `MilestoneMementoManager` object.
5. The `createMemento` method returns a freshly created `MilestoneMemento` object. The `MilestoneMementoManager` object adds the new `MilestoneMemento` object to its collection of `MilestoneMementoIF` objects.

When a player's character dies, the `UserInterface` object offers the player the option for the character to start from a previously achieved milestone, rather than from the very beginning. It offers the player a list of milestones to choose from by calling the `MilestoneMementoManager` object's `getMilestoneMementos` method. This method returns an array of `Milestone-Memento` objects that the `MilestoneMementoManager` object has collected.

If the player indicates that he or she wants the character to start from one of its previously achieved milestones, the `UserInterface` object passes the corresponding `MilestoneMemento` object to the `MilestoneMemento-Manager` object's `restoreFromMemento` method. This method, in turn, calls the `GameModel` object's `setMemento` method, passing it the chosen `MilestoneMemento` object. Using the information in the `MilestoneMemento` object, the `GameModel` object restores its state.

The other snapshot mechanism saves the complete state of the game to a file, including the `MilestoneMementoManager` object and its collection of `MilestoneMemento` objects. This mechanism is based on Java's serialization facility.

If you are unfamiliar with Java's serialization facility, it is a way to copy the state of an object to a stream of bytes and then create a copy of the original object from the contents of the byte stream. There is a somewhat more detailed description of serialization under the Implementation heading of this pattern.

The classes that are involved in saving and restoring a complete snapshot of the game's state to and from a file are:

Serializer. The `Serializer` class is responsible for serializing a `GameModel` object. It copies the state information of the `GameModel` object and all other objects it refers to that are part of the game's state as a byte stream to a file.

FileOutputStream. This is the standard Java class `java.io.FileOutputStream`. It writes a stream of bytes to a file.

Deserializer. The `Deserializer` class is responsible for reading a serialized byte stream and creating a copy of the `GameModel` object and other objects that were serialized to create the byte stream.

FileInputStream. This is the standard Java class `java.io.FileInputStream`. It reads a stream of bytes from a file.

Here is the sequence of events that occurs when the user requests that the game be saved to a file or restored from a file:

1. The player tells the user interface that he or she wants to save the game to a file. The `UserInterface` object then creates a `Serializer`

object, passing the name of the file and a reference to the GameModel object to its constructor. The Serializer object creates an ObjectOutputStream object and a FileOutputStream object. It uses the ObjectOutputStream object to serialize the GameModel object and all other game-related objects it refers to into a byte stream. It uses the FileOutputStream object to write that byte stream to a file.

2. When the player wants to restore the game from a file, he or she tells the user interface. The UserInterface object creates a Deserializer object, passing the name of the file and a reference to the GameModel object to its constructor. The Deserializer object creates an ObjectInputStream object and a FileInputStream object. It uses the FileInputStream object to read a serialized byte stream from a file. It uses the ObjectInputStream object to deserialize the GameModel object and all other game-related objects it refers to from the byte stream.

Most of the patterns in this book describe only one way to solve a problem. The Snapshot pattern is different. It describes two ways of solving the problem of making a snapshot of an object's state.

FORCES

☺ You need to create a snapshot of an object's state and also be able to restore the state of the object.

☺ You want a mechanism that saves and restores an object's state to be independent of the object's internal structure, so that the internal structure can change without having to modify the save/restore mechanism.

SOLUTION

The following are two general solutions to the problem of saving a snapshot of an object's state and restoring its state from the snapshot. First is a description of using Memento objects to create a nonpersistent copy of an object's partial state. Then there is a description of how to use serialization to save and restore an object's state. That is followed by a comparison of the two techniques.

Figure 8.15 shows the general organization for objects that use Memento objects to save and restore an object's state.

Here are descriptions of the roles the classes play in the variation of the Snapshot pattern that uses Memento objects:

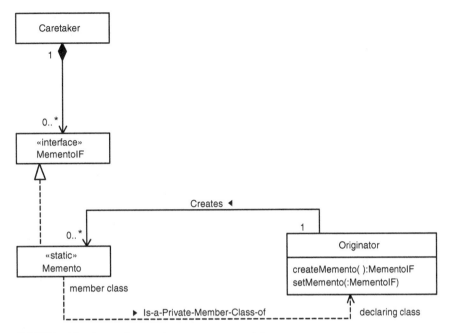

FIGURE 8.15 Snapshot using memento objects.

Originator. A class in this role is a class whose instance's state information is to be saved and restored. When its `createMemento` method is called, it creates a `Memento` object that contains a copy of the `Originator` object's state information. Later, you can restore the `Originator` object's state by passing a `Memento` object to its `setMemento` method.

Memento. A class in this role is a private static class of the `Originator` class that implements the `MementoIF` interface. Its purpose is to encapsulate snapshots of an `Originator` object's state. Because it is a private member of the `Originator` class, only the `Originator` class is able to access it. Other classes must access instances of the `Memento` class either as instances of `Object` or through the `MementoIF` interface.

MementoIF. Classes other than the `Originator` class access `Memento` objects through this interface. Interfaces in this role may declare no methods. If they do declare any methods, the methods should not allow the encapsulated state to be changed. This ensures the consistency and integrity of the state information. Interfaces in this role are designed using the Read-Only Interface pattern.

Caretaker.   Instances of classes in this role maintain a collection of `Memento` objects. After a `Memento` object is created, it is usually added to a `Caretaker` object's collection. When an undo operation is to be performed, a `Caretaker` object typically collaborates with another object to select a `Memento` object. After the `Memento` object is selected, it is typically the `Caretaker` object that calls the `Originator` object's `setMemento` method to restore its state.

The other mechanism for creating a snapshot of an object's state is serialization. Serialization is different from most other object-oriented techniques in that it works by violating the encapsulation of the object being serialized. Most, but not necessarily all, of the violation is through Java's reflection mechanism. This is explained more fully by Figure 8.16 and the following descriptions of roles that classes play in this form of the Snapshot pattern.

Here are descriptions of the roles classes play in the variation of the Snapshot pattern that uses serialization:

Target.   An `ObjectOutputStream` object converts the state of instances of classes in this role to a byte stream. An `ObjectInputStream` object restores the state of instances of classes in this role from a byte stream. The role of the `Target` object in these activities is purely passive. The `ObjectOutputStream` object or `ObjectInputStream` object does all of the work.

ObjectOutputStream.   The class in this role is usually the standard Java class `java.io.ObjectOutputStream`. It discovers and accesses a `Target` object's state information and writes it to a byte stream with additional information that allows an `ObjectInputStream` object to restore the state information.

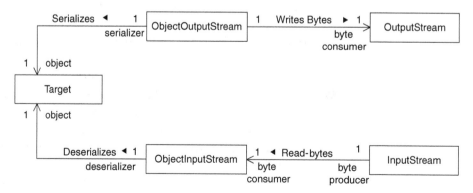

FIGURE 8.16 Snapshot using serialization.

OutputStream. An object in this role is an instance of a subclass of the standard Java class `java.io.OutputStream`. If the state information needs to be saved indefinitely, then the `OutputStream` object may be a `FileOutputStream`. If the state information needs to be saved no longer than the duration of a program run, then the `OutputStream` object may be a `ByteArrayOutputStream`.

ObjectInputStream. The class in this role is a subclass of the standard Java class `java.io.ObjectInputStream`. Instances of these classes read serialized state information from a byte stream and restore it.

If you do not override the default behavior, an `ObjectInputStream` object puts the original `Target` object's state information in a new instance of the `Target` object's class. Using techniques described under the Implementation heading, you can arrange for `ObjectInputStream` objects to restore the saved state to an existing instance of the `Target` class.

Table 8.3 shows some key differences between the two techniques for creating and managing snapshots of an object's state.

IMPLEMENTATION

Using `Memento` objects to make snapshots of an object's state is very straightforward to implement. Using serialization requires additional expertise and sometimes additional complexity. A complete description of serialization is beyond the scope of this book.[1] What follows is a description of some features of serialization relevant to the Snapshot pattern.

To serialize an object you first create an `ObjectOutputStream` object. You can do this by passing an `OutputStream` object to its constructor, like this:

```
FileOutputStream fout = new FileOutputStream("filename.ser");
ObjectOutputStream obOut = new ObjectOutputStream(fout);
```

The `ObjectOutputStream` object will write the byte stream it produces to the `OutputStream` object passed to its constructor.

Once you have created an `ObjectOutputStream` object, you can serialize an object by passing it to the `ObjectOutputStream` object's `writeObject` method, like this:

---

[1] You can find a complete description of serialization on Sun's Java Web page. java.sun.com. At the time of this writing, the URL for the serialization specification is http://java.sun.com/j2se/1.3/docs/guide/serialization/.

TABLE 8.3 Comparison of State Saving by Serialization and Memento Objects

	Serialization	Memento
Persistence	You can use serialization to save state in a persistent form by serializing it to a file.	Using `Memento` objects does not provide persistence.
Complexity of implementation	Serialization can be the simpler technique for saving the entire state of an object. This is especially true for objects whose state includes references to other objects whose state must be also be saved.	Using `Memento` objects is often a simpler way to capture part of an object's state.
Object Identity	Absolute object identity is lost unless you supply additional code to preserve it. The default way that serialization restores an object's state is by creating a copy of the object. If the original object contains other objects and there are multiple references to the same object, then the duplicate object will contain references to an identical but distinct object. Among the objects referred to by the restored object, serialization preserves relative object identity.	Object identity is preserved. Using `Memento` objects is a simpler way to restore the state of an object so that it refers to the same object that it referred to before.
Overhead	Using serialization adds considerable overhead to the process of creating a snapshot to be saved in memory. The bulk of the overhead comes from the fact that serialization works through Java's reflection mechanism and creates new objects when restoring state.	There is no particular overhead associated with using `Memento` objects.
Expertise Required	In cases where you need to make a snapshot of an object's complete state, all of the objects involved implement the `Serializable` interface, and preserving object identity is not important, serialization requires minimal expertise. As situations vary from these constraints, the required level of expertise quickly increases. Some situations may require an in-depth knowledge of serialization internals, reflection, and other arcane aspects of Java.	Using `Memento` objects requires no specialized knowledge.

```
ObOut.writeObject(foo);
```

The `writeObject` method uses Java's reflection facility to discover the instance variables of the object that `foo` references and access them. If the value of an instance variable is a primitive type such as `int` or `double`, its value is written directly to the byte stream. If the value of an instance variable is a reference to another object, then the `writeObject` method also serializes that object.

Turning a serialized byte stream into an object is called *deserialization*. To deserialize a byte stream, you first create an `ObjectInputStream` object. You can do that by passing an `InputStream` object to its constructor, like this:

```
FileInputStream fin = new FileInputStream("filename.ser");
ObjectInputStream obIn = new ObjectInputStream(fin);
```

The `ObjectInputStream` object will read bytes from the input stream passed to its constructor.

Once you have created an `ObjectInputStream` object, you can deserialize its associated byte stream by calling its `readObject` method, like this:

```
GameModel g = (GameModel)obIn.readObject();
```

The `readObject` method is declared to return a reference to an `Object`. Since you will usually want to treat the object it returns as an instance of a more specialized class, you will usually typecast the result of the `readObject` method to a more specialized class.

There is one other thing that you must do in order to serialize an object. You can serialize an instance of a class only if the class gives its permission to be serialized. A class permits the serialization of its instances if the class implements the interface `java.io.Serializable`, like this:

```
import java.io.serializable;
...
class foo extends bar implements Serializable {
```

The `Serializable` interface is a marker interface. It does not declare any members. Declaring that a class implements the `Serializable` interface is simply a way to indicate that it may be serialized. If you pass an object to an `ObjectOutputStream` object's `writeObject` method that does not implement the `Serializable` interface, then the method throws an exception.

So far, serialization seems simple. Though there are many situations in which the preceding details are all that you need to know, there are also many situations that are more complex.

The default behavior, when serializing an object, is to also serialize all of the objects that it refers to and all of the objects that they refer to, until the complete set has been serialized. Though an object may be an instance of a class that implements the Serializable interface, if it refers to any objects that are not Serializable, then any attempt to serialize the object will fail. It will fail when the ObjectOutputStream object's writeObject method calls itself recursively to serialize the object that cannot be serialized and throws an exception. There is a way to avoid this problem.

You can specify that the serialization mechanism should ignore some of an object's instance variables. The simplest way to do this is to declare the variable with the transient modifier, like this:

```
transient ObjectOutputStream obOut;
```

Because the serialization mechanism ignores transient variables, it does not matter to the serialization mechanism if a transient variable refers to an object that cannot be serialized.

There is another problem that can be solved by declaring some instance variables transient. Instances of some classes refer to other objects that refer to many objects that do not need to be saved. Serializing those objects would just add overhead to serialization and deserialization. If the value of an instance variable does not need to be part of an object's serialized state, then declaring the instance variable transient avoids the overhead of unnecessarily serializing and deserializing its values.

Declaring instance variables transient solves a few problems during serialization. It also creates a problem during deserialization. The serialized byte stream does not contain values for transient variables. If you make no other arrangements, after deserialization an object's transient variables will contain the default value for their declared type. For example, transient variables declared with a numeric type will have the value 0. Transient variables that are declared as an object type will have the value null. Serialization ignores initializers and constructors. Unless it is acceptable for an object to suddenly find its transient variables unexpectedly set to null or zero, this is a problem.

The ObjectInputStream class provides mechanisms that allow you to modify the default way that deserialization handles transient variables. What it allows you to do is to provide code that is executed after deserialization has performed its default actions. Often, that code requires information to reconstruct the values of transient variables that are not provided by the default actions of serialization. The ObjectOutputStream class provides mechanisms that allow you to add additional information to the information provided by the default actions of serialization. If you can add enough information to a serialized byte steam to be able to reconstruct the values of an object's transient variables, then you have solved the problem.

To add information to what the ObjectOutputStream class's writeObject method normally provides, you can add a method called writeObject to a serializable class. If an object is an instance of a class that defines a `writeObject` method in the required way, then instead of deciding how to handle the object's instance variables internally, an `ObjectOutputStream` object calls that object's `writeObject` method. This allows a class to determine how its own instance variables will be serialized.

To take responsibility for the serialization of its instance's instance variables, a class should have a method like this:

```
private void writeObject(ObjectOutputStream stream)
                                        throws IOException {
    stream.defaultWriteObject();
    . . .
} // writeObject(ObjectOutputStream)
```

Notice that the method is private. It must be private to be recognized by an `ObjectOutputStream` object. These private `writeObject` methods are responsible for writing only those instance variables that their own classes declare. They are not responsible for variables declared by superclasses.

The first thing that most private `writeObject` methods do is to call the `ObjectOutputStream` object's `defaultWriteObject` method. Calling this method causes the `ObjectOutputStream` object to perform default serialization actions for the class that called it. Next, a private `writeObject` method calls other methods of the `ObjectOutputStream` object to write any additional information that will be needed to reconstruct the values of transient variables. The `ObjectOutputStream` class is a subclass of `DataOutputStream`. It inherits methods to write strings and all of the primitive data types.

To make use of the additional information during deserialization, a class must also define a `readObject` method, like this:

```
private void readObject(ObjectInputStream stream)
                                        throws IOException {
    try {
        stream.defaultReadObject();
    } catch (ClassNotFoundException e) {
        . . .
    } // try
    . . .
} // readObject(ObjectInputStream)
```

Just as the `writeObject` method must be private, the `readObject` method must also be private for it to be recognized. It begins by calling the `ObjectInputStream` object's `defaultReadObject` method. Calling this method causes the `ObjectInputStream` object to perform default deserialization actions for the class that called it. After this, a private `readObject` method will call other methods of the `ObjectInputStream` object to read any additional information that was supplied to reconstruct the values of transient variables. The ObjectInputStream class is a subclass of DataInputStream. It inherits methods to read strings and all of the primitive data types.

Here is an example to show how these private methods can fit together:

```
public class TextFileReader implements Serializable {
    private transient RandomAccessFile file;
    private String browseFileName;
    ...
    private
    void writeObject(ObjectOutputStream stream)
                                     throws IOException{
        stream.defaultWriteObject();
        stream.writeLong(file.getFilePointer());
    } // writeObject(ObjectOutputStream)

    private
    void readObject(ObjectInputStream stream)
                                     throws IOException {
        try {
            stream.defaultReadObject();
        } catch (ClassNotFoundException e) {
            String msg = "Unable to find class";
            if (e.getMessage() != null)
                msg += ": " + e.getMessage();
            throw new IOException(msg);
        } // try
        file = new RandomAccessFile(browseFileName,
                                    "r");
        file.seek(stream.readLong());
    } // readObject(ObjectInputStream)
} // class TextFileReader
```

This class is called TextFileReader. It has an instance variable named file that refers to a RandomAccessFile object. The RandomAccessFile class does not implement the Serializable interface. For instances of TextFileReader to be successfully serialized and deserialized, it is not sufficient that the TextFileReader class implements the Serializable interface. It must also do the following:

● Prevent its reference to a RandomAccessFile object from being serialized.
● Add additional information to the serialized byte stream so that it is possible to reconstruct the RandomAccessFile object.
● Provide logic to allow the RandomAccessFile object to be reconstructed during deserialization.

To prevent its reference to a RandomAccessFile object from being serialized, the TextFileReader class declares its file variable to be transient.

The `TextFileReader` class has an instance variable that refers to a string that is the name of the file that the `RandomAccessFile` object accesses. This is sufficient information to create another `RandomAccessFile` object that accesses that file. However to make the state of the new `RandomAccessFile` object match the state of the original, it is necessary to add to the byte stream the `RandomAccessFile` object's current position in the file. The `TextFileReader` class's private `writeObject` method accomplished that.

To reconstruct the original object's `RandomAccessFile` object, the `TextFileReader` class defines a private `readObject` method. This method reads the file position that was written to the serialized byte stream and passes it to the new `RandomAccessFile` object's `seek` method.

Another issue you may need to deal with is the fact that the `ObjectInputStream` class's `readObject` method normally returns a newly created object. In situations like the role-playing game described under the Context heading, this can be inconvenient. The inconvenience is that other objects already refer to the existing object. To modify their references to refer to the new object would be to involve those objects in the details of another object's deserialization. The `ObjectInputStream` class allows you to resolve the situation without involving any class other than the one it is deserializing.

If the class being deserialized has a method named `readResolve`, then it can control which of its instances is returned by an `ObjectInputStream` object's `readObject` method. The signature of the `readObject` method must look like this:

```
Object readResolve() throws ObjectStreamException ;
```

It does not matter whether the method is public, protected, or private. After an `ObjectInputStream` object's `readObject` method has created an object that it is otherwise ready to return, it checks to see whether the object has a `readResolve` method. If the object does have a `readResolve` method, then the `readObject` method calls it and returns whatever objects the `readResolve` method returns. If the object that the `readResolve` method returns is not the newly created object, then it is up to the `readResolve` method to arrange for the object that it does return to contain the proper state information. You can see this technique used in the example that follows.

CONSEQUENCES

☺ Both forms of the Snapshot pattern keep a lot of the complexity of saving and restoring an object's state out of its class.

⊗ The Snapshot pattern is not very suitable for undoing a fine-grained sequence of commands. Making many snapshots of an object can consume a prohibitive amount of storage. Capturing the changes to an object's state (the Command pattern) may be more efficient.

CODE EXAMPLE

The following is some of the code to implement the design discussed under the Context heading. First is the code for the GameModel class, which is very central to any state-saving operation:

```
public class GameModel implements Serializable {
    private static GameModel theInstance = new GameModel();
    private MilestoneMementoManager mementoManager;
...
    /**
     * This constructor is private. Other classes must call
     * this class's getGameModel method to get an instance.
     */
    private GameModel() {
        mementoManager = new MilestoneMementoManager(this);
        ...
    } // constructor()

    /**
     * Return the single instance of this class.
     */
    public static GameModel getGameModel() {
        return theInstance;
    }
```

The point of the preceding portion of the GameModel class is to make the GameModel class a singleton class. By making its constructor private, other classes are unable to use its constructor. This forces them to get an instance of the GameModel class by calling its getGameModel method.

When an ObjectInputStream object deserializes a byte stream, it uses a special mechanism that creates objects without calling constructors or evaluating variables' initializers. After it has an instance of a class, it sets the object's instance variables to the values it finds in the serialized byte stream.

After an ObjectInputStream object finishes deserializing an object, it checks to see whether the object has a readResolve method. If it does have a readResolve method, then it calls the object's readResolve method and returns the object that the readResolve method returns rather than the object it just created.

Here is the GameModel class's readResolve method, which sets the instance variables in the program's GameModel object to the values in the deserialized `GameModel` object. It then returns the program's `GameModel` object.

```
public Object readResolve() {
      GameModel theModel = getGameModel();
      theModel.mementoManager = mementoManager;
      ...
      return theModel;
  } // readResolve()
```

The remaining portions of the `GameModel` class related to the Snapshot pattern are involved in the management of memento objects.

There are a few noteworthy things about the implementation of the `MilestoneMemento` class. It is a private class of the `GameModel` class. This prevents any class other than the `GameModel` class from directly accessing its members. The `MilestoneMemento` class is declared static. This is a minor optimization that saves the expense of having `MilestoneMemento` objects maintain a reference to their enclosing `GameModel` object.

One other noteworthy aspect of the implementation of the `MilestoneMemento` class is its lack of access methods. Normally, it is good practice to require other classes to access an object's instance variables only through accessor (get and set) methods. This practice results in well-encapsulated objects. Because of the close relationship between the `MilestoneMemento` class and the `GameModel` class, `GameModel` objects directly access the instance variables of `MilestoneMemento` objects. Because other classes can access the `MilestoneMemento` class only through the `MilestoneMementoIF` interface, a `MilestoneMemento` object's instance variables are hidden from all other classes.

```
private static class MilestoneMemento
                          implements MilestoneMementoIF {
      private String description;
...
      /**
       * constructor
       * @param description
       *        The reason for this object's creation.
       */
      MilestoneMemento(String description) {
         this.description = description;
      } // constructor(String)

      /**
       * Return the reason why this memento was created.
       */
      public String getDescription() { return description; }

      // These variables are set by a GameModel object
      MilestoneMementoManager mementoManager;
```

```
    ...
} // class MilestoneMemento
```

We will want to be able to serialize `MilestoneMemento` objects. You may notice that the `MilestoneMemento` class does not declare that it implements the `Serializable` interface. This is not necessary because it implements the `MilestoneMementoIF` interface and the `MilestoneMementoIF` interface extends the `Serializable` interface.

Following are methods that the `GameModel` class provides for creating memento objects and for restoring state from a memento object:

```
/**
 * Create a memento object that encapsulates a snapshot
 * of this object's state.
 */
MilestoneMementoIF createMemento(String description) {
    // Create a memento object
    // and set its instance variables.
    MilestoneMemento memento;
    memento = new MilestoneMemento(description);
    memento.mementoManager = mementoManager;
    ...
    return memento;
} // createMemento(String)

/**
 * Restore this object's state from the given memento
 * object.
 */
void setMemento(MilestoneMementoIF memento) {
    MilestoneMemento m = (MilestoneMemento)memento;
    mementoManager = m.mementoManager;
    ...
} // setMemento(MilestoneMemento)
```

RELATED PATTERNS

Command. The Command pattern allows state changes to be undone on a command-by-command basis without having to make a snapshot of an object's entire state after every command.

Read-Only Interface. Interfaces in the `MementoIF` role are designed using the Read-Only Interface pattern.

Observer

The Observer pattern is very well known and widely used. Since it was originally documented, patterns have evolved. It is important to know about the Observer pattern when working with existing designs that use it.

The Delegation Event Model is a superior choice for new designs. It produces designs that are more reusable. Use of the Delegation Event Model complies with the JavaBean specification. A number of Computer-Aided Software Engineering (CASE) and programming tools provide assistance for the construction and use of classes designed to work with the Delegation Event Model.

The Observer pattern was previously described in [GoF95].

SYNOPSIS

Allow objects to dynamically register dependencies between objects so that an object will notify those objects that are dependent on it when its state changes.

CONTEXT

Suppose that you are working for a company that manufactures smoke detectors, motion sensors, and other security devices. To take advantage of new market opportunities, your company plans to introduce a new line of devices. These devices will be able to send a signal to a security card that can be installed in most computers. The hope is that companies that make security-monitoring systems will integrate these devices and cards with their systems. To make it easy to integrate the cards with monitoring systems, you have been given the task of creating an easy-to-use API.

The API must allow your future customers to easily integrate their programs with it so their programs will receive notifications from the security card. It must work without forcing the customers to alter the architecture of their existing software. All that the API may assume about the customer's software is that at least one, and possibly more than one, object will have a method that should be called when a notification is received from a security device. Figure 8.17 is a design for the API.

Instances of the `SecurityNotifier` class receive notifications from the security card. They, in turn, notify objects that previously requested to

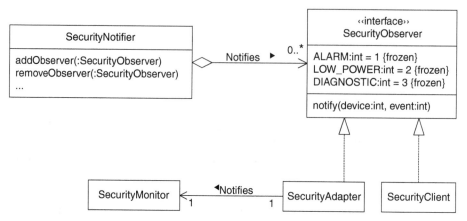

FIGURE 8.17 Security notification API.

receive notifications. Only objects that implement the SecurityObserver interface can be registered with a SecurityNotifier object to receive notifications from it. A SecurityObserver object becomes registered to receive notifications from a SecurityNotifier object when it is passed to the SecurityNotifier object's addObserver method. Passing it to the Security-Notifier object's removeObserver method ends the SecurityObserver object's registration to receive notifications.

A SecurityNotifier object passes a notification to a SecurityObserver object by calling its notify method. The parameters it passes to its notify method are a number that uniquely identifies the security device that the original notification came from and a number that specifies the type of notification.

The remaining classes in the diagram are not part of the API. They are classes that would already exist or be added to potential customers' monitoring software. The class indicated in the diagram as SecurityClient corresponds to any class a customer adds to his or her monitoring software that implements the SecurityObserver interface. Customers may add such classes to their monitoring software to process notifications from a SecurityNotifier object.

The class indicated in the diagram as SecurityMonitor corresponds to an existing class in a customer's monitoring software that does not implement the SecurityObserver interface but does have a method that should be called to process notifications from security devices. The customer is able to have instances of such a class receive notifications without modifying the class. The customer is able to do this by writing an adapter class that implements the SecurityObserver interface so its notify method calls the appropriate method of the SecurityMonitor class.

FORCES

☺ You are implementing two otherwise independent classes. An instance of one will need to notify other objects when its state changes. An instance of the other will need to be notified when an object it has a dependency on changes state. However, the two classes are not specifically intended to work with each other. To promote reuse, one should not have direct knowledge of the other.

☺ You have a one-to-many dependency relationship that may require an object to notify multiple objects when it changes its state.

☹ Some logic is required to route or prioritize notifications. The logic is independent of the sender and recipients of the notifications.

SOLUTION

Figure 8.18 is a class diagram that shows the roles that classes and interfaces play in the Observer pattern.

You will notice that Figure 8.18 is more complicated than Figure 8.17. Figure 8.17 incorporates some simplifications that are described in the Implementation section.

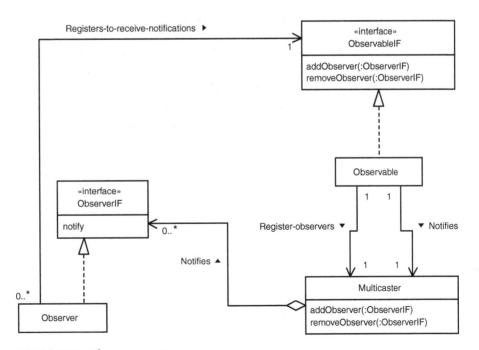

FIGURE 8.18 Observer pattern.

Following are descriptions of the roles that the classes and interfaces in Figure 8.18 play in the Observer pattern:

ObserverIF. An interface in this role defines a method that is typically called `notify` or `update`. An `Observable` object calls the method to provide a notification that its state has changed, passing it whatever arguments are appropriate. In many cases, a reference to the `Observable` object is one of the arguments that allow the method to know what object provided the notification.

Observer. Instances of classes in this role implement the `ObserverIF` interface and receive state change notifications from `Observable` objects.

ObservableIF. `Observable` objects implement an interface in this role. The interface defines two methods that allow `Observer` objects to register and unregister to receive notifications.

Observable. A class in this role implements the `ObservableIF` interface. Its instances are responsible for managing the registration of `ObserverIF` objects that want to receive notifications of state changes. Its instances are also responsible for delivering the notifications. The `Observable` class does not directly implement these responsibilities. Instead, it delegates these responsibilities to a `Multicaster` object.

Multicaster. Instances of a class in this role manage registration of `ObserverIF` objects and deliver notifications to them on behalf of an `Observable` object. The purpose of this role is to increase reuse of code. Delegating these responsibilities to a `Multicaster` class allows their implementation to be reused by all `Observable` classes that implement the same `ObservableIF` interface or deliver notifications to objects that implement the same `ObserverIF` interface.

Figure 8.19 summarizes the collaborations between the objects that participate in the Observer pattern.

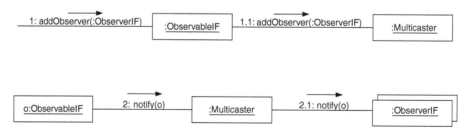

FIGURE 8.19 Observer collaboration.

1. Objects that implement an `ObserverIF` interface are passed to the `addObserver` method of an `ObservableIF` object.

   1.1 The `ObservableIF` object delegates the `addObserver` call to its associated `Multicaster` object. The `Multicaster` object adds the `ObservableIF` object to the collection of `ObserverIF` objects that it maintains.

2. The `ObservableIF` object labeled o needs to notify other objects that its state has changed. It initiates the notification by calling the `notify` method of its associated `Multicaster` object.

   2.1 The `Multicaster` object calls the notify method of each one of the `ObserverIF` objects in its collection.

IMPLEMENTATION

OBSERVING THE OBSERVABLE

An `Observable` object normally passes a self-reference as a parameter to an `Observer` object's `notify` method. In most cases, the `Observer` object needs access to the `Observable` object's attributes in order to act on the notification. Here are some ways to provide that access:

- Add methods to the `ObservableIF` interface for fetching attribute values. This is usually the best solution. However, it works only if all the classes that implement the `ObservableIF` interface have a common set of attributes sufficient for `Observer` objects to act on notifications.
- You can have multiple `ObservableIF` interfaces, with each providing access to enough attributes for an `Observer` object to act on notifications. To make that work, `ObserverIF` interfaces must declare a version of their notify method for each one of the `ObservableIF` interfaces. However, requiring observer objects to be aware of multiple interfaces removes much of the original motivation for having `ObservableIF` interfaces. Requiring a class to be aware of multiple interfaces is not much better than requiring it to be aware of multiple classes, so this is not a very good solution.
- You can pass attributes that `ObserverIF` objects need as parameters to their `notify` methods. The main disadvantage of this solution is that it requires `Observable` objects to know enough about `ObserverIF` objects to provide them with the correct attribute values. If the set of attributes required by `ObserverIF` objects changes, then you must modify all of the `Observable` classes accordingly.

- You can dispense with the `ObservableIF` interface and pass the `Observable` objects to `ObserverIF` objects as instances of their actual class. This implies overloading the `ObserverIF` interface's `notify` method, so that there is a `notify` method for each `Observable` class that will deliver notifications to `ObserverIF` objects.

The main disadvantage of this approach is that `Observer` classes must be aware of the `Observable` classes that will be delivering notifications to its instances and know how to fetch the attributes it needs from them. On the other hand, if only one `Observable` class will be delivering notifications to `Observer` classes, then this is the best solution. It adds no complexity to any classes. It substitutes a dependency on a single interface for a dependency on a single class. Then it simplifies the design by eliminating the `ObservableIF` interface.

The example under the Context heading uses this simplified solution.

ELIMINATING THE MULTICASTER

Another simplification often made to the Observer pattern is to eliminate the `Multicaster` class. If an `Observable` class is the only class delivering notifications to objects that implement a particular interface, then there is no need for the reusability a `Multicaster` class provides. This is the reason that the example under the Context heading does not have a class in the `Multicaster` role. Another reason not to have a `Multicaster` class is that an `Observable` object will never have to deliver notifications to more than one object. In this case, the management and delivery of notifications to `Observer` objects is so simple that a `Multicaster` class adds more complexity than it saves.

BATCHING NOTIFICATIONS

It may not be necessary or useful to notify `Observer` objects of every change to an `observable` object. If this is the case, you can avoid unnecessary notifications by batching state changes and waiting until an entire batch of state changes is complete before delivering notifications. If another object makes changes to an `Observable` object's state, then providing a single notification for a batch of changes is more complicated. You will have to add a method to the `Observable` object's class that other objects can call to indicate the beginning of a batch of state changes. When a state change is part of a batch, it should not cause the object to deliver any notifications to its registered observers. You will also have to add a method to the `Observable` object's class that other objects call to indicate the end of a batch of state changes. When this method is called, if any state changes occurred since the beginning of the batch, the object should deliver notifications to its registered observers.

If multiple objects will initiate changes to an `Observable` object's state, then determining the end of a batch of changes may be more complicated. A good way to manage this complexity is to add an additional object that coordinates state changes initiated by the other objects and understands their logic well enough to determine the end of a batch of changes. See the description of the Mediator pattern for a more detailed description of how to use one object to coordinate the actions of other objects.

VETO

The Observer pattern is usually used to notify other objects that an object's state has changed. A common variation is to define an alternate `ObservableIF` interface that allows objects to request that they receive a notification before an object's state changes. The usual reason for sending state change notifications after a state change is to allow the change to propagate to other objects. The usual reason for sending a notification before a state change is so that other objects can veto a state change. The usual way to implement this is to have an object throw an exception to prevent a proposed state change.

CONSEQUENCES

The Observer pattern allows an object to deliver notifications to other objects without the sender or receiver of the notifications being aware of each other's class.

There are some situations in which the Observer pattern can have unforeseen and undesirable results:

- Delivering notifications can take a long time if an object has a large number of objects to deliver the notification to. That can happen because one object has many observers directly registered to receive its notifications. It can also happen because an object has many indirect observers since its notifications are cascaded by other objects. You can sometimes lessen the impact of this by making the delivery of notification happen asynchronously in its own thread. However, asynchronous delivery of notifications can introduce its own problems.
- A more serious problem happens if there are cyclic dependencies. Objects call each other's `notify` methods until the stack fills up and a `StackOverflowError` is thrown. Though serious, the problem can be easily solved by adding an internal flag to one of the classes involved in the cycle that detects a recursive notification like this:

```
    . . .
    private boolean inNotify = false;
    public void notify(ObservableIF source) {
        if (inNotify)
          return;
        inNotify = true;
        . . .
        inNotify = false;
    }
```

● If a notification can be delivered asynchronously of other threads, as is the case in the example under the Context heading, there are some additional consequences to consider. You need to ensure that the asynchronous delivery of notifications is done in a way that ensures the consistency of the objects that receive the notifications. It may also be important that notification does not block waiting for another thread for any length of time.

When an `observer` object receives a notification, it knows which object changed, but it does not know in what way it changed. Avoid requiring an `Observer` object to determine which attributes of an `ObservableIF` object changed. It is usually simpler for an observer to act on all of an `ObservableIF` object's attributes rather than going to the trouble of determining which have changed and then acting on just those.

JAVA API USAGE

Java's delegation event model is a specialized form of the Observer pattern. Classes whose instances can be event sources participate in the `Observable` role. Event listener interfaces participate in the `ObserverIF` role. Classes that implement event listener interfaces participate in the `Observer` role. Because there are a number of classes that deliver various subclasses of `java.awt.AwtEvent` to their listeners, there is a `Multicaster` class that they use called `java.awt.AWTEventMulticaster`.

CODE EXAMPLE

The following is code that implements some of the security monitoring design presented under the Context heading. The first piece of code is the `SecurityObserver` interface. For instances of a class to be able to receive notifications, it must implement the `SecurityObserver` interface.

```
public interface SecurityObserver {
    public final int ALARM = 1;
```

```
    public final int LOW_POWER = 2;
    public final int DIAGNOSTIC = 3;

    /**
     * This method is called to deliver a security
     * notification.
     * @param device
     *        ID of the device this notification came from.
     * @param event
     *        This should be one of the above constants.
     */
    public void notify(int device, int event);
} // interface SecurityObserver
```

The following piece of code is the `SecurityNotifier` class responsible for delivering the notifications that a computer receives from security devices.

```
class SecurityNotifier {
    private ArraySet observers = new ArraySet();
...
    public void addObserver(SecurityObserver observer) {
        observers.add(observer);
    } // addObserver(SecurityObserver)

    public void removeObserver(SecurityObserver observer) {
        observers.remove(observer);
    } // removeObserver(SecurityObserver)

    private void notify(int device, int event) {
        Iterator iterator = observers.iterator();
        while (iterator.hasNext()) {
            ((SecurityObserver)iterator.next()).notify(device,
                                                        event);
        } // while
    } // notify(int, int)
} // class SecurityNotifier
```

The last class shown here is an adapter class that allows instances of the `SecurityMonitor` class to receive notifications, even though the `SecurityMonitor` class does not implement the `SecurityObserver` class.

```
class SecurityAdapter implements SecurityObserver {
    private SecurityMonitor sm;

    SecurityAdapter(SecurityMonitor sm) {
        this.sm = sm;
    } // Constructor(SecurityMonitor)

    /**
     * This method is called to deliver a security
     * notification.
```

```
 *  @param device
 *         ID of the device this notification came from.
 *  @param event
 *         This should be one of the above constants.
 */
public void notify(int device, int event) {
    switch (event) {
      case ALARM:
        sm.securityAlert(device);
        break;
      case LOW_POWER:
      case DIAGNOSTIC:
        sm.diagnosticAlert(device);
        break;
    } // switch
  } // notify(int, int)
} // class SecurityAdapter
```

RELATED PATTERNS

Adapter.   The Adapter pattern can be used to allow objects that do not implement the required interface to participate in the Observer pattern by receiving notifications on their behalf.

Delegation.   The Observer pattern uses the Delegation pattern.

Mediator.   The Mediator pattern is sometimes used to coordinate state changes initiated by multiple objects to an Observable object.

Publish-Subscribe.   The Publish-Subscribe pattern (described in *Patterns in Java, Volume 3*) is a specialized version of the Observer pattern for delivery of notifications to remote and distributed objects.

State

This pattern was previously described in [GoF95].

SYNOPSIS

Encapsulate the states of an object as discrete objects, each extending a common superclass.

CONTEXT

Many objects are required to have a dynamically changing set of attributes called their *state*. Such objects are called *stateful objects*. An object's state will usually be one of a predetermined set of values. When a stateful object becomes aware of an external event, its state may change. The behavior of a stateful object is in some ways determined by its state.

For an example of a stateful object, suppose that you are writing a dialog for editing parameters of a program. The dialog will have buttons for specifying the disposition of changes you have made:

- The dialog will have an OK button that saves the parameter values in the dialog to both a file and the program's working values.
- The dialog will have a Save button that saves the parameter values only to a file.
- The dialog will have an Apply button that saves the parameter values only to the program's working values.
- The dialog will have a Revert button that restores the dialog values from the file.

It is possible to design such a dialog so that it is stateless. If a dialog is stateless, then it will always behave the same way. The OK button will be enabled whether or not you have edited the values in the dialog. The Revert button will be enabled even if the user has just reverted the dialog values to the contents of the file. If there are no other considerations, then designing this dialog to be stateless is satisfactory.

In some cases, the dialog's stateless behavior may be a problem. Updating the values of the program's working values may be disruptive. Storing parameter values to a file might take an annoyingly long time if the file is on a remote shared file server. A way to avoid unnecessary saves to the file or unnecessary setting of the program's working parameter values is to make the dialog stateful so that it will not perform these operations when they are not useful. Instead, it will allow them only when updating the file or working values with values different from those that they already contain. Figure 8.20 is a state diagram showing the four states needed to produce this behavior.

To implement the state diagram in Figure 8.20, you can implement the classes shown in Figure 8.21.

Figure 8.21 shows four classes that correspond to the four states in the state diagram and their common superclass. The superclass, DirtyState, has a public method called processEvent. The processEvent method takes an event identifier as its argument and returns the next state. It determines the next state by calling the abstract nextState method. Each subclass of DirtyState overrides the nextState method in an appropri-

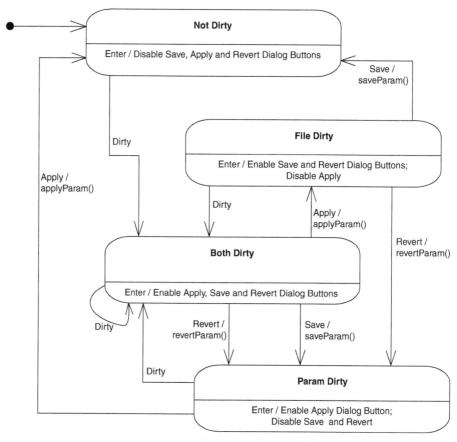

FIGURE 8.20 Parameter dialog state diagram.

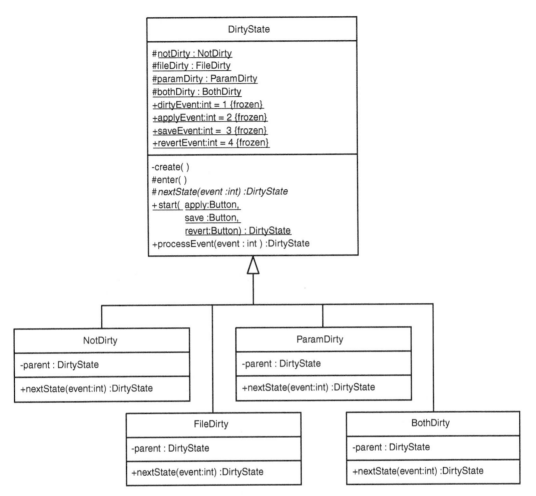

FIGURE 8.21 DirtyState class diagram.

ate way to determine the next state. The DirtyState class also has a static method called *start*.

The start method gets things going by creating an instance of each subclass of the DirtyState class and returning the initial state. The start method also creates an instance of the DirtyState class and assigns its variables notDirty, fileDirty, paramDirty, and bothDirty to the corresponding subclass instances that it creates.

The DirtyState class defines a protected method called enter. A DirtyState object's enter method is called when it becomes the current state. It is called by the start method and the processEvent method. The enter method defined by the DirtyState class doesn't do anything. However, subclasses override the enter method to implement their entry actions.

The DirtyState class defines some static constants. The constants identify event codes that are passed to the processEvent method.

FORCES

☺ An object's behavior is determined by an internal state that changes in response to events.

☺ The organization of logic that manages an object's state should be able to scale up to many states without becoming one unmanageably large piece of code.

SOLUTION

Figure 8.22 shows the basic class organization for the State pattern.

Here is an explanation of the roles classes play in the State pattern:

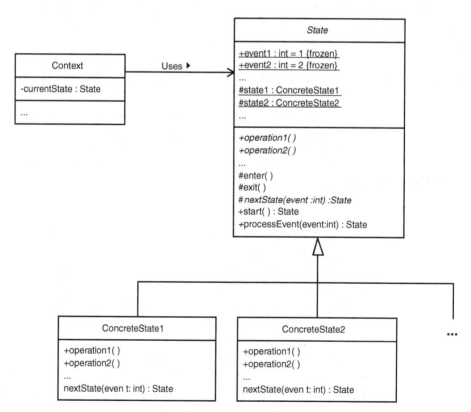

FIGURE 8.22 State class diagram.

Context. Instances of classes in this role exhibit stateful behavior. Instances of `Context` determine their current state by keeping a reference to an instance of a concrete subclass of the `State` class. The subclass of the `State` class determines the state.

State. The `State` class is the superclass of all classes used to represent the state of `Context` objects. A `State` class defines these methods:

- A `State` object's enter method is called when the state that the object represents becomes the current state. The `State` class provides a default implementation of this method that does nothing. It is very common for subclasses of the `State` class to override this method.

- The `start` method performs any necessary initialization of state management objects and returns an object corresponding to the client object's initial state. Before it returns the `State` object that represents the initial state, it calls the `State` object's enter method.

- The `nextState` method is an abstract method that takes an argument that indicates the occurrence of an event and returns the next state. Each concrete subclass of `State` overrides the `nextState` method to determine the correct next state.

- A `State` object's `exit` method is called when the state that the object represents ceases to be the current state. The `State` class provides a default implementation of this method that does nothing. It is very common for subclasses of the `State` class to override this method.

- The `processEvent` method is a public method that takes an argument that indicates the occurrence of an event and returns the new current state. The `processEvent` method calls the `nextState` method. If the object that `nextState` method returns is a different object than the current `State` object, then there will be a new current state. In this case, the `processEvent` method calls the old current state's `exit` method and then calls the new current state's enter method.

- The methods `operation1`, `operation2`, and so on, implement operations that behave differently for each state. For example, if an object has states associated with it called `On` and `Off`, the implementation for an operation for the `On` state might do something, and the implementation for the `Off` state might do nothing. The design of these methods is an application of the Polymorphism pattern described in *Patterns in Java, Volume 2*.

The `State` class defines constants that are symbolic names for the event codes passed to the `processEvent` method.

Unless a `State` class has instance variables, there is no need to have more than one instance of it. If there is only one instance of a concrete subclass of `State`, then the `State` class will have a static variable that refers to that instance. Implementations of the `processEvent` method return the instances referred to by those variables rather than create additional instances.

ConcreteState1, ConcreteState2, and so on. These are concrete subclasses of `State`. They must implement the `operation1`, `operation2`, and so on, methods in an appropriate way. They must also implement the `nextState` method to determine the appropriate next state for each event. `ConcreteState` classes may override the `enter` method and/or `exit` method to implement appropriate actions to be performed when entering or exiting a state.

IMPLEMENTATION

No class other than the `State` class needs to be aware of the subclasses of the `State` class. You can ensure that no class other than the `State` class is aware of its subclasses by declaring the subclasses of the `State` class as private member classes of the `ContextState` class.

CONSEQUENCES

☺ The code for each state is in its own class. This organization makes it easy to add new states without unintended consequences. For this reason, the State pattern works well for small and large numbers of states.

☺ To clients of state objects, state transitions appear to be atomic. A client calls the current state's `processEvent` method. When it returns, the client has its new state.

☺ A procedural implementation of stateful behavior typically involves multiple methods that contain `switch` statements or chains of `if-else` statements for dispatching to state-specific code. These can be large and difficult to understand. Using the State pattern eliminates these `switch` statements or chains of `if-else` statements. It organizes the logic in a more cohesive way that results in classes that have smaller methods.

☺ Using the State pattern results in fewer lines of code and fewer execution paths. This makes it easer to test a program using the White Box Testing pattern described in *Patterns in Java, Volume 2*.

☺ State objects that represent nonparametric states can be shared as singletons if there is no need to create a direct instance of the State class. In some cases, such as the example shown under the Context heading, there is a need to create an instance of the State class to provide a set of state objects with a way of sharing data. Even in those cases, for each subclass of the State class that represents a non-parametric state, there can be a single instance of that class associated with an instance of the State class.

● Using the State pattern eliminates the need for code in a method to dispatch to state-specific code. It does not eliminate state-specific switch statements that dispatch to a state's handling of an event.

CODE EXAMPLE

Here is code that implements the class diagram shown under the Context heading:

```
class DirtyState {
    // Symbolic constants for events
    public static final int DIRTY_EVENT  = 1;
    public static final int APPLY_EVENT  = 2;
    public static final int SAVE_EVENT   = 3;
    public static final int REVERT_EVENT = 4;

    // Symbolic constants for states
    private static BothDirty  bothDirty;
    private static FileDirty  fileDirty;
    private static ParamDirty paramDirty;
    private static NotDirty   notDirty;

    private Parameters parameters;
    private Button apply, save, revert;

    /**
     * Having this private constructor prevents classes outside
     * of this class from creating an instance of this class.
     */
    DirtyState() {
        if (bothDirty==null) {
            bothDirty  = new BothDirty();
            fileDirty  = new FileDirty();
            paramDirty = new ParamDirty();
            notDirty   = new NotDirty();
        } // if
    } // constructor()
```

The DirtyState class's start method initializes the state machine. Its arguments are the Parameters object that the state machine can use to update the program's working values and the buttons that the state machine will enable and disable. The start method returns the initial state.

```
public static DirtyState start(Parameters p,
                               Button apply,
                               Button save,
                               Button revert){
    DirtyState d = new DirtyState();
    d.parameters = p;
    d.apply = apply;
    d.save  = save;
    d.revert= revert;
    d.notDirty.enter();
    return d.notDirty;
} // start(Button, Button, Button)

/**
 * Respond to a given event with the next state.
 * @param event An event code.
 * @return the next state.
 */
protected DirtyState nextState(int event) {
    // This non-overridden method should never be called.
    throw new IllegalAccessError();
} // nextState(int)

/**
 * Respond to the given event by determining the next
 * current state and transitioning to it if it is a
 * different state.
 */
public final DirtyState processEvent(int event) {
    DirtyState myNextState = nextState(event);
    if (this!=myNextState) {
        myNextState.enter();
    } // if
    return myNextState;
} // processEvent(int)

/**
 * This method is called when this object becomes the
 * current state.
 */
protected void enter() { }
```

The four concrete subclasses of DirtyState are implemented as private classes. For the sake of brevity, only one of them is shown here.

```
/**
 * class to represent state for when the fields of the
 * dialog do not match the file or the working parameter
```

```
         * values.
         */
        private class BothDirty extends DirtyState {
            /**
             * Respond to a given event.
             * @return the next state.
             */
            public DirtyState nextState(int event) {
                switch (event) {
                  case DIRTY_EVENT:
                      return this;
                  case APPLY_EVENT:
                      if (parameters.applyParam()) {
                          fileDirty.enter();
                          return fileDirty;
                      } // if
                  case SAVE_EVENT:
                      if (parameters.saveParam()) {
                          paramDirty.enter();
                          return paramDirty;
                      } // if
                  case REVERT_EVENT:
                      if (parameters.revertParam()) {
                          paramDirty.enter();
                          return paramDirty;
                      } // if
                  default:
                      String msg = "unexpected event "+event;
                      throw new IllegalArgumentException(msg);
                } // switch (event)
            } // nextState(int)

            /**
             * This method is called when this object becomes
             * the current state.
             */
            protected void enter() {
                apply.setEnabled(true);
                revert.setEnabled(true);
                save.setEnabled(true);
            } // enter
        } // class BothDirty
} // class DirtyState
```

RELATED PATTERNS

Flyweight. You can use the Flyweight pattern to share state objects.

Mediator. The State pattern is often used with the Mediator pattern when implementing user interfaces.

Singleton.   You can implement nonparametric states using the Singleton pattern.

Polymorphism.   The design of state-specific operations implemented by concrete state classes follows the Polymorphism pattern discussed in *Patterns in Java, Volume 2.*

Null Object

This pattern was previously described in [Woolf97].

SYNOPSIS

The Null Object pattern provides an alternative to using `null` to indicate the absence of an object to delegate an operation to. Using `null` to indicate the absence of such an object requires a test for `null` before each call to the other object's methods. Instead of using null, the Null Object pattern uses a reference to an object that doesn't do anything.

CONTEXT

You have been given the task of writing classes to encapsulate an enterprise's business rules.[2] Because these classes will be used in a variety of environments, there is a requirement that these objects be able to route warning messages to a dialog box, a log file, other destinations, or nowhere at all. A simple way to arrange this is to define an interface called `WarningRouter` for routing warning messages and then have the classes you write delegate the routing of warnings to objects that implement that interface, as shown in Figure 8.23.

To handle the situation where warning messages should not be routed anywhere, you could have the variable that would otherwise refer to a `WarningRouter` object containing `null`. Using this technique means that a `BusinessRule` object must first test to see if a variable is `null` before it can issue a warning message. Depending on the specific business rule class, there may be just one or many places that refer to a `WarningRouter` object. There are procedural techniques for limiting the amount of additional complexity implied by those tests for `null`. However, every call to a `WarningRouter` object's methods is an opportunity for someone to forget to put a test for null in the code. Such an omission will cause a `NullPointerException` to be thrown at runtime.

---

[2] A business rule is a rule that governs the behavior of a business's information systems. Examples of things determined by such rules are when to reorder stock or when the creditworthiness of a customer needs to be scrutinized. Business rules change over time, so the implementation of business rules should allow changing them to be as painless as possible.

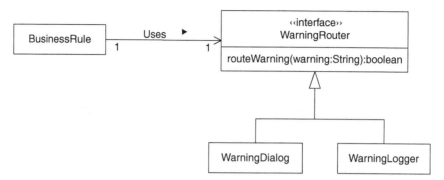

FIGURE 8.23 WarningRouter interface.

An alternative to using `null` to indicate no action is to create a class that implements `WarningRouter` and does nothing with a warning message, as shown in Figure 8.24.

The advantage of having an `IgnoreWarning` class is that you can use it just like any other class that implements the `WarningRouter` interface. It does not require a test for null or any other special logic.

FORCES

- ☺ A class delegates an operation to another class. The delegating class does not usually take into account how the other class implements the operation. However, it sometimes does require that the operation be implemented by doing nothing.
- ☺ You want the class delegating the operation to delegate it in all cases, including the do-nothing case. You do not want the do-nothing case to require any special code.

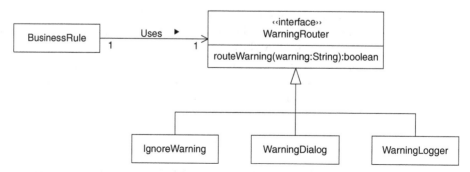

FIGURE 8.24 Ignore warning class.

SOLUTION

Figure 8.25 presents a class diagram that shows the structure of the Null Object pattern.

Here are descriptions of the roles that classes and interfaces play in the Null Object pattern:

Delegator. A class in this role participates in the Null Object pattern by delegating an operation to an interface or an abstract class. It performs this delegation without taking responsibility for the do-nothing case of an operation. It simply assumes that the object it delegates to will encapsulate the correct behavior, even if that is to do nothing.

In particular, an object in the Delegator role does not need to test for null before invoking methods of the object it is delegating to.

OperationIF. A class in the Delegator role delegates an operation to an interface in this role. An abstract class can also fill this role.

RealOperation. Classes in this role implement the operation the Delegator class delegates to the OperationIF interface.

NullOperation. Classes in this role provide a do-nothing implementation of the operation that the Delegator class delegates to the OperationIF interface.

IMPLEMENTATION

It is often the case that instances of NullOperation classes contain no instance-specific information. When this is the case, you may save time and memory by implementing the NullOperation class as a singleton class.

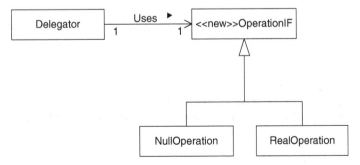

FIGURE 8.25 Null Object pattern.

CONSEQUENCES

☺ The Null Object pattern relieves a class that delegates an operation to another class of the responsibility of implementing the do-nothing version of that operation. This results in simpler code that does not have to test for null before calling the method that implements the delegated operation. It results in more reliable code because the Null Object pattern eliminates some opportunities to create bugs by omitting a test for `null` from code.

☺ The do-nothing behavior encapsulated by a class in the `NullOperation` role is reusable if there is one consistent do-nothing behavior that works for all `Delegator` classes.

☹ The Null Object pattern increases the number of classes in a program. If there is not already an interface in the `OperationIF` role, then the Null Object pattern may introduce more complexity through the introduction of additional classes than it removes by the simplification of code.

CODE EXAMPLE

Following is the code that implements the classes presented under the Context heading. First is the `WarningRouter` interface that is implemented by classes that provide environment-appropriate handling for warning messages.

```java
public interface WarningRouter {
    /**
     * This method sends a warning message to whatever
     * destination it considers appropriate.
     * @return true if caller should proceed with its current
     *          operation.
     */
    public boolean routeWarning(String msg) ;
} // interface WarningRouter
```

Next is some code from the `BusinessRule` class that delegates the handling of warning messages to objects that implement the `WarningRouter` interface.

```java
class BusinessRule {
    private WarningRouter warning;
    private Date expirationDate = new Date(Long.MAX_VALUE);
    ...
    BusinessRule() {
        ...
        if (new Date().after(expirationDate)) {
```

```
            String msg = getClass().getName()+" has expired.";
            warning.routeWarning(msg);
        } // if
        ...
    } // constructor()
} // class BusinessRule
```

Next is a class that implements the `WarningRouter` interface by popping up a dialog box that displays the warning message.

```
class WarningDialog implements WarningRouter {
    public boolean routeWarning(String warning) {
        int r;
        r = JOptionPane.showConfirmDialog(null,
                                warning,
                                "Warning",
                        JOptionPane.OK_CANCEL_OPTION,
                        JOptionPane.WARNING_MESSAGE);
        return r == 0;
    } // routeWarning(String)
} // class WarningDialog
```

The `WarningDialog` class's `routeWarning` method returns true if the user clicks the dialog box's OK button or false if the user clicks its Cancel button. The following listing is of the `IgnoreWarning` class. Because it encapsulates do-nothing behavior, its `routeWarning` method always returns true.

```
class IgnoreWarning implements WarningRouter {
    public boolean routeWarning(String warning) {
        return true;
    } // routeWarning(String)
} // class IgnoreWarning
```

RELATED PATTERNS

Strategy. The Null Object pattern is often used with the Strategy pattern.

Singleton. If instances of a `NullOperation` class contain no instance-specific information, then you may save time and memory by implementing the `NullOperation` class as a singleton class.

Strategy

This pattern was previously described in [GoF95].

SYNOPSIS

Encapsulate related algorithms in classes that implement a common interface. This allows the selection of algorithm to vary by object. It also allows the selection of algorithm to vary over time.

CONTEXT

Suppose you have to write a program that displays calendars. One of the requirements for the program is that it be able to display sets of holidays celebrated by different nations and different religious groups. The user must be able to specify which sets of holidays to display.

You would like to satisfy the requirement by putting the logic for each set of holidays in a separate class. This will give you a set of small classes to which you could easily add more classes. You want classes that use these holiday classes to be unaware of any specific set of holidays. This brings you to the design shown in Figure 8.26.

Here is how classes in Figure 8.26 work with each other. If a Calendar-Display object has a HolidaySetIF object to work with, it consults with that

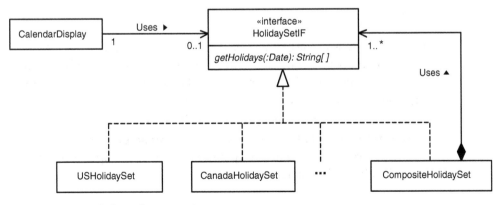

FIGURE 8.26 Holiday classes.

object about each day it displays, in order to find out if that day is a holiday. Such objects are either an instance of a class like USHoliday that identifies a single set of dates or they are an instance of CompositeHoliday. The CompositeHoliday class is used when the user requests the display of multiple sets of holidays. It is instantiated by passing an array of Holiday objects to its constructor.

This arrangement allows a CalendarDisplay object to find out what holidays fall on a particular date by just calling a HolidaySetIF object's getHolidays method.

FORCES

☺ A program must provide multiple variations of an algorithm or behavior.

☺ You need to vary the behavior of each instance of a class.

☺ You need to vary the behavior of objects at runtime.

☺ Delegating behavior to an interface allows classes that use the behavior to be unaware of the classes that implement the interface and the behavior.

☹ If a behavior of a class's instances does not vary from instance to instance or over time, then it is simplest for the class to directly contain the behavior or directly contain a static reference to the behavior.

SOLUTION

Figure 8.27 is a class diagram that shows the roles that classes play in the Strategy pattern.

Here are descriptions of the roles that interfaces and classes play in Figure 8.27:

Client. A class in the Client role delegates an operation to an interface. It does so without knowing the actual class of the object it delegates the operation to or how the class implements the operation.

StrategyIF. An interface in this role provides a common way to access operations encapsulated by its subclasses.

ConcreteStrategy1, ConcreteStrategy2, and so on. Classes in this role provide alternative implementations of the operation that the client class delegates.

The Strategy pattern always occurs with a mechanism for determining the actual ConcreteStrategy object that the client object will use. The

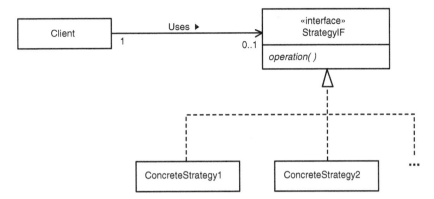

FIGURE 8.27   Strategy pattern.

selection of a strategy is often driven by configuration information or events. However, the actual mechanism varies greatly. For this reason, no particular strategy-selecting mechanism is included in the pattern.

IMPLEMENTATION

It is common for ConcreteStrategy classes to share some common behavior. You should factor the common behavior that they share into a common superclass.

There may be situations where none of the behaviors encapsulated in ConcreteStrategy classes are appropriate. A common way to handle a situation like that is for the Client object to have a null instead of a reference to a Strategy object. This means having to check for null before calling a Strategy object's method. If the structure of the Client object makes this inconvenient, consider using the Null Object pattern.

CONSEQUENCES

☺ The Strategy pattern allows the behavior of Client objects to be dynamically determined on a per-object basis.

☺ The Strategy pattern simplifies Client classes by relieving them of any responsibility for selecting behavior or implementing alternate behaviors. It simplifies the code for Client objects by eliminating if and switch statements. In some cases, it can also increase the speed of Client objects because they do not need to spend any time selecting a behavior.

JAVA API USAGE

The java.util.zip package contains some classes that use the Strategy pattern. Both the CheckedInputStream and CheckedOutputStream classes use the Strategy pattern to compute checksums on byte streams. Both these classes participate as Client classes. The constructors for both classes take a Checksum argument. Checksum is an interface that participates in the AbstractStrategy role. Two classes implement the Checksum interface: Adler32 and CRC32. These classes participate in the ConcreteStrategy role. Figure 8.28 is a diagram that shows the relationship between these classes.

CODE EXAMPLE

Here is the code that implements the design presented under the Context heading. The first listing is for the HolidaySetIF interface. The HolidaySetIF interface defines a method that returns an array of the names of holidays that fall on a given date. It participates in the Strategy pattern in the StrategyIF role.

```
public interface HolidaySetIF {
    public String[] NO_HOLIDAY = new String[0];
    /**
     * Return array of strings describing holidays falling on
     * given date.  If no holidays on the given date, returns
     * NO HOLIDAY.
     */
    public String[] getHolidays(Date dt) ;
} // interface HolidaySetIF
```

The HolidaySetIF interface has a zero length array that implementations of the getHolidays method may return to indicate no holiday falls on a date. Returning this array saves the expense of creating another zero length array for every day that is not a holiday.

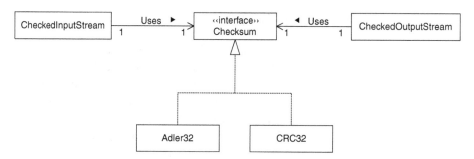

FIGURE 8.28 Checksum-related classes.

Next is a partial listing of the `CalendarDisplay` class, which participates in the Strategy pattern as a `Client` class.

```
class CalendarDisplay {
    private HolidaySetIF holiday;
    ...
    /**
     * Instances of this private class are used to cache
     * information about dates that are to be displayed.
     */
    private class DateCache {
        private Date date;
        private String[] holidayStrings;

        DateCache(Date dt) {
            date = dt;
            ...
            if (holiday == null) {
                holidayStrings = holiday.NO_HOLIDAY;
            } else {
                holidayStrings = holiday.getHolidays(date);
            } // if
            ...
        } // constructor(Date)
    } // class DateCache
} // class CalendarDisplay
```

Notice that, aside from having to handle the possibility of not having any `Holiday` object to work with, the `CalendarDisplay` class is totally unburdened with any details of determining which holidays fall on a date.

The various subclasses of `Holiday` participate in the Strategy pattern in the `ConcreteStrategy` role. They are not particularly interesting with respect to the Strategy pattern and have this basic structure:

```
public class USHoliday implements HolidaySetIF {
    public String[] getHolidays(Date dt) {
        String[] holidays = HolidaySetIF.NO_HOLIDAY;
        ...
        return holidays;
    } // getHolidays(Date)
} // class USHoliday
```

RELATED PATTERNS

Adapter. The Adapter pattern is structurally similar to the Strategy pattern. The difference is in the intent. The Adapter pattern allows a `Client` object to carry out its originally intended function by calling a method of objects that implement a particular interface. The Strategy pattern provides objects that implement a particular interface for the purpose of altering or determining the behavior of a `Client` object.

Flyweight.   If there are many client objects, `ConcreteStrategy` objects may be best implemented as Flyweight objects.

Null Object.   The Strategy pattern is often used with the Null Object pattern.

Template Method.   The Template method pattern manages alternate behaviors through subclassing rather than delegation.

Template Method

This pattern was previously described in [GoF95].

SYNOPSIS

Write an abstract class that contains only part of the logic needed to accomplish its purpose. Organize the class so that its concrete methods call an abstract method where the missing logic would have appeared. Provide the missing logic in the subclass's methods that override the abstract methods.

CONTEXT

Suppose that you have the task of writing a reusable class for logging users into an application or applet. In addition to being reusable and easy to use, the tasks of the class will be to:

- Prompt the user for a user ID and password.
- Authenticate the user ID and password. The result of the authentication operation should be an object. If the authentication operation produces some information needed later as proof of authentication, then the object produced by the authentication operation should encapsulate the information.
- While the authentication operation is in progress, the user should see a changing and possibly animated display that tells the user that authentication is in progress and all is well.
- Notify the rest of the application or applet that login is complete and make the object produced by the authentication operation available to the rest of the application.

Two of these tasks—prompting the user and assuring the user that authentication is in progress—are application independent. Though the strings and images displayed to the user may vary with the application, the underlying logic will always be the same.

The other two tasks—authenticating the user and notifying the rest of the application—are application specific. Every application or applet will have to provide its own logic for these tasks.

The way that you organize your Logon class will be a large factor in how easy it is for developers to use. Delegation is a very flexible mechanism. You could simply organize a Logon class so that it delegates the tasks of authenticating the user and notifying the rest of the application. Though this approach gives a programmer a lot of freedom, it does not help guide a programmer to a correct solution.

Programmers are unlikely to make frequent use of your Logon class. This means that when they use it, they will probably not be very familiar with it. Just as it can be easier to fill in the blanks of a preprinted form than to write a document from scratch, giving your Logon class a fill-in-the-blanks organization can guide programmers to the correct use of the Logon class. You can achieve a fill-in-the-blanks organization by defining the Logon class to be an abstract class that defines abstract methods that correspond to the application-dependent tasks that the programmer must supply code for. To use the Logon class, a programmer must define a subclass of the Logon class. Because the methods corresponding to the tasks that the programmer must code are abstract methods, a Java compiler will complain if the programmer does not fill in the blanks by overriding the abstract methods.

Figure 8.29 presents a diagram that shows the organization of a Logon class organized in that way and its subclass.

The AbstractLogon class has a method called logon that contains the top-level logic for the top-level task of logging a user on to a program. It calls the abstract methods authenticate and notifyAuthentication to perform the program-specific tasks of authenticating a user and notifying the rest of the program when the authentication is accomplished.

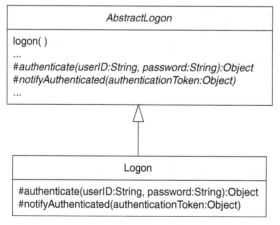

FIGURE 8.29 Logon class and subclass.

FORCES

☺ You have to design a class for reuse in multiple programs.

☺ The overall responsibility of the class will be the same for all applications. However, portions of its behavior will be different in each program in which it is used.

☺ You can make the class easier for programmers unfamiliar with the class to use by designing it in a way that reminds programmers who use the class to supply logic for all its program-specific responsibilities.

☺ If a Java class that is not abstract inherits an abstract method but does not override it, then Java compilers will complain when compiling it.

☹ Designing a class to remind programmers to supply logic for its program-specific responsibilities requires additional effort. If the class is not reused, then the additional effort is wasted.

SOLUTION

Organize reusable logic into an abstract class that calls application-specific logic through place markers in the form of abstract methods. To use the abstract class, the programmer must create a subclass that overrides the abstract methods with application-specific logic.

Figure 8.30 is a class diagram that shows the organization of the Template Method pattern.

Following are descriptions of the roles played by classes in the Template Method pattern:

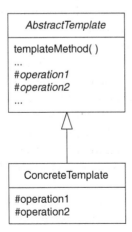

FIGURE 8.30 Template Method pattern.

AbstractTemplate.   A class in this role has a concrete method that contains the class's top-level logic. The method is indicated in the diagram as `templateMethod`. This method calls other methods, defined in the `AbstractTemplate` class as abstract methods, to invoke lower-level logic that varies with each subclass of the `AbstractTemplate` class.

ConcreteTemplate.   A class in this role is a concrete subclass of an `AbstractTemplate` class. It overrides the abstract methods defined by its superclass to provide the logic needed to complete the logic of the `templateMethod` method.

IMPLEMENTATION

The basic way an `AbstractTemplate` class provides guidance to a programmer is by forcing him or her to override abstract methods with the intention of providing logic to fill in the blanks of its template method's logic. You can add more structure by providing additional methods for subclasses to override with supplemental or optional logic. For example, consider a reusable class called `Paragraph` that represents paragraphs in a word processor document.

One of the `Paragraph` class's responsibilities is to determine how to wrap the words it contains into lines that fit within specified margins. The `Paragraph` class has a template method responsible for wrapping the words in a paragraph. Because some word processors allow paragraphs to wrap around graphics, the `Paragraph` class defines an abstract method that the class's word-wrapping logic calls to determine the margins for a line of text. Concrete subclasses of the paragraph class are forced to provide an implementation of that method to determine the margins for each line.

Some word processors include a hyphenation engine that automatically determines where words can be hyphenated. This feature allows longer words to be split between lines so the lines of a paragraph can be of more even lengths. Since not every word processor will require the `Paragraph` class to support hyphenation, it does not make sense for the `Paragraph` class to define an abstract hyphenation method and force subclasses to override it. However, it is helpful for the `Paragraph` class to define a concrete hyphenation method that is called by the word-wrapping logic and does nothing. The point of such a method is that a subclass of `Paragraph` can override the method in those cases where hyphenation needs to be supported.

Methods such as those that can be optionally overridden to provide additional or customized functionality are called *hook methods*. To make it easier for a programmer to be aware of the hook methods that a class provides, you can apply a naming convention to hook methods. Two of the more common naming conventions for hook methods are to either begin the names of hook methods with the prefix do- or end the names of hook methods with the suffix -Hook. For example, following those naming conventions, the name of the `Paragraph` class's hyphenation method might be doHyphenation or hyphenationHook.

CONSEQUENCES

A programmer writing a subclass of an `AbstractTemplate` class is forced to override those methods that must be overridden to complete the logic of the superclass. A well-designed template method class has a structure that provides a programmer with guidance in providing the basic structure of its subclasses.

CODE EXAMPLE

Following is some code that implements the design presented under the Context heading. First is the `AbstractLogon` class. It participates in the Template Method pattern in the `AbstractTemplate` role. Its template method is called `logon`. The `logon` method puts up a dialog that prompts the user for a user ID and password. After the user supplies a user ID and password, the `logon` method pops up a window telling the user that authentication is in progress. The window stays up while the `logon` method calls the abstract method `authenticate` to authenticate the user id and password. If the authentication is successful, it takes down the dialog boxes and calls the abstract method `notifyAuthentication` to notify the rest of the program that the user has been authenticated.

```
public abstract class AbstractLogon {
    /**
     * This method authenticates a user.
     * @param frame
     *          The parent frame of dialogs this method pops up.
     * @param programName The name of the program
     */
public void logon(Frame frame, String programName) {
        Object authenticationToken;
        LogonDialog logonDialog;
        logonDialog = new LogonDialog(frame,
                                 "Log on to "+programName);
        JDialog waitDialog = createWaitDialog(frame);
```

The LogonDialog class implements a dialog to prompt the user for logon information. The waitDialog variable refers to a window containing a message for the user that authentication is in progress.

```
while(true) {
    waitDialog.setVisible(false);
    logonDialog.setVisible(true);
    waitDialog.setVisible(true);
    try {
        String userID = logonDialog.getUserID();
        String password = logonDialog.getPassword();
        authenticationToken = authenticate(userID,
                                           password);
        break;
    } catch (Exception e) {
        // Tell user that Authentication failed
        JOptionPane.showMessageDialog(frame,
                                 e.getMessage(),
                           "Authentication Failure",
                           JOptionPane.ERROR_MESSAGE);
    } // try
}
// Authentication successful
waitDialog.setVisible(false);
logonDialog.setVisible(false);
notifyAuthentication(authenticationToken);
} // logon()
...
```

The remainder of this listing simply shows the abstract methods the AbstractLogon class defines that the logon method calls.

```
/**
 * Authenticate user based on the supplied user id and
 * password.
 * @param userID the supplied user id
 * @param password the supplied password
 * @return object encapsulating proof of authentication.
 */
abstract protected Object authenticate(String userID,
                                       String password)
                    throws Exception;

/**
 * Notify the rest of program that user is authenticated.
 * @param authToken
 *          What the authenticate method returned.
 */
abstract
protected void notifyAuthentication(Object authToken) ;
} // class AbstractLogon
```

Subclasses of the `AbstractLogon` class must override its abstract methods like this:

```
public class Logon extends AbstractLogon {
    . . .
    protected Object authenticate(String userID,
                                  String password)
                throws Exception {
      if (userID.equals("abc") && password.equals("123"))
        return userID;
      throw new Exception("bad userID");
    } // authenticate

    protected void notifyAuthentication(Object authToken) {
      . . .
    } // notify(Object)
} // class Logon
```

RELATED PATTERNS

Strategy.   The Strategy pattern modifies the logic of individual objects at runtime. The Template Method pattern modifies the logic of an entire class at compile time.

Visitor

This pattern was previously described in [GoF95].

SYNOPSIS

One way to implement an operation that involves the objects in a complex structure is to provide logic in each of their classes to support the operation. The Visitor pattern provides an alternate way to implement such operations that avoids complicating the classes of the objects in the structure by putting all the necessary logic in a separate class. The Visitor pattern also allows the logic to be varied by using different Visitor classes.

CONTEXT

Suppose you have the assignment of adding new features to a word processor related to its ability to produce a table of contents. From the viewpoint of a user, there will be a dialog that allows the user to specify information that guides the building of a table of contents. The word processor allows a style name to be associated with each paragraph. The dialog will allow the user to specify which paragraph styles correspond to headings that should appear in the table of contents.

The word processor uses information specified in the dialog to build an internal table that contains all the information it needs to build a multilevel table of contents. In the rest of this description, the table is referred to as the *internal ToC table*. The information in each row of the table will include a level number that can correspond to chapter, section, and subsection or any other hierarchical organization the user wants to represent. The rows of the table will also include a paragraph style and other information for formatting the table of contents. If a paragraph style appears in the table, it means paragraphs with that style are headings whose first line will appear in that level of a table of contents.

In addition to adding the dialog and internal ToC table to the word processor, you will have to add these table-of-contents-related features:

- Generate and insert a table of contents for a single file document into that document.

● Reorganize a single file document into a multifile document, based on a heading level in the internal ToC table.

Since these operations involve manipulating a word processing document, any design for implementing the table-of-contents features will involve classes that the word processor uses to represent documents. Figure 8.31 shows some of the classes that the word processor uses to represent documents.

The classes that will be of interest to a table-of-contents mechanism are Document, Paragraph, and LineOfText. A document contains paragraphs, which contain lines of text. Any design for generating a table of contents should recognize that Document objects may contain other objects that are not Paragraph objects. It should also recognize that other kinds of objects than Document objects may contain Paragraph objects. Finally, the design should not add complexity to the classes that represent documents.

There are two basic approaches that you could take toward implementing the table-of-contents features. One approach is to put the necessary logic in the various classes that represent a document. For the reasons discussed in the previous paragraph, this is not a good solution.

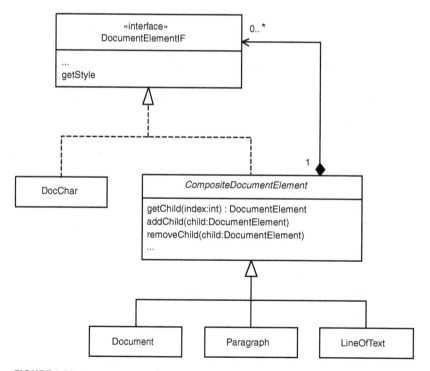

FIGURE 8.31 Document classes.

The other approach is to put all the logic for each feature in a separate class. When a table-of-contents operation is to be done, the object responsible for the operation examines a Document object and objects that it contains. It looks for Paragraph objects that the Document object directly contains. When it finds Paragraph objects that have a style that is in the internal ToC table driving the table-of-contents operation, it takes the appropriate action. This is the approach shown in Figure 8.32.

Figure 8.32 includes the classes for representing word processing documents that were shown in Figure 8.31. It also includes the following classes:

WordProcessor. The WordProcessor class is responsible for creating and editing the objects that represent a document. It uses the other classes in the diagram to edit a document.

DocumentVisitor. This is an abstract class. Its subclasses explore the objects that constitute a document in order to produce a

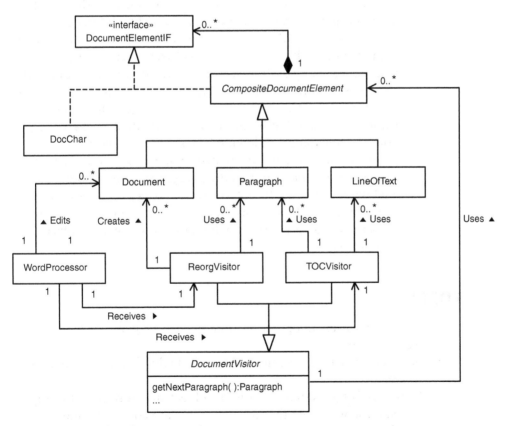

FIGURE 8.32 Table-of-contents classes.

table of contents or reorganize a document into multiple files. The `DocumentVisitor` class provides logic that its subclasses use to navigate among the objects that constitute a document.

The concept is that instances of subclasses of the `DocumentVisitor` class visit the objects that constitute a document, gathering information from each object, and then act on the information.

TOCVisitor. This subclass of the `DocumentVisitor` class is responsible for generating a table of contents. It works by examining each `Paragraph` object directly owned by a `Document` object. When it finds a `Paragraph` object with a style that is in the internal ToC table, it generates a corresponding table-of-contents entry. The table-of-contents entry uses the contents of the first `LineOfText` object that belongs to the `Paragraph` object.

ReorgVisitor. This subclass of `DocumentVisitor` class is responsible for automatically separating a document into multiple files. It begins by being told to look for paragraphs that correspond to a certain level of organization in a document. It finds that level of organization in the internal ToC table. It fetches the style associated with that level of organization from the table. It then examines all of the `Paragraph` objects that directly belong to a `Document` object. It looks for `Paragraph` objects that have the style it fetched from the table. When it finds a `Paragraph` object with that style, it creates a new `Document` object. It moves the `Paragraph` object that it found, along with all of the `Paragraph` objects immediately following it that are at a lower level of organization to the newly created `Document` object. It writes the new `Document` object and all the paragraph objects now associated with it to a file. It replaces the `Paragraph` objects it moved from the original `Document` object with a new object that contains the name of the file in which the moved paragraphs are now stored.

FORCES

☺ There are a variety of operations that need to be performed on an object structure.

☺ The object structure is composed of objects that belong to different classes.

☺ The types of objects that occur in the object structure do not change often and the ways that they are connected are consistent and predictable.

SOLUTION

This section contains two versions of the Visitor pattern. The first is an ideal solution that produces a very clean result. Unfortunately, there are many situations for which the ideal solution will not work or will be inefficient. The second version of the Visitor pattern works for a wider range of situations at the expense of introducing additional dependencies between classes.

Figure 8.33 is a class diagram that shows the roles that classes play in the ideal version of the Visitor pattern.

Here is a description of the roles that classes play in Figure 8.33.

> **Client.** Instances of classes in this role are responsible for manipulating an object structure and the objects that compose it. They use ConcreteVisitor objects to perform computations on the object structures for which they are responsible.

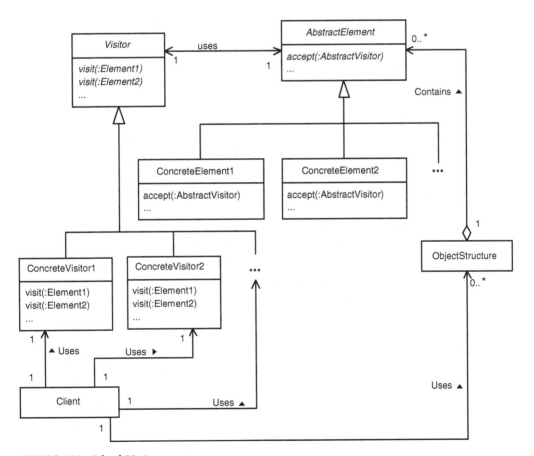

FIGURE 8.33 Ideal Visitor pattern.

ObjectStructure. An instance of a class in this role serves as the root object of an object structure. When visiting objects in an object structure, a `Visitor` object begins with an instance of an `ObjectStructure` class and then moves on to other objects in the object structure.

It is possible for a class to participate in the Visitor pattern in the `ObjectStructure` role and also to participate in the `ConcreteElement` role as an element of the object structure.

AbstractElement. A class in this role is an abstract superclass of the objects that constitute an object structure. It defines an abstract method, shown in Figure 8.33, as `accept`. It takes an `AbstractVisitor` object as its argument. Subclasses of an `AbstractElement` class provide an implementation of `accept` that calls a method of the `AbstractVisitor` object and then passes the `AbstractVisitor` object to the `accept` method of other `AbstractElement` objects.

ConcreteElement1, ConcreteElement2, and so on. Instances of classes in this role are elements of an object structure. Computations are done on the objects of an object structure by passing an `AbstractVisitor` object to a `ConcreteElement` object's `accept` method. The `accept` method passes the `ConcreteElement` object to one of the `AbstractVisitor` object's methods so that it can include the `ConcreteElement` object in its computation. When that is done, the `ConcreteElement` object passes the `AbstractVisitor` object to the other `ConcreteElement` object's `accept` method.

Visitor. A class in this role is an abstract superclass of classes that perform computations on the elements of an object structure. It defines a method for each class that its subclasses will visit, so that their instances can pass themselves to `Visitor` objects to be included in their computations.

ConcreteVisitor1, ConcreteVisitor2, and so on. Instances of classes in this role visit objects that constitute an object structure.

Figure 8.34 presents a collaboration diagram that shows more clearly how `Visitor` objects collaborate with object structures.

What is shown in Figure 8.34 is the collaboration between a `Visitor` object and the elements of an object structure. After a `Visitor` object is presented to an `ObjectStructure` object, the `ObjectStructure` object passes the `Visitor` object to a `ConcreteElement` object's `accept` method. The `ConcreteElement` object passes itself to the `Visitor` object's `visit` method to allow the object to include the `Visitor` object in its computa-

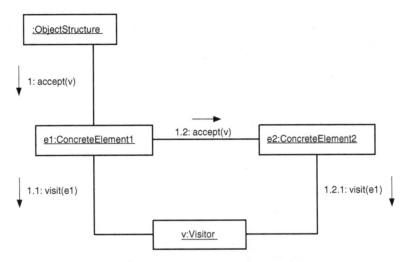

FIGURE 8.34 Ideal visitor collaboration.

tion. The `ConcreteElement` object then passes the `Visitor` object to another `ConcreteElement` object so that the `Visitor` object may visit it. The cycle continues on, with the `Visitor` object being passed on to other `ConcreteElement` objects. A `ConcreteElement` object may be associated with any number of other `ConcreteElement` objects. It may pass a visitor object to some, all, or none of its associated `ConcreteElement` objects.

In this version of the Visitor pattern, the `AbstractElement` objects determine which elements of an object structure a `Visitor` object visits and the order in which it visits them. This works well only if it works for all kinds of `Visitor` objects to follow the same path in visiting elements of an object structure. It has the advantage of keeping `Visitor` classes independent of the structure of the object structure. However, there are situations where this does not work. These situations include:

- Visitors that modify an object structure. The example in the Context section of a visitor object that splits a document into multiple files is such a situation.
- Object structures that are so large that it would add an unacceptable amount of execution time for a `Visitor` to visit every object when it needs to visit only a small subset of the objects in the structure.

Figure 8.35 is a class diagram that shows another version of the Visitor pattern. In this version of the Visitor pattern, `Visitor` classes are responsible for navigating their own way through an object structure. Visitors organized in this way are able to modify an object structure or

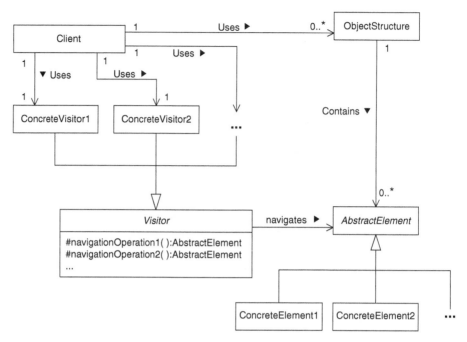

FIGURE 8.35 Visitor pattern.

selectively navigate it. The drawback to this organization is that the Visitor classes are not as reusable because they have to make assumptions about the structure of an object structure in order to navigate through it.

In this version of the Visitor pattern, the AbstractElement class does not contain any methods specifically related to Visitor objects. Instead, the Visitor class defines methods that its subclasses use to navigate an object structure.

IMPLEMENTATION

When implementing the Visitor pattern, the first decision you will have to make is whether you can use the ideal version of the pattern. When it is possible, you should use the ideal version of the Visitor pattern because it takes less effort to implement and maintain. When you can't use the ideal version of the Visitor pattern, put as much of the logic as possible for navigating the object structure in the Visitor class rather than its subclasses. This will minimize the number of dependencies that ConcreteVisitor objects have on the object structure and make maintenance easier.

CONSEQUENCES

☺ The Visitor pattern makes it easy to add new operations on an object structure. Because the `ConcreteElement` classes have no dependencies on `Visitor` classes, adding a new `Visitor` class does not require making any changes to an `AbstractElement` class or any of its subclasses.

☺ The Visitor pattern puts the logic for an operation in one cohesive `ConcreteVisitor` class. This is easier to maintain than operations that are spread out over multiple `ConcreteElement` classes.

☺ A single `Visitor` object captures the state needed to perform an operation on an object structure. This is easier to maintain and more efficient than the way state information has to be passed as discrete values from one object to another.

☹ Another consequence of the Visitor pattern is the additional work it takes to add new `ConcreteElement` classes. The ideal version of the Visitor pattern requires you to add a new `visit` method to each `ConcreteVisitor` class for each `ConcreteElement` class that you add. For the other version of the Visitor pattern, you may need to change the logic that `Visitor` classes use to navigate the object structure.

☹ A direct consequence of the Visitor pattern is that `ConcreteElement` classes must provide access to enough of their state to allow `Visitor` objects to perform their computations. This may mean that you expose information that would otherwise be hidden by the class's encapsulation.

CODE EXAMPLE

The following is code for some of the classes presented in the table-of-contents design under the Context heading. First is code for the `WordProcessor` class that contains top-level logic for a word processor. It is responsible for initiating operations that manipulate documents.

```
public class WordProcessor {
    // The document currently being edited
    private Document activeDocument;
...
    /**
     * Reorganize a document into subfiles.
     */
    private void reorg(int level) {
        new ReorgVisitor(activeDocument, level);
    } // reorg(int)

    /**
     * Build a table of contents
```

```
            */
        private TOC buildTOC() {
            return new TOCVisitor(activeDocument).buildTOC();
        } // buildTOC()
    } // class WordProcessor
```

The next listing is for the `DocumentVisitor` class. The `DocumentVisitor` class is an abstract superclass of classes that implement operations that have to visit many of the objects that constitute a document.

```
abstract class DocumentVisitor {
    private Document document;
    private int docIndex = 0;    // Index for navigating
                                 // children of document.
    DocumentVisitor(Document document) {
        this.document = document;
    } // constructor(Document)

    protected Document getDocument() { return document; }

    /**
     * Return the next paragraph that is a direct part of the
     * document
     */
    protected Paragraph getNextParagraph() {
        Document myDocument = document;
        while (docIndex < myDocument.getChildCount()) {
            DocumentElementIF docElement;
            docElement = myDocument.getChild(docIndex);
            docIndex += 1;
            if (docElement instanceof Paragraph)
              return (Paragraph)docElement;
        }
        return null;
    } // getNextParagraph()
    ...
} // class DocumentVisitor
```

The next listing is for the `ReorgVisitor` class, which is responsible for visiting the paragraphs of a document and moving those that are at a specified level of organization in the table of contents to a separate document.

```
class ReorgVisitor extends DocumentVisitor {
    private TocLevel[] levels;

    ReorgVisitor(Document document, int level) {
        super(document);
        this.levels = document.getTocLevels();
        Paragraph p;
        while ((p = getNextParagraph()) != null) {
            ...
```

```
        } // while
    } // constructor(Document)
} // class ReorgVisitor
```

As you can see from this listing, the ReorgVisitor class concerns itself with Document and Paragraph objects.

The final listing is for the TOCVisitor class. The TOCVisitor class is responsible for building a table of contents. It navigates more deeply into a document's object structure, concerning itself with Document objects, Paragraph objects, and LineOfText objects. Its interest in LineOfText objects is that a table-of-contents entry will contain the text of the first LineOfText object in the paragraph that the table-of-contents entry corresponds to.

```
class TOCVisitor extends DocumentVisitor {
    private Hashtable tocStyles = new Hashtable();

    TOCVisitor(Document document) {
        super(document);
        TocLevel[] levels = document.getTocLevels();
        // put styles in a hashtable.
        for (int i=0; i < levels.length; i++) {
            tocStyles.put(levels[i].getStyle(), levels[i]);
        } // for
    } // constructor(Document)

    TOC buildTOC() {
        TOC toc = new TOC();
        Paragraph p;
        while ((p = getNextParagraph()) != null) {
            String styleName = p.getStyle();
            if (styleName != null) {
                TocLevel level;
                level = (TocLevel)tocStyles.get(styleName);
                if (level != null) {
                    LineOfText firstLine = null;
                    for (int i = 0; i < p.getChildCount();i++){
                        DocumentElementIF e = p.getChild(i);
                        if (e instanceof LineOfText) {
                            firstLine = (LineOfText)e;
                            break;
                        } // if
                        ...
                    } // for
                } // if
            } // if
        } // while
        return toc;
    } // buildTOC()
} // class TOCVisitor
```

RELATED PATTERNS

Iterator.   The Iterator pattern is an alternative to the Visitor pattern when the object structure to be navigated has a linear structure.

Little Language.   In the Little Language pattern, you can use the Visitor Pattern to implement the interpreter part of the pattern.

Composite.   The Visitor pattern is often used with object structures that are organized according to the Composite pattern.

Concurrency Patterns

The patterns in this chapter involve coordinating concurrent operations. These patterns primarily address two types of problems:

Shared resources. When concurrent operations access the same data or another type of shared resource, operations may interfere with each other if they access the resource at the same time. To ensure that operations on shared resources execute correctly, the operations must be sufficiently constrained to access their shared resource one at a time. However, if the operations are overly constrained, then they may deadlock and not be able to finish executing.

Deadlock is a situation where one operation waits for another operation to do something before it proceeds. Because each operation is waiting for the other to do something, they wait forever and never do anything.

Sequence of operations.   If operations are constrained to access a shared resource one at a time, it may be necessary to ensure that they access the shared resource in a particular order. For example, an object cannot be removed from a data structure before it is added to the data structure.

The Single Threaded Execution pattern is the most important pattern in this chapter. Most shared-resource issues can be resolved with just the Single Threaded Execution pattern, which ensures that no more than one thread at a time can access a resource. Situations where the sequence of operations matters are less common. Such situations can be handled using the Scheduler pattern.

The Guarded Suspension pattern provides guidance on what to do when a thread has exclusive access to a resource and discovers that it cannot complete the operation on that resource because something is not yet ready.

When an operation may require exclusive access to multiple resources, the Lock Object pattern is a way to simplify coordination of access to the multiple resources.

The Balking pattern is useful if an operation must be done either immediately or not at all.

The Read/Write Lock pattern is an alternative to one-at-a-time access if some operations can share the same resource and some operations cannot share.

The Producer-Consumer pattern is useful for coordinating objects that produce a resource with objects that consume the resource.

The Two-Phase Termination pattern is used to shut down threads in an orderly way.

The Double Buffering pattern is a specialized form of the Producer-Consumer pattern that makes it more likely resources will be produced before they are needed.

The Asynchronous Processing pattern describes how to avoid waiting for the results of an operation when you don't need to know the result immediately.

The Future pattern describes how to keep classes that invoke an operation from having to know whether the operation is synchronous or asynchronous.

Single Threaded Execution

The Single Threaded Execution pattern is also known as Critical Section.

SYNOPSIS

Some methods access data or other shared resources in a way that produces incorrect results if concurrent calls to a method access the data or another resource at the same time. The Single Threaded Execution pattern solves this problem by preventing concurrent calls to the method from resulting in concurrent executions of the method.

CONTEXT

Suppose you are writing software for a system that monitors the flow of traffic on a major highway. At strategic locations on the highway, sensors in the road monitor the number of passing cars per minute. The sensors send information to a central computer. The central computer controls electronic signs located near major interchanges. The signs display messages to drivers, advising them of traffic conditions so that they can select alternate routes.

At the places in the road where sensors measure the flow of cars, there is a sensor for each traffic lane. The sensor in each lane is wired to a controller that totals the number of cars passing that place in the road each minute. The controller is attached to a transmitter that transmits each minute's total to the central computer. Figure 9.1 is a class diagram showing these relationships.

Here are descriptions of the classes that appear in Figure 9.1:

TrafficSensor.   Each instance of this class corresponds to a physical sensor device. Each time a vehicle passes a physical sensor device, the corresponding instance of the TrafficSensor class calls a TrafficSensorController object's vehiclePassed method. Each TrafficSensor object will have its own thread, allowing it to handle inputs from its associated sensor asynchronously of other sensors.

TrafficTransmitter.   Instances of this class are responsible for transmitting the number of vehicles that pass a place on the

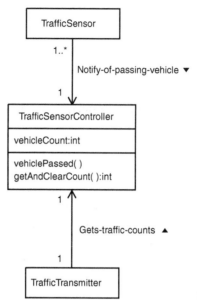

FIGURE 9.1 Traffic sensor classes.

road each minute. A `TrafficTransmitter` object gets the number of vehicles that have passed a place on the road by calling the `getAndClearCount` method of its corresponding `TrafficSensorController` object. The `TrafficSensorController` object's `getAndClearCount` method returns the number of vehicles that have passed the sensors since the previous call to the `getAndClearCount` method.

TrafficSensorController. Instances of the `TrafficSensor` class and the `TrafficTransmitter` class call the methods of the `TrafficSensorController` class to update, fetch, and clear the number of vehicles that have passed a place on the road.

It is possible for two `TrafficSensor` objects to call a `TrafficSensorController` object's `vehiclePassed` method at the same time. If both calls were to execute at the same time, they would produce an incorrect result. Each call to the `vehiclePassed` method is supposed to increase the vehicle count by one. However, if two calls to the `vehiclePassed` method execute at the same time, the vehicle count is incremented by one instead of two. Here is the sequence of events that would occur if both calls execute at the same time:

1. Both calls fetch the same value of `vehicleCount` at the same time.
2. Both calls add one to the same value.
3. Both calls store the same value in `vehicleCount`.

Clearly, allowing more than one call to the `vehiclePassed` method to execute at the same time will result in undercounting vehicles. A slight undercount of vehicles is not a serious problem for this application. However, there is a similar problem that is more serious.

A `TrafficTransmitter` object periodically calls a `TrafficSensorController` object's `getAndClearCount` method. The `getAndClearCount` method fetches the value of the `TrafficSensorController` object's `vehicleCount` variable and then sets it to zero. If a `TrafficSensorController` object's `vehiclePassed` method and `getAndClearCount` method are called at the same time, it creates a situation called a *race condition*.

A race condition is a situation whose outcome depends on the order in which concurrent operations finish. If the `getAndClearCount` method finishes last, then it sets the value of the `vehicleCount` variable to zero, wiping out the result of the call to the `vehiclePassed` method. This is just another way for small undercounts to happen. However, the problem is more serious if the `vehiclePassed` method finishes last.

If the `vehiclePassed` method finishes last, it replaces the zero set by the `getAndClearCount` method with a value one greater than the value it fetched. This means the next call to the `getAndClearCount` method will return a value that includes vehicles counted before the previous call to the `getAndClearCount` method. Vehicles may be double counted, triple counted, or worse.

An overcount like this could be large enough to convince the central computer that a traffic jam is starting. It will respond to this sort of situation by displaying messages on electronic signs suggesting that drivers follow alternate routes. An error like this could cause a traffic jam.

A simple way to avoid these problems is to require that no more than one thread at a time execute a `TrafficSensorController` object's `vehiclePassed` method or `getAndClearCount` method. You can indicate this design decision by indicating that the concurrency of these methods is guarded; in a UML drawing, indicating that a method's concurrency is guarded is equivalent to declaring it synchronized in Java. This is shown in Figure 9.2.

Any number of threads may call the guarded methods of the same object at the same time. However, only one thread at a time is allowed to execute the object's guarded methods. While one thread is executing an object's guarded methods, other threads wait until the thread is finished executing the object's guarded methods. When the thread is finished, a waiting thread is arbitrarily selected to execute the object's guarded methods next. This ensures single-threaded execution of an object's guarded methods.

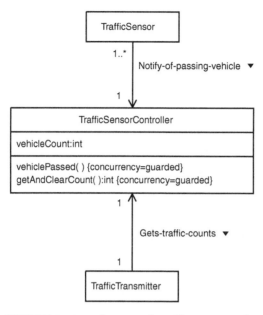

FIGURE 9.2 Synchronized traffic sensor classes.

FORCES

- ☺ A class has methods that update or set instance or class variables.
- ☺ A method manipulates external resources that support only one operation at a time.
- ☺ The class's methods may be called concurrently by different threads.
- ☺ No time constraint requires a method to execute immediately when it is called.

SOLUTION

Ensure that operations that cannot correctly be performed concurrently are not performed concurrently. Accomplish this by making methods that should not be executed concurrently guarded. Figure 9.3 shows the general case.

The class in Figure 9.3 has two kinds of methods. It has unguarded methods named safeOp1, safeOp2, and so on, that can safely execute concurrently. It has guarded methods named unsafeOp1, unsafeOp2, and so on, that are unsafe if executed concurrently. When different threads call the guarded methods of a `Resource` object at the same time, only one thread at a time is allowed to execute the method. The rest of the threads wait for that thread to finish.

```
                    Resource
        safeOp1
        safeOp2
        ...
        unsafeOp1 {concurrency=guarded}
        unsafeOp2 {concurrency=guarded}
        ...
```

FIGURE 9.3 Single Threaded Execution pattern.

IMPLEMENTATION

Guarded methods are implemented in Java by declaring methods to be synchronized. It may take longer to call a synchronized method than an unsynchronized method. Consider the collaboration diagram in Figure 9.4.

Figure 9.4 shows that a synchronized method in class A calls class B's doIt method. The doIt method is synchronized. If the doIt method is called only from synchronized methods of class A, then as an optimization, it is possible to make the doIt method an unsynchronized method. It will still be executed by only one thread at a time, because it is only called by methods that are executed by one thread at a time.

This optimization is called *synchronization factoring*. Synchronization factoring is an unsafe optimization in the sense that if the program is modified so that concurrent calls can be made to the doIt method, it will stop working correctly. If you decide this optimization is worth doing manually, you should put comments in design diagrams and code to warn and remind people that the optimization has been performed.

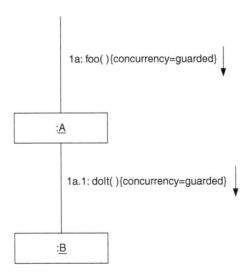

FIGURE 9.4 Synchronization factoring.

448 ■ CHAPTER NINE

There are compilers and JVMs that perform this optimization automatically. JVMs that use Sun's HotSpot technology do this. There are compilers that are able to do synchronization factoring in some cases. If you
use a JVM or compiler that performs this optimization automatically, then
it is best not to do this manually.

CONSEQUENCES

☺ If a class has methods that access variables or other resources in a
way that is not thread safe, you can make the class's methods thread
safe by making them guarded.

● Making methods guarded that do not need to be can reduce performance. There are two reasons for this. One reason is that there may
be some additional overhead in just calling a guarded method. The
other reason is that if a method is guarded but does not need to be,
then its callers may wait for a lock when there is no need to wait.

☹ Making methods guarded can introduce the opportunity for threads
to become *deadlocked*. Deadlock occurs when two threads each have
exclusive use of a resource and each thread is waiting for the other to
release its resource before continuing. Since each thread is waiting
for a resource that the other thread already has exclusive access to,
both threads will wait forever without gaining access to the resource
they are waiting for. Consider the example in Figure 9.5.

In Figure 9.5, thread 1a calls object x's foo method and thread 1b calls
object y's bar method at the same time. Thread 1a then calls object y's bar

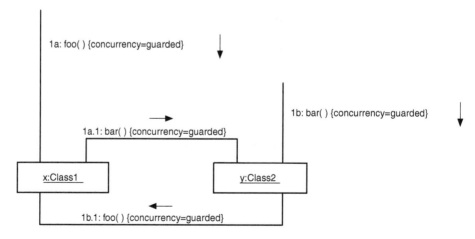

FIGURE 9.5 Deadlock.

method and waits for thread 1b to finish its call to that method. Thread 1b calls object x's `foo` method and waits for thread 1a to finish its call to that method. At that point, the two threads are deadlocked. Each is waiting for the other to finish its call.

Deadlock can also involve more than two threads. Deadlock is sometimes called *deadly embrace*.

JAVA API USAGE

Many of the methods of the `java.util.Vector` class are synchronized to ensure single-threaded access to the internal data structures of `Vector` objects.

CODE EXAMPLE

The following is some of the code that implements the traffic sensor design discussed under the Context heading. The first class shown is the `Traffic-Sensor` class. Instances of the `TrafficSensor` class are associated with a traffic sensor. A traffic sensor detects the passing of a vehicle over a place in a traffic lane. When the traffic sensor associated with an instance of the `TrafficSensor` class detects a passing vehicle, the instance's `detect` method is called. Its `detect` method is responsible for notifying other interested objects of the passing vehicle.

```java
public class TrafficSensor implements Runnable {
    private TrafficObserver observer;

    /**
     * Constructor
     * @param observer
     *         The object to notify when this object's
     *         associated traffic sensor detects a passing
     *         vehicle.
     */
    public TrafficSensor(TrafficObserver observer) {
        this.observer = observer;
        new Thread(this).start();
    } // constructor(TrafficObserver)

    /**
     * Top-level logic for this object's thread.
     */
    public void run() {
        monitorSensor();
    } // run()
```

```
    // This method calls this object's detect method when its
    // associated traffic sensor detects a passing vehicle.
    private native void monitorSensor() ;

     // This method is called by the monitorSensor method to
     // report the passing of a vehicle to this object's
     // observer.
    private void detect() {
        observer.vehiclePassed();
    } // detect()
...
    /**
     * Classes must implement this interface to be notified
     * of passing vehicles by a TrafficSensor object.
     */
    public interface TrafficObserver {
        /**
         * This is called when a TrafficSensor detects a passing
         * vehicle.
         */
        public void vehiclePassed();
    } // interface TrafficObserver
} // class TrafficSensor
```

The next class shown is the TrafficTransmitter class. Instances of the TrafficTransmitter class are responsible for transmitting the number of vehicles that have passed a place in the road each minute.

```
public class TrafficTransmitter implements Runnable {
    private TrafficSensorController controller;
    private Thread myThread;

    /**
     * constructor.
     * @param controller The TrafficSensorController this
     *                    object will get vehicle counts from.
     */
    public
    TrafficTransmitter(TrafficSensorController controller) {
        this.controller = controller;
        ...
        myThread = new Thread(this);
        myThread.start();
    } // constructor(TrafficSensorController)

    /**
     * Transmit a vehicle count every minute
     */
    public void run() {
        while (true) {
            try {
                myThread.sleep(60*1000);
                transmit(controller.getAndClearCount());
```

```
            } catch (InterruptedException e) {
            } // try
        } // while
    } // run()

    // Transmit a vehicle count.
    private native void transmit(int count);
} // class TrafficTransmitter
```

The final class shown here is the `TrafficSensorController` class. Instances of the `TrafficSensorController` class maintain a running total of the number of vehicles that have passed the traffic sensors associated with the instance. Notice that its methods are implemented as synchronized methods.

```
public class TrafficSensorController
            implements TrafficSensor.TrafficObserver {
    private int vehicleCount = 0;
...
    /**
     * This method is called when a traffic sensor detects a
     * passing vehicle.  It increments the vehicle count.
     */
    public synchronized void vehiclePassed() {
        vehicleCount++;
    } // vehiclePassed()

    /**
     * Set the vehicle count to 0
     * @return the previous vehicle count.
     */
    public synchronized int getAndClearCount() {
        int count = vehicleCount;
        vehicleCount = 0;
        return count;
    } // getAndClearCount()
} // class TrafficSensorController
```

RELATED PATTERNS

Most of the other concurrency patterns use the Single Threaded Execution pattern.

Lock Object

SYNOPSIS

An operation that requires single-threaded access to multiple objects is to be performed. Save time and complexity by having an additional object that gets locked instead of the multiple objects that participate directly in the operation.

CONTEXT

Suppose you are writing a multi-player game program. The game is played in real time. Each player is able to initiate operations that affect the state of multiple game objects. To ensure that each object's state change happens correctly, you use the Single Threaded Execution pattern.

For the game to work correctly, changes to some game objects must appear to happen at the same time. To happen at the same time without interference from the actions of another player, you want to ensure that the thread responsible for changing the state of the objects has exclusive access to the objects.

One way to arrange for threads to have exclusive access to the objects is to require threads to get a lock on each of the objects before they try to modify any of the objects' states. There are some difficulties with this type of solution:

- Simply having to get a lock on multiple objects requires a few extra CPU cycles, but that is the smallest of the problems.
- You need to ensure that when threads try to lock multiple objects, they do not get stuck in a deadlock. You don't want one thread to be waiting to get a lock on an object that another thread has a lock on and will not release until it can get a lock on an object that the first thread has a lock on.
  - It is possible to avoid deadlocks such as these by using the Static Locking Order pattern described in *Patterns in Java, Volume 3*. You ensure that threads first sort the objects in the order of the value the `System.identityHashCode` returns for them and then locks them in that order.

○ It seems clear that deadlock avoidance adds complexity and over-head.

● Locking a collection of objects is an awkward thing to code in Java. To lock an arbitrary number of objects, you need to execute synchro-nized statements in a self-recursive method. Here is an example:

```
public class ObjectLocker {
    /**
     * This method locks all of the objects in given array and
     * then passes the array to the given ObjectManipulationIF
     * object.
     *
     * @param objs
     *          An array of the objects that the given
     *          ObjectManipulationIF object is to act on.
     * @param operation
     *          The operation to be performed
     */
    public void doIt(Object[] objs, ObjectManipulationIF op) {
        doItHelper(objs, op, objs.length-1);
    } // doIt(Object[], ObjectManipulationIF)

    private void doItHelper(Object[] objs,
                            ObjectManipulationIF op,
                            int ndx) {
        synchronized (objs[ndx]){
            if (ndx==0) {
                op.doObject(objs);
            } else {
                doItHelper(objs, op, ndx-1);
            } // if
        } // synchronized
    } // doItHelper(Object[], ObjectManipulationIF, int)
} // class ObjectLocker
```

Clearly, there are good reasons to look for an alternate solution to the problem of ensuring that a thread has exclusive access to multiple game objects. You want a solution that avoids the complexity and overhead of locking individual objects.

A way to simplify this problem is to insist that only one thread at a time will have access to any game objects. This restriction will sometimes force threads to wait that would not otherwise need to wait. However, you decide that the complexity and overhead that this saves you is more valuable.

To implement this simplified strategy, you create one additional object that will be used only as a lock object. The rule will be that no thread will do anything to affect the state of a game object unless it holds the lock on the lock object.

FORCES

☺ Operations are to be performed that require exclusive access to the objects they affect to ensure that they are correct.

☺ Having to lock an arbitrary set of objects in order to perform an operation adds complexity and overhead to the operation.

☺ It is acceptable if operations sometimes have to wait for other operations to complete before starting. Your performance requirements are soft enough that sometimes having to wait for another operation to complete even when it is not strictly necessary is acceptable.

SOLUTION

Arrange for threads to have exclusive access to a set of objects by having the threads acquire a synchronization lock on an object that exists only for this purpose. An object that exists only for the purpose of being the subject of locks is called a *lock object*. Collaborations involving a lock object follow the pattern shown in Figure 9.6.

In Figure 9.6, a `Foo` object's `doIt` method is called. The `doIt` method begins by getting a lock on the object `lockObject`. Once it has a lock on the `lockObject` object, it performs operations on other objects and then releases its lock on the lock object.

There are different ways that a lock object can be incorporated into the organization of some classes. Figure 9.7 shows a simple organization.

Figure 9.7 shows an abstract class. The class has a static method called `getLockObject`. Subclasses of the abstract class call the `getLockObject` method to get the lock object to synchronize operations. This way of managing a lock object works well when you want all instances of one or more classes to share the same lock object.

Other ways of managing lock objects are discussed under the Implementation heading. Because there are a variety of reasonable ways to manage access to lock objects, they are not really part of the pattern. This pattern is about using a lock object, not managing access to it.

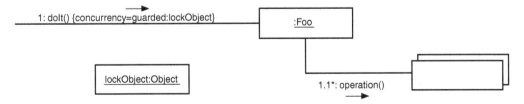

FIGURE 9.6 Lock object collaboration.

IMPLEMENTATION

There are a variety of ways to manage access to a lock object. The main considerations in choosing the way to manage a lock object are the diversity of the objects that will use the lock object and whether you need more than one lock object.

The example of lock object management shown under the Solution heading in Figure 9.7 shows classes accessing a lock object through a static method that they inherit. This organization works well when it is appropriate to lock all the instances of a class or classes to perform an operation.

When the set of objects that you need to lock for an operation are not mostly instances of the same class, there are typically multiple other groupings. In these cases, the way that the lock object is managed is typically driven by whatever organization is shared by the objects involved in operations the lock object is for. For example, consider the case of objects organized into a tree, as shown in Figure 9.8.

Figure 9.8 shows objects organized into a tree. The objects are instances of different classes. However, all the objects have a method named getLockObject that returns the lock object to use for operations on these objects. The way that these objects implement the getLockObject method is that if they are not the root of the tree, their getLockObject method calls the parent object's getLockObject method. If the object is the root of the tree, then it provides the actual lock object.

If an operation is going to need exclusive access to any of the objects in the tree, it arbitrarily picks one of the objects it needs exclusive access to and calls its getLockObject method. The getLockObject method of any of the objects in the tree returns the same lock object. Once the operation has a lock on the lock object, it has exclusive access to all of the objects in the tree.

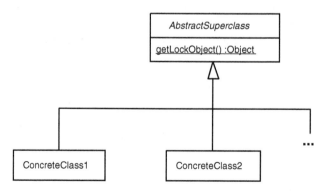

FIGURE 9.7 Lock object.

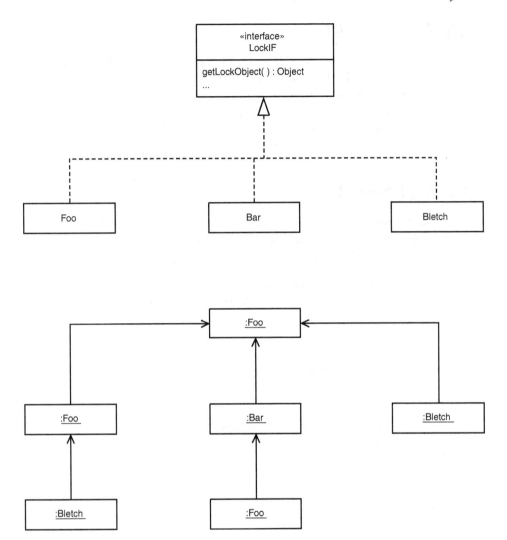

FIGURE 9.8 Objects in a tree.

CONSEQUENCES

☺ By using the Lock Object pattern, you can ensure that only one thread at a time is accessing a set of objects. You are able to accomplish this with very little complexity or overhead.

☹ An operation that uses the Lock Object pattern has exclusive access to all objects that may possibly be affected by the operation or any other operation. This means that if two operations could otherwise execute concurrently because they do not affect any of the same objects, they won't.

JAVA API USAGE

The java.awt.Component class has a method called getTreeLock. The getTreeLock method returns an object that is used as a lock object by the Component class and all of its subclasses. The getTreeLock method of every Component object returns the same lock object.

Subclasses of the Component class are used to build Abstract Windows Toolkit (AWT)_ and Swing-based GUIs.

CODE EXAMPLE

The code example for this pattern involves some classes that follow the game object scenario described under the Context heading. Here is part of the abstract superclass for classes used to model game classes.

```java
public abstract class AbstractGameObject {
    private static final Object lockObject = new Object();
    ...
    /**
     * True if this object is glowing.
     */
    private boolean glowing;

    ...

    public static final Object getLockObject() {
        return lockObject;
    } // getLockObject()

    ...

    public boolean isGlowing() {
        return glowing;
    } // isGlowing()

    public void setGlowing(boolean newValue) {
        glowing = newValue;
    } // setGlowing(boolean)
} // class AbstractGameObject
```

Notice that the AbstractGameObject class has a getLockObject method. The getLockObject method returns an object to use as a lock object. The class also has a boolean property to determine whether an object is glowing. The next listing is for a subclass of the AbstractGameObject class that uses both of these.

```java
class GameCharacter extends AbstractGameObject {
    ...
    private ArrayList myWeapons = new ArrayList();
```

```
public void dropAllWeapons() {
    synchronized (getLockObject()) {
        for (int i = myWeapons.size()-1; i>=0; i—) {
            ((Weapon)myWeapons.get(i)).setGlowing(true);
        } // for
        ...
    } // synchronized
} // dropAllWeapons()

...
} // class GameCharacter
```

The GameCharacter class has a method called dropAllWeapons that begins by getting a lock on the lock object returned by the getLockObject method. It inherits this method from the AbstractGameObject class. It then sets to true the glowing property of the weapon objects associated with the character. It continues on doing other things while having exclusive access to all game objects.

RELATED PATTERNS

Single Threaded Execution.   The Lock Object pattern is a refinement of the Single Threaded Execution pattern.

Guarded Suspension

This pattern is based on material that appeared in [Lea97].

SYNOPSIS

If a condition exists that prevents a method from doing what it is supposed to do, suspend execution of the method until the condition no longer exists.

CONTEXT

Suppose that you have to create a class that implements a queue data structure. A queue is a first-in_first-out data structure. Objects are removed from a queue in the same order they are added. Figure 9.9 shows a Queue class.

The Queue class has two methods that are of particular interest:

● The push method adds objects to a queue.
● The pull method removes objects from the queue.

If a Queue object's pull method is called when the queue is empty, it does not return until there is an object in the queue for it to return. An object can be added to the queue while the pull method is waiting to return if another thread calls the push method. These two methods are synchronized to allow multiple threads to safely make concurrent calls.

Simply making both methods synchronized creates a problem when there is a call to a Queue object's pull method and the queue is empty. The pull method waits for a call to the push method to provide it with an object to return. However, because they are both synchronized, calls to the push method cannot execute until the pull method returns and the pull method will never return until a call to the push method executes.

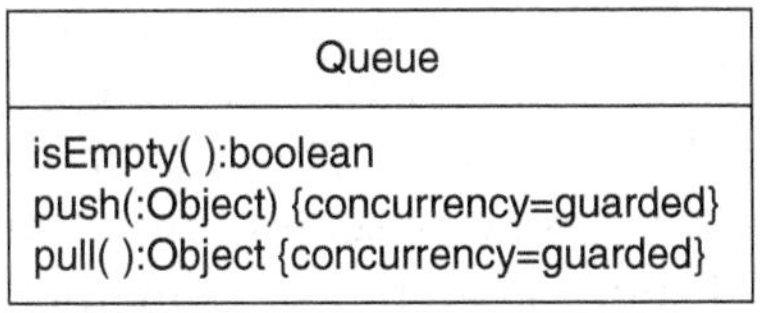

Queue
isEmpty( ):boolean push(:Object) {concurrency=guarded} pull( ):Object {concurrency=guarded}

FIGURE 9.9 Queue class.

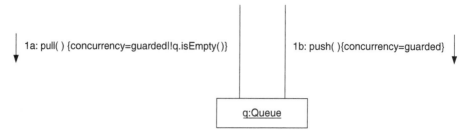

FIGURE 9.10 Queue collaboration.

A solution to the problem is to add a precondition to the `pull` method so that it does not execute when the queue is empty. Consider the collaboration diagram in Figure 9.10.

The collaboration diagram in Figure 9.10 shows concurrent calls to a `Queue` object's `push` and `pull` methods. If the `pull` method is called when the `Queue` object's `isEmpty` method returns true, then the thread waits until `isEmpty` returns false before executing the `pull` method. Because it does not actually execute the `pull` method while the queue is empty, there is no problem with a call to the `push` method being able to add objects to an empty queue.

FORCES

☺ A class's methods must be synchronized to allow safe concurrent calls.

☺ An object may be in a state that makes it impossible for one of its synchronized methods to execute to completion. In order for the object to leave that state, a call to one of the object's other synchronized methods must execute. If a call to the first method is allowed to proceed while the object is in that state, it deadlocks and will never complete. Calls to the state-changing method that allows the first method to complete will have to wait until it does complete, which will never happen.

SOLUTION

Consider Figure 9.11. Figure 9.11 shows a class named `Widget`. It has two synchronized methods named `foo` and `bar`. There is an exceptional state that `Widget` objects can enter. While a `Widget` object is in the exceptional state, its `isOK` method returns false; otherwise, it returns true. When a widget object is in the exceptional state, a call to its `bar` method may take it

```
┌─────────────────────────────────────┐
│               Widget                 │
├─────────────────────────────────────┤
│ isOK( ):boolean                      │
│ foo( ) {concurrency=guarded}         │
│ bar(:int) {concurrency=guarded}      │
└─────────────────────────────────────┘
```

FIGURE 9.11 Unguarded suspension class.

out of that state. There is no way to take it out of the exceptional state other than a call to `bar`. Taking a `Widget` object out of its exceptional state is a side effect of the `bar` method's main purpose, so it is not acceptable to call the `bar` method just to take a widget object out of its exceptional state.

A call to a `Widget` object's `foo` method cannot complete if the `Widget` object is in its exceptional state. If this happens, because the `foo` and `bar` methods are synchronized, subsequent calls to the `Widget` object's `foo` and `bar` methods will not execute until the pending call to `foo` returns. The call to `foo` will not return until a call to `bar` takes the `Widget` object out of its exceptional state.

The purpose of the Guarded Suspension pattern is to avoid the deadlock situation that can occur when a thread is about to execute an object's synchronized method and the state of the object prevents the method from completing. If a method call occurs when an object is in a state that prevents the method from executing to completion, the Guarded Suspension pattern suspends the thread until the object is in a state that allows the method to complete. This is illustrated in the collaboration diagram in Figure 9.12.

Notice that Figure 9.12 indicates a precondition that must be satisfied before a call to a `Widget` object's `foo` method executes. If a thread tries to call a `Widget` object's `foo` method when the `Widget` object's `isOK` method returns false, the thread is forced to wait until `isOK` returns true before it is able to execute the `foo` method. While the thread is waiting for `isOK` to return true, other threads are free to call the `bar` method.

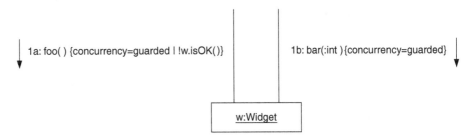

FIGURE 9.12 Guarded suspension collaboration.

IMPLEMENTATION

The Guarded Suspension pattern is implemented using the `wait` and `notify` methods, like this:

```
class Widget {
    synchronized void foo(){
        while (!isOK()) {
            wait();
        }
        ...
    }

    synchronized void bar(x int) {
        ...
        notify();
    }
}
```

The way this works is that a method such as `foo` must satisfy preconditions before it actually begins executing. The first thing such a method does is test its preconditions in a while loop. While the preconditions are false, it calls the `wait` method.

Every class inherits the `wait` method from the `Object` class. When a thread calls an object's `wait` method, the `wait` method causes the thread to release the synchronization lock it holds on the object. The method then waits until it is notified that it may return. Then, as soon as the thread is able to recapture the lock, the `wait` method returns.

When the `wait` method returns, control returns to the top of the while loop, which tests the preconditions again. The reason for testing the preconditions in a loop is that between the time that the thread first tries to recapture the synchronization lock and the time that it does capture it, another thread may have made the preconditions false.

The call to the `wait` method is notified that it should return when another method, such as `bar`, calls the object's `notify` method. Such methods call the `notify` method after they have changed the state of the object in a way that may satisfy a method's preconditions. The `notify` method is another method that all classes inherit from the `Object` class. What the `notify` method does is notify another thread that is waiting for the `wait` method to return that it should return.

If more than one thread is waiting, the `notify` method chooses one to notify arbitrarily. Arbitrary selection works well in most situations. It does not work well for objects that have methods with different preconditions. Consider a situation in which multiple method calls are waiting to have their different preconditions satisfied. Arbitrary selection can result in a situation where the preconditions of one method call are satisfied, but the

thread that gets notified is waiting to execute a method with different preconditions that are not yet satisfied. In a situation like this, it is possible
for a method call to never complete because the method is never notified
when its preconditions are satisfied.

There is an alternative for classes where arbitrary selection is not
a good way to decide which thread to notify. Their methods can call
the `notifyAll` method. Rather than choosing one thread to notify, the
`notifyAll` method notifies all waiting threads. This avoids the problem of
not notifying the right thread. However, it may result in wasted machine
cycles as a result of waking up threads waiting to execute method calls
whose preconditions are not satisfied.

CONSEQUENCES

☺ Using the Guarded Suspension pattern allows a thread to cope with
an object unable to perform an operation by waiting until the object
is able to perform the operation.

● The Guarded Suspension pattern uses synchronized methods or synchronized statements. It is possible for multiple threads to be waiting
to execute a call to the same method. The Guarded Suspension pattern specifically does not deal with selecting which of the waiting
threads will be allowed to proceed when the object is in a state that
will allow the method to be executed. You can use the Scheduler pattern to accomplish this.

☹ A situation that can make it difficult to use the Guarded Suspension
pattern is nested synchronization. Consider the collaboration diagram in Figure 9.13.

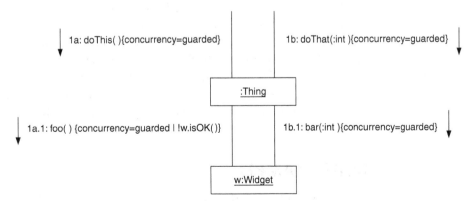

FIGURE 9.13 Guarded suspension under nested synchronization.

In Figure 9.13, access to the `Widget` object is through the synchronized methods of a `Thing` object. This means that when thread 1a calls the `Widget` object's `foo` method when the state of the `Widget` object causes its `isOK` method to return false, the thread will wait forever for the `Widget` object's `isOK` method to return true. The reason for this is that the methods of the `Thing` object are synchronized without any preconditions. This presents the same problem that the Guarded Suspension pattern was intended to solve.

JAVA API USAGE

The `java.net.InetAddress` class uses the Guarded Suspension pattern to manage an internal optimization. One of the responsibilities of the `InetAddress` class is to find the network address that corresponds to the name of a host. Because determining the network address that corresponds to a name may involve consulting one or more remote servers, it is a relatively expensive operation.

Once the `InetAddress` class determines the network address that corresponds to a hostname, it caches the network address. The cache is shared by all `InetAddress` objects. When an `InetAddress` object needs to determine the network address that corresponds to a hostname, the first place that it looks is in the cache. If the address is in the cache, then the `InetAddress` object does not need to consult any remote servers.

While an `InetAddress` object is getting the address corresponding to a hostname, another `InetAddress` object may want the address corresponding to the same hostname. While the first object is in the process of getting the address, there is no point in the second object looking for the address in the cache. The address will not be in the cache until after the first `InetAddress` object finishes getting the address. The best thing that the second `InetAddress` object can do is to wait until the first `InetAddress` object has finished getting the address. This is when the `InetAddress` class's use of the Guarded Suspension pattern comes in.

Before an `InetAddress` object checks to see if the cache contains the address for a hostname, it checks to see if another `InetAddress` object is getting the address for the hostname in question. If another `InetAddress` is getting the address, then the `InetAddress` object waits until the other `InetAddress` object has finished getting the address and has put it in the cache. Only then does it proceed to look in the cache for the hostname's address.

CODE EXAMPLE

The following is code that implements the `Queue` class design discussed under the Context heading.

```
public class Queue {
    private ArrayList data = new ArrayList();

    /**
     * Put an object on the end of the queue
     */
    synchronized public void put(Object obj) {
        data.add(obj);
        notify();
    } // put(Object)

    /**
     * Get an object from the front of the queue
     * If queue is empty, waits until it is not empty.
     */
    synchronized public Object get() {
        while (data.size() == 0){
            try {
                wait();
            } catch (InterruptedException e) {
            } // try
        } // while
        Object obj = data.get(0);
        data.remove(0);
        return obj;
    } // get()
} // class Queue
```

Notice that in the preceding listing, the call to the wait method is wrapped in a try statement to catch the InterruptedException that calls to the wait method may throw. Simply ignoring the InterruptedException that the wait method is declared to throw is the simplest thing to do for programs that do not expect the wait method to actually throw an InterruptedException. See the discussion of the Two-Phase Termination pattern for an explanation of when the wait method throws an InterruptedException and what you should do about it.

RELATED PATTERNS

Balking.　The Balking pattern provides a different strategy for handling method calls to objects not in an appropriate state to execute the method call.

Two-Phase Termination.　Because the implementation of the Two-Phase Termination pattern usually involves the throwing and handling of InterruptedException, its implementation usually interacts with the Guarded Suspension pattern.

Balking

This pattern is based on material that appeared in [Lea97].

SYNOPSIS

If an object's method is called when the object is not in an appropriate state to execute the method, have the method return without doing anything.

CONTEXT

Suppose you are writing a program to control an electronic toilet flusher. Such devices are intended for use in public bathrooms. They have a light sensor on the front of the flusher. When the light sensor detects an increased light level, it assumes that a person has left the toilet and triggers a flush. Electronic toilet flushers also have a button to manually trigger a flush. Figure 9.14 is a class diagram showing classes to model this behavior.

As shown in Figure 9.14, when a LightSensor object or a FlushButton object decides that there should be a flush, it requests the Flusher object to start a flush by calling its flush method. The flush method starts a flush and then returns once the flush is started. This arrangement raises some concurrency issues to resolve.

You will need to decide what happens when the flush method is called while a flush is already in progress. You will also need to decide what happens when both the LightSensor object and the FlushButton object call the Flusher object's flush method at the same time.

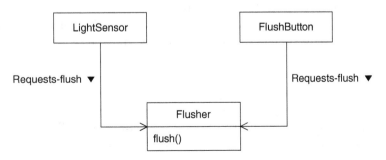

FIGURE 9.14 Flusher classes.

These are the three most obvious choices for how to handle a call to the `flush` method while there is a flush in progress:

Start a new flush immediately.   Starting a new flush while a flush is already in progress has the same effect as making the flush in progress last longer than a normal flush. The optimal length of a normal flush has been determined through experience. A longer flush will waste water, so this is not a good option.

Wait until the current flush finishes and immediately start another flush.   This option effectively doubles the length of a flush. It is a bigger waste of water than the first option.

Do nothing.   This option wastes no water, so it is the best choice.

When there are two concurrent calls to the flush method, allowing one to execute and ignoring the other is also a good strategy.

Suppose a call is made to an object's method when the object is not in a state to properly execute the method. If the method handles the situation by returning without performing its normal function, we say that the method balked. UML does not have a standard way of indicating a method call with balking behavior. This book represents a method call that exhibits balking behavior with an arrow that curves back on itself, as shown in Figure 9.15.

Figure 9.15 shows the balking behavior of the `Flusher` class's `flush` method.

FORCES

☺ An object may be in a state in which it is inappropriate to execute a method call.

☺ Postponing execution of a method call is not a good policy for the problem at hand. The method call must be executed immediately to produce the correct result.

☺ Calls made to an object's method when the object is not in an appropriate state to execute the method may be safely ignored.

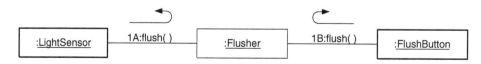

FIGURE 9.15 Flusher collaboration.

SOLUTION

The collaboration diagram in Figure 9.16 shows objects collaborating in the Balking pattern.

In Figure 9.16, a `Client` object calls the `doIt` method of a `Service` object. The bent-back arrow indicates that the call may balk. If the `Service` object's `doIt` method is called when the `Service` object is in a state inappropriate for executing a call to its `doIt` method, then the method returns without having performed its usual functions.

The `doIt` method returns a result, indicated in the diagram as `didIt`. The result is either true or false, indicating whether the method performed its normal functions or balked.

IMPLEMENTATION

If a method can balk, then, generally, the first thing it does is check the state of the object it belongs to, to determine whether it should balk.

While an object's method is executing, after it has decided not to balk, you do not want the state of the object to become inappropriate for the method to execute. You can use the Single Threaded Execution pattern to prevent this inconsistency.

Instead of telling its callers that it balked by returning a value, it is also reasonable for a method to notify its callers that it balked by throwing an exception. If a method's callers do not need to be interested in whether it balked, the method does not need to return this information.

CONSEQUENCES

☺ Method calls are not executed if they are made when then method's object is in an inappropriate state.

● Calling a method that can balk means that the method may not perform its expected functions but may do nothing instead.

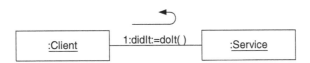

FIGURE 9.16 Balking collaboration.

CODE EXAMPLE

The following is code for the `Flusher` class discussed under the Context heading.

```
public class Flusher {
    private boolean flushInProgress = false;

    /**
     * This method is called to start a flush.
     */
    public void flush() {
        synchronized (this) {
            if (flushInProgress)
                return;
            flushInProgress = true;
        }
        // code to start flush goes here.
        ...
    }


    /**
     * This method is called to notify this object that a
     * flush has completed.
     */
    void flushCompleted() {
        flushInProgress = false;
    } // flushCompleted()
} // class Flusher
```

If the `flush` method is called while a flush is in progress, the method balks.

Notice the use of the synchronized statement in the `flush` method. It is there to ensure that if multiple calls to the `flush` method occur at the same time, the result is predictable. Exactly one of the calls will proceed normally and the others will balk. Without the synchronized statement, multiple calls could proceed normally at the same time.

Also, notice that the `flushCompleted` method is not synchronized. This is because there is never a time when setting the `flushInProgress` variable to false causes a problem. Since the `flushCompleted` method does not modify any other state information, concurrent calls to the `flush-Completed` method are safe. However, there never should be concurrent calls to the `flushCompleted` method, because the nature of the flusher mechanism makes it physically impossible for two flushes to complete at the same time.

RELATED PATTERNS

Guarded Suspension.   The Guarded Suspension pattern provides an alternate way to handle method calls to objects that are not in an appropriate state to execute the method call.

Single Threaded Execution.   The Balking pattern is often combined with the Single Threaded Execution pattern to coordinate changes to an object's state.

Scheduler

This pattern is based on material that appeared in [Lea97].

SYNOPSIS

Control the order in which threads are scheduled to execute single-threaded code using an object that explicitly sequences waiting threads. The Scheduler pattern provides a mechanism for implementing a scheduling policy. It is independent of any specific scheduling policy.

CONTEXT

Suppose you are designing software to manage a building's physical security. The security system will support security checkpoints. At each checkpoint, a person must pass his or her identification badge through a scanner before passing through the checkpoint. When someone passes an identification badge through a checkpoint's scanner, the checkpoint either allows the person to pass through or rejects the badge. Whenever someone passes through a security checkpoint or a badge is rejected, an entry is printed on a hard-copy log in a central security office. Figure 9.17 shows the basic collaboration.

The interactions in Figure 9.17 show SecurityCheckpoint objects creating JournalEntry objects and passing them to a Printer object's print method. Simple though it is, there is a problem with this organization. The problem occurs when people go through three or more checkpoints at

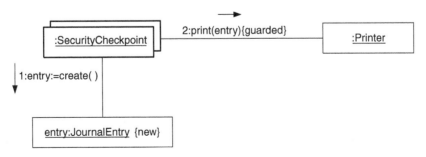

FIGURE 9.17 Security journal collaboration.

almost the same time. While the printer is printing the first of the log entries, the other print calls wait. After the first log entry is printed, there is no guarantee which log entry will be printed next. This means the log entries may not be printed in the same order the security checkpoints send them to the printer.

To ensure that journal entries are printed in the proper order, you could simply put each journal entry in a queue and then print the journal entries in the order they arrived in the queue. Though this still leaves open the possibility of three or more journal entries arriving at the same time, the likelihood is greatly reduced. It may take as long as a second to print a journal entry. For the problem to occur, both the other two journal entries must arrive within that time period. Queuing a journal entry may take only about a microsecond. This reduces the likelihood of journal entries printing out of sequence by a factor of 1 million.

You could make the queuing of journal entries to be printed the responsibility of the `Printer` class. However, the queuing of method calls to be executed sequentially is a capability that has a lot of potential reuse if it is implemented as a separate class. The interaction diagram in Figure 9.18 shows how a printer object could collaborate with another object to queue the execution of calls to its `print` method.

In Figure 9.18, a `SecurityCheckpoint` object calls the `printer` object's `print` method. The `print` method begins by calling the `Scheduler` object's `enter` method. The `enter` method does not return until the `Scheduler` object decides that it should. When the `print` method is finished, it calls the `Scheduler` object's `done` method. Between the time that the `enter` method returns and the `done` method is called, the `Scheduler` object assumes that the resource it is managing is busy. No call to the `enter` method will return while the `Scheduler` object believes that the resource it is managing is busy. This ensures that only one thread at a time executes the portion of the `print` method after its call to the `Scheduler` object's `enter` method until it calls the `Scheduler` object's `done` method.

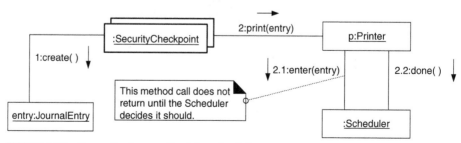

FIGURE 9.18 Security journal with scheduler.

The actual policy the Scheduler object uses to decide when a call to the enter method returns is encapsulated in the Scheduler object. This allows the policy to change without affecting other objects. In this example, the policy you want when more than one call to the enter method is waiting to return is as follows:

- If the Scheduler object is not waiting for a call to its done method, then a call to its enter method returns immediately. The Scheduler object then waits for a call to its done method.
- While the Scheduler object is waiting for a call to its done method, a call to its enter method will wait to return until a call to the Scheduler object's done method. When the Scheduler object's done method is called, if any calls to its enter method are waiting to return, then one of those enter method calls is chosen to return.
- If multiple calls to a Scheduler object's enter method are waiting to return, then the Scheduler object must select the next enter method call that will return. It selects the one passed a JournalEntry object with the earliest timestamp. If more than one JournalEntry object has the same earliest timestamp, then one of them is chosen arbitrarily.

In order for the Scheduler class to be able to compare the timestamps of JournalEntry objects and still be reusable, the Scheduler class must not refer directly to the JournalEntry class. However, it can refer to the JournalEntry class through an interface and still remain reusable. This is shown in Figure 9.19.

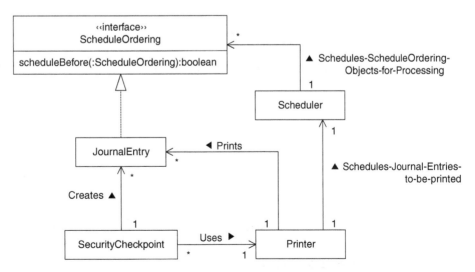

FIGURE 9.19 Journal entry scheduling classes.

The Scheduler class does not know about the JournalEntry class. It just schedules processing for objects that implement the ScheduleOrdering interface. This interface declares the scheduleBefore method that the Scheduler class calls to determine which of two ScheduleOrdering objects it should schedule first. Though the Scheduler class encapsulates a policy governing when processing will be allowed for a ScheduleOrdering object, it delegates the determination of the order in which they will be allowed to process to the ScheduleOrdering object.

FORCES

☺ Multiple threads may need to access a resource at the same time, and only one thread at a time may access the resource.
☺ The program's requirements imply constraints on the order in which threads should access the resource.

SOLUTION

The Scheduler pattern uses an object to explicitly schedule concurrent requests by threads for non-concurrent processing. The class diagram in Figure 9.20 shows the roles classes play in the Scheduler pattern.

Here are descriptions of the roles the classes play in the Scheduler pattern:

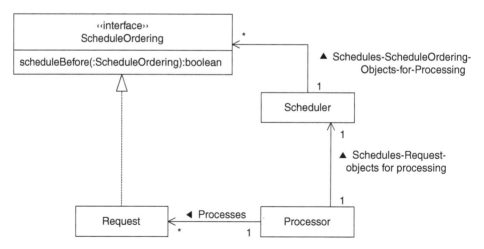

FIGURE 9.20 Scheduler classes.

Request. Classes in this role must implement the interface in the ScheduleOrdering role. Request objects encapsulate a request for a Processor object to do something.

Processor. Instances of classes in this role perform a computation described by a Request object. They may be presented with more than one Request object to process at a time, but they can process only one at a time. A Processor object delegates to a Scheduler object the responsibility for scheduling Request objects for processing, one at a time.

Scheduler. Instances of classes in this role schedule Request objects for processing by a Processor object. To promote reusability, a Scheduler class does not have any knowledge of the Request class that it schedules. Instead, it accesses Request objects through the ScheduleOrdering interface that they implement.

A class in this role is responsible for deciding when the next request will run. It is not responsible for the order in which the requests will run. It delegates that responsibility to a ScheduleOrdering interface.

ScheduleOrdering. Request objects implement the interface that is in this role. Interfaces in this role serve two purposes:

- By referring to a ScheduleOrdering interface, Processor classes avoid a dependency on a Request class.
- By calling methods defined by the ScheduleOrdering interface, Scheduler classes are able to delegate the decision about which Request object will be processed next. This increases the reusability of Scheduler classes. The class diagram in Figure 9.20 indicates one such method, named scheduleBefore.

The interaction between a Processor object and a Scheduler object occurs in two stages, as shown by the collaboration diagram in Figure 9.21.

The first interaction in Figure 9.21 is a call to a Processor object's doIt method. The first thing the doIt method does is call the enter method of the Scheduler object associated with the Processor object. If there is no other thread currently executing the rest of the doIt method, then the enter method returns immediately. After the enter method returns, the Scheduler object knows that the resource it manages is busy. While its resource is busy, any calls to the Scheduler object's enter method will not return until the resource is not busy and the Scheduler object decides it is that call's turn to return.

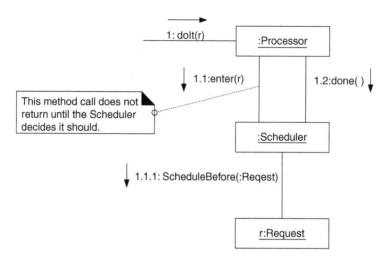

FIGURE 9.21 Scheduler interaction.

A Scheduler object considers the resource it manages to be busy until the Scheduler object's done method is called. When one thread makes a valid call to a Scheduler object's done method, if any threads are waiting to return from the Scheduler object's enter method, then one of them returns.

If a call to a Scheduler object's enter method must wait before it returns and there are other calls waiting to return from the enter method, then the Scheduler object must decide which call will return next. It decides by consulting the Request objects that were passed into those calls to decide which call will return next. It does this indirectly by calling methods declared for the purpose by the ScheduleOrdering interface and implemented by the Request object.

IMPLEMENTATION

In some applications, the Scheduler class has a scheduling policy that does not require it to consult Request objects to determine the order in which calls to its enter method will return. An example of such a policy is to allow calls to the enter method to return in the order in which they were called. In such cases, there is no need to pass Request objects into the enter method or to have a ScheduleOrdering interface. Another example of such a policy is to not take into account the order in which requests are scheduled but to require at least five minutes between the end of one task and the beginning of another.

CONSEQUENCES

☺ The Scheduler pattern provides a way to explicitly control when threads may execute a piece of code.

☺ The scheduling policy is encapsulated in its own class and is reusable.

☹ Using the Scheduler pattern adds significant overhead beyond what is required to make a simple call to a synchronized method.

CODE EXAMPLE

The following is some of the code that implements the print scheduling design discussed under the Context heading. The first listing is of the `Printer` class that manages the printing of security checkpoint journal entries.

```
class Printer {
    private Scheduler scheduler = new Scheduler();

    public void print(JournalEntry j) {
        try {
            scheduler.enter(j);
            try {
                ...
            } finally {
                scheduler.done();
            } // try
        } catch (InterruptedException e) {
        } //try
} // class Printer
```

Each `Printer` object uses a `Scheduler` object to schedule concurrent calls to its `print` method so that they print sequentially in the order of their timestamps. It begins by calling the `Scheduler` object's `enter` method, passing it the `JournalEntry` object to be printed. The call does not return until the `Scheduler` object decides that it is the `JournalEntry` object's turn to print.

The `print` method ends by calling the `Scheduler` object's `done` method. A call to the `done` method tells the `Scheduler` object that the `JournalEntry` object has been printed and another `JournalEntry` object can have its turn to be printed.

Following is the source code for the `Scheduler` class.

```
public class Scheduler {
    private Thread runningThread;
```

The runningThread variable is null when the resource a Scheduler object manages is not busy. It contains a reference to the thread using the resource when the resource is busy.

```
private ArrayList waitingRequests = new ArrayList();
private ArrayList waitingThreads = new ArrayList();
```

An invariant for this class is that a request and its corresponding thread are only in waitingRequests and waitingThreads while its call to the enter method is waiting to return. The purpose of keeping requests that are waiting to run and the corresponding threads in parallel ArrayList objects is to facilitate the determination of which request should be processed next.

The enter method is called before a thread starts using a managed resource. The enter method does not return until the managed resource is not busy and this Scheduler object decides it is the method call's turn to return.

```
public void enter(ScheduleOrdering s)
                        throws InterruptedException {
    Thread thisThread = Thread.currentThread();

    // For the case when the managed resource is not
    // busy, synchronize on this object to ensure that two
    // concurrent calls to enter do not both return
    // immediately.
    synchronized (this) {
        if (runningThread == null) {
            runningThread = thisThread;
            return;
        } // if
        waitingThreads.add(thisThread);
        waitingRequests.add(s);
    } // synchronized (this)
    synchronized (thisThread) {
        // Wait until another thread's call to the done
        // method decides that it is this thread's turn.
        while (thisThread != runningThread) {
            thisThread.wait();
        } // while
    } // synchronized (thisThread)
    synchronized (this) {
        int i = waitingThreads.indexOf(thisThread);
        waitingThreads.remove(i);
        waitingRequests.remove(i);
    } // synchronized (this)
} // enter(ScheduleOrdering)
```

A call to the done method indicates that the current thread is finished with the managed resource.

```
synchronized public void done() {
    if (runningThread != Thread.currentThread())
        throw new IllegalStateException("Wrong Thread");
    int waitCount = waitingThreads.size();
    if (waitCount <= 0) {
        runningThread = null;
    } else if (waitCount == 1) {
        runningThread = (Thread)waitingThreads.get(0);
        waitingThreads.remove(0);
    } else {
        int next = waitCount - 1;
        ScheduleOrdering nextRequest;
        nextRequest
            = (ScheduleOrdering)waitingRequests.get(next);
        for (int i = waitCount-2; i>=0; i-) {
            ScheduleOrdering r;
            r = (ScheduleOrdering)waitingRequests.get(i);
            if (r.scheduleBefore(nextRequest)) {
                next = i;
                nextRequest = (ScheduleOrdering)
                              waitingRequests.get(next);
            } // if
        } // for
        runningThread = (Thread)waitingThreads.get(next);
        synchronized (runningThread) {
            runningThread.notifyAll();
        } // synchronized (runningThread)
    } // if waitCount
} // done()
} // class Scheduler
```

The done method uses the notifyAll method to wake up a thread, rather than the notify method, because it has no guarantee that there will not be another thread waiting to regain ownership of the lock on the runningThread object. If it used the notify method, and there were additional threads waiting to regain ownership of the runningThread object's lock, then the notify method could fail to wake up the right thread.

The Scheduler class is independent of the specific type of resource it is scheduling the resource to. However, it does require that the class responsible for representing operations on the resource implement the ScheduleOrdering interface. When there are multiple operations waiting for access to a resource, the Scheduler class uses the ScheduleOrdering interface to determine the order in which it should schedule operations. Here is a listing of the ScheduleOrdering interface.

```
public interface ScheduleOrdering {
    public boolean scheduleBefore(ScheduleOrdering s);
} // interface ScheduleOrdering
```

The final listing in this code example is a skeletal listing of the JournalEntry class that the Printer class is responsible for printing.

```
public class JournalEntry implements ScheduleOrdering {
    ...
    private Date time = new Date();
...

    /**
     * return the time that this JournalEntry was created.
     */
    public Date getTime() { return time; }

    /**
     * Return true if the given request should be scheduled
     * before this one.
     */
    public boolean scheduleBefore(ScheduleOrdering s) {
        if (s instanceof JournalEntry)
            return getTime().before(((JournalEntry)s).getTime());
        return false;
    } // scheduleBefore(ScheduleOrdering)
} // class JournalEntry
```

RELATED PATTERNS

Read/Write Lock. Implementations of the Read/Write Lock pattern usually use the Scheduler pattern to ensure fairness in scheduling.

Read/Write Lock

This pattern is based on material that appeared in [Lea97].

SYNOPSIS

Allow concurrent read access to an object, but require exclusive access for write operations.

CONTEXT

Suppose that you are developing software for conducting online auctions. The way these auctions work is that an item will be put up for auction. People will access the online auction to see the current bid for an item. People can then decide to make a bid for an item that is greater than the current bid. At a predetermined time, the auction closes and the highest bidder at that time gets the item at the final bid price.

You expect that there will be many more requests to read the current bid for an item than to update it. You could use the Single Threaded Execution pattern to coordinate access to bids. Though this will ensure correct results, it can unnecessarily limit responsiveness. When multiple users want to read a current bid at the same time, Single Threaded Execution requires that only one user at a time is allowed to read the current bid. This forces users who just want to read the current bid to unnecessarily wait for other users who just want to read the current bid.

There is no reason to prevent multiple users from reading the current bid at the same time. Single-threaded execution is only required for updates to the current bid. Updates to the current bid must be processed one at a time to ensure that updates that would not increase the value of the current bid are ignored.

You can avoid unnecessary waiting to read data by allowing concurrent reads of data but only single-threaded access to data when it is being updated. Consider the collaboration diagram in Figure 9.22.

Figure 9.22 shows multiple user-interface objects calling a bid object's `getBid` and `setBid` methods. The `getBid` method waits until there are no calls to `setBid` waiting to complete before it returns the current bid. The `setBid` method waits for any executing calls to `getBid` or `setBid` to complete before it updates the current bid. The `readWriteLock` object

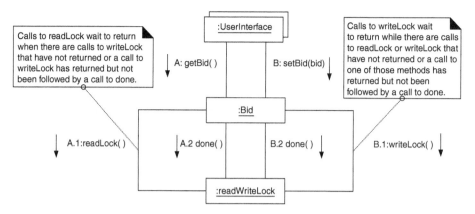

FIGURE 9.22 Bid collaboration.

encapsulates the logic that coordinates the execution of the getBid and setBid methods to allow it to be reused.

All calls to a readWriteLock object's readLock method return immediately, unless there are any outstanding write locks. A write lock is considered to be outstanding from the time that a call to a readWriteLock object's writeLock returns until it is released by a corresponding call to the readWriteLock object's done method. Calls to the readLock method wait until all outstanding write locks have been released.

Calls to a readWriteLock object's writeLock method return immediately, unless one or more of the following are true:

● A previous call to writeLock is waiting to execute.
● A previous call to writeLock has finished executing, but there has been no corresponding call to the readWriteLock object's done method.
● There are any executing calls to the readWriteLock object's readLock method or there are outstanding read locks.

If a call to a readWriteLock object is made when any of the preceding conditions are true, it will not return until all of the preceding conditions are false.

FORCES

☺ There is a need for read and write access to an object's state information.
☺ Any number of read operations may be performed on the object's state information concurrently. However, read operations are guaran-

teed to return the correct value only if there are no write operations executing at the same time as a read operation.

☺ Write operations on the object's state information must be performed one at a time, to ensure their correctness.

☺ There will be concurrently initiated read and write operations.

☺ Allowing concurrently initiated read operations to execute concurrently will improve responsiveness and throughput.

☺ The logic for coordinating read and write operations should be reusable.

SOLUTION

Organize a class so concurrent calls to methods that fetch and store its instance information are coordinated by an instance of another class. The class diagram in Figure 9.23 shows the roles classes play in the Read/Write Lock pattern.

A class in the Data role has methods to get and set its instance information. Any number of threads may concurrently get a Data object's instance information, so long as no thread is setting its instance information at the same time. On the other hand, its set operations must occur one at a time, while there are no get operations being executed. Data objects must coordinate their set and get operations so they obey these restrictions.

Data objects use an abstraction to coordinate get operations. The abstraction is a read lock. A Data object's get methods do not fetch any information until they get a read lock. Associated with each Data object is a ReadWriteLock object. Before one of its get methods gets anything, it calls the ReadWriteLock object's readLock method, which issues a read lock to

FIGURE 9.23 Read/write lock classes.

the current thread. While the thread has a read lock, the get method can be sure it is safe to get data from the object. This is because while there are any outstanding read locks, the `ReadWriteLock` object will not issue any write locks. If there are any outstanding write locks when the `ReadWrite-Lock` object's `readLock` method is called, it does not return until all the outstanding write locks have been relinquished by calls to the `ReadWriteLock` object's `done` method. Otherwise, calls to the `ReadWriteLock` object's `readLock` method return immediately.

When a `Data` object's get method is finished getting data from the object, it calls the `ReadWriteLock` object's `done` method. A call to that method causes the current thread to relinquish its read lock.

Similarly, `Data` objects use a write lock abstraction to coordinate set operations. A `Data` object's `set` methods do not store any information until they get a write lock. Before one of a `Data` object's `set` methods stores any information, it calls the associated `ReadWriteLock` object's `writeLock` method, which issues a write lock to the current thread. While the thread has a write lock, the set method can be sure that it is safe for it to store data in the object. This is because the `ReadWriteLock` object issues write locks only when there are no outstanding read locks and no outstanding write locks. If there are any outstanding locks when the `ReadWriteLock` object's `writeLock` method is called, it does not return until all of the outstanding locks have been relinquished by calls to the `ReadWriteLock` object's `done` method.

The preceding constraints that govern when read and write locks are issued do not address the order in which read and write locks are issued. The order in which read locks are issued does not matter, so long as get operations can be performed concurrently. Since write operations are performed one at a time, the order in which write locks are issued should be the order in which the write locks are requested.

The one remaining ambiguity occurs when there are calls to both of a `ReadWriteLock` object's `readLock` and `writeLock` methods waiting to return and there are no outstanding locks. If get operations are intended to return the most current information, then that situation should result in the `writeLock` method returning first.

IMPLEMENTATION

Since read locks and write locks do not contain any information, there is no need to represent them as explicit objects. It is sufficient to just count them.

The scheduling policies described elsewhere in this description of the Read/Write Lock pattern give preference to granting read locks. If there is a call waiting to get a write lock because there are outstanding read locks, then any requests for additional read locks in this circumstance will be granted immediately. This is a good policy for many applications. However, there are some applications where it is more appropriate to have scheduling policies that give preference to granting write locks.

If the scheduling policy gives preference to write locks, it means that no read locks will be granted while there is a call waiting for a write lock to be granted. Other policies are possible. Preference-based policies, however, are the most common.

CONSEQUENCES

☺ The Read/Write Lock pattern coordinates concurrent calls to an object's `get` and `set` methods so that calls to the object's `set` methods do not interfere with each other or with calls to the object's `get` methods.

☺ If there are many concurrent calls to an object's `get` methods, using the Read/Write Lock pattern to coordinate the calls can result in better responsiveness and throughput than using the Single Threaded Execution pattern. This is because the Read/Write Lock pattern allows concurrent calls to the object's `get` methods to execute concurrently.

● If there are relatively few concurrent calls to an object's `get` methods, using the Read/Write Lock pattern will result in lower throughput than using the Single Threaded Execution pattern. This is because the Read/Write Lock pattern spends more time managing individual calls. When there are concurrent `get` calls for it to manage, this results in a net improvement.

☹ If the scheduling policy is to give preference to granting read locks, then it is possible that write locks will never be granted. If there is a steady enough stream of read lock requests for there to always be at least one outstanding read lock, then no write lock will ever be granted. This results in a situation called *write starvation*.

☹ Similarly, if the scheduling policy is to give preference to granting write locks, then it is possible that read locks will never be granted. If there is a steady enough stream of write lock requests for there to always be at least one call waiting to be granted a write lock, then no read lock will ever be granted. This results in a situation called *read starvation*.

One policy that avoids starvation problems is to reverse the read or write lock preference if the number of waiting requests exceeds a predetermined limit. Another way to avoid starvation is to determine preference randomly each time a scheduling choice is to be made. The drawback to policies like these is that they make the behavior of the `ReadWriteLock` class more difficult to analyze and debug.

CODE EXAMPLE

Following is code that implements the design discussed under the Context heading. The first listing is the Bid class, which is rather straightforward.

```
public class Bid {
    private int bid = 0;
    private ReadWriteLock lockManager = new ReadWriteLock();
...
    public int getBid() throws InterruptedException{
        lockManager.readLock();
        int bid = this.bid;
        lockManager.done();
        return bid;
    } // getBid()

    public void setBid(int bid) throws InterruptedException {
        lockManager.writeLock();
        if (bid > this.bid) {
            this.bid = bid;
        } // if
        lockManager.done();
    } // setBid(int)
} // class Bid
```

As you can see, the methods of the Bid class use a ReadWriteLock object to coordinate concurrent calls. They begin by calling the appropriate lock method before getting or setting values. When finished, they call the ReadWriteLock object's done method to release the lock.

The ReadWriteLock class is more complex. As you read through its listing, you will notice that there are two main things it focuses on:

● It carefully tracks state information in a way that will be consistent for all threads.
● It ensures that all preconditions are met before its lock methods return.

Any other class that is responsible for enforcing a scheduling policy will have these implementation concerns.

```
public class ReadWriteLock {
    private int waitingForReadLock = 0;
    private int outstandingReadLocks = 0;
    private ArrayList waitingForWriteLock = new ArrayList();
    private Thread writeLockedThread;
```

A ReadWriteLock object uses these instance variables to keep track of threads that have requested or been issued a read or write lock. It uses the list referred to by the waitingForWriteLock variable to keep track of threads that are waiting to get a write lock. Using this list, it is able to ensure that write locks are issued in the same order they are requested.

A ReadWriteLock object uses the waitingForReadLock variable to count the number of threads waiting to get a read lock. Simple counting is sufficient for this because all threads waiting for a read lock will be allowed to get them at the same time. There is no reason to keep track of the order in which threads requested read locks.

A ReadWriteLock object uses the outstandingReadLocks variable to count the number of read locks that it has issued to but that have not yet been released by the threads they were issued to.

A ReadWriteLock object uses the writeLockedThread variable to refer to the thread that currently has a write lock. If no thread currently has a write lock from the ReadWriteLock object, then the value of the write-LockedThread variable is null. By having a variable that refers to the thread that has been issued the write lock, the ReadWriteLock object can tell whether it awakened the thread to receive a write lock or the thread was awakened for another reason.

The ReadWriteLock class's readLock method appears as follows. It issues a read lock and returns immediately, unless there is an outstanding write lock. All it does to issue a read lock is increment the outstandingReadLocks variable.

```
synchronized public void readLock() throws InterruptedException {
    if (writeLockedThread != null) {
        waitingForReadLock++;
        while (writeLockedThread != null) {
            wait();
        } // while
        waitingForReadLock-;
    } // if
    outstandingReadLocks++;
} // readLock()
```

A listing of the writeLock method appears as follows. You will notice that it is longer than the readLock method listing. This is because it manages threads and a data structure. It begins by checking for the case in which there are no outstanding locks. If there are no outstanding locks, it issues a write lock immediately. Otherwise, it adds the current thread to a list that the done method uses as a queue. The current thread waits until the done method issues it a write lock. The writeLock method then finishes by removing the current thread from the list of threads waiting for a write lock.

```
public void writeLock() throws InterruptedException {
    Thread thisThread;
    synchronized (this) {
```

```
        if ( writeLockedThread==null
             && outstandingReadLocks==0) {
          writeLockedThread = Thread.currentThread();
          return;
        } // if
        thisThread = Thread.currentThread();
        waitingForWriteLock.add(thisThread);
      } // synchronized(this)
      synchronized (thisThread) {
        while (thisThread != writeLockedThread) {
          thisThread.wait();
        } // while
      } // synchronized (thisThread)
      synchronized (this) {
        waitingForWriteLock.remove(thisThread);
      } // synchronized (this)
    } // writeLock
```

The final part of the ReadWriteLock class is the done method. Threads call a ReadWriteLock object's done method to relinquish a lock that the ReadWriteLock object previously issued to them. The done method considers three cases:

There are outstanding read locks, which implies that there is no outstanding write lock. It relinquishes the read lock by decrementing the outstandingReadLocks variable. If there are no more outstanding read locks and threads are waiting to get a write lock, then it issues a write lock to the thread that has been waiting the longest to get a write lock. Finally, it wakes up the waiting thread.

There is an outstanding write lock. It causes the current thread to relinquish the write lock. If there are threads waiting to get a read lock, then it grants read locks to all of the threads that are waiting for a read lock. If there are no outstanding read locks and there are threads waiting to get the write lock, it transfers the write lock to the thread that has been waiting the longest by having the writeLockedThread variable refer to that thread instead of the current thread.

There are no outstanding locks. If there are no outstanding locks, then the done method has been called at an inappropriate time, so it throws an IllegalStateException.

```
synchronized public void done() {
    if (outstandingReadLocks > 0) {
        outstandingReadLocks-;
        if ( outstandingReadLocks==0
```

```
                && waitingForWriteLock.size()>0) {
              writeLockedThread
                = (Thread)waitingForWriteLock.get(0);
              writeLockedThread.notifyAll();
          } // if
      } else if (Thread.currentThread()
                              == writeLockedThread) {
          if ( outstandingReadLocks==0
              && waitingForWriteLock.size()>0) {
              writeLockedThread
                = (Thread)waitingForWriteLock.get(0);
              writeLockedThread.notifyAll();
          } else {
              writeLockedThread = null;
              if (waitingForReadLock > 0)
                notifyAll();
          } // if
      } else {
          String msg = "Thread does not have lock";
          throw new IllegalStateException(msg);
      } // if
  } // done()
} // class ReadWriteLock
```

One last detail to notice about the done method is that is uses the notifyAll method, rather than the notify method. When it wants to allow read locks to be issued, it calls the ReadWriteLock object's notifyAll method to allow all of the threads waiting to get a read lock to proceed. When it issues the write lock to a thread, it calls that thread's notifyAll method. Calling its notify method will work in most cases. However, in the case that another thread is waiting to gain the synchronization lock of the thread to be issued the write lock, using the notify method could cause the wrong thread to wake up. Using the notifyAll method guarantees that the right thread will wake up.

There is a more industrial-strength version of the ReadWriteLock class that is part of the clickblocks software you can download at www.click-blocks.org. It is in the package named org.clickblocks.util.

RELATED PATTERNS

Single Threaded Execution.   The Single Threaded Execution pattern is a good and simpler alternative to the Read/Write Lock pattern when most of the accesses to data are write accesses.

Scheduler.   The Read/Write Lock pattern is a specialized form of the Scheduler pattern.

Producer-Consumer

SYNOPSIS

Coordinate the asynchronous production and consumption of information or objects.

CONTEXT

Suppose you are designing a trouble ticket dispatching system. Customers will enter trouble tickets through Web pages. Dispatchers will review the trouble tickets and forward them to the person or organization best suited to resolve the problem.

Any number of people may submit trouble tickets at any given time. There will usually be multiple dispatchers on duty. If any dispatchers are not busy when a trouble ticket comes in, the system immediately gives the trouble ticket to one of them. Otherwise, it places the trouble ticket in a queue, where the trouble ticket waits its turn to be seen by a dispatcher and be dispatched. Figure 9.24 is a class diagram showing a design for classes that implement this behavior.

Figure 9.24 shows a `Client` class whose instances are responsible for getting trouble tickets filled out by users and placed in a `Queue` object. Trouble tickets stay in the `Queue` object until a `Dispatcher` object pulls them out of the `Queue` object.

The `Dispatcher` class is responsible for displaying trouble tickets to a dispatcher and then forwarding them to the destination selected by the dispatcher. When an instance of the `Dispatcher` class is not displaying a

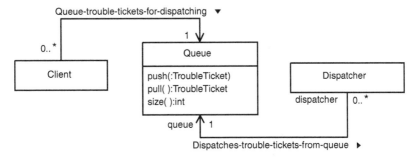

FIGURE 9.24   Trouble ticket classes.

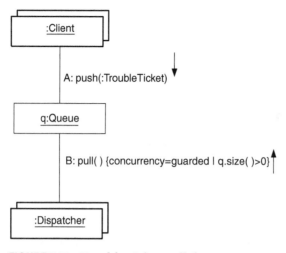

FIGURE 9.25 Trouble ticket collaboration.

trouble ticket or forwarding it, it calls the `Queue` object's `pull` method to get another trouble ticket. If there are no trouble tickets in the `Queue` object, the `pull` method waits until it has a trouble ticket to return.

Figure 9.25 is a collaboration diagram that shows the interactions previously described.

FORCES

- ☺ Objects are produced or received asynchronously of their use or consumption.
- ☺ When an object is received or produced, there may not be any object available to use or consume it.

SOLUTION

The class diagram in Figure 9.26 shows the roles in which classes participate in the Producer-Consumer pattern.

Here are descriptions of the roles that classes can play in the Producer-Consumer pattern.

Producer.   Instances of classes in this role supply objects that are used by `Consumer` objects. Instances of `Producer` classes produce objects asynchronously of threads that consume them. This

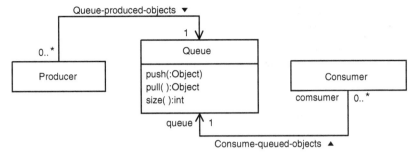

FIGURE 9.26 Producer-consumer classes.

means that sometimes a `Producer` object will produce an object when all `Consumer` objects are busy processing other objects. Rather than wait for a `Consumer` object to become available, instances of `Producer` classes put objects they produce in a queue and then continue with whatever they do.

Queue. Instances of classes in this role act as a buffer for objects produced by instances of `Producer` classes. Instances of `Producer` classes place the objects that they produce in an instance of a `Queue` class. The objects remain there until a `Consumer` object pulls them out of the `Queue` object.

Consumer. Instances of `Consumer` classes use objects produced by `Producer` objects. They get the objects that they use from a `Queue` object. If the `Queue` object is empty, a `Consumer` object that wants to get an object from it must wait until a `Producer` object puts an object in the `Queue` object.

The collaboration diagram in Figure 9.27 shows the interactions between objects that participate in the Producer-Consumer pattern.

IMPLEMENTATION

Some implementations of the Producer-Consumer pattern limit the queue to a maximum size. In such implementations, a special case to consider is when the queue is at its maximum size and a producer thread wants to put an object in the queue. The usual way to handle this is for the queue to use the Guarded Suspension pattern to force the producer thread to wait until a consumer thread removes an object from the queue. When there is room for the object that the producer wants to put in the queue, the producer thread is allowed to finish and proceed with whatever else it does.

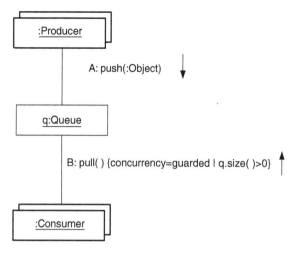

FIGURE 9.27 Producer-consumer collaboration.

CONSEQUENCES

☺ Producer objects can deliver the objects they produce to a Queue object without having to wait for a Consumer object.

● When there are objects in the Queue object, Consumer objects can pull an object out of the queue without waiting. However, when the queue is empty and a Consumer object calls the Queue object's pull method, the pull method does not return until a Producer object puts an object in the queue.

JAVA API USAGE

The core Java API includes the classes java.io.PipedInputStream and java.io.PipedOutputStream. Together, they implement a variant of the Producer-Consumer pattern called the Pipe pattern. The Pipe pattern involves only one Producer object and only one Consumer object. The Pipe pattern usually refers to the Producer object as a data source and the Consumer object as a data sink.

The java.io.PipedInputStream and java.io.PipedOutputStream classes jointly fill the role of Queue class. They allow one thread to write a stream of bytes to one other thread. The threads perform their writes and read asynchronously of each other, unless the internal buffer they use is empty or full.

CODE EXAMPLE

The following listings show code that implements the design discussed under the Context heading; the first two listings shown are skeletal listings of the `Client` and `Dispatcher` classes.

```
public class Client implements Runnable {
    private Queue myQueue;
    ...
    public Client(Queue myQueue) {
        this.myQueue = myQueue;
        ...
    } // constructor(Queue)
    ...
    public void run() {
        TroubleTicket tkt = null;
        ...
        myQueue.push(tkt);
    } // run()
} // class Client

public class Dispatcher implements Runnable {
    private Queue myQueue;
    ...
    public Dispatcher(Queue myQueue) {
        this.myQueue = myQueue;
    } // constructor(Queue)
    ...
    public void run() {
        TroubleTicket tkt = myQueue.pull();
        ...
    } // run()
} // class Dispatcher
```

The last listing is of the `Queue` class.

```
public class Queue {
    private ArrayList data = new ArrayList();

    /**
     * Put an object on the end of the queue
     * @param obj the object to put at end of queue
     */
    synchronized public void push(TroubleTicket tkt) {
        data.add(tkt);
        notify();
    } // push(TroubleTicket)

    /**
     * Get a TroubleTicket from the front of the queue
     * If queue is empty, wait until it is not empty.
     */
```

```
synchronized public TroubleTicket pull() {
    while (data.size() == 0){
        try {
            wait();
        } catch (InterruptedException e) {
        } // try
    } // while
    TroubleTicket tkt = (TroubleTicket)data.get(0);
    data.remove(0);
    return tkt;
} // pull()

/**
 * Return the number of trouble tickets in this queue.
 */
public int size() {
    return data.size();
} // size()
} // class Queue
```

RELATED PATTERNS

Guarded Suspension.   The Producer-Consumer pattern uses the Guarded Suspension pattern to manage the situation of a `Consumer` object wanting to get an object from an empty queue.

Pipe.   The Pipe pattern is a special case of the Producer-Consumer pattern that involves only one `Producer` object and only one `Consumer` object. The Pipe pattern usually refers to the `Producer` object as a data source and the `Consumer` object as a data sink.

Scheduler.   The Producer-Consumer pattern can be viewed as a special form of the Scheduler pattern that has a scheduling policy with two notable features:

- The scheduling policy is based on the availability of a resource.
- The scheduler assigns the resource to a thread but does not need to regain control of the resource when the thread is done, so it can reassign the resource to another thread.

Two-Phase Termination

SYNOPSIS

Provide for the orderly shutdown of a thread or process through the setting of a latch. The thread or process checks the value of the latch at strategic points in its execution.

CONTEXT

Suppose you are responsible for writing a server that provides middle-tier logic for a stock trading workstation. A client connects to the server. The client then indicates that it is interested in certain stocks. The server sends the current price of those stocks to the client. When the server receives information that shares of a stock have been traded, it reports the trade to clients who are interested in the stock.

The server's internal mechanism creates a thread for each client. This thread is responsible for delivering information about stock trades to the client it serves.

The server must respond to some administrative commands. One of these is a command that forces the disconnection of a client. When the server is asked to disconnect a client, it must shut down the thread that services the client and release the related set of resources the thread is using.

Another administrative command that the server must respond to is a command to shut down the entire server.

The commands are similar in what they do. The main difference is their scope. One command shuts down a single thread. The other command shuts down an entire process. In both cases, the implementation techniques are similar. Figure 9.28 is a collaboration diagram that shows how a server thread could be organized to shut down cleanly on request.

The collaboration shown in Figure 9.28 begins with a call to a Session object's run method. The run method first calls the Session object's initialize method. It then repeatedly calls the Portfolio object's send-TransactionsToClient method. It keeps calling the method as long as the Session object's isInterrupted method returns false. The Session object's isInterrupted method returns false until the Session object's interrupt method is called.

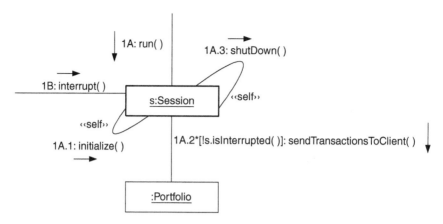

FIGURE 9.28 Server thread shutdown.

The normal sequence of events that shuts down a session begins with a different thread than the one that called the `run` method. That other thread calls the `Session` object's `interrupt` method. The next time that the `Session` object calls its `isInterrupted` method, it returns true. The `run` method then stops calling the `Portfolio` object's `sendTransactionsToClient` method. It then calls the `Session` object's `shutDown` method, which performs any necessary cleanup operations.

The technique for shutting down a process in an orderly manner is similar to the technique for threads. When a command is received to shut down an entire process, it sets a latch that causes every thread in the process to shut down.

FORCES

☺ A thread or process is designed to run indefinitely.
☺ There could be unfortunate results if a thread or process is forcibly shut down without first having the chance to clean up after itself.
☺ When a thread or process is asked to shut down, it is acceptable for the thread or process to take a reasonable amount of time to clean up before shutting down.

SOLUTION

There are two basic techniques for shutting down a thread or a process. One way is to immediately terminate them. The other way is to ask the

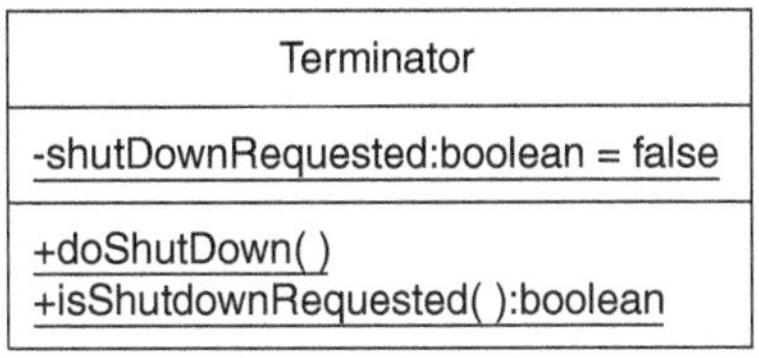

FIGURE 9.29 Process shutdown.

thread or process to terminate and then expect it to comply with the request by first performing any necessary cleanup and then terminating.

The class diagram in Figure 9.29 shows a class that you might use to coordinate the shutdown of a process. A class such as this is used to allow a process to receive a request to shut down and then clean up after itself before shutting down. Each of the process's threads calls the isShutdownRequested method at strategic points in its execution. If it returns true, the thread cleans up and shuts down. When all the application threads have died, the process exits.

Shutting down an individual thread involves using a thread-specific latch. Every Java thread has one because it is part of the Thread class. It is set to true by calling the thread's interrupt method. It is queried by calling the thread's isInterrupted method.

IMPLEMENTATION

After a process or thread has been requested to shut down, it can be difficult or impossible to determine whether the process or thread will actually terminate until it does. For this reason, if there is any uncertainty that the thread or process will terminate after it has been requested to do so, after a predetermined amount of time the thread or process should be forcibly terminated.

You can forcibly terminate a thread by calling its stop method. The mechanism for forcibly terminating a process varies with the operating system.

Methods that set a termination latch to true do not need to be synchronized. Flag setting is idempotent. One or more threads can perform the operation, concurrently or not, and the result is still that the termination latch is set to true.

CONSEQUENCES

☺ Using the Two-Phase Termination pattern allows processes and threads to clean up after themselves before they terminate.

☹ Using the Two-Phase Termination pattern can delay the termination of a process or thread for an unpredictable amount of time.

JAVA API USAGE

The core Java API does not make use of the Two-Phase Termination pattern. However, it does have features to support the Two-Phase Termination pattern.

To support the two-phase termination of threads, the `Thread` class provides the `interrupt` method to request a thread's termination. The `Thread` class also provides the `isInterrupted` method to allow a thread to find out whether its termination has been requested.

There are some methods such as `sleep` that are known to put a thread in a wait state. There is an assumption that if a thread is asked to shut down while waiting for one of these methods to return, the thread will detect the request for its termination and comply as soon as the waiting method returns. To help ensure the timeliness of a thread's shutdown, some methods that cause a thread to wait for something throw an `InterruptedException` if a thread is waiting for one of those methods to return when its `interrupt` method is called. The methods that can throw an `InterruptedException` include `Thread.sleep`, `Thread.join`, and `Object.wait`. There are a number of others.

To support the shutdown of a process, when a thread dies, if no threads are still alive and are not daemon threads, then the process shuts down.

Note that Java does not provide any direct way of detecting or catching signals or interrupts from an operating system that cause a process to shut down. The `java.lang.Runtime` class has a method named `add-ShutdownHook` that can be used to request that some code will be run when the JVM shuts down. The documentation for the method just promises that the JVM will make a best effort to run the code. There is no guarantee that it will run.

CODE EXAMPLE

The following listing shows code that implements the design discussed under the Context heading.

```
public class Session implements Runnable {
    private Thread myThread;
    private Portfolio portfolio;
    private Socket mySocket;
```

```
...
    public Session(Socket s) {
        myThread = new Thread(this);
        mySocket = s;
        ...
    } // constructor()

    public void run() {
        initialize();
        while (!myThread.interrupted()) {
            portfolio.sendTransactionsToClient(mySocket);
        } // while
        shutDown();
    } // run()

    /**
     * Request that this session terminate.
     */
    public void interrupt() {
        myThread.interrupt();
    } // interrupt()

    /**
     * Initialize ths object.
     */
    private void initialize() {
        ...
    } // initialize()

    /**
     * perform cleanup for this object.
     */
    private void shutDown() {
        //...
    } // shutDown()
...
} // class Session
```

Double Buffering

This pattern is also known as Exchange Buffering.

SYNOPSIS

You have an object that consumes data. Avoid delays in the consumption of data by asynchronously producing data with the goal of the data being ready for consumption before the consumer needs it.

CONTEXT

Suppose you are maintaining software that loads a day's transactions from a point-of-sale (POS) system into a database that supports a data warehouse. Your task is to reduce the amount of time that it takes to load POS transactions into the database.

You discover that one significant performance bottleneck is that the program is spending a lot of time reading the files that contain the transaction records. You notice that the program is using an instance of `java.io.BufferedInputStream` to buffer reads. To reduce the number of read operations that it needs to perform, you try increasing the size of the buffer that the `BufferedInputStream` object is using.

The result of increasing the buffer size is that the program spends less time reading POS transaction records. However, the program is still waiting for the transactions to be read from a file before adding them to the database. Since the database is stored on different physical disks than the transaction files, you know that it is possible for the reading of transactions and the updating of the database to happen concurrently. While some POS transactions are being added to the database, you would like the next transaction records to have already been read by the time the preceding POS transactions have been added to the database. This way the program does not have to wait for more POS transactions to be read.

You decide to solve the problem of the program having to wait for POS transactions to be read by creating a class similar to `BufferedInput-Stream`. The new class will be called `DoubleBufferedInputStream`. This new class will use two buffers instead of one. The first time one of its read methods is called, it synchronously fills one of its buffers. From this point on, each buffer will fill one of two roles.

One role is called *active buffer;* the other role is called *reserve buffer.* The buffer that is synchronously filled during the first read call is initially the active buffer. The other buffer is initially the reserve buffer. As soon as the active buffer is full of its initial contents, two things happen:

- The read method reads bytes from the active buffer.
- At the same time, bytes are asynchronously read from the underlying input stream to fill the reserve buffer.

When the active buffer is empty and the asynchronous filling of the reserve buffer is finished, the two buffers switch roles. If the reading of bytes into the reserve buffer has not yet finished, the role switch is delayed until the reading is finished. After the role switch, the read method reads bytes from the active buffer and bytes are asynchronously read from the underlying input stream to fill the reserve buffer. Figure 9.30 shows these interactions.

FORCES

- ☺ An object consumes many pieces of data at once.
- ☺ Data is pulled by the consuming object from a data-producing object. The data-producing object has no control over when the data-consuming object will want more data.
- ☺ If data is not available when a consuming object wants it, the performance of the consuming object will suffer in some way.

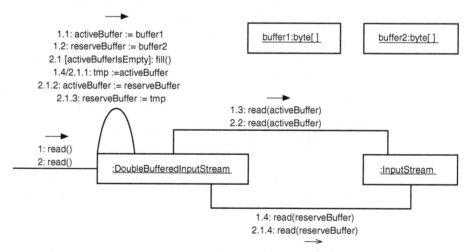

FIGURE 9.30 DoubleBufferedInputStream collaboration.

☺ Over time, the average rate at which data is consumed is not faster than the rate at which it can be produced.

SOLUTION

You have an object that consumes data. Avoid delays in the consumption of data by asynchronously producing the data with the goal of the data being ready for consumption before the consumer needs it. You do this by putting data in a buffer before it is needed.

The behavior of some data-consuming objects is that they consume an entire buffer of data and then don't want another buffer for some indeterminate amount of time. If that amount of time is generally more than the amount of time that it takes to fill the buffer with data again, then you can reuse the same buffer. However, if the data-consuming objects do not use the entire buffer of data all at once or do not wait long enough between the times that they want data to refill a buffer, then you will need more than one buffer. The general case is that you will need more than one buffer.

Figure 9.31 shows the interactions between objects that participate in the Double Buffering pattern. The `dataProvider` object provides data to objects that call its `getData` method. The `buffer1` and `buffer2` objects are used by the `DataProvider` object to temporarily keep data in memory from when the data is fetched or created until the time it is returned by the `getData` method. The `DataSource` object is responsible for fetching or creating data.

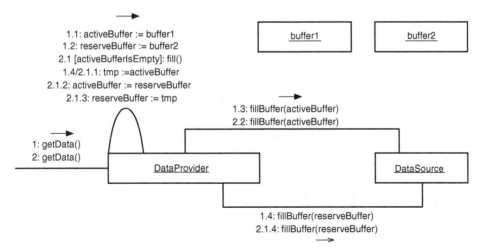

FIGURE 9.31 Double buffering collaboration.

Here are descriptions of the interactions shown in Figure 9.31.

1. This is the first request to get data from wherever it comes from.

   1.1 The `buffer1` object becomes the active buffer.
   1.2 The `buffer2` object becomes the reserve buffer.
   1.3 The active buffer is synchronously filled.
   1.4 The reserve buffer is asynchronously filled. This method call returns immediately without waiting until the reserve buffer is filled. A separate thread is responsible for filling the reserve buffer.

2. This is a request for more data. If there is sufficient data in the active buffer, the data is used to satisfy the request. Otherwise, more data is needed and the call continues to 2.1. After 2.1 is complete, there is more data available, which is used to satisfy the request for more data.

   2.1 This step happens only if the active buffer is empty. The purpose of this step is to ensure that the buffer being used as the active buffer is full—or as full as it is going to get.

      2.1.1 If the asynchronous filling of the reserve buffer is not finished, then this step waits until it is finished before proceeding. When this step does proceed, it is the first step in swapping the buffers that are functioning as the active and reserve buffers.
      2.1.2, 2.1.3 These steps complete the swapping of the active and reserve buffers. After step 2.1.3, the buffer that was the reserve buffer before 2.1.1 is the active buffer and the buffer that was the active buffer is the reserve buffer.
      2.1.4 The reserve buffer is asynchronously filled. This method call returns immediately without waiting until the reserve buffer is filled. A separate thread is responsible for filling the reserve buffer.

IMPLEMENTATION

Each request for data consumes some amount of data. The buffers should be sufficiently large to hold enough data to satisfy one request.

MULTIPLE BUFFERS

One of the assumptions underlying the Double Buffering pattern is that over time the average rate at which data is produced is at least as fast as the rate at which it is consumed. Some applications may occasionally have multiple requests for data in rapid succession and then none for a while. In situations like this, data is sometimes consumed faster than a buffer can be filled. To avoid having to wait for data when requests for data come in bursts, use more buffers.

The additional buffers are used as reserve buffers. Having enough reserve buffers filled in advance of when their contents are needed means that bursts of requests for data will not have to wait for data.

EXCEPTION HANDLING

Asynchronous operations are performed to fill reserve buffers with data before the data is needed. These operations may throw an exception. Exceptions thrown from these operations require some special handling. There are two difficulties associated with handling these exceptions.

The first problem is that these exceptions are thrown in a thread that is probably being used just for the asynchronous read-ahead. It will usually be more inconvenient and less useful to handle exceptions in the read-ahead thread than to handle the exceptions in the data-requesting thread. To make this happen, you will need to catch exceptions in the read-ahead thread and re-throw them in the data-requesting thread. However, simply re-throwing the exceptions is usually not good enough. There is a timing issue.

When an exception is thrown in the read-ahead thread, it will usually be at a point in the data beyond the data that has already been returned by requests for data. If you immediately re-throw the exception in the data-requesting thread, the data-requesting thread might not get to see the good data between what it has already seen and the place where the exception was thrown. It would be better not to re-throw the exception in the data-requesting thread until the data-requesting thread sees all the data up to the point at which the exception occurred.

The example under the Code Example heading includes a code that handles exceptions in this way.

CONSEQUENCES

☺ Using the Double Buffering pattern avoids situations where an application must wait for more data to be fetched or created before it can continue processing data.

- The Double Buffering pattern increases the amount of memory that a program uses so that it can run faster.
- ☹ The Double Buffering pattern is an optimization that adds complexity to a program.

JAVA API USAGE

Java's Swing user-interface toolkit uses the Double Buffering pattern. Most Swing GUI components are a subclass of `javax.swing.JComponent`. The `JComponent` class has a method named `setDoubleBuffered`. This method is used to turn double buffering on or off.

Under the Solutions heading, there is a special case mentioned in which you need only one buffer to implement the Double Buffering pattern. The specific circumstance in which you need only one buffer is when exactly one buffer full of data is consumed at one time and the amount of time between data requests is generally greater than the amount of time it takes to fill a buffer. Swing and user interfaces in general are examples of this special case.

Swing implements the Double Buffering pattern with only one buffer. It can do this because even when there are rapid updates to what is being displayed on the screen, they are more than a few milliseconds apart. That is generally more than enough time to draw a screen image in a buffer before it is needed.

CODE EXAMPLE

The code example for this pattern is a subclass of `java.io.InputStream`. It is similar to the `java.io.BufferedInputStream` class, except that instead of using single buffering to just reduce the number of physical read operations needed to read a file, it uses double buffering to also avoid having to wait for physical reads.

```
public
class DoubleBufferedInputStream extends FilterInputStream {
    private static final int DEFAULT_BUFFER_COUNT = 2;
    private static final int DEFAULT_BUFFER_SIZE = 4096;

    private byte[][] buffers;
```

The double buffering is done using the array of arrays referred to by the `buffers` variable. The active buffer is the array whose index in the top-level array matches the value of the `activeBuffer` variable. The other arrays are used as reserve buffers.

```
private int activeBuffer = 0;

/**
 * The number of bytes in each buffer.
 */
private int[] counts;
```

When buffers are filled, this class tries to fill them completely. However, that is not always possible. The actual number of bytes of data that a buffer contains is in the element of the counts array that corresponds to the buffer.

```
/**
 * The index of the next character to be read from the
 * active buffer.
 *
 * It will always be the case that
 *     0 <= pos <= counts[activeBuffer]
 *
 * If pos==counts[activeBuffer] then the
 * active buffer is empty.
 */
private int pos;

/**
 * If an exception is thrown while reading ahead to fill a
 * reserve buffer, this variable is set to the exception
 * object so that it can be re-thrown later in a data-
 * requesting thread when the data-requesting thread gets
 * to the point that the exception was thrown.
 */
private Throwable exception;

/**
 * If this is true then the underlying input stream has
 * been exhausted.
 */
private boolean exhausted;

/**
 * This is true after the entire underlying input stream
 * has been read into buffers.
 */
private boolean eof;

/**
 * This object is responsible for asynchronously filling
 * reserve buffers.
 */
private BufferFiller myBufferFiller;
```

The BufferFiller class is a private class that appears toward the end of this listing.

```
/**
 * A lock object used to synchronize data-requesting
 * threads with the filling of buffers.
 */
private Object lockObject = new Object();
```

The following method throws an IOException if it is called after a DoubleBufferedInputStream object's close method. It is called by some of the class's read and skip methods so that they throw an IOException if they are called after the stream has been closed. The method works by checking whether the value of the buffers variable is null. The buffers variable is set to reference an array or arrays by the class's constructor; it is set to null by the close method.

```
private void checkClosed() throws IOException {
    if (buffers == null) {
        throw new IOException("Stream closed");
    } // if
} // checkClosed()

/**
 * Construct a DoubleBufferedInputStream that will read
 * input from the given input stream using a default
 * buffer size and two buffers.
 */
public DoubleBufferedInputStream(InputStream in) {
    this(in, DEFAULT_BUFFER_SIZE);
} // constructor(InputStream)

/**
 * Construct a DoubleBufferedInputStream that will read
 * input from the given input stream using two buffers
 * having the given size.
 */
public DoubleBufferedInputStream(InputStream in, int size){
    this(in, size, DEFAULT_BUFFER_COUNT);
} // constructor(InputStream, int)

/**
 * Construct a DoubleBufferedInputStream
 * that will read input from the given input stream using
 * given number of buffers having the given size.
 */
public DoubleBufferedInputStream(InputStream in,
                                 int size,
                                 int bufferCount){
    super(in);
    if (size < 1) {
        String msg = "Buffer size < 1";
        throw new IllegalArgumentException(msg);
    } // if size
```

```
        if (bufferCount < 2) {
            bufferCount = 2;
        } // if

        buffers = new byte[bufferCount][size];
        counts = new int[bufferCount];
        myBufferFiller = new BufferFiller();
    } // constructor(InputStream, int, int)

    /**
     * Return the next byte of data, or -1 if the end of the
     * stream is reached.
     */
    public synchronized int read() throws IOException {
        checkClosed();
        if (eof) {
            return -1;
        } // if eof
        if (pos >= counts[activeBuffer]) {
            eof = !advanceBuffer();
        } // if empty
        if (eof) {
            return -1;
        } // if eof

        // Return the next character anded with 0xff so that
        // the values 0x80-0xff are not treated as negative
        // values.
        int c =  buffers[activeBuffer][pos++] & 0xff;
        if (pos >= counts[activeBuffer]) {
            eof = !advanceBuffer();
        } // if empty
        return c;
    } // read()

    /**
     * Read the given number of bytes from this input stream
     * into the given byte array, starting at the given offset.
     *
     * @return the number of bytes read, or -1 if
     *         the end of the stream has been reached.
     */
    public synchronized int read(byte b[], int off, int len)
                                        throws IOException {
        checkClosed();
        if ((off | len | (off + len) | (b.length - (off + len))) < 0) {
            throw new IndexOutOfBoundsException();
        } else if (eof) {
            return -1;
        } else if (len == 0) {
            return 0;
        } // if
```

```
                int howMany = 0;
                do {
                    if (len <= counts[activeBuffer]-pos) {
                        System.arraycopy(buffers[activeBuffer], pos,
                                         b, off, len);
                        howMany += len;
                        pos += len;
                        len = 0;
                    } else {
                        int remaining = counts[activeBuffer]-pos;
                        System.arraycopy(buffers[activeBuffer], pos,
                                         b, off, remaining);
                        howMany += remaining;
                        pos += remaining;
                        len -= remaining;
                        off += remaining;
                    } // if len
                    if (pos >= counts[activeBuffer]) {
                        eof = !advanceBuffer();
                    } // if empty
                } while (!eof && len>0) ;
                return howMany;
            } // read(byte[], int, int)

            /**
             * This method makes the current active buffer an empty
             * reserve buffer and the next reserve buffer the new
             * active buffer.  If the next reserve buffer has not yet
             * been filled and there is reason to believe that it will
             * be filled then this method waits until then.
             *
             * @return true if this call was successful in
             *         advancing to another filled buffer.
             */
            private boolean advanceBuffer() throws IOException {
                int nextActiveBuffer = (activeBuffer+1)%counts.length;
                if (counts[nextActiveBuffer]==0) {
                    if (exhausted) {
                        rethrowException();
                        return false;
                    } // if exhausted

                    // We don't know if there is a pending request to
                    // fill reserve buffers or not so make sure that
                    // there is.
                    myBufferFiller.fillReserve();

                    synchronized (lockObject) {
                        while ( counts[nextActiveBuffer]==0
                                && !exhausted) {
                            try {
                                lockObject.wait();
                            } catch (InterruptedException e) {
```

```
                    IOException ioe
                      = new InterruptedIOException();
                    ioe.initCause(e);
                    throw ioe;
                } // try
            } // while
        } // synchronized

        if (counts[nextActiveBuffer]==0 && exhausted) {
            rethrowException();
            return false;
        } // if exhausted
    } // if ==0

    // At this point we know that the next buffer has data
    // in it, so we can make that the active buffer.
    counts[activeBuffer] = 0;
    activeBuffer = nextActiveBuffer;
    pos = 0;

    // Now that the former active buffer is an empty
    // reserve buffer, try to fill it before we need it.
    myBufferFiller.fillReserve();
    return true;
} // advanceBuffer()

/**
 * Re-throw the exception that was caught by the read-ahead
 * thread in the current thread.
 */
private void rethrowException() throws IOException {
    if (exception!=null) {
        Throwable e = exception;
        exception = null;
        close();
        if (e instanceof IOException) {
            throw (IOException)e;
        } else if (e instanceof RuntimeException) {
            throw (RuntimeException)e;
        } else if (e instanceof Error) {
            throw (Error)e;
        } else {
            IOException ioe;
            ioe = new IOException("An error occurred");
            ioe.initCause(e);
            throw ioe;
        } // if
    } // if
} // rethrowException()

/**
 * This method skips over the given number of bytes, or
 * possibly fewer.  To avoid the problem of this method
```

```
 * waiting for a read-ahead operation to finish, this
 * implementation of skip will not skip more bytes than
 * are currently in the active and reserve buffers.
 * @return    the actual number of bytes skipped.
 */
public synchronized long skip(long n) throws IOException {
    checkClosed();
    if (n <= 0) {
        return 0;
    }
    long skipped = 0;
    int thisBuffer = activeBuffer;
    do {
        int remaining = counts[thisBuffer]-pos;
        if (remaining >= n) {
            pos += n;
            skipped += n;
            break;
        } // if
        pos = 0;
        n -= remaining;
        skipped += remaining;
        thisBuffer = (thisBuffer+1)%counts.length;
    } while (thisBuffer!=activeBuffer);

    activeBuffer = thisBuffer;
    myBufferFiller.fillReserve();
    return skipped;
} // skip(long)


/**
 * Return the number of bytes that can be read from this
 * input stream without blocking.
 *
 * This implementation returns the combined number of
 * bytes of data in the active and reserve buffers.
 */
public synchronized int available() throws IOException {
    checkClosed();

    int count = 0;
    for (int i=0; i<counts.length; i++) {
        count += counts[i];
    } // for
    return count;
} // available()


/**
 * Close this input stream and release any system resources
 * associated with the stream.
 */
public void close() throws IOException {
    if (buffers == null)
```

```
            return;
        myBufferFiller.close();
        buffers = null;
        counts = null;
    } // close


    /**
     * This inner class is responsible for asynchronously
     * filling reserve buffers.
     */
    private class BufferFiller implements Runnable {
        /**
         * This is true after a call to fillReserve has
         * completed and remains true until the requested
         * asynchronous filling of the reserve buffers has
         * completed.
         */
        private boolean outstandingFillRequest;

        /**
         * This is the thread responsible for the
         * asynchronous filling of reserve buffers.
         */
        private Thread myThread;

        BufferFiller() {
            myThread = new Thread(this, "Buffer Filler");
            myThread.start();
        } // constructor()

        /**
         * Synchronously fill one buffer.  Assume any
         * synchronization issues have been handled by this
         * method's caller.
         *
         * @param ndx
         *        the index of the buffer to fill.
         * @return the number of bytes read into the buffer.
         */
        private int fillOneBuffer(int ndx) throws IOException {
            counts[ndx] = in.read(buffers[ndx]);
            return counts[ndx];
        } // fillOneBuffer(int)

        /**
         * Fill any empty reserve buffers.
         */
        private void fill() throws IOException {
            for ( int i = (activeBuffer+1)%counts.length;
                    i != activeBuffer
                        && !myThread.isInterrupted();
                    i = (i+1)%counts.length) {
                if (counts[i]==0) {
```

```
                int thisCount = fillOneBuffer(i);
                if (thisCount == -1) {
                    // end of file
                    exhausted = true;
                    Thread.currentThread().interrupt();
                } else {
                    // notify any thread waiting most
                    // recently filled buffer
                    synchronized (lockObject) {
                        lockObject.notifyAll();
                    } // synchronized
                } // if eof
            } // if ==0
        } // for
} // fill()


/**
 * This is the top-level logic for the prefilling of
 * reserve buffers.
 */
public synchronized void run() {
    try {
        while ( !myThread.isInterrupted()
                && !exhausted){
            synchronized (this) {
                while (!outstandingFillRequest) {
                    wait();
                } // while
            } // synchronized
            fill();
            outstandingFillRequest = false;
        } // while
    } catch (InterruptedException e) {
        // Do nothing.  This is normal.
    } catch (ThreadDeath e) {
        throw e;
    } catch (Throwable e) {
        exception = e;
    } finally {
        exhausted = true;

        // Notify any thread waiting for fill to
        // finish.
        synchronized (lockObject) {
            lockObject.notifyAll();
        } // synchronized
        try {
            in.close();
        } catch (IOException e) {
            if (exception==null) {
                exception = e;
            } // if
        } // try
```

```
            in = null;
        } // try
    } // run()

    /**
     * Request that the reserve buffers be asynchronously
     * filled.  If an asynchronous fill operation is
     * currently underway, this method has no effect.
     */
    synchronized void fillReserve() {
        outstandingFillRequest = true;
        notify();
    } // fillReserve

    /**
     * Shut down the asynchronous buffer filling.
     */
    void close() {
        myThread.interrupt();
    } // close()
} // class BufferFiller
} // class DoubleBufferedInputStream
```

Something to note about the `DoubleBufferedInputStream` class is that because its instances have a thread associated with them, they will never be garbage-collected until they are closed. The `close` method shuts down the thread.

RELATED PATTERNS

Producer-Consumer. The Double Buffering pattern is a specialized form of the Producer-Consumer pattern.

Guarded Suspension. The Guarded Suspension pattern is used in the implementation of the Double Buffering pattern to coordinate the actions of data-requesting threads with the read-ahead thread.

Two-Phase Termination. The Two-Phase Termination pattern may be used in the implementation of the Double Buffering pattern to shut down the read-ahead thread in an orderly way.

Asynchronous Processing

SYNOPSIS

An object receives requests to do something. Do not process the requests synchronously. Instead, queue them and process them asynchronously.

CONTEXT

Because objects are requested to process things in very diverse circumstances, the description of this pattern includes two different scenarios to make clear the breadth of the problem that this pattern solves: a server scenario and a client scenario. First we consider the server-based scenario.

Suppose you are designing a server that will generate form letters on behalf of applications. The way it is supposed to work is that applications will pass an object to the server that contains the information needed to generate a form letter. If the server determines that the object contains valid data, then it returns an ID number to the application. The ID number can be used later by the application to uniquely refer to the generated form letter and send it on.

The simplest way for this server software to work would be to generate a form letter synchronously. This would mean that the server would have a thread that receives a request, generates the form letter, returns the letter's ID to the requesting application, and then waits for the next request. Figure 9.32 shows these interactions. However, there are some problems with this design that lead you to decide to look for an alternative.

The first problem is a performance problem. The simplest way for clients to work with a form letter server is to pass the data for a form letter to the server and then wait for the server to return the letter's ID.

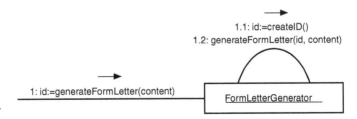

FIGURE 9.32 Synchronous form letter generation.

The longer an application finds itself waiting for the server to return a letter's ID, the more likely there is something more useful it could be doing than waiting. If the server processes requests synchronously, then there is no telling how long a client might find itself waiting for the server.

Applications can be designed to work around this problem by firing off a thread whose only purpose is to wait for the form letter ID. Designing applications to work this way avoids the problem of their having to wait for the server. This is at the expense of the added complexity of coordinating the additional thread on each application.

There is another problem with the synchronous design that is more serious. The problem manifests itself when the server is subject to a burst of requests arriving at about the same time. To service each request synchronously, the server needs to have at least as many active threads as there are pending requests.

If the server does not limit the number of threads it allows to run concurrently, then a sufficiently big burst of requests will overload the server. When the number of threads exceeds some number, performance quickly goes down. A sufficiently large number of threads (perhaps just a few hundred) will cause the server to run out of memory.

If the server does limit the number of threads it allows to run concurrently, then a problem can occur when the server is using its maximum number of threads. Since the server needs a thread for every request it processes, it must refuse to process requests until some pending requests complete and the threads running them become available to process other requests.

The alternative to processing requests synchronously is to process them asynchronously. Figure 9.33 shows how this interaction works. Here are descriptions of the interactions that appear in Figure 9.33:

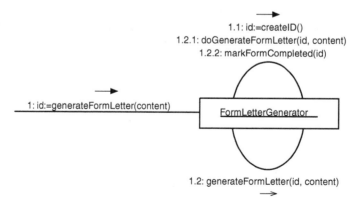

FIGURE 9.33 Asynchronous form letter generation.

1. A client asks the server to generate a form letter based on data in a given object. This call returns after the form letter has been assigned an ID number but usually before the form letter is generated.

   1.1 The server assigns an ID to the form letter prior to its generation.

   1.2 The server initiates the asynchronous generation of the form letter.

      1.2.1 The form letter is generated.

      1.2.2 The form letter is put in a database, where it can be the subject of further operations.

Making the generation of form letters asynchronous solves the problems that we had with synchronous processing. Clients do not have to wait any longer than it takes to assign an ID to the form letter. The server can limit the number of threads that it devotes to generating form letters to as few a one. If there isn't a thread immediately available to process a request, it can queue the request using the Producer-Consumer pattern. Putting the asynchronous processing in the server does complicate the server slightly. However, the server is the only place that has this complication. All of its clients are relieved of this complexity.

Now let us consider a client-based scenario.

Suppose that you are designing the implementation of a GUI using Swing. The GUI is supposed to look like the picture shown in Figure 9.34.

When the menu item labeled "Do It" is clicked, a lengthy operation takes place that lasts a few seconds. If the operation is not run asynchronously of the GUI event that triggered it, the GUI and the operation will not behave properly. The problem stems from the fact that delivery of Swing events is single threaded. If a command is run synchronously in response to the GUI event, then no other GUI events will be processed until the command completes.

The first implication you will notice in a Swing GUI if a lengthy command runs synchronously is that no screen refresh is done until the command finishes. This is because Swing normally refreshes the screen in response to a screen refresh event. Swing generates screen refresh events internally. Calls to a Swing component's `refresh` method also generate screen refresh events.

After you click on a pull-down menu item, the pull-down menu normally disappears. If a lengthy command is synchronously run in response to clicking on a pull-down menu item, the pull-down menu will not disappear until the command finishes. The reason for this is that the next screen refresh event is not processed until after the command finishes.

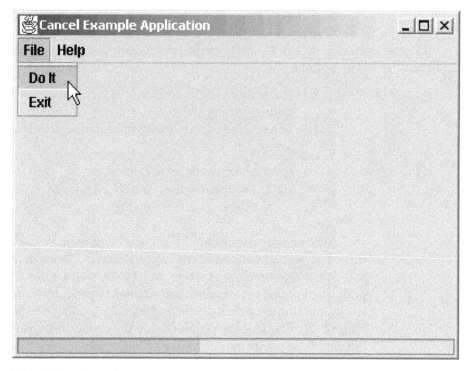

FIGURE 9.34 Simple GUI.

Swing does provide a way to run a command asynchronously of the event that triggers the command without using another thread. The `javax.swing.SwingUtilities` class has a method named `invokeLater` for this purpose. This method generates a special event that directly invokes a piece of code. The event is queued like any other event. The event is executed when it comes to the front of the queue. Invoking a command this way when a menu item is clicked allows the screen refresh event that is already in the event queue to execute before the command is run. This solves the problem of the pull-down menu not going away.

If the command does something that is supposed to change the appearance of the user interface, then running it through the `invokeLater` method is not good enough. It must be run in a separate thread. For example, suppose that the command wants to display and update a progress bar. If the command is run through the `invokeLater` method, then the progress bar will not appear until after the command has finished. When the progress bar does appear, it will simply be in the last state that the command put it in. This happens because the screen is not refreshed until the command has finished. To get a progress bar to appear and be visually updated while the command is running, the command must run in a different thread than the thread that delivers events.

Some readers may feel that modal dialog boxes are exceptions to the rule that a command must run in a separate thread if it is to make visible changes in the appearance of a GUI while it is running. A command can invoke a modal dialog box synchronously. The dialog works quite well. When the dialog box is dismissed, the command that invoked the dialog continues and completes without any strange things happening in the user interface.

The exception is only apparent, however. Swing implements modal dialogs by starting a new thread to process user-interface events while the modal dialog is up.

FORCES

- ☺ An object is expected to respond to requests to process things.
- ☺ An object's clients may not need to wait for its response to a request.
- ☺ Requests arrive asynchronously of each other.
- ☺ It is possible for an object to receive a request while it is still in the process of responding to previous requests.
- ☺ There may be no practical limit on how many requests arrive at about the same time.
- ☹ An object is required to respond to a request within a specified amount of time from when it received the request.

SOLUTION

Design objects to process requests asynchronously of when it receives them. The general organization of this is shown in Figure 9.35.

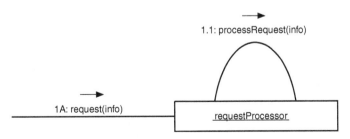

FIGURE 9.35 Asynchronous processing.

Conceptually, this is one of the simplest patterns in this book. However, like many conceptually simple ideas, there are numerous implementation-specific details to be filled in.

IMPLEMENTATION

There are two main issues in designing an implementation of this pattern. The first issue is how the requests will be managed and how the threads that will process them will be allocated. The second issue arises if the other objects need to know that the request has been processed or what the outcome of its processing was.

REQUEST MANAGEMENT AND THREAD ALLOCATION

There are many ways to manage requests and the allocation of threads to process them. What is meant here by managing requests is determining when a request *may not be* processed. The possibilities include the following:

- Allow a request to be scheduled for processing immediately.
- Postpone processing a request for a specific period of time.
- Postpone processing a request until a condition is satisfied.
- Reject a request so that it will never be processed.

What is meant here by allocating a thread to process a request is to determine when a request *may be* processed. This involves allocating a thread to process the request and may also involve setting the thread's priority.

The simplest way of matching requests with threads is to start a new thread every time a request is to be processed. This has the virtue of simplicity. The drawbacks are that it provides minimal control over request management and thread allocation. This organization allows a request to be rejected but provides no way to postpone its processing. There is no real thread allocation policy or limit on the number of threads. This is a problem if it is possible for multiple events notifications to arrive at about the same time. If too many events are being processed at the same time, then the sheer number of threads may cause the request processing to slow down or break due to a lack of resources.

A simple thread allocation policy is to have a fixed number of threads available to process events and arbitrarily assign events to threads as each becomes available. This is essentially an application of the Producer-

Consumer pattern. The thread responsible for receiving and queuing requests is the producer. The threads that process the requests are consumers.

A more sophisticated thread allocation policy can be implemented using the Thread Pool pattern (described in *Patterns in Java, Volume 3*). Passing requests to a thread pool allows more sophisticated thread allocation policies. The number of threads in use may be allowed to vary, based on the demand. The priority of threads may also be varied, based on the nature of the request.

Request management may be accomplished by using the Scheduler pattern. The nature of a scheduler object is that it prevents threads from running until a condition is met. Using a scheduler object can allow you to postpone the processing of a request using almost any criteria.

Figure 9.36 shows the interactions between a schedule object and a thread pool. If you use a simple queue instead of a thread pool, the interactions are similar.

1A A request is delivered to the object labeled `requestProcessor`.

> **1A.1** The `requestProcessor` object passes the request information to the `scheduler` object.

1B When the `scheduler` object decides that it is time to process a request, it passes the request information to the `threadPool` object.

1C The `threadPool` object allocates a thread to process the request, and the `requestProcessor` provides the logic and state information.

The `scheduler` object shown in Figure 9.36 is an active object that has its own thread. It is able to recognize when a request is ready to be processed and pass it to the thread pool independently of what any other thread is doing.

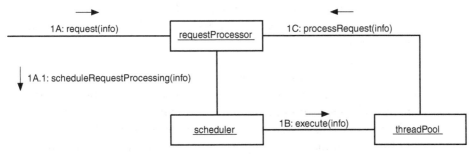

FIGURE 9.36 Request processing with scheduler and thread pool.

If there is a need to conserve threads, you can implement the `scheduler` object as a passive object that does not have its own thread. The way this works is that every time a request is passed to a `scheduler` object, the `scheduler` object checks whether it has any requests ready to be passed to the thread pool. Optionally, when one of the thread pool's threads finishes processing a request, it may call a method of the `scheduler` object that checks for requests ready to process.

OUTCOME MANAGEMENT

In some cases, after the processing of a request is completed, another object is supposed to discover the fact that the request processing is completed. Most commonly, the object that is supposed to be aware of the completed request processing is the object that originated the request. Here are two common ways that other objects learn that the processing of a request has completed:

- The object responsible for the completed request processing may send an event to objects that have been registered to receive such events.
- The outcome of the request processing may be stored in a place that interested objects will poll for the purpose of discovering requests and their outcomes.

If the object that originated a request is supposed to become aware of the outcome of request processing, it may use the Future pattern to coordinate the outcome of the request processing with any other activities it is involved in.

CONSEQUENCES

- ☺ An object that is the source of a request does not have to wait for the request to be processed before it can do other things, such as send out more events.
- ☺ A request can be queued for processing without having a thread allocated to it. This is a big savings on resources, as each thread consumes a significant amount of memory even if it is doing nothing.
- ☺ The Asynchronous Processing pattern makes it possible to have explicit policies to determine when or if a request will be processed.
- ☹ The Asynchronous Processing pattern makes it difficult to guarantee that a request will be processed within a fixed amount of time.

JAVA API USAGE

Swing- and AWT-based user interfaces use the Asynchronous Processing pattern. They manage keyboard and mouse events using the Producer-Consumer pattern and schedule them sequentially using a single thread.

The process works as follows: When the user does something with the mouse or keyboard, a platform-specific mechanism creates an appropriate object that describes the event. It then puts the event in a queue. The queue object is an instance of the `java.awt.EventQueue` class. The Event-Queue object has a thread associated with it that pulls event objects from the queue and dispatches them so that they are delivered to appropriate listeners.

You can get the `EventQueue` object being used to supply keyboard and mouse events to any Swing or AWT component using code like this:

```
import java.awt.Component;
java.awt.EventQueue
...
    Component c;
    EventQueue evtQueue;
...
    evtQueue = c.getToolkit().getSystemEventQueue();
```

CODE EXAMPLE

The code example for this pattern is an example of a client program that processes some user-interface events asynchronously. It is a subclass of Swing's `JFrame` class that looks like the picture in Figure 9.34. On its `File` pull-down menu is a menu item labeled "Do It." There is also a progress bar at the bottom of the frame.

When a user clicks the Do It menu option, the progress bar goes from 0 to 100 percent over the course of about 4 seconds. While the progress bar is being incremented, the Do It menu item does not appear on the `File` pull-down menu. In its place, there appears a menu item labeled "Stop Doing It." If the user clicks on the Stop Doing It menu item, then the progress bar stops changing.

Regardless of whether it is because the progress bar is at 100 percent or because the user clicks the Stop Doing It menu item, when the progress bar stops changing, the Stop Doing It menu item is replaced by the Do It menu item.

```
public class CancelFrame extends JFrame {
    JMenuItem menuHelpAbout = new JMenuItem();
    JMenu menuHelp = new JMenu();
```

```java
JMenuItem menuFileDoIt = new JMenuItem();
JMenuItem menuFileStopDoingIt = new JMenuItem();
JMenuItem menuFileExit = new JMenuItem();
JMenu menuFile = new JMenu();
JMenuBar menuBar1 = new JMenuBar();
BorderLayout borderLayout1 = new BorderLayout();
JProgressBar myProgress = new JProgressBar();
Thread doItThread;

public CancelFrame() {
    try {
        jbInit();
    } catch(Exception e) {
        e.printStackTrace();
    } // try
} // constructor()

/**
 * Initialize the contents of this frame.
 */
private void jbInit() throws Exception {
    this.setJMenuBar(menuBar1);
    this.getContentPane().setLayout(borderLayout1);
    this.setSize(new Dimension(400, 300));
    this.setTitle("Cancel Example Application");
    menuFile.setText("File");
    menuFileDoIt.setText("Do It");
    menuFileDoIt.addActionListener(new ActionListener() {
            public void actionPerformed(ActionEvent ae) {
                fileDoIt_ActionPerformed(ae);
            } // actionPerformed(ActionEvent)
        });
    menuFileStopDoingIt.setText("Stop Doing It");
    menuFileStopDoingIt.addActionListener(
                                        new ActionListener() {
            public void actionPerformed(ActionEvent ae) {
                fileStopDoingIt_ActionPerformed(ae);
            } // actionPerformed(ActionEvent)
        });
    menuFileExit.setText("Exit");
    menuFileExit.addActionListener(new ActionListener() {
            public void actionPerformed(ActionEvent ae) {
                fileExit_ActionPerformed(ae);
            } // actionPerformed(ActionEvent)
        });
    menuHelp.setText("Help");
    menuHelpAbout.setText("About");
    menuHelpAbout.addActionListener(new ActionListener() {
            public void actionPerformed(ActionEvent ae) {
                helpAbout_ActionPerformed(ae);
            } // actionPerformed(ActionEvent)
        });
    menuFile.add(menuFileDoIt);
```

```
        menuFile.add(menuFileExit);
        menuBar1.add(menuFile);
        menuHelp.add(menuHelpAbout);
        menuBar1.add(menuHelp);
        this.getContentPane().add(myProgress,
                                    BorderLayout.SOUTH);
    } // jbInit()


    /**
     * Asynchronously set the progress bar to zero and then
     * progressively update it to 100% over a few seconds.
     */
    void fileDoIt_ActionPerformed(ActionEvent e) {
        doItThread = new Thread() {
                public void run() {
                    try {
                        installStopItMenuItem();
                        myProgress.setMinimum(0);
                        myProgress.setMaximum(19);
                        myProgress.setValue(0);
                        myProgress.repaint();
                        for (int i=0; i<20; i++) {
                            Thread.currentThread().sleep(300);
                            myProgress.setValue(i);
                            myProgress.repaint();
                        } // for
                    } catch (InterruptedException e) {
                    } finally {
                        installDoItMenuItem();
                        doItThread = null;
                    } // try
                } // run()
            };
        doItThread.start();
    } // fileDoIt_ActionPerformed(ActionEvent)

    private void installStopItMenuItem() {
        menuFile.remove(menuFileDoIt);
        menuFile.insert(menuFileStopDoingIt, 0);
        menuFile.repaint();
    } // installStopItMenuItem()

    private void installDoItMenuItem() {
        menuFile.remove(menuFileStopDoingIt);
        menuFile.insert(menuFileDoIt, 0);
        menuFile.repaint();
    } // installDoItMenuItem()

    void fileStopDoingIt_ActionPerformed(ActionEvent e) {
        if (doItThread != null) {
            doItThread.interrupt();
        } // if
    } // fileStopDoingIt_ActionPerformed(ActionEvent)
```

```
    void fileExit_ActionPerformed(ActionEvent e) {
        System.exit(0);
    } // fileExit_ActionPerformed(ActionEvent)

    void helpAbout_ActionPerformed(ActionEvent e) {
        JPanel aboutPanel = new CancelFrame_AboutBoxPanel1();
        JOptionPane.showMessageDialog(this,
                                      aboutPanel,
                                      "About",
                                      JOptionPane.PLAIN_MESSAGE);
    } // helpAbout_ActionPerformed;
} // class CancelFrame
```

RELATED PATTERNS

Thread Pool.   The Thread Pool pattern (described in *Patterns in Java, Volume 3*) may be used in implementing the Asynchronous Processing pattern.

Producer-Consumer.   The Producer-Consumer pattern may be used in implementing the Asynchronous Processing pattern.

Scheduler.   The Scheduler pattern may be used in implementing the Asynchronous Processing pattern.

Façade.   An implementation of a request processing class may use classes that are artifacts of using the Thread Pool, Producer-Consumer, or Scheduler patterns. Request processing classes generally act as a façade to hide these details from their client classes.

Future.   The object that originates a request may need to be aware of the outcome of the request being asynchronously processed by another object. The originating object may use the Future pattern to coordinate the outcome of processing with any other activities the originating object is involved in.

Active Object.   The Active Object pattern described in [SSRB00] describes a way of combining the Future pattern with the Asynchronous Processing pattern.

Future

This pattern is also known as Promise.

SYNOPSIS

Use an object to encapsulate the result of a computation in a way that hides from its clients whether the computation is synchronous or asynchronous. The object will have a method to get the result of the computation. The method waits for the result if the computation is asynchronous and in progress or performs the computation if it is synchronous and not yet performed.

CONTEXT

Suppose you are designing a reusable class that will allow a program to get current weather data for a given location. A common type of application for this weather class is expected to be a display that includes weather information along with many other pieces of information. For example, the weather class might be used as part of a servlet that generates the HTML for a Web page that displays weather information to the side of some news.

The amount of time it will take to get weather information will vary greatly. It could be a fraction of a second or it could be many minutes. You want to design the weather class in a way that minimizes the impact on its clients.

You consider having instances of the weather class send an event to interested objects when it receives requested weather information. You decide against this. You are concerned that requiring the weather class's clients to receive an asynchronous call that delivers an event notification forces too much complexity on them. A method to receive such a notification must arrange for the client to take notice of the new weather information in a thread-safe way.

Finally, you decide on the organization shown in Figure 9.37. Here are descriptions of the classes shown in Figure 9.37:

> **Weather.** Instances of this class encapsulate information about the current weather conditions at a particular location.

Client.   Instances of a class in this role use the information in
`Weather` objects.

WeatherRequester.   When a `Client` object wants to get a `Weather`
object that contains the current information for a given location,
it asks a `WeatherRequester` object to request the information on
its behalf. The `Client` object does this by calling the `Weather-`
`Requester` object's `getWeather` method. The `getWeather` method
does not wait for the weather information to be fetched. It
returns immediately. The value it returns is a `WeatherFuture`
object. The requested weather information is fetched
asynchronously.

WeatherFuture.   This class is responsible for allowing other
threads to coordinate their actions with a thread that is fetching
weather information. When a `WeatherRequester` object's
`getWeather` method is called, it initiates the asynchronous fetching of requested weather information. It immediately returns a
`WeatherFuture` object that is associated with the request.

A `WeatherFuture` object has a method named `check` that
returns false if it is called before the requested information has
been fetched and a `Weather` object containing the information
has been created. After the `Weather` object has been created, calls
to the `check` method return true.

A `WeatherFuture` object has another method named
`waitForWeather`. If this method is called before the `Weather`
object has been created, it waits until the `Weather` object has
been created. Once the `Weather` object has been created, calls to
the `waitForWeather` method immediately return the `Weather`
object.

FORCES

☺ A computation takes place asynchronously of other threads that use
the result of the computation.

☺ An asynchronous computation can notify objects that use its result
that the result is available by using the Observer pattern or passing
the object an event of some sort. For this to work properly, it may be
necessary to have single-threaded access to some methods or sections
of code. In some situations, this may add an unacceptable level of
overhead or complexity to a class.

☺ You want to encapsulate a computation so that its clients do not need
to know whether it is synchronous or asynchronous.

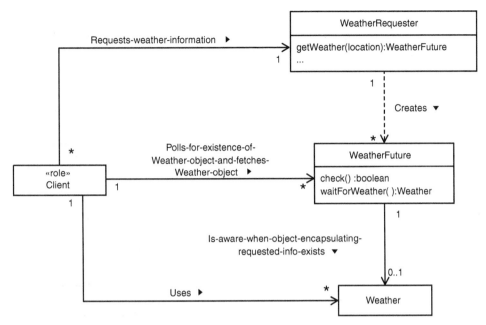

FIGURE 9.37 Weather information classes.

SOLUTION

Instead of designing a method to directly return the result of a computation, have it return an object that encapsulates the computation. The object that encapsulates the computation will have a method that can be called to get the result of the computation. Callers of this method do not know whether the computation is performed synchronously or asynchronously of their thread.

Figure 9.38 shows the roles that classes play in this solution. Here are descriptions of the roles that classes play in the Future pattern.

Result. Instances of a class in this role encapsulate the result of a computation.

Client. Instances of classes in this role use `Result` objects. `Client` objects initiate the process of getting a `Result` object by passing the appropriate parameters to a `Requester` object's `doIt` method.

Requester. A class in this role has a method that can be called to initiate the computation of a `Result` object. In Figure 9.38, this method is indicated with the name `doIt`. The `doIt` method returns a `Future` object that encapsulates that computation.

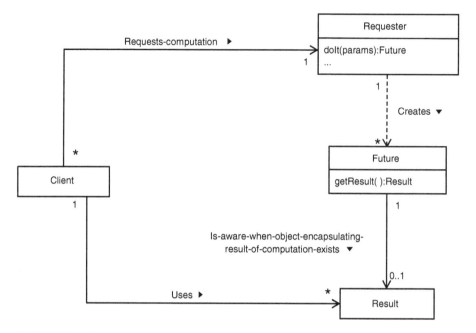

FIGURE 9.38 Future pattern.

Future.   Each instance of a class in this role encapsulates the computation of a Result object. The computation may be synchronous or asynchronous. If the computation is asynchronous, then it is computed in its own thread. An asynchronous computation may already be underway when the Future object that encapsulates it is created.

Future objects have a method that Client objects call to get the result of a computation. In Figure 9.38, this method is indicated with the name getResult. The way that this method works depends on whether the computation is synchronous or asynchronous.

If the computation is asynchronous and the method is called before the computation has completed, then the method waits until the computation is complete and then returns the result. If the method is called after the computation has completed, then the method immediately returns the result.

If the computation is synchronous, the first time the method is called the computation is synchronously performed and its result is returned. Subsequent calls to the method just return the result. Alternatively, the computation may be performed when the Future object is created.

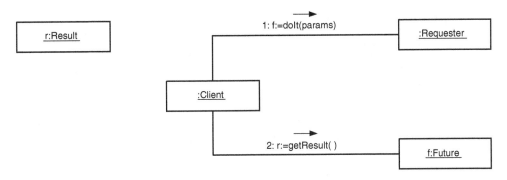

FIGURE 9.39 Future interactions.

Figure 9.39 is a collaboration diagram that shows the interactions between objects in the Future pattern. Here are descriptions of the interactions shown in Figure 9.39:

1. A `Client` object calls a `Requester` object's `doIt` method. This initiates a computation that is encapsulated by the `Future` object that the `doIt` method returns.
2. After spending some time doing other things, the `Client` object calls the `Future` object's `getResult` method. The `getResult` method returns the result of the computation.

IMPLEMENTATION

POLLING

A common usage pattern for the Future pattern is for the `Client` object to call a `Requester` object's `doIt` method to start a computation before it needs the result. It then does some other things. When it finally needs the result of the computation, it calls the `Future` object's `getResult` method. If the computation is asynchronous, initiating the computation as soon as possible and then getting its result as late as possible maximizes the advantages of the asynchronous processing.

In some situations this usage is not appropriate. One such situation is when the client has an ongoing task that it performs continuously. Consider the example of a servlet that serves a Web page containing news articles and weather information. Suppose this servlet uses the weather-related classes discussed under the Context heading. After it has requested weather information, there is no one point in what this servlet does that you can regard as the latest possible time to get the weather information. The servlet is continuously updating the information it uses for the content for the Web page it serves. You don't want any request for the servlet to provide Web content to be delayed by having to wait for an update to weather information.

One way to resolve this problem would be to have a separate thread for each request for weather information. Using a thread for this purpose does not add much value and seems like a waste of resources.

A better solution is to add another method to the `Future` class. Typically, this method will have a name that begins with the word *check*, such as `checkComputation`. The purpose of this `check` method is to check whether a `Client` object will wait idly if it calls the `Future` object's `getResult` method. A `check` method may be helpful if the encapsulated computation is asynchronous. The `check` method will return false if it is called before the computation has completed or true if it is called after the computation has completed. If the computation is synchronous, then the `check` method always returns true.

Having a `check` method allows `Client` objects to poll `Future` objects. Each request for content can poll a `Future` object by calling its `check` method. If the `check` method returns true, the servlet updates the weather information that is used for the Web page's content. If the `check` method returns false, then the servlet continues to use the information that it already has.

PROXY

The Future pattern is sometimes used with the Proxy pattern. This is generally done by having the class in the `Future` role implement an interface that allows it to be used as a proxy to the class performing the computation. When used this way, the object that initiates the computation and creation of the `Future` object and the object that gets the result from the `Future` object are usually not the same object.

An object will initiate the creation of the `Future` object. It will pass the `Future` object to other objects that will access the object through an interface without any knowledge of the `Future` object's class or its participation in the Future pattern. When the Future and Proxy patterns are combined in this way and the computation is synchronous, the result is the Virtual Proxy pattern.

LAUNCHING A SYNCHRONOUS COMPUTATION

If a `Future` object encapsulates a synchronous computation, it must be able to launch the computation the first time that its `getResult` method is called. To launch the computation, the `Future` object must be able to provide the computation with its parameters. For this reason, if a `Future` class encapsulates a synchronous computation, the class's constructor will take the necessary parameters to provide the parameter values to the computation.

RENDEZVOUS

Implementing a `Future` class to work with an asynchronous computation involves getting the thread that calls its `getResult` method to wait until the computation is finished. There is a name for the technique of getting multiple threads to wait until one or more of them reach a certain point. The name of this technique is *rendezvous*.

The `java.lang.Thread` class has a method named `join` that provides a convenient way of implementing rendezvous. A `Thread` object's `join` method does not return until the thread dies. If a thread will perform the asynchronous computation associated with a `Future` object and then die, then the `Future` object can call the thread's `join` method to rendezvous with it.

A thread does not necessarily die when it finishes a computation. It may have something else to do. It may be under the management of a thread pool (the Thread Pool pattern is described in *Patterns in Java, Volume 3*) that will reuse the thread for another computation. To implement rendezvous in a way that does not assume what a thread will do after it finishes an asynchronous computation, you should use `wait` and `notifyAll`. The code listing of the `AsynchronousFuture` class under the Code Example heading shows an example of this technique.

EXCEPTIONS

If the computation associated with a `Future` object throws an exception, you want the exception to be thrown out of the `Future` object's `getResult` method. If the computation is performed synchronously, then any exceptions that it throws will, as a natural consequence, be thrown out of the `Future` object's `getResult` method.

If the computation is asynchronous and it throws an exception, the natural course of events is for it to throw the exception in the currently running thread. In order for the exception to be thrown out of the `Future` object's `getResult` method, you will need to catch the exception and set one of the `Future` object's instance variables to refer to it. You can then code the `getResult` method so that if the instance variable is not null, the `getResult` method throws the exception that it refers to.

CONSEQUENCES

☺ The classes that use a computation are relieved of any responsibility for concurrency.

☺ If the computation is asynchronous, all of the complexity related to synchronization is in the Future class.

JAVA API USAGE

The java.awt.MediaTracker class is an example of the Future pattern in the Java API. The MediaTracker class encapsulates the process of asynchronously loading image data into the ImageProducer object associated with an Image object. It fills both the Requester and the Future roles.

The MediaTracker class does not encapsulate the result of loading the image data. It just encapsulates the process of loading the data. The ImageProducer object fills the Result role.

CODE EXAMPLE

The code example for this pattern is based on the design for reusable classes to fetch current weather information that was discussed under the Context heading. The first class presented is the WeatherRequester class that fills the requester role.

```
public class WeatherRequester {
    /**
     * The object that does the real work of fetching weather
     * information.
     */
    WeatherFetchIF fetcher;

    public WeatherRequester(WeatherFetchIF fetcher) {
        this.fetcher = fetcher;
    } // constructor(WeatherFetchIF)

    /**
     * Initiate the process of getting current weather data for
     * the given geographical coordinates.
     */
    public synchronized WeatherFuture getWeather(Coordinate location) {
        return new WeatherFuture(fetcher, location);
    } // getWeather(Coordinate)
} // class WeatherRequester
```

The constructor for the WeatherRequester class is passed the object that will do the real work of fetching current weather information for a given location. Its getWeather method is passed a location and creates a WeatherFuture object by passing the weather fetching object and the location to the WeatherFuture class's constructor. The WeatherFuture class fills the Future role.

```
public class WeatherFuture {
   /**
    * When a coordinate is passed to the constructor, it puts
    * the coordinate for the request in this instance variable
    * so that it is visible to the new thread that it starts.
    */
   private Coordinate location;

   /**
    * The object to use to fetch current weather information.
    */
   private WeatherFetchIF fetcher ;

   /**
    * An object to provide support logic.
    */
   private AsynchronousFuture futureSupport ;

   /**
    * Construct a WeatherFuture object that encapsulates the
    * fetching of weather information for the given coordinate
    * using the given WeatherFetchIF object.
    */
   public WeatherFuture(WeatherFetchIF fetcher,
                        Coordinate location) {
      this.fetcher = fetcher;
      this.location = location;
      futureSupport = new AsynchronousFuture();
      new Runner().start();
   } // constructor(WeatherFetchIF, Coordinate)

   /**
    * Return true if the requested weather info has been
    * fetched.
    */
   public boolean check() {
       return futureSupport.checkResult();
   } // checkResult()

   /**
    * Return the result object for this future.  If it has not
    * yet been set, wait until it is set.
    */
```

```java
public synchronized WeatherIF waitForWeather() throws Exception {
    return (WeatherIF)futureSupport.getResult();
} // getResult()


/**
 * This private class provides the top-level logic for
 * asynchronously fetching current weather information.
 */
private class Runner extends Thread {
    public void run() {
        try {
            WeatherIF info = fetcher.fetchWeather(location);
            futureSupport.setResult(info);
        } catch (Exception e) {
            futureSupport.setException(e);
        } // try
    } // run()
} // class runner
} // class WeatherFuture
```

When the weather information has been fetched, it is encapsulated in an instance of a class that implements an interface named WeatherIF. The core logic for managing the asynchronous computation is delegated to a reusable class named AsynchronousFuture.

```java
public class AsynchronousFuture {
    private Object result;
    private boolean resultIsSet;
    private Exception problem;

    /**
     * Return true if the result has been set.
     */
    public boolean checkResult() {
        return resultIsSet;
    } // checkResult()

    /**
     * Return the result object for this future.  If it has not
     * yet been set, wait until it is set.
     */
    public synchronized Object getResult() throws Exception {
        while (!resultIsSet) {
            wait();
        } // while
        if (problem!=null) {
            throw problem;
        } // if problem
        return result;
    } // getResult()
```

```
/**
 * Call this method to set the result of a computation.
 * This method should only be called once.
 */
public synchronized void setResult(Object result) {
    if (resultIsSet) {
        String msg = "Result is already set";
        throw new IllegalStateException(msg);
    } // if
    this.result = result;
    resultIsSet = true;
    notifyAll();
} // setResult(Object)

/**
 * If the asynchronous computation associated with this
 * object throws an exception, pass the exception to this
 * method and the exception will be rethrown by the
 * getResult method.
 */
public synchronized void setException(Exception e) {
    problem = e;
    resultIsSet = true;
    notifyAll();
} // setException(Exception)
} // class AsynchronousFuture
```

RELATED PATTERNS

Asynchronous Processing.   The Asynchronous Processing pattern
provides guidance on when to make a computation asynchronous. It is often used with the Future pattern.

Observer.   Using the Observer pattern is an alternative to polling a
`Future` object to determine whether its associated asynchronous
computation has completed.

Proxy.   The Future pattern can be combined with the Proxy pattern
so that the `Future` object is also a proxy for the object that performs that underlying computation.

Virtual Proxy.   If the Future pattern is combined with the Proxy
pattern and the computation is synchronous, then what you
have is equivalent to the Virtual Proxy pattern.

Active Object.   The Active Object pattern described in [SSRB00]
describes a way of combining the Future pattern with the
Asynchronous Processing pattern.

A P P E N D I X

Overview of *Patterns in Java,* Volumes 1 through 3

Volume 1

Fundamental Design Patterns

547

Interface and Abstract Class

You need to keep client classes independent of classes that implement a behavior and ensure consistency of behavior between the behavior-implementing classes. Don't choose between using an interface and using an abstract class. Have the classes implement an interface and extend an abstract class.

Immutable

The Immutable pattern increases the robustness of objects that share references to the same object and reduces the overhead of concurrent access to an object. It accomplishes this by not allowing an object's state information to change after it is constructed. The Immutable pattern also avoids the need to synchronize multiple threads of execution that share an object.

Marker Interface

The Marker Interface pattern uses the fact that a class implements an interface to indicate semantic boolean attributes of the class. It works particularly well with utility classes that must determine something about objects without assuming they are an instance of any particular class.

Proxy

The Proxy pattern forces method calls to an object to occur indirectly through a proxy object that acts as a surrogate for the other object, delegating method calls to that object. Classes for proxy objects are declared in a way that usually eliminates a client object's awareness that it is dealing with a proxy.

Creational Patterns

Factory Method

You need to create an object to represent external data or process an external event. The type of object depends on the contents of the external data or type of event. You want neither the data source, the event source, nor the object's clients to be aware of the actual type of object created. You encapsulate the decision of what class of object to create in its own class.

Abstract Factory

Given a set of related interfaces, the Abstract Factory pattern provides a way to create objects that implement those interfaces from a matched set of concrete classes. The Abstract Factory pattern can be very useful for allowing a program to work with a variety of complex external entities such as different windowing systems with similar functionality.

Builder

The Builder pattern allows a client object to construct a complex object by specifying only its type and content. The client is shielded from the details of the object's construction.

Prototype

The Prototype pattern allows an object to create customized objects without knowing their class or any details of how to create them. It works by giving prototypical objects to an object that initiates object creation. The creation-initiating object then creates objects by asking the prototypical objects to make copies of themselves.

Singleton

The Singleton pattern ensures that only one instance of a class is created. All objects that use an instance of that class use the same instance.

Object Pool

Manage the reuse of objects for a type of object that is expensive to create or those for which only a limited number of a kind of object can be created.

Partitioning Patterns

Filter

The Filter pattern allows objects that perform different transformations and computations on streams of data and have compatible interfaces to be dynamically connected to perform combinations of operations on streams of data.

Composite

The Composite pattern allows you to build complex objects by recursively composing similar objects in a treelike manner. The Composite pattern also allows the objects in the tree to be manipulated in a consistent manner, by requiring all of the objects in the tree to have a common superclass or interface.

Read-Only Interface

An object is supposed to be modified by some of its clients and not by others. Ensure that clients that are not supposed to modify an object don't modify an object by forcing them to access the object through an interface that does not include any methods that modify the object.

Structural Patterns

Adapter
page 209

An Adapter class implements an interface known to its clients and provides access to an instance of a class not known to its clients. An adapter object provides the functionality promised by an interface without having to assume what class is being used to implement that interface.

Iterator
page 217

The Iterator pattern defines an interface that declares methods for sequentially accessing the objects in a collection. A class that accesses a collection only through such an interface remains independent of the class that implements the interface and the class of the collection.

Bridge
page 223

The Bridge pattern is useful when there is a hierarchy of abstractions and a corresponding hierarchy of implementations. Rather than combining the abstractions and implementations into many distinct classes, the Bridge pattern implements the abstractions and implementations as independent classes that can be combined dynamically.

Façade
page 235

The Façade pattern simplifies access to a related set of objects by providing one object that all objects outside the set use to communicate with the set.

Flyweight
page 243

If instances of a class that contain the same information can be used interchangeably, the Flyweight pattern allows a program to avoid the expense of multiple instances that contain the same information by sharing one instance.

Dynamic Linkage
page 255

Allow a program, upon request, to load and use arbitrary classes that implement a known interface.

Virtual Proxy
page 265

If an object is expensive to instantiate and may not be needed, it may be advantageous to postpone its instantiation until the object is needed. The Virtual Proxy pattern hides from its clients the fact that an object may not yet exist, by having the clients access the object indirectly through a proxy object that implements the same interface as the object that may not exist. The technique of delaying the instantiation of an object until it is actually needed is sometimes called *lazy instantiation*.

Behavioral Patterns

restoration of the state does not need to know anything about the state information. It only needs to know that the object whose state it is restoring or capturing implements a particular interface.

Observer   page 387

Allow objects to dynamically register dependencies between objects, so that an object will notify those objects that are dependent on it when its state changes.

State   page 397

Encapsulate the states of an object as discrete objects, each belonging to a separate subclass of an abstract state class.

Null Object   page 407

The Null Object pattern provides an alternative to using null to indicate the absence of an object to delegate an operation to. Using null to indicate the absence of such an object requires a test for null before each call to the other object's methods. Instead of using null, the Null Object pattern uses a reference to an object that doesn't do anything.

Strategy   page 413

Encapsulate related algorithms in classes that are subclasses of a common superclass. This allows the selection of algorithm to vary by object and also allows it to vary over time.

Template Method   page 419

Write an abstract class that contains only part of the logic needed to accomplish its purpose. Organize the class so that its concrete methods call an abstract method where the missing logic would have appeared. Provide the missing logic in the subclass's methods that override the abstract methods.

Visitor   page 427

One way to implement an operation that involves the objects in a complex structure is to provide logic in each of their classes to support the operation. The Visitor pattern provides an alternate way to implement such operations that avoids complicating the classes of the objects in the structure by putting all the necessary logic in a separate class. The Visitor pattern also allows the logic to be varied by using different Visitor classes.

Concurrency Patterns

Single Threaded Execution   page 443

Some methods access data or other shared resources in a way that produces incorrect results if there are concurrent calls to a method and both calls access the data or other resource at the same time. The Single Threaded Execution pattern solves this problem by preventing concurrent calls to the method from resulting in concurrent executions of the method.

Lock Object   page 453

An operation is to be performed that requires single-threaded access to multiple objects. Save time and complexity by having an additional object that gets locked instead of the multiple objects that participate directly in the operation.

Guarded Suspension   page 461

Suspend execution of a method call until a precondition is satisfied.

Balking   page 469

If an object's method is called when the object is not in an appropriate state to execute that method, have the method return without doing anything.

Scheduler   page 475

Control the order in which threads are scheduled to execute single-threaded code using an object that explicitly sequences waiting threads. The Scheduler pattern provides a mechanism for implementing a scheduling policy. It is independent of any specific scheduling policy.

Read/Write Lock   page 485

Allow concurrent read access to an object but require exclusive access for write operations.

Producer-Consumer   page 495

Coordinate the asynchronous production and consumption of information or objects.

Two-Phase Termination   page 501

Provide for the orderly shutdown of a thread or process through the setting of a latch. The thread or process checks the value of the latch at strategic points in its execution.

Double Buffering   page 507

You have an object that consumes data. Avoid delays in the consumption of data by asynchronously producing data with the goal of the data being ready for consumption before the consumer needs it.

Asynchronous Processing   page 523

An object receives requests to do something. Do not process the requests synchronously. Instead, queue them and process them asynchronously.

Future   page 535

Use an object to encapsulate the result of a computation in a
way that hides from its clients whether the computation is synchronous or asynchronous. The object will have a method to get
the result of the computation. The method waits for the result
if the computation is asynchronous and in progress or performs
the computation if it is synchronous and not yet performed.

Volume 2

GRASP Patterns

Low Coupling/High Cohesion   page 53

If you find that a class is so highly coupled or lacking in cohesion as to make a design brittle or difficult to modify, then apply
other appropriate GRASP patterns to reassign the class's responsibilities.

Expert   page 59

Assign a responsibility to the class that has the information
needed to carry out the responsibility.

Creator   page 65

Determine which class should create instances of a class based
on the relationship between the potential creator classes and the
class to be instantiated.

Polymorphism   page 69

When alternate behaviors are selected based on the type of an
object, use a polymorphic method call to select the behavior,
rather than using if statements to test the type.

Pure Fabrication   page 73

Fabricate a class that does not represent a problem domain
entity when you must assign a responsibility to a class, but
assigning it to a class that represents a problem domain entity
would ruin its low coupling or high cohesion.

Law of Demeter   page 77

If two classes have no other reason to be directly aware of each
other or otherwise coupled, then the two classes should not
directly interact. Instead of having a class call the methods of
another class that it has no other reason to be coupled with, it
should call that method indirectly through another class.
Insisting on such indirection keeps a design's overall level of
coupling down.

Organizational Coding Patterns

Code Optimization Patterns

Robustness Coding Patterns

object. This prevents changes to the passed object from also changing the state of the object associated with the method or constructor.

Testing Patterns

Black Box Testing   page 285

Ensure that software satisfies requirements by designing tests based solely on requirements. Do not base tests on the way that the software is implemented.

White Box Testing   page 289

Design a suite of test cases to exhaustively test software by testing it in all meaningful situations. The set of meaningful situations is determined from knowledge of the software's internal structure. A complete set of tests will exercise all the execution paths through the software.

Unit Testing   page 293

Test individual classes in isolation from the other classes of the program under development.

Integration Testing   page 297

Test individually developed classes together for the first time.

System Testing   page 301

Test a program as a whole entity, in an environment similar to the one in which it is intended to be run, to ensure that it conforms to its specifications.

Regression Testing   page 309

Keep track of the outcomes of testing software with a suite of tests over time. This allows you to monitor the progress of programmers in completing their coding as they make incremental changes. It allows you to determine whether a change to a program introduced new bugs.

Acceptance Testing   page 313

Acceptance testing is testing done to ensure that delivered software meets the needs of the customer or organization for which the software was developed. Such testing is usually performed by the organization for which the software was developed. Acceptance testing is done according to a plan. The purpose of an acceptance testing plan is to ensure that software developers and the organization for which they develop a software system agree on when the software is ready to be delivered by the developers.

Volume 3

Transaction Patterns

Distributed Architecture Patterns

Objects in a distributed environment need to call methods of remote objects. For remote calls to work, many details must be just right. Provide an infrastructure that allows objects to make remote calls, with most of the details of the call hidden and handled automatically by the infrastructure.

You need to improve the throughput or availability of a distributed computation. A distributed computation is a computation that involves objects that reside on multiple computing elements and are able to communicate with each other. In some circumstances, it is possible to improve the availability and throughput of a computation by replicating an object onto multiple computing elements while maintaining the illusion to the object's clients that there is only a single object.

You need to ensure the availability of an object even if it or the platform on which it is running experiences a failure. You accomplish this by providing redundant objects that do not rely on any single common resource.

When one of a set of redundant independent objects fails, one fewer failures must occur before the entire set of redundant objects becomes unavailable. To minimize the likelihood of a catastrophic failure, repair the failed object as soon as possible.

An object needs to access a very large volume of remote data. To conserve network bandwidth, instead of bringing data to an object, move the object to the data.

You don't want hackers to be able to gain access to servers containing sensitive information if they are able to compromise the security of a publicly accessible server. Put servers that are accessible to the public Internet on a publicly accessible local-area network (LAN) that connects with both between your private network firewall and the public Internet.

To keep a process or software component highly available, you want it to be automatically restarted if it fails. Organize highly available software components in pairs, so that if one fails the other restarts it.

Distributed Computing Patterns

for the client to download the objects without the attributes and then lazily download the attributes on an as-needed basis.

Heartbeat   page 209

While a remote object is performing an operation on behalf of a client, periodically send a message back to the client indicating that the remote object is still alive.

Connection Multiplexing   page 229

You are designing a distributed system in which one object may establish many connections with another object. To avoid the overhead of setting up and shutting down many connections between the same two objects, you arrange for one actual connection to carry the contents of multiple virtual connections.

Concurrency Patterns

Session Object   page 277

A server's sessions with clients have state information associated with them, but you don't want to duplicate a lot of objects for each session. Use a single object to contain all the state information needed during a session by the server, and make that object accessible to all other objects that need state information for the current session.

Lock File   page 285

A program will need to have exclusive access to an external resource. You design the program to check for the existence of a lock file prior to accessing the resource. If the lock file exists, the program does not use the resource. If the lock file does not exist, the program creates the file and then uses the resource.

Static Locking Order   page 291

If two objects need exclusive access to the same set of resources, they can become deadlocked, with each holding a lock on one resource and waiting for the other to release its resource. You can avoid such deadlocks by ensuring that all objects acquire locks on resources in the same order.

Optimistic Concurrency   page 297

Improve throughput of transaction processing by not waiting for locks that a transaction will need. Instead, be optimistic and perform the transaction logic on private copies of the records or objects involved. Do insist that the locks be granted before the updates can be committed, but abort the transaction if conflicting updates were made prior to the granting of the locks.

Thread Pool   page 303

The nature of many servers is that they are presented with a steady stream of tasks to perform that must each be performed in its own thread. Creating a thread is a relatively expensive operation. Avoid the expense of creating a thread for each task by reusing threads.

Ephemeral Cache Item   page 325

A cache can be used to keep a local copy of data from a remote data source. From time to time, the content of the data in the remote data source may change. You want a local cache to reflect such changes in a remote data source. Ensure that the data in the local cache matches the remote data source within a bounded amount of time by considering data in a cache to have a maximum useful lifetime.

Transaction Stack State   page 337

Implement the ability to restore the original state of objects altered by possibly nested atomic transactions by saving the state of an object on a stack. This technique is most commonly used for transactions that alter only local objects or objects that are otherwise cheap to access.

Temporal Patterns

Time Server   page 349

In order for some distributed applications to function correctly, the clocks on the computers they run on must be synchronized. Ensure that clocks on multiple computers are synchronized by synchronizing them with a common clock.

Versioned Object   page 355

You may need to access previous or future states of an object. When an object gets a new state, keep both the object's new state and its previous states. Identify the states by a timestamp or a version number. Allow access to a specific state of an object by identifying its timestamp or version number.

Temporal Property   page 373

The values of an object's attributes may change over time. They usually change independently of each other. Keep historical values of attributes in a way that allows clients to get the effective value of a particular attribute as of a particular time.

Database Patterns

BIBLIOGRAPHY

[Appleton97] Brad Appleton. "Patterns and Software: Essential Concepts and Terminology." www.enteract.com/"bradapp/docs/patterns-intro .html.

[ASU86] Alfred V. Aho, Ravi Seti, and Jeffery D. Ullman. *Compilers, Principles, Techniques and Tools*. Reading, Mass.: Addison-Wesley, 1986.

[Bentley86] Jon Louis Bentley. *Programming Pearls*. New York: ACM, 1986.

[BMRSS96] Frank Buschmann, Regine Meunier, Hans Rohnert, Peter Sommerlad, and Michael Stal. *Pattern-Oriented Software Architecture, Volume 1: A System of Patterns*. Chichester, England: John Wiley & Sons, 1996.

[GoF95] Erich Gamma, Richard Helm, Ralph Johnson, and John Vlissides. *Design Patterns: Elements of Reusable Object-Oriented Software*. Reading, Mass.: Addison-Wesley, 1995.

[Larman98] Craig Larman. *Applying UML and Patterns*. Upper Saddle River, N.J.: Prentice Hall PTR, 1998.

[Lea97] Doug Lea. *Concurrent Programming in Java*. Reading, Mass.: Addison-Wesley, 1997.

[LL01] Timothy C. Lethbridge and Robert Laganière. *Object-Oriented Software Engineering: Practical Software Development Using UML and Java*. New York: McGraw-Hill, 2001.

[Rhiel00] Dirk Rhiel. *Fundamental Class Patterns in Java*. Unpublished manuscript (in 2000). www.riehle.org/papers/2000/plop-2000-class-patterns.html.

[Ritchie84] D. Ritchie. "A Stream Input-Output System," *AT&T Bell Labs Technical Journal,* vol. 63, pp. 311—324. October 1984.

[SSRB00] Douglas Schmidt, Micheal Stal, Hans Rohnert, and Frank Buschmann. *Pattern Oriented Software Architecture, Volume 2.* Chichester, England: John Wiley & Sons, 2000.

[Woolf97] Bobby Woolf. "The Null Object Pattern."www.ksccary.com /nullobj.htm.

I N D E X

9 780471 227298